Heidegger's Topology

philosophy

Heidegger's Topology: Being, Place, World

Jeff Malpas

The MIT Press
Cambridge, Massachusetts
London, England

First MIT Press paperback edition, 2008
© 2006 Massachusetts Institute of Technology

MIT Press books may be purchased at special quantity discounts for business or sales
promotional use. For information, please e-mail special_sales@mitpress.mit.edu or
write to Special Sales Department, The MIT Press, 55 Hayward Street, Cambridge,
MA 02142.

This book was set in Stone Serif and Stone Sans by SNP Best-set Typesetter Ltd., Hong
Kong, and was printed and bound in the United States of America.

Library of Congress Cataloging-in-Publication Data

Malpas, J. E.
Heidegger's topology : being, place, world / by Jeff Malpas.
    p. cm.
Includes bibliographical references and index.
ISBN 978-0-262-13470-5 (hc : alk. paper)—978-0-262-63368-0 (pb : alk. paper)
1. Heidegger, Martin, 1889–1976. 2. Place (Philosophy). I. Title.
B3279.H49M272   2007
111'.092—dc22

                                                                2006046709

10 9 8 7 6 5 4 3

Contents

Things exist rooted in the flesh,
Stone, tree and flower. . . . Space and time
Are not the mathematics that your will
Imposes, but a green calendar
Your heart observes; how else could you
Find your way home or know when to die. . . .
—R. S. Thomas, "Green Categories"

Acknowledgments

This book has taken rather longer to write than I ever anticipated. Indeed, it is a book for which a partial version already existed at the beginning of 1999. Administrative and other duties prevented me from pursuing the project, however, and the final version actually represents a major reworking and rewriting of the original material—indeed, there is very little of the original that remains. Although a considerable amount of work had thus already been undertaken beforehand, the core elements in the book were actually developed in a series of articles published between 2001 and 2004 and in the reworking of that material between the end of 2003 and the middle of 2004. Over this period the research was supported by the School of Philosophy at the University of Tasmania, by a Large Grant from the Australian Research Council (from 2001–2003), and by a six-month stay, from May to October of 2004, at Ludwig-Maximilians-Universität in Munich, where I was fortunate enough to be able to resume the Humboldt Fellowship that I had originally held at the University of Heidelberg in 1998–1999.

I would like to thank the University of Tasmania and Ludwig-Maximilians-Universität Munich, as well the Australian Research Council and the Alexander von Humboldt Foundation for the support they have given this project. Special thanks are also due to a number of individuals: Andrew Benjamin, Ed Casey, Bert Dreyfus, Stuart Elden, Joseph Fell, Karl Homann (my host in Munich), Marcelo Stamm (who deserves special thanks and acknowledgment for his generosity in allowing my wife and myself to use his Munich apartment during the time this book was written), Peter Steiner, Reinhard Steiner, James Phillips (for being one of my best-ever postgraduate students and also for assisting with the final corrections and revisions), and Julian Young (for many long discussions on dwelling and other topics over the years and for much else besides).

A note on referencing: Except in a few cases in which the English text appears in a dual English/German edition, all references in the text to English translations of Heidegger's works are followed by a reference to the original German source in parentheses—where the relevant volume appears in Heidegger's *Gesamtausgabe* (*Complete Works*), the reference is given as *GA* followed by volume number and page number, for example: (*GA*, 13:84).

1 Introduction: Heidegger, Place, and Topology

But poetry that thinks is in truth the topology of Being. . . .
—Heidegger, "The Thinker as Poet"[1]

This book has its origins in two ideas: first, that a central, if neglected, concept at the heart of philosophical inquiry is that of place; and, second, that the concept of place is also central to the thinking of the key twenti-eth-century philosopher, Martin Heidegger. Originally the material dealt with in these pages was intended to form part of a single investigation into the nature and significance of place. As work on that volume proceeded, however, it soon became obvious that it would be difficult to deal with the Heidegger material in a way that did justice to it while also allowing the development of the broader inquiry into place as such. As a result, the volume that appeared with Cambridge University Press in 1999, *Place and Experience: A Philosophical Topography*, while it included some brief discussion of Heidegger, was focused on the task of establishing the philosophical nature and significance of place, leaving the main investigation of the role of place in Heidegger for another work—a work that was projected in the pages of *Place and Experience* under the title "Heidegger's Topology of Being."

The title may have changed slightly, but the present volume aims to make good on that original commitment and can be regarded as something of a companion volume to *Place and Experience* (in fact, since I am now working on a third volume, *Triangulating Davidson*, that will develop a place-oriented reading of Donald Davidson's work on language, mind, and understanding, the original project now seems to have turned into a trilogy of works). Moreover, while Heidegger is a central focus here, and the work aims to provide an account of the role and significance of place in relation to Heidegger, the book also contains material that can be viewed as expanding and supplementing elements of the original analysis in *Place and Experience*. This is especially so as regards a number of methodological issues surrounding the idea of what I have called "topography" and that appears in Heidegger as "topology." In this respect, *Heidegger's Topology* can be viewed as providing, not only a particular way of reading Heidegger's thought in its entirety, but also a more detailed investigation of the way in which the concept of place relates to certain core philosophical issues such as the nature of ground, of the transcendental, and of concepts of unity, limit, and bound, as well as a further defense of the philosophical significance and legitimacy of place.

In taking place as the central concept in Heidegger's thought, the aim is to be able to arrive at a more basic and, one hopes, more illuminating understanding of that thought and so also, perhaps, a more basic and illuminating appropriation of it into an English-speaking context—an understanding, moreover, that shows how that thought originates, not in some peculiar and special "intuition" of being, but rather in the simple and immediate grasp of being in our own "being-in" the open-ness of place. In this respect, what I offer here is a very specific "reading" of Heidegger, one that aims to understand him as responding to a particular problem or set of problems and that aims to bring to the fore an issue that is otherwise not always directly apparent in Heidegger's thinking either as he himself formulates it or as it is interpreted by others, but which is nevertheless foundational to that thinking. The aim, in fact, is to bring to light something in Heidegger's thinking that perhaps he could not have himself fully articulated and that indeed remains, to some extent, to be "recovered" from that work. That the task of reading Heidegger will indeed involve a certain "struggle" both with Heidegger, and sometimes even against him, seems to me an inevitable result of any attempt to engage with Heidegger as a "live" thinker rather than a mere "text." It also means, however, that my account may be viewed as simply putting too much stress on certain elements at the expense of others. This is a criticism that I am happy to accept, although I leave it up to the reader to judge whether the way of reading proposed does not bring certain advantages with it—not least in terms of advancing the understanding of the underlying concepts and problems that seem to be at issue here.

The plan of the book is fairly simple inasmuch as it follows the development of Heidegger's topology through three main stages: the early period of the 1910s and 1920s (up to and including *Being and Time*) centered on the "meaning of being" (chapters 2 and 3); the middle period of the 1930s and extending into the 1940s, centered on the "truth of being" (chapter 4);[2] and the late period from the mid-1940s onwards in which the "place of being" comes properly to the fore (chapter 5). The chapters that are of most importance in explicating the dynamics that underpin the shifts in Heidegger's thinking across these three broad stages are chapters 3 and 4, and it is these that focus most closely on what may be viewed as the more "technical" issues of Heidegger interpretation—issues that are likely to be of greater interest to Heidegger specialists than to the general reader. Indeed, readers whose interest is more on place than on Heidegger as such may wish to be more selective in their reading of these two chapters and perhaps give closer attention to chapters 1, 2, 5, and 6—it is in the latter two chapters (5 and 6) that the idea of Heideggerian topology is most fully articulated.

1.1   The Significance of Place

Heidegger's work is of special relevance to any place-oriented thinker. As Edward Casey has so admirably set out in his *The Fate of Place*,[3] the history of place within the Western philosophical tradition has generally been one in which place has increasingly been seen as secondary to space—typically to a particular notion of space as homogeneous, measurable extension— and so reduced to a notion of position, simple location, or else mere "site." The way in which place relates to space, time, and other concepts and the manner in which these concepts are configured has seldom been the object of detailed philosophical exploration. Although Casey argues that place has reemerged in recent thought through the work of a number of writers, of whom he takes Heidegger to be one, the way in which place appears in Heidegger's thought seems to me to be especially significant and also quite special. Unlike Casey, who views Heidegger as proceeding to place by "indirection,"[4] I take Heidegger to have attempted a thinking of being that is centrally oriented to the concept of place as such. In this respect, I concur with Joseph Fell when he writes that, "The entirety of Heidegger's thinking turned out to be a protracted effort at remembering the place in which all human experience—practical or theoretical, willed or reasoned, poetic or technical—has always come to pass."[5] Indeed, I would argue that Heidegger's work provides us with perhaps the most important and sustained inquiry into place to be found in the history of Western thought.

In this latter respect, the significance of Heidegger as a thinker of place is evident, not only in terms of the way in which spatial and topographic concepts figure in his own work, nor even the way in which he might be taken as a focus for exploration of some of the problematic aspects of these

ideas, but in terms of the manner in which spatial and topographic thinking has flowed from Heidegger's work into that of other key thinkers over
the last sixty years or more, both through the reaction against those ideas,
or against certain interpretations of them, as well as their positive appropriation. This is an aspect of Heidegger's work that is gradually being
explored in more detail. Stuart Elden, for instance, has argued for a significant Heideggerian influence, specifically in relation to ideas of spatiality, on the work of Michel Foucault;[6] while if one accepts Casey's claim
that recent philosophy has seen something of a resurgence in the concept
of place, much of that resurgence has to be seen as due to the pivotal influence of Heidegger's thought and of Heidegger's own focus, particularly in
his later work, on notions of space and place. Understanding the way such
notions figure in Heidegger's work may thus be viewed as foundational to
understanding a good deal of contemporary thinking, and recognition of
this point seems to be evident in the appearance of a small but steady flow
of works over the last few years that do indeed take up aspects of spatial
and topological ideas in Heidegger's work. Stuart Elden's book on Heidegger and Foucault, referred to above, is one example of this, while Julian
Young's work has been especially important in tracing ideas of place and
dwelling in Heidegger's later thinking, particularly as these ideas arise in
relation to Heidegger's engagement with the early nineteenth-century
German poet Friedrich Hölderlin.[7]

Nevertheless, while there is an increasing recognition of the importance
of space and place, it remains the case, especially so far as place itself is
concerned, that there has been relatively little analysis of the way in which
spatial and topological concepts operate in Heidegger's thinking as a
whole.[8] Undoubtedly, this is partly a result of the fact that Heidegger's early
thought has always tended to command more attention than the later, and
in that early work, as I discuss further below (see chapter 3), space and
place have a problematic status, while in Heidegger's later thinking, in
which topological notions are more explicitly to the fore, the focus on
place comes as part of what has often been seen as an obscure and barely
philosophical mysticism. At a more fundamental level, however, the apparent neglect of place in Heidegger's work undoubtedly reflects the more
general neglect of place that Casey brings to our attention and so the rel-
ative lack of analytical attention that has hitherto been paid to place as
such. Although concepts of space and place have become commonplace
in recent discussions across the humanities, arts, and social sciences, there
have been few attempts to provide any detailed account of what these concepts actually involve.[9] This is true even of such influential thinkers of

place and space such as Lefebvre and Foucault in whose works spatial notions, in particular, function as key analytic tools and yet are not themselves investigated in any detailed fashion. More generally, and especially in regard to place, the tendency is either to assume the notion, or to assume some specific reading of it, or else to view it as a secondary and derivative concept. Indeed, all too often, place is viewed as a function of human responsiveness or affectivity,[10] as a social or cultural "construction,"[11] or else as nothing other than a sort of neutral "site" (perhaps understood in terms of a more or less arbitrary region of physical space) that draws any qualities it might have from that which is located within it.[12] The neglect of place that is evident here can be seen, to some extent, as a result of the seeming "obscurity" that attaches to place as such—place seems an evanescent concept, disappearing in the face of any attempt to inquire into it[13]— we are thus easily led, no matter how persistently the concept may intrude into our thinking, to look to articulate place in other terms (within a Heideggerian frame, the "obscurity" that attaches to place may be seen to reflect the same "obscurity" that attaches to being as such). In some ways, in fact, this is a tendency to which Heidegger himself seems to succumb (at least around the period of *Being and Time*).

Yet what place is and how it ought to be understood is just what is in question—and while the obscurity of place may render answers to such questions all the more elusive, those questions are no less pressing or significant. Building on the foundations already laid in *Place and Experience*, the present book aims to go some way toward providing more of the analysis that seems to be needed here, and in doing so, to go a little further in establishing the centrality and necessity of place, not only in Heidegger, but in all philosophical inquiry. In attempting to address the question of place as such, the analysis advanced in the following pages should not be seen, any more or less than the analysis in *Place and Experience* that preceded it, as *necessarily* incompatible with those many other accounts that deploy spatial and topological notions in analysis and description from more specifically sociological, anthropological, geographical, political, economic, linguistic, literary, or cultural perspectives.[14] In this respect, the hope is that any general account of place will be complementary to the more specific accounts that arise within particular disciplinary approaches (which is not to say that it will be consistent with all such accounts or that it will be inconsistent with all of them either), providing a broader framework within which the analytic and descriptive use of spatial and topological notions can be guided and better understood. Certainly such a hope underpinned my own earlier work in *Place and Experience*, and the same is true of the investigations that are pursued here in more direct relation to Heidegger.

I have already noted the way in which spatial and topological notions have a problematic status in Heidegger's early work, and there is no doubt that the idea of topology emerges as an explicit and central idea for Heidegger quite late in his thinking. Yet the claim I will advance here is that what guides that thinking, if only implicitly, almost from the start, is a conception of philosophy as having its origin in a particular idea, problem, and, we may also say, experience: our finding ourselves already "there," in the world, in "place." The famous question of being that is so often referred to by Heidegger himself as the primary focus for his thought thus has to be understood as itself a question determined by this starting point. In his book on the young Heidegger, John van Buren writes that:

Heideggerians in their search for "Being" have for years been after the wrong thing. Despite Heidegger's continued use of such phrases as "the question of being," "being as being," and "being itself," right up until the unfinished introduction to his collected edition, his question was never really the question of being , but rather the more radical question of what gives or produces being as an effect.[15]

Much of my argument here could be put in terms of the idea that the question of being is indeed underlain by a "more radical question"—namely, the question of place—so that, in van Buren's terminology, being has to be understood as, one might say, an "effect" of place. Strictly speaking, however, I would prefer to say that being and place are inextricably bound together in a way that does not allow one to be seen merely as an "effect" of the other, rather being emerges only in and through place. The question of being must be understood in this light, such that the question of being itself unfolds into the question of place. Moreover, one of the intriguing features of van Buren's work is that, while he does not thematize the concept of place in any significant way, he nevertheless paints a picture of Heidegger's early thinking in terms of a proliferation of ideas and images of place, home, situatedness, and involvement[16]—even suggesting, at one point, that "in 1921 Heidegger already used the term Dasein in the sense of a site of being."[17]

There is much in van Buren's work, then, as well as in that of Theodore Kisiel on which van Buren often draws, that is important for filling out the place-oriented character even of Heidegger's earliest thought—and van Buren and Kisiel will be important sources for my discussion of the early Heidegger. Yet just as van Buren does not thematize the topological character of Heidegger's early thought, so his work differs from mine in a number of important respects. While van Buren takes the early Heidegger to be an "an-archic" and even "anti-philosophical" thinker, I see Heidegger, through his career, as concerned to engage with philosophy's own topological origin. As a consequence of this, my reading of Heidegger is probably a rather more unified and systematic one than van Buren would find congenial. On my account, then, and in contrast with van Buren's, the Heideggerian project is to find a way of adequately responding to and articulating the *topos*, the place, that is at stake in all philosophical thinking. Heidegger's engagements with the mystical tradition, with medieval theology, with Christian personalist thinking, with the foundations of logic, with phenomenology, and with German idealism do not constitute merely different elements or strains in his thought (there is in this sense, *contra* John Caputo, no mystical *"element"* in Heidegger),[18] instead all are part of the one attempt to think philosophy, and the most basic philosophical concerns, in as essential manner as possible—which, on my reading, means to think philosophy in terms of place. In drawing on these various sources, Heidegger can be seen to be working through a topology of Western thought that aims at unearthing the fundamentally topological character and orientation of that thought. One of the reasons for Heidegger's significance to place-oriented thinking is thus the way in which his work can be seen as just such an "unearthing" or "working out" of the topological character of the Western philosophical tradition—a character that is present throughout that tradition, as Edward Casey's work suggests, and yet is so often present as something overlooked or obscured.[19]

In discussing his own "transcendental" reading of the early Heidegger and the contrast between that reading and the reading offered by John van Buren in his book *The Young Heidegger*, Steven Galt Crowell writes that:

Readers of Heidegger quickly sense the presence of two voices in his work. There is, first, the Heidegger who seeks the proper name of being; the Heidegger who, in spite of his best insights into the ontological difference, often seems to imagine being as some primal cosmic "event," a hidden source or power. Seeking the "meaning of being," this Heidegger appears to want philosophy to "eff the ineffable." There is, second, the Heidegger who is concerned with the reflexive issue of the possibility of philosophy itself, the Heidegger who constantly chastises other thinkers for not being rigorous enough, for succumbing to metaphysical prejudice and losing sight of the things themselves. This Heidegger seems precisely to shun the excesses of what the first Heidegger appears to embrace . . . Van Buren gives the palm to the first, "mystical" and "antiphilosophical," voice, while I follow the second "transcendental" and "critical" one.[20]

My own approach can be seen as taking something of a middle path between van Buren and Crowell—an approach that aims to hear these two voices as one and the same. Both the mystical and the transcendental have to be understood as focused on the same question, namely, the question of the place, the "situatedness," of philosophy and the place, the *topos*, of being as such. One might argue that mysticism places its emphasis on the need to retain a sense of the originary unity of that place and its essential ungroundedness in anything other than itself, while the transcendental focuses on the attempt to articulate the structure of that place and the way place functions as a ground. Yet it turns out that these two approaches converge. The mystical and the transcendental do not constitute different ways of taking up the same question except inasmuch as they have come to be seen as different ways because of the way they have emerged as separate within the philosophical tradition. Yet the transcendental is no less concerned to preserve the originary character of the place of being than is the mystical. Indeed, when we understand the real character of the transcendental, both in terms of that which it aims to address and the manner in which it aims to do so, then the transcendental and the mystical can be seen to speak with a single voice. If the transcendental drops away in Heidegger's later thinking, it is not because we cannot understand Heidegger's later thought in those terms, but rather because Heidegger himself adopts a particular conception of the transcendental as tied to the concept of transcendence and that notion does prove to be problematic in the way Heidegger comes to understand matters. Yet we can also maintain a sense of the transcendental, and the hermeneutic and phenomenological, as continuing into later Heidegger, so long as we maintain a core conception of the transcendental, and the hermeneutic and phenomenological, as essentially topological in character.[21]

That place is indeed at issue here, at least in the way Heidegger views matters, is evident from the way Heidegger takes philosophical thinking to itself arise out a certain sort of situatedness (something that will be the focus for much of my discussion in chapter 2 below); but it also becomes evident fairly quickly once one begins to explore Heidegger's understanding of the question of being that, van Buren's comments notwithstanding, he clearly takes as the fundamental question of philosophical inquiry. As I noted in discussing van Buren above, my claim is that the question of being already implies ("unfolds into") the question of place, and it is worth setting out, if only in summary form, how this connection seems to emerge, and, indeed, how it is already evident in the way Heidegger understands the question of being as such.

Although many discussions of Heidegger's work begin by trying to say just what is the question of being—and so trying to give some account of what "being" itself "is"—it should be clear that there is a certain difficulty associated with such attempts since the meaning of the question, and so how being itself should be understood, is precisely what is at issue. We can certainly say how being has been understood historically, and Heidegger does this on many occasions, but this does not answer the question of being so much as provide a way into that question. We may also give a preliminary account of the understanding of being that seems to be developed in Heidegger's thought, but if this is taken as a way of establishing the character of the question to which Heidegger's work provides an answer, then the risk will always be that an appearance of circularity will be the result—as Heidegger himself acknowledges.[22] Yet the appearance of circularity is only that—an appearance—and reflects the fact that thought must have some orientation to its subject matter if it is even to begin.

To a large extent, however, when it comes to the question of being, our orientation to that question is first given as a certain form of disorientation. For while we can talk about being, there is indeed a question as to what such talk—what "being"—means. In this respect, the fact that we look for some account of what being is as a way into Heidegger's thinking is itself indicative of the difficulty that the question of being itself presents from the start. It is just this difficulty, this "disorientation" with respect to being, that is indicated by the passage from Plato's *Sophist* that Heidegger places at the beginning of *Being and Time*: "For manifestly you have long been aware of what you mean when you use the expression 'being.' We, however, who used to think we understood it, have become perplexed."[23] In some ways, then, the proper starting point for thinking about being in Heidegger is simply its questionability—indeed, such questionability is itself central to Heidegger's understanding of being as such. It may seem trivial to say that there can be no question of being in the absence of questionability, but the point is nevertheless an important one in the Heideggerian context. For what is at issue in the question of being is, in the simplest terms, how anything can be the thing that it is. For something to be what it is, however, is for the thing to stand forth in a certain fashion—to stand forth so that its own being is disclosed. Yet to be disclosed in this way is also for the thing to stand forth in such a way that its being is also open to question—for it to be possible for the question "what is it?" (in Aristotle, the question of the "*ti esti*") to be possible.

One way of moving forward in the face of such questionability is, as I noted above, by reference to the way the question of being has been understood within the preceding philosophical tradition. Heidegger, of course, looks especially to the Greek understanding of the question as determinative of the understanding of being within the Western philosophical tradition as a whole, and for Greek thought, the focus of the question of being is what Aristotle called "*ousia*," the really real, the primary being, "substance." Heidegger claimed that one of the great breakthroughs in his own thinking was to realize that this Greek understanding of being was based in the prioritization of a certain mode of temporality, namely the present, and so understood the being of things in terms of the "presence" or "presencing" of things in the present[24]—in terms of the way they "stand fast" here and now. The way in which temporality comes to be at issue here (and so the connection between "presence" and "the present") is important, but its entrance into the discussion should not distract us from the way in which the issue of being is indeed tied here directly to the idea of presence or presencing as such. The introduction of this idea of "presence" or "presencing" is indicative of a key problem in contemporary discussion of Heidegger's thought—although it is an issue that, for those not especially interested in the details of Heideggerian interpretation, may seem somewhat obscure. Yet the issue is one that is important to address before I proceed much further. The interpolated excursus on presence that follows is thus something that some readers may choose merely to skim or completely skip over—but I would hope that it is a discussion to which such readers would later return.

In the very late lecture "Time and Being," Heidegger tells us that "Ever since the beginning of Western thinking with the Greeks, all saying of 'Being' and 'Is' is held in remembrance of the determination of Being as presencing which is binding for thinking,"[25] and again, "From the early period of Greek civilization to the recent period of our century, 'being' [*Sein*] has meant: presencing [*Anwesen*]."[26] But this seeming identification of being with presence or presencing (which has not always gone unchallenged),[27] nevertheless leaves open as a question just what is meant by presence as such and whether what Heidegger means by presence is always one and the same. The matter is also complicated by the range of terms in German that can be used to refer to presence including: (*das*) "*Anwesen*," (*die*) "*Anwesenheit*,"[28] (*das*) "*Anwesende*," (*das*) "*Präsens*," and (*die*) "*Gegenwart*" (which refers to the temporal "present" as well as having a sense that can be used to mean just "presence"). Does "presence" always mean just the presence of things in the present? Might not this Greek understanding of presence itself call upon, and yet at the same time obscure, a sense of presence that extends beyond one single mode of temporality? Might "presence" be ambiguous between that which is present as present and the coming to presence, the "presenting" or "presencing," of what is present? It seems to me that Heidegger does indeed tend to think of being always in terms of presence, but that presence does not always mean presence in the sense of standing fast in the present, and so, when Heidegger refers to the way in which being has always meant "presence" or "presencing," what remains at issue is just how "presence" should be understood. In fact, "presence" encompasses both presence or "presentness" (in the sense of that which is present *as* present) and the happening of such presentness (as the presenting or presencing of that which is present). Thus Heidegger comments, again in "Time and Being," that "Presence means: the constant abiding that approaches man, reaches him, is extended to him. . . . Not every presencing is necessarily the present. A curious matter. But we find such presencing, the approaching that reaches us, in the present, too. In the present, too, presencing is given."[29] This distinction between two modes of presence is close to the distinction between presence and that which presences for which Julian Young also argues. Young writes that: "being is, as Heidegger puts it, 'presence,' or sometimes 'presencing.' Presence (*Anwesenheit*) is contrasted with 'what presences [*das Anwesende*].' Since the essence of a being is that it is something present, noticeable, capable of being 'of concern' to us, 'what presences' is just another name for beings."[30] Not only does Young distinguish between presence (what I have termed presencing) and what presences, however, he also argues for a distinction between two senses of presence, presence as intelligibility and presence as the unintelligible in which intelligibility is grounded: "For many readers [of Heidegger] . . . *all* there is to say about *Sein* is that it is 'intelligibility.' I oppose this view of things. Though there is indeed *a* sense of *Sein* in which it is just presence (truth as disclosure, 'world' in the onto-logical sense, intelligibility), there is another sense in which what is crucial about it is precisely the opposite—unintelligibility ('un-truth')."[31] Young uses "being" and "Being" to mark out these two senses ("being" is being in the sense of intelligibility and "Being" is being in the sense of the unin-telligible ground of being). Perhaps the main difference between Young's account and mine is that I take "presence" itself to be ambiguous between both the entity that presences (what Young refers to as "what presences"— "*das Anwesende*") as well as presencing as such and thus take it to be ambiguous between beings and being,[32] as well as between that which is intelligible and that in which intelligibility is grounded—so we do not need both the distinction between "what presences" and "presence," as well as a distinction between two modes of "presence," but just the distinction between two senses of presence, which can itself apply in at least two different ways.

Yet in drawing attention to these distinctions, it is also important to recognize that they do not provide a simple and unequivocal tool with which to analyze Heidegger's texts—indeed, this is one reason why I would rather say that there is one distinction here (between presence and what presences) that plays out in at least two ways (in terms of being and beings, as well as between the ground of intelligibility and what is intelligible), rather than that there are two separate distinctions (between presence and what presences and between two senses of presence). In this respect, although I wholeheartedly agree with Young that being cannot simply be equated with intelligibility but also encompasses a certain "unintelligibility"—it encompasses both clarity and opacity, or, in the language of "The Origin of the Work of Art" (see the discussion in chapter 4 below), both "world" (or "clearing") and "earth"—I do not see the distinction Young presents in terms of the distinction between the two senses of "presence" or of "being" as quite so clear-cut as it might seem—there is a constant play between shadow and light here, between intelligibility and its ground, so that what may appear as intelligible may also appear as a ground for intelligibility, while sometimes what appears as ground may appear as, even if only partially, that which is intelligible (a particularly good example of this is "world," which sometimes may appear as intelligible and sometimes as that which grounds intelligibility even while not being fully intelligible in itself). Indeed, I would view the distinctions that are in play here—between being and beings, between presencing and what is present, between the ground of intelligibility and intelligibility—as having an irreducible equivocity to them (what I refer to below as "iridescence") that is common to many of Heidegger's terms and in accordance with which they always have a tendency to shimmer and shift in relation to one another, sometimes overlapping, sometimes not. Consequently, and dependent on the particular context, Heidegger may use "being" or "presencing" to refer either to intelligibility, or its unintelligible ground, or to the complex of both; he may use some variation on "presence" to refer to "what is present" either in the sense of some entity that is present or to the world as that which presents itself as the horizon of intelligibility. While it is important to be aware of the possible distinctions here and not to construe Heidegger's language in ways that are oblivious to its various facets, it is equally important not to treat those distinctions in too rigid a fashion and to recognize the way those facets reflect one complex of thought.

If this distinction between these two senses of "presence"—presence as that which is present *as* present and presence as the happening of such presentness—is accepted, then much of Heidegger's thinking can be seen as an attempt to recover the latter of these two senses and, in so doing, to recover the necessary belonging-together of the former sense with the latter. The ambiguity that attaches to talk of both being and presence here means that we can understand how Heidegger may indeed be said, in *Being and Time*, to reject the idea that being is presence, while nevertheless insisting, in his later writing, that being means presence.[33] In *Being and Time*, the focus is on a rethinking of being against the prevailing, and especially Greek, understanding of being as presence in the present. This does not entirely disappear in the later thinking,[34] but *Being and Time* takes this issue up in a very specific way through the focus on the role of temporality that is already evident in the connection between presence and the present (where "the present" is itself equivocal between the originary "present" as it figures in the ecstatic unity of originary time and the "present" as it is ordinarily understood). *Being and Time* is directed at the articulation of the meaning of being in terms of time and so also at a re-thinking of time in terms of directionality and possibility—in terms of the "ecstatic" unity of past, present, and future. It is this specific focus on temporality as giving the proper meaning of being that largely disappears from Heidegger's later thinking, in which there is no longer the same imperative to re-think the idea of presence in its specific relation to temporality (as presence in the present), and in which the focus is on understanding presence as a coming to presence in terms of what is already indicated in *Being and Time* in the idea of "disclosedness" (*Erschlossenheit*).[35] As a result, in the later work, "presence" is more often employed in its broader senses in which it is not tied to the idea of presence in the present and in which there seems to be a clearer and stronger emphasis on keeping open the way in which presence captures something central to the understanding of being.

The idea that being and presence are connected is especially significant for the inquiry into the connection between being and place. Presence does not mean being in some indeterminate or general sense—presence is always a matter of a specific "there." Similarly, disclosedness, whether as it appears in *Being and Time* or elsewhere, does not occur in some general or abstract fashion but always takes the form of a certain "clearing"—a "*Lichtung*"—it is indeed the establishing and opening up of a "place." Thus Heidegger's inquiry into being always takes the form, almost from the very beginning and certainly to the very end of his thinking, of an inquiry into

presencing or disclosedness as this occurs in terms of the happening of a
"*Da,*" a there, a *topos*. Inasmuch as "presencing" always involves such a
"placing," so the presence or disclosedness that is the focus of Heidegger's
inquiry into being is never a matter simply of the coming to presence of
a single being—as if presence was something that could attach to a single
self-sufficient entity. The presencing or disclosedness of a being is always
a matter of its coming to presence in relation to other beings. This is why,
for Heidegger, presencing or disclosedness is inseparable from the happening of a world. When Heidegger tells us, as he does in *Being and Time*,
that what is at issue in the inquiry into being is the inquiry into that by
means of which beings can be the beings that they are, this does not mean
that he aims to inquire into the way the being of each being is somehow
separately determined, but rather that what is at issue is how beings can
emerge in a way such that their own being is both in the midst of, and
yet also distinct from, that of other beings. The question of being concerns
the presencing of beings as what they are, and so as they emerge both in
their relatedness and their differentiation.

The question of being does not, at least not initially, require any distinction between beings such that the question of being must be seen to
privilege some beings over others. Yet inasmuch as the question concerns
all and every being, so our own being is not excluded from the question
either—the question of the presencing of things is indeed a question that
encompasses both the way in which other beings come to presence in relation to us, as well as to one another, and the way we ourselves come to
presence also. This means that the question of being will always involve
our own being. Yet this does not imply that the question of being should
therefore be construed as simply a question about the possibility of *knowledge* since what is at issue is the original presence that is necessary if that
specific type of relation to things that is called "knowledge" is to be possible. Neither should the question of being be construed as already, from
the start, a question only about how things can be present to human
beings. The question of being is the question of how beings—any and every
being—can emerge in their relatedness to, and their distinctiveness from,
one another. The question of being concerns, in short, the possibility of
"world." It soon becomes apparent, of course, that in the possibility of
world human beings play an essential role. In *Being and Time*, in fact, it
looks as if the being that is characteristic of human beings is actually that
in which world is grounded, although this cannot be so in any straightforward sense since the question of that in which the ground is grounded
also points toward a question about the ground of human being as such.[36]

Yet the way in which human being comes to be itself at issue here should not be taken to mean that the question of being as Heidegger understands it is somehow already a question, from the start, about being only as it stands in relation to human being. Rather, it turns out that the question of being is itself always a question in which human being is necessarily enmeshed. This is so simply in virtue of the way in which Heidegger understands the question of being as indeed a matter of the happening of presence, where presence is not some simple "standing there" of the thing independently of all else, but is, indeed, a matter of coming into relatedness with things in their sameness and difference, in their unity and multiplicity.[37] This coming into presence is what Heidegger refers to in a variety of ways in terms of disclosedness or unhiddenness, and for much of his thought, it is seen as identical with the happening of "truth."

If we begin with the question of how it is that things can first come to presence, are indeed first "disclosed," then our starting point would seem to lie in what can only be referred to as a fundamental happening that is the happening of presence or disclosedness—the happening of world—as such. It is this happening that turns out to be at the very heart of Heidegger's "question of being." This "happening" is not some abstract or standardized occurrence—of the sort, for instance, that we may attempt to repeat in a laboratory experiment or that we may reduce to a mathematical equation—nor does it lie in a realm removed from ordinary experience. Instead, the "happening" that is at issue here is the "happening" of the very things that we encounter in our concrete and immediate experience of the world. The sense in which the "question of being" does indeed lie at the center of Heidegger's thought is just the sense in which this question of the "happening" of the presence or disclosedness of things remains the question that always preoccupies him. Yet inasmuch as this question is central, so the attempt to address that question forces us to reflect upon the character of the happening that is at issue here. In doing so, what soon becomes evident is that this happening of presence or disclosedness is always the happening of a certain open realm in which, not only things, but we ourselves are disclosed and come to presence—in which we are gathered together with the things around us. This does not reflect a subjectivist bias on Heidegger's part but rather the simple fact that what we find given to us from the start is a disclosedness in which we are already involved. The inevitable starting point for any question about the happening or gathering that occurs in the disclosedness of things, regardless of what we may conclude later, is thus a happening that encompasses ourselves as well as things.

This happening or gathering is, moreover, not something that occurs in some general and anonymous fashion. What is gathered is always gathered in its concreteness and particularity—it is "I" who is gathered, together with this thing and that—and so is itself constituted as a gathering that has its own particularity, its own character, its own unity and bounds. It seems natural, and inevitable, to describe such a gathering as a gathering that occurs in and through place since place names just such gathering in particularity. The idea and image of place, particularly as understood through the idea of topology, is indeed just the idea and image of a concrete gathering of otherwise multiple elements in a single unity—as places are themselves gathered into a single locality (and in Heidegger's later thinking, notably, as we shall see in chapter 5 below, in the late essay "Art and Space," this idea of the gathering of place in place, the happening of the "settled locality" or "*Ortschaft*" becomes an important theme). As it functions to embody and articulate the idea and image of such a gathered unity, so place embodies and articulates an idea that Heidegger takes to be central to the thinking of being as such—the idea of unity. It is this idea, understood in one way in terms of the Aristotelian claim concerning the equivocity of being ("being is said in many ways"), to which Heidegger famously refers as providing the initial inspiration for his thinking, but the emphasis on unity, its necessary relation to difference, and the way this is intimately connected with the question of being occurs throughout his thinking, often specifically in connection with Greek thought but in a way that also makes clear its wider relevance. Thus, in 1969, he says that "To be able to see the parts (as such) there must be a relation to the unity . . . since Heraclitus, this unity is called ἕν, and . . . since this inception, the One is the other name of being,"[38] and before this, in the 1940s, he comments that:

Greek thinking equates beings, τὸ ὄν, early on with τo ἕν, the one, and, indeed already in pre-Platonic thinking being is distinguished by "unity." Until today, "philosophy" has neglected to reflect at all upon what the ancient thinkers mean with this ἕν. Above all, it does not ask why, at the inception of Western thinking, "unity" is so decisively attributed to beings as their essential feature.[39]

One way of understanding Heidegger's thinking in its entirety—a way of understanding that also picks up on the supposed importance of the Aristotelian equivocity of being—is in terms of the attempt to articulate the nature of the unity that is at issue here, since that task is at one with the question of being. The claim I would make, however, is that this attempt is one that is already determined, in Heidegger's thinking (and I would suggest in all thinking), by the necessary role of place.[40] Thus, in addressing the matter concerning the unity of Heidegger's thought as such, Joseph Fell responds by saying that "The answer to [Heidegger's] early, and only, question about what is common to the manifold uses of the word 'Being' is precisely his later meditation on the 'single,' 'simple,' and 'remaining' place, the common place where every being is 'as' it is."[41] The path along which Heidegger's thought moves is a path that constantly turns back toward this place, and in which the place-bound direction of that thinking, sometimes in spite of itself, becomes ever clearer. In this latter respect, however, while my (and Fell's) emphasis on Heidegger's thinking as essentially determined by the thinking of place implies the assertion of a fundamental unity and consistency to Heidegger's thinking as such, it is a consistency that is fully compatible with the character of that thinking as exhibiting certain breaks, shifts, misunderstandings, and even certain misrepresentations,[42] as it constantly articulates and rearticulates the "question" of being as it arises in terms of the "experience" of place. Heidegger's thinking is thus always "on the way" (*unterwegs*), but that which it is on the way toward is the place in which it already begins.

1.2 The Problem of Place

If place is indeed a significant concept both for philosophical inquiry and for the understanding of Heidegger's own thought, it is also, however, a concept that brings certain characteristic problems with it—problems that often threaten to block the investigation of place right from the start. This is especially so for any attempt to take up place as it relates to Heidegger's work, and in large part it arises out of Heidegger's well-known involvement with Nazism. Heidegger became a member of the National Socialist Party ("saying yes" as he put it "to the Nationalist and the Socialist"[43]) in 1933, and a little later in the same year, he was appointed rector of the University of Freiburg by the National Socialist Party, but resigned the position in 1934, after having apparently found it increasingly difficult to accommodate himself to the demands of the new regime.

There has, over at least the last twenty years, been an ongoing debate, not merely over the nature and extent of Heidegger's commitment to National Socialism, but also over the extent to which that commitment compromises or taints his thinking as a whole.[44] Yet there has also been a strong tendency to assume that, whatever the exact details of Heidegger's involvement, his entanglement with Nazism is itself tied to his espousal of a mode of thinking that emphasized notions of place and belonging. At this point, it becomes apparent that far from being merely a question of Heidegger's own politics, what is at issue here concerns the politics of place as such. Indeed, Heidegger's Nazi associations, coupled with the evident centrality of place and associated notions in his thinking (especially notions of belonging, rootedness, homeland, and so forth), seem often to be taken as providing a self-evident demonstration of the politically reactionary and "dangerous" character of place-based thinking.

A particularly clear example of this approach is to be found in the work of the geographer and cultural theorist David Harvey. In his influential text *The Condition of Post-Modernity*, Harvey writes that:

> The German philosopher Heidegger . . . in part based his allegiance to the principles (if not the practices) of Nazism on his rejection of a universalizing machine rationality as an appropriate mythology for modern life. He proposed, instead, a counter-myth of rootedness in place and environmentally-bound traditions as the only secure foundation for political and social action in a manifestly troubled world.[45]

And later in the same work Harvey writes of the "sorts of sentiments of place, Being, and community that brought Heidegger into the embrace of national socialism."[46] Harvey's comments are echoed by another major figure within geographical theory, Doreen Massey. Although her work has also been important in bringing ideas of place and space to greater prominence in contemporary theory, nevertheless, Massey explicitly criticizes what she takes to be the "Heideggerian view of Space/Place as Being" and raises a variety of objections to such an account, claiming that:

> There are a number of distinct ways in which the notion of place which is derived from Heidegger is problematical. One is the idea that places have single essential identities. Another is the idea that the identity of place—the sense of place—is constructed out of an introverted, inward-looking history based on delving into the past for internalized origins. . . . Another problem with the conception of place which derives from Heidegger is that it seems to require the drawing of boundaries. . . . [Another aspect of] the Heideggerian approach, and one which from the point of view of the physical sciences now looks out of date, is the strict dichotomization of time and space. . . .[47]

While Massey is concerned to argue against Heidegger precisely because of the rise of Heideggerian-influenced notions of place and space within geography and cultural theory (and to argue for certain alternative conceptions), it is clear that she regards this as problematic, not only because of a supposed incompatibility of these notions with modern physics,[48] but more properly because of what she appears to view as the theoretically conservative and politically reactionary character of the Heideggerian concern with place.[49]

More recently, and from within an architectural frame, the architectural theorist Neil Leach argues against the Heideggerian idea of "dwelling" (closely associated in the later thinking with notions of place), and associated notions, on grounds that echo the criticisms found in Harvey and Massey. Following on from Jean-François Lyotard's critique of Heidegger in "*Domus* and Megalopolis,"[50] Leach claims that Heidegger's appeal to notions of, for instance, "*Heimat*" (a term sometimes, although somewhat inadequately, translated as "homeland"):

would appear to be part of a consistent nationalistic outlook in his [Heidegger's] thought, which is echoed in a series of forced etymological strategies in his writings which attempt to lend authority to the German language by tracing the origins of certain German words to ancient Greek. All this would seem to infer that there is a potential nationalism that permeates the whole of his thought, a nationalism which in the context of prewar Germany, shared something in common with fascism.[51]

Leach goes on to argue more specifically against the emphasis on the notion of dwelling (an idea that will be explored in more detail in chapter 5), which he presents through Lyotard's term "*domus*" as an essentially mythic concept that does not acknowledge its own character *as* mythic:

The *domus* . . . can be seen as a myth of the present, and it is within this framework that we can now also begin to understand regionalism as a movement grounded in myth. Thus what purports to be a sentimental evocation of traditional forms can be seen as part of a larger project of constructing and reinforcing a regional or national identity. We might therefore recognise within regionalism not only the potential dangers inherent in all such calls for a regional or national identity, but also the essential complicity of the concept within the cultural conditions of late capitalism. . . . These values are particularly suspect in an age when there has been a fundamental shift in the ways in which we relate to the world. Not only must we question the primacy of a concept such as "dwelling" as a source of identification, but we must also ask whether a concept which is so place-specific can any longer retain much authority. . . . All this begins to suggest that there is a potential problem in too readily adopting a Heideggerian model as the basis for a theoretical framework for a new Europe. . . . For the *domus* as domestication is potentially totalitarian.[52]

Leach opposes the concepts of dwelling and the "*domus*" with the ideas of the urban and the cosmopolitan, arguing that these provide a more politically positive and productive source for thinking about contemporary architecture, especially in the fractured landscapes of Central and Eastern Europe.[53]

It is notable that neither Harvey nor Massey, nor even Leach, pays much detailed attention to Heidegger's texts as such.[54] Indeed, one of the intriguing features of these comments is that they seem to be directed at a Heideggerian position—one that gives explicit emphasis to ideas of place and also "dwelling"—that only becomes evident in Heidegger's thinking in the period after 1935, and most clearly not until after 1947. Thus the addresses from the early 1930s in which Heidegger seems to align himself with elements of Nazi ideology combine the vocabulary of *Being and Time* with ideas and images also present in Nazi rhetoric, including notions of *"Volk"* and of *"Blut und Boden,"* but they do not deploy any developed notions of place or dwelling as such (and the distinction is an important one, both within Heidegger's own thinking and within thought, politics, and culture more generally). Talk of *"Blut and Boden"* seems to feature in Heidegger's vocabulary in only a few places,[55] and although the notion of *"Volk"* does have a greater persistence and significance,[56] it too is almost entirely absent from Heidegger's postwar thought. Significantly, it is in his engagement with Hölderlin, immediately *after* his resignation of the rectorate, in 1934–1935, that ideas of place and dwelling begin to emerge more explicitly (though still in a relatively undeveloped form) as a focus for Heidegger's thinking. Moreover, the influence of Heidegger on contemporary thinking about place does not stem from the work of the 1920s and early 1930s, but rather from that of the middle to late 1930s and, especially, of the period from 1945 onwards, particularly essays such as "Building Dwelling Thinking."[57] In this respect, the strategy that appears in Harvey, Massey, and Leach seems to be one that attempts to discredit ideas explicit in the later thinking largely on the basis of the political engagement apparently present in the earlier.[58]

If there is an argument that seems to underpin the criticisms of Harvey, Massey, and Leach, among others, it would seem to be that notions of place and dwelling are politically reactionary because they are somehow intrinsically exclusionary. Yet there seems very little in the way of any general argument that is advanced to support this claim. Certainly an exclusionary politics presupposes the idea of that from which "others" are excluded, but this does not establish that place is an intrinsically exclusionary or reactionary idea, only that it may be employed to reactionary or exclusionary ends—and this would seem to be true of just about any important concept one may care to name. Yet although there is certainly much with which one could take issue in the passages from which I have quoted above, both in terms of their reading of Heidegger and of the "politics" of place,[59] my aim in quoting from these writers is not to initiate a sustained critique of their work as such, so much as simply to demonstrate the way in which, particularly in relation to Heidegger's thought, place has indeed emerged as politically problematic. Heidegger's entanglement with Nazism has thus provided a powerful base, irrespective of the actual strength of the arguments advanced,[60] from which to inveigh against place-oriented modes of thinking.[61] Yet having established that place does present a prima facie "problem" in this respect, it is worth attending, in more general terms, to the connections that might be at issue here, as well as to the possible connections that might exist, both in Heidegger and more broadly, between ideas of place and reactionary, perhaps even totalitarian, forms of politics.

It has to be noted, from the very start, that there is no doubt that there are elements of Heidegger's thought and action that those of us who are committed to a broadly liberal, democratic form of life must find repugnant. It is not merely that Heidegger seems himself not to have been a committed democrat (declaring in the *Der Spiegel* interview of 1966 that he remained unconvinced that democracy was the political system best fitted to the demands of the modern technological world),[62] or that he was willing to use people and situations to his own personal-political ends,[63] but that he also seems to have espoused a set of political commitments, at least in the 1930s, that were indeed consonant with elements of Nazi ideology, including the commitment to the special role of Germany in the world, to the role of the "Leader" (*der Führer*) as the focus for the people and the State, and to the need for Germany to expand her borders in order to allow for the expansion of the German nation.[64]

The fact of such commitment is certainly a reason for caution, and even suspicion, in dealing with Heidegger's work, yet equally, the fact of such commitment does not, as such, tell us very much about how we should then regard Heidegger's philosophy. In this respect, there is a tendency in many discussions of the issues at stake here to assume a fairly simplistic view of the relation between the elements that make up a body of thought, and between philosophical thinking and the political and personal involvement of the philosopher. Although we may wish or hope it to be otherwise, possession of a measure of philosophical insight and erudition is no guarantee of the possession, in like measure, of qualities of personal courage, compassion, or even moral conscience, let alone of political judgment or ability. This would seem to be a simple fact of human psychology that is unaffected by general claims about any sort of necessary connection between philosophy and the philosopher. Moreover, to the extent that there will always be some connection between philosophical and political commitments, or between philosophical theory and personal actions, the connection will be no different in kind from the connection that obtains between the various components of individual psychology more broadly—and that means that there will always be a measure of inconsistency and indeterminacy, as well as scope for interpretation and reinterpretation. Just as we may well find that elements within Heidegger's philosophical writings are inconsistent with one another, or else fail to display the interrelation that might be claimed or expected, so the same will be true of Heidegger's political pronouncements and actions.

Of course, it is often argued that Heidegger himself asserted the inextricability of philosophical thinking with the personal life of the philosopher, and so, even if the assertion of a strong connection does not hold in general, we are nevertheless obliged to assume some such connection in Heidegger's case. Here, however, not only does such reasoning seem at fault in formal terms (there is no reason why we cannot simply say that Heidegger was mistaken on this point—in his own case as well as in general), but more importantly, inasmuch as Heidegger does assert such a connection, this line of argument also involves a misunderstanding of the nature of that connection as Heidegger seems to have intended it. The way in which philosophical thinking connects with, or is grounded in, the life of the philosopher is not primarily at the level of a consistency of ideas, but rather in terms of the way philosophical thinking has its origin, and so is determined as philosophical, in the philosopher's own personal "situatedness." This will turn out to be an important point in the topological character of Heidegger's thought, but it certainly does not warrant the idea that there is a simple passage from the content of Heidegger's politics or his personal life to the content of his philosophy or vice versa. Neither does it rule this out, of course, but it provides no basis for the assertion of any such connection independently of actually working through the ideas at issue. Thus, on purely general grounds, it seems that neither Heidegger's politics nor his personal actions, no matter that we may find them distasteful and even abhorrent, preempt the need, if we wish to understand his thinking, to engage with his philosophy. There can be no "shortcuts" here.

A large part of the story of Heidegger's politics in the 1930s certainly involves his adoption of a set of reactionary ideas, common among many Germans of the period, including writers and intellectuals, that harked back to the notions of German greatness and "mission" prior to the First World War (the so-called ideas of 1914).[65] In Heidegger's case those ideas were also coupled with a conviction that the advent of the Nazi "Revolution" offered the chance for a radical reform of the German universities, and so, presumably, of German science and culture, under Heidegger's own leadership.[66] Nevertheless, there seems little doubt that the underlying philosophical basis for Heidegger's political engagement in the 1930s, and so for Heidegger's engagement with Nazism as such, was his particular understanding of the idea of a "folk" or "people" (*Volk*) as of central historical-political significance.[67] This is the point at which the connection with the idea of place comes into view since the idea of a people is itself a notion tied up, certainly in Heidegger's thought, as well as in the ideology and rhetoric of National Socialism, with the idea of a particular "place" or "homeland"—in German, "*Vaterland*" (Fatherland), or, more appropriately in Heidegger's case, a "*Heimat*" (one's "home," sometimes translated as "homeland," but lacking any exact English equivalent)—to which that people belongs.

The racial ideology of Nazism took the idea of the people and the connection with the "homeland" to be one based in race: the "homeland" was understood as the particular geographical space or region in which the racial identity of the people was formed—hence the near-literal use of the language of "blood and soil" (*Blut und Boden*) as exemplifying the relation between people and place. Heidegger, however, never seems to have himself subscribed to such biologically based notions. His conception of both the "people" and the "homeland" appears to have had its foundation in notions of "spirit," "culture," and "community"[68] understood as quite separate from notions of race and biology (a distinction for which there could be no place within Nazi ideology), or, indeed, of mere geographical location. Indeed, James Phillips has argued that while the idea of "the people" was the basis for Heidegger's involvement with Nazism, it also turned out to be, in large part, the basis for his disengagement from it (as I noted above, Heidegger's engagement with Hölderlin, and so with the ideas of place and dwelling that come to the fore there, also plays an important role here).[69] The biologistic and racist character of Nazi thinking about the concept of the "people," and so of the connection between the people and their "place," is evident in many writings from the period. It is, for instance, clearly evident in the writing of Ludwig Ferdinand Clauss, whose book *Die nordische Seele: Eine Einführung in die Rassensee-lenkunde* (The Nordic Soul: An Introduction to Racial Psychology) was first published in 1932 and in a number of editions thereafter. In this work, Clauss presents a view of the soul as both determined by the landscape in which it is located while also determining that landscape in a more basic fashion. Thus Clauss writes that:

The manner in which the soul reaches out into its world fashions the geographical area of this world into a "landscape." A landscape is not something that the soul alights upon, as it were, something ready-made. Rather it is something that it fashions by virtue of its species-determined way of viewing its environment. . . . It cannot, of course, arbitrarily fashion any landscape out of any kind of geographical area. The area is the matter, so to speak, into which the soul projects its style and thus transforms it into a landscape. But not every matter lends itself to the same formative activity of the soul. . . . When. . . . persons whose inner landscape is the north succumb to the enticement of the south and stay there and settle down . . . the first generations will live in opposition, albeit unconsciously, to the landscape which is alien to their kind. Gradually, then, the style of the souls undergoes a change. They do not change their race, they will not become Mediterranean people . . . but their Nordic style will undergo a transformation which will ultimately make them into a southern variety of Nordic man. . . . The landscape forms the soul, but the soul also forms the landscape . . . every authentic racial stock is bound up with its space.[70]

Given what we know about the subsequent history of the Third Reich, the last sentence of this quotation is ominous. "Every authentic racial stock is bound up with its space," writes Clauss. What then of a "racial stock" or a people that lack such a space? The conclusion, presumably, is that they are not an "authentic racial stock"—not an authentic people—at all. Such a conclusion was readily employed to justify the Nazi persecution and, ultimately, the destruction of those deemed to be of Jewish "stock." Dispersed throughout Europe and the Middle East, the Jews could have no homeland, no landscape, no space nor place of their own. Thus the stereotype of the Jews as cosmopolitan and rootless fed into a view of individual identity as tied to racial identity, understood in terms of geographical and territorial locatedness, that left them with no authentic identity at all.[71]

Clauss might seem to provide an excellent example of the reactionary character of place-based thinking. It is important to notice, however, the way in which the type of argument advanced by Clauss depends, not only on the assertion of a connection between human identity and place, but, perhaps more importantly, on the ideas that the way in which place and identity are connected is by means of *race*, and so by the "species-determined" soul that itself "reaches out" and fashions its landscape (which is itself understood in terms of certain general forms—the landscape of the "south," of the "north"), and that there is such a thing as "authentic racial stock." All of these latter claims can readily be contested without touching the idea of a fundamental connection between place and identity. Indeed, it is significant that in Clauss's account and in Nazi ideology more generally, the key concept is not that of place as such, but rather of race, or the "species-determined" soul.[72] Moreover, in Clauss, and in Nazism, the tendency to understand human identity as based in general forms, whether of "racial stock" or of landscape type, can actually be seen to constitute a move that diminishes the significance of place—it is the *general type* that is important in Nazi ideology, in contrast to which the thinking that is oriented toward place typically gives emphasis to the specific and the local.

This latter issue turns out to be a crucial point of difference when one looks to the way Nazi ideology is related to the German *"Heimat"* tradition. Although there has been a tendency in the past simply to assimilate this tradition (which, in common with "folkloric" movements elsewhere, including Great Britain, has its origins in developments in the nineteenth century that are partly reactions to developing urbanization and industrialization) to the same "folkish" and nationalist ideology that is present in Nazism, more recent research has emphasized the distinction between them. In many cases the *Heimat* tradition in Germany was connected with reactionary, even racist political tendencies, but this is not always true, and the connection does not, therefore, appear to be an intrinsic one[73]— Celia Applegate, whose work has been particularly important here, argues that such a connection did not generally hold true in the Pfalz region that is the focus for her study, [74] while William Rollins argues that the *Heimatschutz* movement in late nineteenth-century Germany represented "a bourgeois-progressive alternative to the Wilhelmine order."[75] Indeed, while the Nazi attempt to appropriate to themselves all things German meant that they also attempted to take up elements of the *Heimat* tradition, in doing so they also tended to undermine its local and associational elements. The result, as Applegate writes, was that

although Heimat cultivation did persist in the Third Reich, its meaning—politicized, paganized, and nationalized—became ultimately abstract. All that had once been vital to Heimat cultivation, from civic pride to a respect for the particularity of local life and tradition, had little resonance in a regime attentive to national grandeur and racial, not simply local, pride. Heimat, because it implied little about race, tribe, or any of the other categories favoured by Nazi ideology, became a term of distinctly secondary importance: the locus of race, perhaps, but not its essence, and not a concept with any intrinsically prior claim to the loyalties of the German Volk.[76]

The subsumption of the individual to the State, the Nation and to the "People" that is characteristic of fascist, and totalitarian, politics would thus seem to be in tension with the emphasis on the particular and the local that is characteristic of the *Heimat* tradition. The way in which the Nazis, and others, nevertheless, tend to draw on that tradition need not be taken to be indicative of the fascist character of the tradition as such, but rather of the need to find content for the otherwise rather nebulous and abstract notions of "nation" and of "people." In many respects, the tension that seems to exist between the emphasis on the local and the particular that is associated with the Heimat tradition and the overarching nationalism and totalitarianism associated with the idea of "the people" as the focus for political-historical thinking itself seems to arise as a source of tension in Heidegger's own work.

My point here, however, is not so much to defend the *Heimat* tradition (although it does seem to me that there are important elements in that tradition that deserve further exploration) as to indicate the complexities that surround the various forms in which notions of place, belonging, and identity may be articulated. Such complexity is often overlooked. This is so, not only with respect to the historical appearance of such notions, but also with respect to the way they play out in more mundane contemporary thinking across almost the entire political spectrum. Whether we inquire into what it is to be "English" or to be "Australian" (both important topics of discussion in the contemporary English and Australian media), the importance of respecting indigenous connections with the land, or the value of regenerating local communities through the regeneration of urban parkland and streetscapes, what is at issue in all such cases are questions that give priority to notions of place, and yet they do not thereby automatically predispose us to a specific political orientation. It is often claimed that to take place as a focus for ideas of identity and belonging is already to presuppose a homogeneity of culture and identity in relation to that place, as well as to exclude others from it—this is the core of the argument that is often used to demonstrate the supposed politically dangerous character of place-oriented thinking. Yet this claim is usually only advanced in particular instances—it is seldom directed, for instance, against indigenous modes of understanding—and typically depends, not so much on the idea of place as such, but rather on a particular, and already rather contentious conception of place (and so of the relation to place) that is often based on the sort of ideas that Massey lists in the passage I quoted above: "single essential identities . . . an introverted, inward-looking history based on delving into the past for internalized origins . . . the strict dichotomization of time and space." In other words, the argument for the reactionary character of place often seems to depend on already construing place in a politically reactionary fashion.

The real question, however, is just *how* place should be understood. And this is an even more pressing question because of the way in which place, and notions associated with place, are indeed given powerful political employment across the political spectrum. In this respect, simply to reject place because of its use by reactionary politics is actually to run the risk of failing to understand why and how place is important, and so of failing to understand how the notion can, and does, serve a range of political ends, including those of fascism and totalitarianism, as well as of progressivism. Thus, just as Heidegger's own politics cannot be taken, in itself, to undermine his philosophy in any direct way, neither can we take the fact that Nazi ideology and rhetoric invoke notions that are connected with ideas of place and belonging as evidence for the politically unacceptable character of the notions of place and belonging as such. Indeed, just as the Nazis deployed other notions that have a power and significance in human life—including ideas of virtue, of ethics and morality, of courage, care, and commitment (even if in ways that seem to invert the very meanings of these ideas)—so the fact that they also deployed notions of place and belonging attests more to the power and significance of those notions than provides any evidence of their essentially reactionary character. In pressing this point, however, the most that can be achieved is to clear a space in which the question of place can be raised as a significant one deserving of further inquiry. In my own case, I have already set out some of the considerations relevant to such an inquiry in my previous work. The task here is to undertake that inquiry with specific reference to Heidegger, and one of the reasons for undertaking such a project, quite apart from the attempt to advance the understanding of Heidegger's thinking, is precisely because of the way in which place appears central to Heidegger's thought, and yet also the way it appears as a problem in his thinking.

1.3   The Language of Place

So far I have used the term "topology," as well as "space" and "place," without any explanation as to what exactly I take these terms to involve. Although the exploration of the meaning of these terms is a large part of what I will be attempting in the pages to come, some preliminary clarification is also required now—all the more so given the German sources that I will address. For the most part, my use of "space," "place," and "topology" draws heavily on the analysis that is set out in *Place and Experience*. In that work, I distinguished place from space, while also allowing that there is a sense of dimensionality to place that also makes for a necessary connection between the two concepts, as well as between place and time. Indeed, in *Place and Experience*, I took place to be a more encompassing notion than either space or time, the latter two being presented as complementary modes of dimensionality tied to simultaneity and succession respectively.[77]

One of the difficulties in clarifying the relation between space and place is, not only that the two are necessarily connected (inasmuch as place carries a spatial element within it even while space is also a certain abstraction from out of place), but that there has been a pervasive tendency for place to be understood in terms that are purely spatial. This is a point that I noted above—a point that is a key element in Casey's account of the history of place—and it means that place is most often treated as either a certain position in space or else as a certain portion of space (formally specifiable in both cases through a framework of coordinates). This way of understanding place is itself tied to a particular conception of space as identical with physical space, that is, with space as it is articulated within the system of the physical sciences, and so as essentially articulated in terms of the measurable and the quantifiable. Heidegger himself comments on the modern concept of space and the way it has come to dominate the idea of place, thus: "For us today space is not determined by way of place; rather, all places, as constellations of points, are determined by infinite space that is everywhere homogeneous and nowhere distinctive."[78]

The concepts of place, and of space, that are at issue for Heidegger cannot be assumed to be identical with any narrowly physicalist conception, nor can it be assumed that place can be taken as derivative of space, or as identical with spatial location, position, area, or volume. In this respect, place should not be assumed to be identical with the "where" of a thing. Although this is one sense of place, it is not the only or the primary sense— place also refers us to that open, cleared, gathered "region" or "locale" in which we find ourselves along with other persons and things. Yet when the concept of place does appear explicitly in early Heidegger, it is often in terms, not of this sort of cleared region, but in terms of location or position. Similarly, there is often a tendency for Heidegger, again more so in his early work, to view space in terms that are tied to a physicalist conception of space—a tendency that is itself tied to the way in which, especially in *Being and Time*, Heidegger associates the prioritization of spatiality with Cartesianism. Nonetheless, there is clearly a topological structure already at work even in Heidegger's early thought, while so far as space is concerned, for the most part, Heidegger sees the physicalist conception of space as secondary to more existential conceptions. Thus in *Being and Time*, as we shall see, there is a notion of space that is directly involved with the character of *Dasein* (being-there) as "being-in-the-world."

Place is, as I noted above, a problematic concept in the early work—although it is not absent, it is not generally thematized as such, and it is only in the period after the 1930s that it comes to be an explicit focus of attention. When Heidegger does take up place directly in this way, then it is place as a certain gathered, but open "region" that is indeed the focus of Heidegger's attention. This conception of place connects, in English, with the way in which the term "place" is itself derived from Greek and Latin roots meaning "broad, or open way," as well as with the sense of "place" associated with the way in which the intersection of roads in a town or village may open out into a square that may itself function as somewhere in which events and people may gather and perhaps even as the center for the town or village as such. The idea of place as tied to a notion of gathering or "focus" is also suggested by the etymology of the German term for place, *Ort*, according to which the term originally indicated the point or edge of a weapon—the point of a spear, for instance—at which all of the energy of the weapon is brought to bear.[79] Indeed, Heidegger himself makes use of this connection in his 1952 essay on the poet Georg Trakl, writing that "Originally the word *Ort* meant the point [*Spitze*] of a spear. In it everything flows together. The *Ort* gathers unto itself into the highest and the most extreme."[80] Inasmuch as this notion of place implies a certain unity to the elements that make it up, so, in Heidegger, it also implies a certain very specific form of boundedness, but it is a form that is quite distinct from the boundedness of which Massey complains—it is a form of boundedness tied to the idea of that from which something begins in its unfolding as what it is, rather than that at which it comes to a stop; a concept of boundary as *origin* rather than as *terminus*.[81] Significantly, both this idea of boundedness and that of focus or gathering are themselves closely tied to a conception of place as constituted through a gathering of elements that are themselves mutually defined only through the way in which they are gathered together within the place they also constitute. This latter feature of place, although it may seem initially somewhat obscure, turns out to be a key element in the Heideggerian conception of place and is something about which I shall say more shortly.[82]

The English term "space" can usually be taken as the straightforward translation of the German term *"Raum"*—a translation that fits most of Heidegger's uses of the term—although the German term can sometimes be translated also by the English "room" (as in "room to move"), as well as figuring in the verb forms *"räumen"* (to make empty, evacuate), *"aufräumen"* (to clear out, to make an end of), and *"ausräumen"* (to empty out).

"Place" is rather more complicated, however, as the term can—and is—used to translate a number of different, if sometimes related, terms. The most important term is that which I mentioned briefly above, "Ort,"[83] and, with it, the related form "Ortschaft" (often used to mean a village, town, or other settled locality). Heidegger uses this term as his usual translation for the Greek term "topos" (which appears in the English "topology" and "topography"). Significantly, both "Ort" and "Ortschaft" become more important terms in Heidegger's thinking as place is itself taken up more directly. Consequently, these terms do not appear with the same frequency or emphasis in the early thought as in the later (when Heidegger does talk of place in the earlier writings, it is often by using terms such as "Stelle" or "Platz"). There is, however, one other term that Heidegger employs, on at least two occasions, in a way that does suggest connections with his later use of "Ort" and "Ortschaft": "Stätte," usually translated simply as "place," but often having the connotation of "home," is used by Heidegger in the 1935–1936 essay "The Origin of the Work of Art," as well as in other works, principally from the 1930s and early 1940s, most notably in some of the Hölderlin lectures.[84] The term does not, however, seem to be used in any significant way outside of works mostly restricted to the 1930s and 1940s. The employment of "Ort" as a term that relates to topos is itself indicated by the way in which both terms figure in ways that can be used to designate a discussion or focus of inquiry. This is true of the English word "topic" and so the idea of "topology" in Heidegger's thinking can sometimes be viewed as relating as much to the idea of a literary or textual "site" as to a place as such.[85] The German term "Erörterung," which contains "Ort" within it, also means a debate or discussion, but Heidegger employs it in a way that plays on the sense of "situating," "locating," or "placing" that it also connotes.[86] This is significant, not because it somehow shows that Heidegger's talk of "topos" or "Ort" is really a reference to something linguistic, but rather because of the way it is indicative of the intimate connection between language and place (something I discuss further in chapter 5, especially sec. 5.4 below).

In *Being and Time*, the concept of place appears most directly in the ideas of "*Platz*" and "*Gegend.*" "*Platz*" usually refers to a particular place in the sense of *location* (typically in relation to other things, although it also has a use in which it comes close to space or "room") and is a term whose significance is largely restricted to the framework of *Being and Time* and the discussion of equipmentality—"equipment has its place [*Platz*]."[87] "*Gegend*" is often translated as "region" (John Macquarrie and Edward Robinson also suggest "realm" or "whereabouts").[88] The term appears in Heidegger's later thinking to refer to a region as it gathers around a particular place (and in this sense may be taken to relate more closely to *"Ort"* or *"Ortschaft,"* although referring to a more encompassing domain), but in *Being and Time* the term refers to the larger realm within which items of equipment are placed in relation to one another (in, for instance, the workroom) and so to what is more like a network of "places" (*Plätze*)—this use of *"Gegend"* in relation to *"Platz"* is indicative of the way *"Platz"* usually indicates a position or location within a larger ordering. Another term that has a similar meaning to *"Platz"* is (*die*) *"Stelle,"* although in the same paragraph in *Being and Time* in which he introduces the idea of the *"Platz"* of equipment, Heidegger uses *"Stelle"* to refer to the way equipment "has its position [*Stelle*] in space" in a way that suggests a contrast between the two notions. Yet in both cases, there is a similar sense to the way in which *"Stelle"* and *"Platz"* always refer to a larger region or domain of positions or locations, whether that be the realm of extended spatiality or of the organized workroom. *"Stelle"* is connected to the verb *"stellen"* (to put or to place), which plays a key role in a number of terms, including *"Ge-stell"* (Heidegger's word for the essence of modern technology), and in this respect the connection of *"Stelle"* with spatiality is itself significant (as will be evident in the discussion in chapter 5). Another term that has a similar sense to *"Platz"* and *"Stelle,"* in the broad sense of location or position, is (*die*) *"Statt,"* which appears in the verb *"stattfinden"* (to take place).

It is crucial to recognize the differing senses that attach to these spatial and topographic terms since failure to do so could lead one to seriously misread the role of place in Heidegger's thinking—all the more so if one is reliant on English translations of Heidegger's text that are not sensitive to the underlying issues of topology at stake here. For the most part, the important distinction is between terms such as *"Ort"* and *"Ortschaft"* (and to a lesser extent *"Stätte"*), and terms such as *"Platz"* and *"Stelle."* All of these terms may be translated as "place," and yet although *"Ort"* and *"Ortschaft"* can be used to refer to place in the ontologically significant sense that I have already outlined above (place as the open region in which things are gathered and disclosed), *"Platz"* and *"Stelle"* invariably refer to place merely in the sense of location or position—usually the location or position of some already identified and determined entity. One of the difficulties, in this respect, in moving from Heidegger's earlier to his later thought is that earlier he tends not to employ *"Ort"* or *"Ortschaft"* in any significant way, but instead, when place is an issue, often talks in terms of *"Platz"* or *"Stelle."* Of course, this means that it is location or position that is thereby thematized rather than place as such, and since both location and position are, in a certain sense, "secondary" notions (they depend upon the idea of the region or domain and, in a deeper sense, as will become evident below, on the opening up of such a domain that occurs through place), so they cannot take on an especially central role. Moreover, since the ideas of position or location always refer us to the position or location of some entity, they will always be notions tied more to beings (or perhaps to the being of beings) rather than to being as such (to use the language of the ontological difference).

Thus, while in later Heidegger we can follow the development of a place-oriented mode of thinking much more directly, through Heidegger's appropriation and deployment of notions of place and *topos* as such, in his early thinking, the task is much more difficult. The exploration of the topological character of Heidegger's early thought, including that of *Being and Time*, requires that we be sensitive to the way such topology emerges, not so much in Heidegger's use of the specific language of place, of *topos, Ort,* and *Ortschaft,* but through his employment of other terms. Most obviously, through his employment of terms such as *"Dasein"* (which I will translate as "being there" and with respect to which I shall have more to say in chapter 2 below, see sec. 2.2), *"Welt"* (world), *"Umwelt"* (environment, environing world), and *"Situation"* or *"Lage"* (both of which can be translated as "situation"), but also through temporally oriented terms such as *"jeweilig"* (meaning "for a time" or "for a while," and which I have translated as "lingering"), and *"Ereignis"* (happening or event, also translated in Heidegger as "event of appropriation" or "enowning"). *"Ereignis"* will turn out to be a particularly important and (from a translational point of view) somewhat problematic term about which I will have much more to say (see chapter 5, below, sec. 5.1). So far as the immediate discussion of the language of place is concerned, however, what matters about the idea of *"Ereignis"* is that it carries with it some of the same sense of gathering and disclosing (as a happening is a unitary unfolding or disclosing) that is central to place in the significant sense I have deployed it here. Moreover, understood as tied to such gathering and disclosing, place already has to be understood as essentially dynamic, that is, as having an essential temporal character. Place, one should recall, is not to be simply identified with space.

Although place may appear the most everyday of terms, it is nonetheless, as should be evident from the discussion above, a term that carries a great deal of complexity within it—all the more so when we want to explore the workings of the concept as it moves across different languages. At least initially, however, the term "topology" appears somewhat more straightforward—it is a direct translation of the German term *"Topologie."* The connotations that attach to the English term are also more or less identical to those that attach to the German. Both "topology" and *"Topologie"* have a specific technical sense that refers to a branch of mathematical geometry that studies the nature of surfaces. Heidegger, however, drawing on the Greek roots that lie embedded in the term—*topos* and *logos*—takes it in the sense of a "saying of place" (*Ort-reden*). The real question—one might say that it is one of the central questions that concerns my project here—is what does it mean to talk of, and to attempt, such a "saying of place"? For the moment, all I can do is sketch out some of the background to this idea, before we move on to explore what might be at issue in more detail as it emerges through the larger analysis undertaken in the pages that follow.

Heidegger uses the term *"Topologie"* in only a very few places: in the Le Thor Seminar from 1969;[89] in a poem from 1947 (the line that stands at the head of this chapter);[90] and in his exchange with Ernst Jünger, "On the Question of Being" (originally "Concerning the Line").[91] However, the idea of topology is clearly very closely connected with the later Heidegger's explicit focus on notions of place and particularly with the idea of his work as concerned to speak or articulate "the place of being" (*die Ortschaft des Seyns*). Indeed, Heidegger makes just this connection in the key passage from the Le Thor Seminar that I mentioned above. There he provides a brief summary of the passage of his thinking in a way that also suggests that this is a passage through which all thinking must go:

With *Being and Time* . . . the "question of Being" . . . concerns the question of being qua being. It becomes thematic in *Being and Time* under the name of "the question of the meaning [*Sinn*] of being." Later this formulation was given up in favor of that of "the question of the truth of being," and finally in favor of that of "the question concerning the place or location of being" [*Ortschaft des Seins*], from which the name topology of being arose [*Topologie des Seins*]. Three terms which succeed one another and at the same time indicate three steps along the way of thinking: MEANING—TRUTH—PLACE (τοπoσ).[92]

This passage is a crucial one for my project here since not only does it bring together certain central concepts, but it also provides the outlines of the pathway that I aim to sketch out in more detail in the chapters to come.

One of the few places in which Heidegger's idea of topology has been explicitly addressed is in the work of Otto Pöggeler, and especially in his book *Martin Heidegger's Path of Thinking*. There Pöggeler writes that "Topology is the Saying (λόγοσ) of the abode (τόπoσ) in which truth as occurring unconcealment gathers itself."[93] Pöggeler's elaboration of this admittedly rather dense statement establishes the way in which he sees Heideggerian "topology" as essentially a meditative concern with the way in which a particular environing "world" comes forth around a particular mode of "emplacement" in that world. Heideggerian topology can thus be understood as an attempt to evoke and illuminate that placed abode. In this respect, topology is an attempt to illuminate a place in which we already find ourselves and in which other things are also disclosed to us. Concerned as it is with a place of *disclosure,* the topology to be found in late Heidegger is continuous with the project pursued in Heidegger's earlier work of uncovering the structure of disclosedness itself—and this is a continuity that will be pursued further in the explorations to follow. Understood as constituting a distinctive way of approaching the task of philosophy, or perhaps better, of thinking, the idea of topology provides a specific form of philosophical "methodology"—though not, as Pöggeler emphasizes, a methodology that establishes us as subjects in some special relationship to an object to be investigated. It is a methodology that begins with what is already present to us—the "phenomenon" of disclosedness as such, our location within a world in which not only ourselves, but the things around us, are accessible to us—and that looks, not to analyze the phenomenon at issue by showing how it is explicable in terms of some single underlying ground, but rather by showing the mutual interconnection of its constituting elements.

In this respect the idea of a "saying" of "place" or "abode" (a *logos* of *topos*) bears comparison with the idea of the writing or "inscribing" of place that is undertaken by the traditional topographer. The topographer who is concerned to map out a particular region and who has nothing to go on but the basic technology of theodolite and chain—along with a good eye, a steady hand, and strong legs—has the task of mapping out that region while located within it. Such a task can only be accomplished by looking to the interconnections among the features of that region and through a process of repeated triangulation and traverse—and a good deal of walking—on the basis of which such interconnections are established. Of course the topographer aims to arrive at a mapping of the region that will in some sense be "objective"—at least within a given set of cartographic parameters—but the topographer is always concerned to understand the region from within that region and by reference to the interconnectedness of the elements within it—an interconnection made concrete in the topographer's case by the crisscrossing pathways that represent the topographer's travels through the landscape. There is no reduction of the landscape down to some underlying foundation from which the features of the landscape could be derived or in which they are founded. For the topographer, there is only the surface of the land itself—the topography is written into that surface and accessible from it, rather than lying beneath or being visible from some point far above.

It was this notion of topography that I chose to use in *Place and Experience* as a way of explicating the idea that, so I argued there and will also argue in more detail here, also appears in Heidegger as topology. The use of "topography" as the key term, and not "topology" (the use of "*grapheme*" instead of "*logos*"), came about, in part, because of a desire to avoid the narrowly geometrical and mathematical interpretation that is all too readily associated with the latter term, but, more importantly, in order to be able to highlight the conceptual and methodological aspects of the focus on place that are brought to light through the analogy with the practice of topographical surveying that is sketched out above and that I take to be key elements both of my own idea of a philosophical topography and Heidegger's conception of a topology of being.[94] Inasmuch as this book is about the explication of the nature and significance of place in Heidegger's work, so it is also about the nature and significance in that work of such a "topographical/topological" orientation and method.

The idea of a topology or topography itself has relevance, moreover, to the question of terminology and language that has been at issue in the last few pages. The idea of topology suggests that it is a mistake to look for simple, reductive accounts—whether we are exploring a concept, or problem, or the meaning of a term, the point is always to look to a larger field of relations in which the matter at issue can be placed. This means, however, that it will seldom be possible to arrive at simple, univocal definitions. Significant terms will generally connect up with other terms in multiple ways and carry a range of connotations and meanings that cannot always be easily or precisely separated out. This is especially so of the terminology that Heidegger employs, and it is one of the reasons why there is so much discussion of how to understand key Heideggerian terms such as "being," "*Ereignis*," "*Dasein*," and so on. Thomas Sheehan suggests that one of the problems of contemporary Heidegger scholarship is that there is no clear understanding of what such terms mean.[95] I agree with some of Sheehan's concerns here, notably the way in which so much contemporary writing on Heidegger seems to lapse into obscure and often impenetrable discourse accessible only to the initiated. However, it also seems to me that the sort of clarity that Sheehan seems to hold up as desirable here—a clarity that appears to consist in a certain supposed univocity of meaning—is simply not achievable in discussions of Heidegger and may well constitute a mistaken philosophical ideal in general.[96] Heidegger himself seems to have regarded the character of language as "*vieldeutig*," that is, capable of carrying multiple meanings or senses, as part of the very essence of language. His own use of language plays to this character such that he constantly uses words in overlapping ways, in ways that play upon their etymology, or similarity of sound or structure, in ways such that the same term will appear slightly differently depending on the other terms with which it is being deployed.

In this respect, the common criticism of Heidegger's supposed reliance on dubious etymologies[97] often seems to misunderstand the way in which what is often at issue here is not the attempt to find the "real" meanings of words in their past histories, but rather to emphasize and pursue the multiple meanings that words may bear. It is thus a means to stimulate a way of thinking with language that is not restricted to the literal and yet is not simply metaphorical either. Sometimes, of course, this reliance on etymology is also taken to be associated with Heidegger's claims for the philosophical priority of German, and thence with a nationalism that is proximate to National Socialism (as in the passage I quoted from Leach in the discussion above).[98] Occasionally Heidegger does allow that other languages can express certain ideas more appropriately than the German,[99] but there seems little doubt that there is a certain parochialism in Heidegger's prioritization of his own language. One could put this down to simple narrow-mindedness on Heidegger's part, as well as a preoccupation with his own German identity; more charitably, one might see it as a reflection of the intimate connection between philosophy and language and the priority that one will almost always accord one's home language in any serious attempt at philosophical thinking—as Heidegger says in his essay on Anaximander from 1946: "We are bound to the language of the saying and we are bound to our own native language."[100]

Heidegger's attempt to draw on words in the multiplicity of their meaning cuts across the usual dichotomy of literal and nonliteral—indeed, when Heidegger rejects the metaphorical reading of certain expressions (as he does in "Letter on Humanism"[101]), it is not in order to insist on the purely literal (whatever that may be), but rather to force us to focus on the concrete matters before us, as well as to undercut the certainty of that distinction itself. Heidegger's interest is in the complex multiplicity of meaning out of which both literality and metaphoricity arise. Heidegger works constantly to evade and avoid the attempt at pinning down his language in a simple set of well-defined terms. Sometimes, it seems that this may indeed serve Heidegger as a means to evade and avoid his readers, but often it reflects the character of the language, and the ideas, as such. Dieter Henrich once said of one of his own terms that "*es irisiert*"—"it iridesces."[102] Almost all of Heidegger's language, especially the language of his later writings, is "iridescent" in the sense of constantly shining and showing different facets. The attempt to delineate the topology of thinking and the topology of being will always carry a certain "iridescence" of this sort. It is an iridescence that may also be compared to the "backwards or forwards" relatedness[103] that is to be found in hermeneutical thinking and that is also tied to the nature of the topological. It is a reflection of the iridescent, the multiple, shifting character of place as such.

2 Beginning in Place

. . . but of the origin / One thinks with difficulty. . . .
—Friedrich Hölderlin, "Bread and Wine"[1]

Whatever conclusions we may finally arrive at, and wherever we may suppose we end up, the place in which we begin our philosophy, the place in which philosophical questioning first arises, is the place in which we first find ourselves—that place is not an abstract world of ideas, not a world of sense-data or "impressions," not a world of theoretical "objects" nor of mere causal *relata*.[2] In finding ourselves "in" the world, we find ourselves already "in" a place, already given over to and involved with things, with persons, with our lives. On this basis the central questions of philosophy, questions of being and existence, as well as of ethics and virtue, must themselves take their determination and their starting point from this same place. Such ideas seem to underpin much of Heidegger's thinking, both early and late, and although the notion of place is not explicitly taken up in the early thinking, the idea that philosophy has its origin in our being already "there," in the world, alongside other persons and things, is a central theme in Heidegger's thinking in the late 1910s and early 1920s. Thus, in the lectures and writings from this early period, we find Heidegger developing a critique of the philosophical tradition that is not only based in the "placed" or "situated" character of thinking as such, but that also takes the tradition as having largely overlooked such "situatedness." The task of this chapter is to explore the development of the topology that seems to be at issue here and that is therefore already evident in Heidegger's early thinking. In doing so, we will not only be exploring the origins of Heideggerian topology, but also, from a Heideggerian perspective, exploring the topological origins of thinking as such.

2.1 Philosophy and "Life"

In a now famous essay written for Heidegger's eightieth birthday, Hannah Arendt draws attention to the way in which, in his teaching in the early 1920s, Heidegger offered a revitalized conception of philosophy, and philosophical practice, that emphasized the idea of philosophy as connected to the problems of "life." This did not imply the promise of some form of *"Lebensphilosophie,"* but rather the articulation of an idea of philosophy, as well as a mode of philosophizing, that saw the central questions of philosophy as questions in which the philosopher is herself already entangled, already bound up—philosophy was thus not to be understood as an abstract and impersonal undertaking, but as relating directly to the philosopher's own life and as drawing on the philosopher's own existential situation. Thus, of the character of his own thinking, Heidegger comments, in a letter from 1921, that: "I work concretely and factically out of my 'I am,' out of my intellectual and wholly factic origin, milieu, life-contexts, and whatever is available to me from these as a vital experience in which I live...."[3] Here it is worth noting from the very first (as if it were not obvious already) that to talk of "situation" almost invariably introduces topological, that is, place-related, considerations. To be in a situation is to be "placed" in a certain way, and, typically, such "placing" involves an orientation such that one's surroundings are configured in a particular way and in a particular relation to oneself—just as one is also related in a particular way to those surroundings.[4]

Yet acknowledging the already topological character of situatedness, what does it mean for philosophy to be "situated"—for it to connect up with the philosopher's own life, or with her own "factic origin, milieu, life-contexts"? What it certainly cannot mean, in this context, is that Heidegger's thought, or, indeed, philosophical thinking in general, can be understood simply by relating it to the personal biography of the philosopher—in the manner suggested, perhaps, by the oft-quoted aphorism from Nietzsche, according to which every great philosophy is "a confession on the part of its author and a kind of involuntary and unconscious memoir."[5] Certainly each and every philosophy will necessarily be articulated in terms that draw on, and will reflect, aspects of the philosopher's own biography, but that does not mean that the significance of such philosophy is purely biographical. Nor does it mean that philosophical thinking must necessarily provide some sort of infallible guide to practical life-decisions—what career to follow, what friends to cultivate, what political party to join—although neither does it mean that it must always be irrelevant in this regard. Philosophy is thus not something to be applied *to* life, but rather comes *out* of life and is lived as a *part* of life. In this respect, it might be said that one of the problematic tendencies of much contemporary philosophy is precisely its attempt to engage with contemporary problems and issues through the "application" of previously developed and general philosophical theories, whether of ethics or anything else, to various "practical" domains. Philosophy is in no wise made relevant in such a fashion— real philosophical engagement comes from working through concrete problems and situations in the terms, at least initially, in which those problems and situations themselves arise and formulating responses that come out of those problems and situations. The idea that there is a simple relation of "application" that obtains between prior theory and practical situation, or that one can simply "derive" practical outcomes from prior theoretical commitments, is one of the assumptions that bedevils much of the discussion of Heidegger's own political involvement in the 1930s.

Similarly, while there can be no doubt that biographical details may enable us better to understand what is at issue in a philosopher's work, through enabling us to identify and interpret the motivations that lie behind it and the shifts that may occur in its development, still this does not mean that the real origin of such work can be construed in terms purely of the particular details that make up each philosopher's life-situation. Even though the fact of situatedness, of the "placed" character of life, will always be articulated in personal terms, what is nevertheless at issue in talk of the connection between philosophy and "life" is not the specific character of such situatedness—whether that of Heidegger or any other thinker—but instead the simple fact of worldly situatedness or placedness as such. It is this that, in every individual case, first calls us to philosophize, and that philosophy, at least as Heidegger understands it, must also be called upon to address. Moreover, the primacy of such situatedness is to be found, not only in the fact that it is in such situatedness that our own existence has its origin and ground, but that in the question of the nature of such situatedness, our own existence is itself brought into question. Philosophical thinking is always a mode of questioning—"The authentic foundation of philosophy is a radical, existentiell grasp of and maturation of questionableness; to pose in questionableness oneself and life and the decisive actualizations is the basic stance of all—including the most radical—clarification"[6]—and, as Heidegger sees it, all questioning emerges only out of, and on the basis of, our own concrete existence.

In the same way in which we find ourselves already given over to the particularity and concreteness of our lives, such that we cannot be anything other than that life, so too is our existence a matter of the way our being is already given over to a situatedness in the world from which we cannot stand aside. Yet to be situated in this way is also for that situatedness always to be in question. This is so in at least two senses. First is the sense in which situatedness always opens out into a set of possibilities that can themselves present as questions (for instance, in the general terms of the Kantian questions: "What can I know?" "What should I do?" "What can I hope?" each of which will take on a more specific form in each particular situation). Such questionability relates to the way in which our being situated is always a matter of our being involved and so being called upon to take a stand on the possibilities that lie before us in that "there." The second sense in which questionability arises here concerns the way in which the possibilities that make up the situation themselves arise out of a set of concrete and already determined circumstances that are simply given to us in a way that may appear as opaque and mysterious. Not merely is there a question as to how I should take up the possibilities in which I am already involved (and which are inevitably taken up *by me* through the simple fact of their being possibilities *for me*), but there is also a question as to how I should understand myself as the sort of being who can stand in relation to possibilities in this way (thus Kant sees the first three questions concerning the possibilities available to us as underlain by a fourth question—"What is man?"—that concerns the character of our own being).[7] Moreover, this is not merely a question about me (or, properly, about my "human" being), but about the emergence of the world as such, since my own existence is an existence already given over to that world.

That our existence is at issue for us is indicated by the apparently "contingent" character of that existence—there is no necessity that grounds existence, and not only is there no necessity to the fact of our having come into existence, but there is no necessity to the continuation of that existence—indeed, in the terms that Heidegger will employ in *Being and Time* and elsewhere, our existence is always oriented toward the nullity of its existence, that is, toward its lack of any independent ground, and so to the limit that is presented to it in death. The way death figures in the structure of existence is something that Heidegger develops in detail in *Being and Time*[8] (and which I discuss further below—see sec. 3.4), but the connection between situatedness and questionability is a theme that runs through much of his early thought. The 1924 lecture *The Concept of Time*, for instance, ends with a discussion of the way the question of time connects with the question of situated existence understood as *"Dasein"* and concludes with the sentence "Then Dasein would be: being questioning."[9] Much the same emphasis carries over into *Being and Time* itself. There Heidegger famously writes of the question of being that "The very asking of this question is an entity's mode of *Being*; and as such it gets its essential character from what is enquired about—namely Being. This entity which each of us is himself and which includes enquiring as one of the possibilities of its Being, we shall denote by the term *Dasein*."[10]

The situatedness at issue in Heidegger's thinking and that is taken up in the idea of "being-there" itself can thus be seen to present itself as having two aspects: it is both open and indeterminate in the sense that it is constituted in terms of a set of possibilities (including the possibility of creating new possibilities—hence there is a certain essential "freedom" that characterizes this situatedness), but it is also closed off and determined in the sense that the freeing up of possibilities itself requires that certain possibilities are also ruled out. These two aspects may be construed in temporal terms, that is, in terms of the way in which our situatedness is always an opening into a future from out of a determined and pregiven past. In addition, however, it has an essentially topological character (one that is not inconsistent with its temporality) inasmuch as it is precisely a gathering, a "happening of belonging," in which elements are brought together within a larger domain or region in a way that also allows those elements to appear in their distinctive ways. Indeed, such a gathering will itself always have a dynamic or "temporalizing" character. Thus, the way in which, in virtue of the questionability of our being, we are caught up in the question of being as such reflects the way in which the fact of our existence always precedes us—we find ourselves already in a situation, already living a certain life, already given over to a particular existence—and as such we find ourselves already involved with things, already engaged in a world.

The connection between situatedness and questionability is central to the argument of *Being and Time*, and Heidegger's claim in that work that the question of being can be approached only through an investigation of that mode of being that is our own is not based in some point concerning our epistemological "access" to being nor in any subjectivist assumption. It is rather questionability as such that brings the question of being and our own being together. The question of being concerns the question as to how being can itself be put in question, and this immediately brings our own "situated" being into view since, in its essence, it is only in relation to such situatedness that the questionability of being arises as an issue. One might argue that this way of putting things elides the difference

between the way in which what is at issue for beings like us is the question of our own being as such. However, not only is the question of being
as such inseparable from the question of being as it arises in respect of any
specific being (the ontological difference can itself be seen as affirming this
point), but so too does all of our questioning already presuppose a question about our own being (a familiar hermeneutic point more commonly
put in terms of the way in which all understanding involves self-
understanding). In general, then, we can say that the question *of being*
already concerns the being *of the question*, and, in this respect, the question of being and the question of the nature of our own being, of situatedness, must always be intertwined. As a result, the way in which our being
is at stake in the question of being, and so the way in which we are ourselves involved in that question, has to do not with the mere fact that it
is we who happen to ask the question, but rather with the way in which
we are already given over to such questioning at the same time as we are
given over to being. Moreover, to be given over in this way is to find ourselves already given over to a certain situatedness, to a world, to a "there."
It is to find ourselves already gathered into place. In this respect, we may
say that questionability always presupposes *topos*, while *topos* always presupposes questionability. Furthermore, the questionability at issue here is
not one to be satisfied by finding any simple answer—as if it were a matter
of finding something that "corresponded" to being that being properly
"is," or finding the one "place" in which we are ourselves finally to be
"located." In fact the questionability at issue is such that it can never be
dispelled. In a way that will become evident as the discussion proceeds, it
is not a matter of "answering" the question of being, so much as recognizing that being and questionability belong together.

The fact of the essential questionability of our situatedness does not
imply, however, that such situatedness cannot be covered over or forgot-
ten. Indeed, for the most part, it remains hidden behind our everyday
engagement with things. Many of the "phenomenological exercises" that
appear in Heidegger's early lectures are thus designed to enable his students to recover a sense of the situatedness in which they already find
themselves and so also to gain a sense of the appropriate starting point for
their own philosophical investigations. Outside of the philosophy lecture,
however, such situatedness may also become apparent to us in a more
spontaneous fashion through our own moods and affectivity—through the
way we "find ourselves" (what Heidegger calls in *Being and Time*, "*Befindlichkeit*" and which is translated by Macquarrie and Robinson as "state-of-
mind"). Boredom is one of the ways in which we can find ourselves in the

world, and, in boredom, the world and our situatedness in the world come to evidence in a striking way through the way in which nothing in the world seems to matter to us. Of course, in boredom it is not that nothing matters, but rather that the only thing that seems to matter is that the world appears as not mattering to us. In this sense, boredom provides one way into philosophical questioning—one way into a grasp of our prior situatedness. Boredom is one of the modes of finding ourselves in the world that is of interest to Heidegger in his thinking in the period up until the mid-1930s[11] (see the discussion in sec. 4.3), as is anxiety (*Angst*), which is of particular importance in *Being and Time*, and wonder (in German, "*Wunder*," in Greek, "*thauma*" or, to use the verb form, *thaumazein*).[12] It is wonder, however, that takes on more significance in the later writing,[13] although it also seems evident even in Heidegger's early thinking— for instance, in his reference to the passage from *Antigone* in which he contrasts the phenomenon of the sunrise as it is investigated by the astronomer with the experience of the sunrise as expressed in the words of the Greek chorus "Thou most beautiful, glance of the sun, / That upon seven-gated Thebes / So long shines. . . ."[14] We may say that in trying to reawaken our sense of our originary "situatedness," Heidegger is also concerned to reconnect us with a sense of the urgency and genuineness of our own lives—to reconnect philosophy with the personal, lived experience that gives it real motive and direction.

   Part of the task that Heidegger sets himself, then, is not merely an investigation of the character of our situatedness and its essential structure, but also of its *retrieval* (one may say that this is another aspect of the connection between situatedness and questionability). Indeed, the task of retrieval is largely what is at issue in the problem of the inquiry into *ground* as Heidegger understands it. The forgetfulness or covering-over of our situatedness, and so of the way in which our existence always involves our being already given over to a world and to a "there," is something that Heidegger takes as characteristic of traditional philosophical thinking. The first task for philosophy is thus a task of properly orienting or re-orienting itself to the situatedness out of which it arises, or, as Heidegger says in an early lecture on phenomenology, of orienting itself to life:

Phenomenology is the investigation of life in itself. . . . Phenomenology is never closed off, it is always provisional in its absolute immersion in life as such. In it no theories are in dispute, but only genuine insights versus the ungenuine. The genuine ones can be obtained only by an honest and unreserved immersion in life itself in its genuineness, and this is ultimately possible only through the genuineness of a personal life.[15]

The genuineness that is at stake here cannot be a matter of a particular form of life or a particular mode of living. If that were so, one might expect Heidegger to give us some account of the particularities of that life. No such account is forthcoming, and what thus seems to be at issue in this talk of the "genuineness of a personal life" is just a matter of a certain mode of "comportment"—of the stand one takes in relation to that life. In discussing the idea of the university in 1921–1922, Heidegger begins by asking: "What about this 'life' at and in university? Is it the way the university is taken up and experienced? Indeed, the question must be posed concretely: how do we here, now, today, take it; how do we live it? We live it the way we ourselves are, namely in and out of our factical existence [*Dasein*]."[16] The emphasis is thus on the genuineness of a personal life as *personal*, that is, as a life that is lived as one's own. Indeed, if philosophy is to attain any sort of objectivity, then this can only be through the personal involvement that is at issue here. Thus, even when Heidegger emphasizes the character of philosophy as a "theoretical" activity, still he is concerned to emphasize the necessary situatedness even of theoretical insight.

Already this way of speaking adumbrates the idea of authenticity (*Eigentlichkeit*) that appears in *Being and Time*, as well as something of what might be at stake in the notion of "resoluteness" (*Entschlossenheit*), both notions being understood in terms of the way in which one recognizes oneself as already given over to the concrete possibilities in which one's life consists and takes up those possibilities as one's own.[17] These ideas are given a much more specific development and take on a particular form in *Being and Time* (a form particular to that work and the thinking that immediately surrounds it), yet what underlies those ideas is nevertheless already present at the very beginning of Heidegger's career: it is just the idea of our existence as something that is irreducibly personal, that is our own. Consequently, John van Buren argues that the emphasis on own-ness and authenticity that appears in Heidegger has nothing to do with notions of subjectivism or "decisionism," but rather with Heidegger's emphasis on the concreteness and particularity of existence and of the personal character of our involvement in the world that is present in his earliest thinking as it derives from a variety of sources including Duns Scotus, Eckhart, Schleiermacher, and Natorp.[18] I would say that it stems from his emphasis on the way in which existence consists in and arises out of an involvement in the world that is always our *own* (*eigen*, hence "*eigentlich*," authentic), that is always placed, that is always "there."

2.2 Situatedness and "Being-There"

The way in which our situatedness, and the involved, "owned" character
of that situatedness, arises as a focus for Heidegger's thinking is most clearly
evident in the way in which he makes use of the German term *"Dasein"*—
a term that can be used to mean "existence" in the sense in which one
might say "it is there" (*Es ist da*). By focusing on existence as *"Dasein,"* Heidegger is able to draw attention to the way in which existence is indeed a
matter of situatedness—to exist, to be "in the world," is to have a concrete
"there." The idea of *"Dasein"* will be familiar even to those who have only
a cursory knowledge of Heidegger's early work, but the notion nevertheless deserves some comment.

I should note, first of all, that rather than leave the German term
"Dasein" untranslated here, and so to treat it simply as a technical term
within the Heideggerian context, I will use the English phrase "being-
there" as its translation—meaning the kind of being that is or has its own
"there"—one reason for doing this, as should already be evident, is precisely in order to draw out the topological issues at stake. Although "being-
there" is sometimes used in English-speaking commentaries as a gloss on
the German term, for the most part the common practice has been to leave
"Dasein" untranslated. Undoubtedly there are drawbacks to employing
"being-there" instead of *"Dasein."* Perhaps the first, and least significant,
is that the English "there" does not correspond exactly to the German *"Da"*
since the latter can carry senses of both "here" and "there." More significantly, Heidegger himself may be taken as warning us against treating
Dasein as a matter of "being-there" in a number of places. Thus, Stuart
Elden draws attention to a passage in the *Heraclitus Seminar* in which Heidegger comments "Dasein is translated as *être-là* [being-there], for example
by Sartre. But with this, everything that was gained as a new position in
Being and Time is lost. Are human beings there like a chair? . . . Dasein does
not mean being there and being here [Dort- und Hiersein] . . . ,"[19] and
Thomas Sheehan quotes a line ("Da ≠ *ibi* und *ubi*")[20] from elsewhere in
Heidegger's work to the same conclusion. Perhaps Heidegger's fullest elaboration on this matter comes, however, in the *Zollikon Seminars* with
Medard Boss, where he explains his use of *"Dasein"* in *Being and Time* as
follows:

In the philosophical tradition, the term "Dasein" means presence-at-hand, existence. In this sense, one speaks, for instance, of proofs for God's existence. However,
Da-sein is understood differently in *Being and Time*. To begin with, French

existentialists also failed to pay attention to it. That is why they translated Da-sein in *Being and Time* as *être-là*, which means being here and not there. The *Da* in *Being and Time* does not mean a statement of place [*Ortsangabe*] for a being, but rather it should designate the openness where beings can be present for the human being, and the human being also for himself. The *Da* of [Da-sein's] *being* distinguishes the humanness of the human being. The talk about human Da-sein is *accordingly* a pleonasm, avoidable in all contexts, including *Being and Time*. The appropriate French translation of Dasein should be: Etre le là, and the meaningful accentuation should be Da-*sein* in German instead of Dasein.[21]

Not only might this passage be taken to show the unacceptability of the translation of *Dasein* as "being-there," but it could also be viewed as casting doubt on the idea that the *Da* of *Dasein* refers us to a notion of place at all.[22] Both conclusions would, however, be much too hasty.

The first point to note is that the French translation Heidegger actually proposes here, *être le là*, "being the there," does not dispense with the idea of the "there" at all, but rather proposes a particular emphasis in the way the "there" is understood to relate to "being" (it does indeed give just the emphasis I noted above when I said that "being-there" means the kind of being that is or has its own "there"). This is reinforced by the fact that the term Heidegger uses in the passage immediately above is not "*Ort*" (place), but "*Ortsangabe*," which is rendered almost literally in the passage above as "statement of place." The point is that the "Da" cannot be treated as the "where" of an entity that might be offered in a statement of its location ("*Ortsangabe*" can also mean "address"). The "there" that is at issue in this case is thus not to be understood in the sense of a mere location for something—"here rather than there"—and this can be taken as a point that applies as much to the concept of "place" as such as it does to the idea of "there."

It is, in fact, the question of place and how to understand it that turns out to underlie the question of the meaning of the "Da" and of "Dasein,"[23] and so it is this that also underlies the difficulty of translation that is at issue here. To repeat a point that was made in the previous chapter, "place" should not be understood as referring primarily to the idea of that in which an entity is located—place is not simple location or position (*Platz, Stelle*). To conceive of place as such already makes place derivative of the idea of a certain realm or domain in which there are multiple places. Often this is tied to the idea of space as that realm of extendedness in which a multiplicity of places, and so of entities, can be located. If one is to allow a sense of place as associated with mere location, then it must be distinguished from the concept of place as itself the open region within which entities come to appearance. It is the latter conception of place that lies at the heart of my discussion here, and that is also, I claim, fundamentally at issue in Heidegger. Rather than the sense of place that is invoked when I give someone my address, or explain where to find a particular book, this latter sense of place is more like that which is at issue in the experience of place as such—whether that be the experience of finding oneself within a particularly striking landscape, of being gathered into the familiarity of friendly surroundings, or of trying to navigate though an unknown countryside or town.

That it is the understanding of place and the "there" that is the underlying question here is itself indicated by the fact that Heidegger is indeed at pains to distinguish "Da" in the sense he employs it from "Da" as associated with simple location. There are thus clearly two senses of the "Da" at issue in Heidegger's discussion (something that can be marked in German through the use of different terms—"Da" and "Dort/Hin"), and this should be seen to apply as much in English, or in French, as it does in the original German. Thus Heidegger can say, in the passage quoted by Elden, that "Dasein does not mean being there and being here" and then immediately add the question "What does the Da mean?"[24] intending to deflect us away, not from the idea that the "Da," the "there," is what is at issue, but from the automatic assumption that "Da" is simple location. It is, in fact, only through leaving "Dasein" and "Da" untranslated that lines such as those referred to by Elden or Sheehan can seem relevant to the translational issue in question. If we acknowledge the way in which "Dasein" can function in German as a quite ordinary compound verb that does indeed mean "being here/there," and so the way in which "Da" can itself mean "here/there," then it is clear that what is in question is how we should understand the idea of "here/there," including the concept of "there," and so too, I might add, how we should understand the concept of place, as well as being. The fact that this is not immediately seen as the key question itself indicates the widespread tendency, sometimes evident even when place is explicitly thematized, to overlook the question of place or to assume that the concept is already understood.

Sheehan argues against the translation of "Da" by "there" on the grounds that Heidegger understands the "Da," whether in Dasein or elsewhere, "not as the 'there' but as das Offene or die Offenheit, the 'open.'"[25] I have no difficulty with this as a point about how the "Da" should be explicated (indeed, the idea of "the open" and its connection with the "there" is, as should already be evident, an important element in my own account), and the passage from the Zollikon Seminars emphasizes just this way of understanding *Dasein*, but the point is nevertheless of little help as a piece of *translational* advice. So far as the translation of *"Dasein"* and *"Da"* is concerned, it is not first a matter of how these terms are to be philosophically explicated (whether in German or in English), nor of the other terms that might be called upon in such explication (as one calls upon *"das Offene"* and *"die Offenheit"* in German), but of what term in English is to be used to correspond to the German. Whatever term is used here, that term will itself require explication and will also need to be connected up with other appropriate English terms (such as "the open" and "openness"). When it comes to a term such as the English "there," not only is this term as much in need of interrogation and explication as the German *"Da,"* but it is also a term, like "place," whose meaning is all too easily passed over as unproblematic or as of no real philosophical significance.

To translate "Dasein" as "being-there," while it does mean that the sense of "here" that can be involved with *"Da"* is lost, nevertheless makes clear the way in which *Dasein* is indeed a mode of being that is characterized by its *"there"*—it *is* its there—although how this "there" is to be understood remains itself in question. On the other hand, leaving *"Dasein"* untranslated can easily lead us to ignore or overlook the way in which, as soon as we understand our being in terms of *Dasein*, we have already understood it topologically (similarly, Heidegger's own employment of *Dasein*, especially in *Being and Time*, as something of a technical term, coupled with his concern to avoid the sense of *"Da"* as spatial location, can serve to conceal the topology that is actually at issue here). As I noted in chapter 1: to come to recognize and understand the topological character of Heidegger's early thought, it is crucial that we become sensitive to the ways in which that topology is developed through concepts of the "there," as well as through concepts such as those of "world" and "event," and that means becoming sensitive to these topological concerns in translation as much as anywhere else.

There is, of course, another obvious English alternative to "being-there" that is sometimes proposed—"there-being"—and this may be thought to fit more closely both with the structure of the German (*Da-sein*) and with Heidegger's point about the emphasis being on the second syllable (Da-*sein*).[26] "There-being" is, however, a somewhat odd construction in contemporary English, and as such it can easily encourage the tendency to overlook the connection with the "there" and so with place, while also contributing somewhat to the continued specialization of the Heideggerian vocabulary. Moreover, while one might argue that "being-there" encourages the idea of something being *"at a there"* as if it were "at a loca-

tion," "there-being" also mirrors the standard English form ("there" followed by "to be" plus a substantive noun) for statements of presence—
"there is . . . a table." The latter is perhaps no less problematic than the
former. The use of "being-there" as a translation for "*Dasein*" is not without
its drawbacks, but it does seem to be the simplest and most direct way of
translating "*Dasein*" into English. At the same time, it also has a small
number of uses in English that do have appropriate connotations for the
task at hand. The use of the phrase as the title for Peter Sellers's famous
portrayal of a man who "is there" almost solely through the way in which
he "is not there" (his own lack of engagement enables the engagement,
the "being there," of those around him)[27] is indicative of the way "being-
there" can be used in English to connote a certain sort of situational
engagement—a sense of engagement that is also carried by phrases such
as "you just had to be there." Admittedly, this is a weaker set of connotations than can be found for the German terms, but it still seems preferable
to hiding the place-oriented connotations of "*Dasein*" by simply taking the
term untranslated into English or by employing the somewhat artificial
construction of "there-being."

2.3   Facticity and World

In his early thinking Heidegger treats "being-there" in close relation to
something he calls "*Faktizität*" (facticity), a notion that first emerges, at
least in this form, in his lectures in the winter semester of 1919–1920.[28]
"Facticity" is a term that Heidegger appropriates from neo-Kantian thinking in which it originally refers to the impenetrability, the "irrationality,"
of sheer existence.[29] In the 1923 lecture course entitled *Ontology—The
Hermeneutics of Facticity*, Heidegger characterizes facticity in terms of the
way in which each being-there "is what it is directly and only through its
having its own lingering 'there' " (Das eigene Dasein ist, was es ist, gerade
und nur in seinem *jeweiligen* "*Da*"—or as John van Buren translates it, "The
being-there of our own Dasein is what it is precisely and only in its *temporally particular 'there,'* its being '*there*' for a while").[30] We may say that the
facticity of being-there thus refers directly to the way in which "being-
there," in being what it is, is a certain concrete, "timely" situatedness or
placedness. Facticity thus carries with it the idea of the "there"—of a
certain sort of "place"—and of existence as a lingering, an "abiding-for-a-
while" of a certain place or placedness.

A central element in the idea of facticity is that our own existence cannot
be construed as coming before (whether temporally or ontologically) the

encounter with other things or other persons. Existence, we might say, is its "there," and in being such, it is not something separate from the there, the place, the world, in which it finds itself. The basis for Heidegger's "factical" conception of the relation between existence and the world would seem, at least initially, to be phenomenological: when we look to the character of experience (where experience is not yet taken as "subjective," but as simply referring us to any sort of meaningful "encounter"), what first confronts us, in the sense of being ontologically primary, is not a sense of our own existence in some detached or abstracted form, nor of being presented with a field of sensory "evidence," but rather our being already involved with things in such a way that we do not even think of them as separate from us nor us from them, and in which things are encountered as already part of a meaningful whole. We thus find ourselves first of all enmeshed in a world, and so in a set of relationships, and it is only subsequent to this that we begin to separate out a sense of ourselves and a sense of things as they are apart from us. That Heidegger himself understands matters in this way is explicit in many places in his early work (as well as later). In the 1923 lectures on "The Hermeneutics of Facticity," for example, Heidegger raises a question as to the character of being-there's encounter with things within the world.

The world, claims Heidegger, is that which environs or surrounds us and also that toward which we are oriented, about which we are concerned, and to which we attend. But how do we encounter the world, and if our encountering the world is always an encounter with respect to particular things and situations, how are these encountered? Heidegger proposes to answer these questions by looking to our everyday, precritical encounter with things, and the example he focuses on is an ordinary thing of the home or the workplace, a table. How is the table first encountered? We might be inclined to say, as a material thing, as something "with such and such a weight, such and such a color, such and such a shape," as a thing that also offers an infinity of possible perceptual appearances. The thing as a material, natural thing might be distinguished from the thing as it might be evaluated or used—as it might be significant or meaningful. Heidegger denies, however, that the thing grasped as mere object, either as natural object or as meaningful object, is what is first encountered. Instead, what is prior is the "in the world" as such that is articulated in and around specific things such as the table, but is not any table, *this* table, the table before us now. Thus Heidegger tells us that "This schema must be avoided: What exists are subjects and objects, consciousness and being." We cannot first posit things aside from our dealings with those things nor the selves involved in those dealings aside from things. To illustrate the point at issue—and the illustration is itself a large part of Heidegger's argument—Heidegger turns to an analysis of an example taken from the circumstances of his own particular being-there, a description of the table in his family home:

What is there in *the* room there at home is *the* table (not "a" table among many other tables in other rooms and other houses) at which one sits *in order to* write, have a meal, sew, play. Everyone sees this right away, e.g., during a visit: it is a writing table, a dining table, a sewing table—such is the primary way in which it is being encountered in itself. This characteristic of "in order to do something" is not merely imposed on the table by relating and assimilating it to something else which it is not. Its standing-there in the room means: Playing this role in such and such characteristic use. This and that about it is "impractical," unsuitable. That part is damaged. It now stands in a better spot in the room than before—there's better lighting, for example. . . . Here and there it shows lines—the boys like to busy themselves at the table. Those lines are not just interruptions in the paint, but rather: it was the boys and it still is. This side is not the east side, and this narrow side so many cm. shorter than the other, but rather the one at which my wife sits in the evening when she wants to stay up and read, there at the table we had such and such a discussion that time, there that decision was made with a *friend* that time, there that *work* was written that time, there that holiday celebrated that time. That is *the* table—as such it is there in the temporality of everydayness. . . .[31]

This aspect of facticity—the way in which our existence as a matter of our being already given over to the world and involved in it—is worth reflecting upon partly because of the way in which it might seem to go against some deeply ingrained and common tendencies in thinking, and also because of the way it may also suggest a bifurcation between two modes of understanding the world and our relation to it—one geared to the "theoretical" and the other to the "practical."

One may question whether it actually is the case that our "first" encounter with the world is indeed "factical" in the way Heidegger suggests. If we proceed in the manner that Descartes does in the first "Meditation," then we may well take the view that what we first encounter is not a world, nor a set of particular things within that world, but just a set of representations—beliefs, ideas, sensory stimulations, or whatever. Yet such a view is not so much a starting point for investigation or a discussion as already a conclusion that depends on a prior set of assumptions—it can only be arrived at on the basis of investigation, but then, what should be the starting point for such an investigation? Certainly, in the order of our own *experience*, we do not first encounter beliefs, ideas, sensory

stimulations, or any of the other entities that are often cited as epistemo-
logically or ontologically primary here. Thus, of his seeing the lectern in
the hall in which he is teaching, Heidegger comments:

Coming into the lecture-room, I see the lectern. . . . What do "I" see? Brown surfaces, at right angles to one another? No, I see something else. A largish box, with
another smaller one set upon it? Not at all. I see the lectern at which I am to speak.
You see the lectern, from which you are to be addressed, and from which I have
spoken to you previously. In pure experience there is no "founding" interconnection, as if I first of all see intersecting brown surfaces, which then reveal themselves
to me as a box, then as a desk, then as an academic lecturing desk, a lectern, so that
I attach lecternhood to the box like a label. All that is simply bad and misguided
interpretation, diversion from a pure seeing into the experience.[32]

A similar point appears later, in *Being and Time*, in relation, not to vision,
but to sound:

What we "first" hear is never noises or complexes of sounds, but the creaking wagon,
the motor-cycle. We hear the column on the march, the north wind, the wood-
pecker tapping, the fire crackling. It requires a very artificial and complicated frame
of mind to "hear" a "pure noise."[33]

The manner of being-there's being-in-the-world, then, is not a matter of
being "alongside" "sensations,"[34] but of being alongside, that is, given
together with, motorcycles, wagons, woodpeckers, and so forth. Similarly,
what comes first in our involvement in the lecture hall in which Heidegger's lectern sits, is not some combination of colors, shapes, and surfaces,
instead:

In the experience of seeing the lectern something is given *to me* from out of an
immediate environment [*Umwelt*]. This environmental milieu (lectern, book, black-
board, notebook, fountain pen, caretaker, student fraternity, tram-car, motor-car,
etc.) does not consist just of things, objects, which are then conceived as meaning
this and this; rather, the meaningful is primary and immediately given to me
without any mental detours across thing-oriented apprehension. Living in an environment, it signifies to me everywhere and always, everything has the character of
world. It is everywhere the case that "*it worlds*" [*es weltet*], which is something different from "it values" [*es wertet*].[35]

The "worlding" of the world is the happening of meaning and of
encounter—a happening that Heidegger will later refer to in terms of "disclosedness" or "unconcealing," as well as simply the "Event." But it is also
a happening of the "there," and so also of place. Indeed, that this is so is
evident from the fact that what occurs here is something that has a con-

crete character—it is not an occurrence of detached meanings or abstracted ideas, but of a concrete place—the lecture hall in which Heidegger now speaks and in which his student listen. Van Buren comments that, for early Heidegger, "The world and each worldly thing in it are a topological Da (here) of being,"[36] meaning that the happening of world is something that always occurs topologically, in relation to a concrete "there," and with respect to particular things. And while van Buren does not take this any further, one might say, in that case, that the worlding of the world is also the placing, or the "taking place," of place.

The concept of world that is apparent here is not the concept of world as simply, in Wittgenstein's phrase, "all that is the case."[37] Instead the world is understood in a way that is much closer to the notion of "*Umwelt*," "environment" or "environing world," in the sense that it is a conception of world as a certain ordered realm within which one always stands in a certain orientation and with a certain directedness. The idea of the "environing world" that appears in twentieth-century ethological thought looks to understand the way in which different creatures always live within a certain configuration of salient features and affordances. Similarly, the "world," as Heidegger uses it, is understood as a particular configuration of meaning—a context of meaning we might say (*Bedeutsamkeit*) or of meaningful involvements (*Bewandtnis*). The world as first encountered is thus not a world of mere causes, of ideas or impressions, or even of states of affairs, but a world of self, of others, of concrete things. Indeed, in this respect, the phenomenological "return to the things" must also be understood, not merely in Heidegger, but in much post-Husserlian phenomenology (as well as in Husserl's own later thinking), as a "return to the world." Thus Merleau-Ponty writes:

To return to things themselves is to return to that world which precedes knowledge, of which knowledge always *speaks*, and in relation to which every scientific schematization is an abstract and derivative sign-language, as is geography in relation to the countryside in which we have learnt beforehand what a forest, a prairie or a river is.[38]

Merleau-Ponty's use of a geographical comparison here is significant. For to return to things as they are in the world is to return to things as they are given in place and in relation to ourselves. It is to return to the concrete immediacy of existence out of which philosophical inquiry itself comes.

2.4 Ground and Unity

If questionability always arises out of its particular *topos* or *place*—out of a particular, meaningful configuration that allows something to appear as questionable—so philosophical thinking itself arises out of such a place, not only in terms of the specific questions that it may ask, but as a mode of questioning as such. The question of being that Heidegger addresses, and that he takes to lie at the heart of philosophical thinking, arises together with the questioning of our own existence and together with that existence. The place in which that question arises is thus our own essential situatedness, the "there" of our own existence in the world, and it is also this place that, as Heidegger sees it, is the place in which philosophical thinking itself has its origin.

The way in which philosophy is itself implicated with the Heideggerian inquiry into the situated character of existence is a central point in Heidegger's thinking. Indeed, it seems impossible to disentangle the question of "being-there" either from the question of being or from the question of the nature and possibility (the ground and "origin") of philosophy, of "thinking," as such. Although it may sometimes appear as if philosophy is something from which Heidegger aims to distance himself (for instance, in his late thought, or, as van Buren suggests, at certain points in his very early thinking), this is more an effect of Heidegger's own ambiguous relationship with the philosophical tradition, and the fact that "philosophy" may name both the real task of thinking and the pathway such thinking must take, as well as the constant tendency toward the forgetting of that task, than an indication of Heidegger's abandonment of philosophy as such. Philosophy is surely broader than the problematic mode of philosophizing that Heidegger refers to as "metaphysics," and so must offer the possibility of disclosure as well as forgetfulness.[39]

It is important to note here that "origin," as Heidegger uses it, almost always refers to the notion of "ground" as that which determines, [40] rather than constituting some nostalgic desire for the recovery of a "lost" beginning. Yet it is precisely in the latter sense that it has often been understood. Thus Allan Megill writes, following on from Derrida's comments in *Margins of Philosophy*,[41] that:

Clearly Heidegger's notion of return to an original (if ideal) past is a departure from presence in the temporal sense. But it is not a departure from presence in the sense of proximity . . . the nostalgic cast of Heidegger's commitment to proximity, to "simple and immediate presence," becomes clear. This commitment turns out to be a longing for what is past—for what cannot be possessed in the temporal present.

Thus, Heidegger joins the Dionysian side of the Appollonian/Dionysian contrast, taking the Appollonian in its active, illusion-creating sense and the Dionysian in the sense of a primitive passivity, of a complete union with the primal flux of things. In short, Heidegger's nostalgia can be read as a longing for the immediate Dionysian presence of the origin, from which all division, all separation, all difference, is excluded.[42]

It should already be clear from my comments on "presence" above that this notion cannot be employed in relation to Heidegger without an awareness of the complexity that the term brings with it. In this respect the idea of commitment to "simple and immediate presence" as applied to Heidegger needs to be approached with caution. Inasmuch as Heidegger does have a commitment to such presence, it is to a rethought conception of what such "presence" might mean. But equally the idea of a return to origin in Heidegger cannot be understood in terms of a longing for what is past. Apart from anything else, this is to misunderstand the way in which the return at issue here is not a return to anything *past*. As Heidegger says in relation to that "remembrance" that is our returning to being:

Remembrance is no historiological activity with the past, as if it wanted to make present, from outside and from what is later, what earlier thinkers "believed" "about" being. Remembrance is placement into being itself, which still presences, even though all previous beings are past. Indeed, even talk about placement into being is misleading because it suggests we are not yet placed into being, while being yet remains closer to us than everything nearest and farther than all that is farthest . . . Hence it is not first a matter of being placed into being, it is a matter of becoming aware of our essential abode in being, and becoming genuinely aware of being beforehand.[43]

As it is not something past, so that to which one returns or that which one remembers—the "origin"—is not something that has somehow been lost from our possession, nor is it something "from which all division, all separation, all difference is excluded." The notion of "origin" at issue here is that origin to which we already belong, that which is the unity of all difference, the difference in all unity; it is just that place or "abode" in which we already find ourselves. The return to the origin that is at the heart of Heidegger's topology is the return to the "place," the proper "*topos*," in which we already find ourselves, and in which philosophy itself arises (for more on this see sec. 6.1 below).[44]

In this respect, just as the Kantian inquiry into the ground and limit of philosophy undertaken through the critique of reason is also an inquiry into the ground of experience and knowledge, so too is the Heideggerian inquiry at one and the same time concerned to ground philosophy, as well as to ground the possibility of the disclosedness of things. The way such grounding occurs in Heidegger is through the analysis of situatedness, but the nature of the grounding is also tied to the character of situatedness as such. In looking to our situatedness as that out of which philosophical questioning arises, as well as that which determines the possibility of the encounter with things—which determines the possibility of their being disclosed—Heidegger does not look to find some underlying principle or element out of which such situatedness is constituted. What is brought to salience in and through the situation, in and through the "there," is also what participates in the very happening of the there—myself, the others who are there with me, the things that I find myself alongside. This structure of situatedness shows the same structure that I described above, in chapter 1, as "topological." It does not allow of any grounding of the structure as a whole by reference to any one element within that structure nor by reference to anything apart from that structure, but rather through the already interconnected—the "gathered"—character of the structure as such.

As we have already seen in the discussion of Heidegger's analysis of world, we do not find ourselves in the world through encountering the world, or the things within it, as something that stands over against us as separate and apart from us. The world is that to which we are already given over and in which we are taken up. This is captured in the way Heidegger talks, not only in terms of our already belonging to the world and its already belonging to us (hence his use of terms that emphasize notions of "ownness" and that come to special prominence in *Being and Time*'s emphasis on the "authenticity," "*Eigentlichkeit*," of being-there), but also of the way this belonging to world is a certain "happening" or "event":

> But something does happen. In seeing the lectern I am fully present in my "I"; it resonates with the experience, as we said. It is an experience proper to me and so do I see it. However, it is not a process but rather an *event of appropriation* [*Ereignis*]. . . . Lived experience does not pass in front of me like a thing, but I appropriate [*er-eigne*] it to myself, and it appropriates itself according to its essence.[45]

Later in the same lecture he tells us that "Every situation is an *Ereignis* and not a 'process.' That which happens has a relation to me; it streams [*strahlt*] into one's own 'I.' "[46] Heidegger's use of the term "Ereignis" here, which normally means just "event," but here also connotes "owning" or "belonging" (especially when written in the hyphenated verb form as "*er-eignen*")[47], prefigures the significant role the term will take on in his later work—the focus of further discussion in chapter 5—as well as prefiguring key elements

in the analysis of *Being and Time* (the account of being-there as fundamentally temporal, the "visionary moment," the *"Augenblick,"* as that in
which being-there grasps its "Situation," the idea of authenticity, can all
be seen as articulations of aspects of this original understanding of situatedness as "eventful"). What is important here, however, is not merely the
appearance of this notion so early in Heidegger's thinking (something that
both Kisiel and van Buren have drawn to our attention)[48], but also the way
this term is already being used by Heidegger, as it will also be used later,
to refer to the way in which the relatedness that occurs in situatedness is
both a certain sort of happening and also a belonging or gathering of what
already belongs. Moreover, the reflexive use of the verb form *"sich ereignen,"* literally "it happens/gathers itself," indicates the way in which the
happening/gathering at issue here is not accomplished by anything other
than the happening/gathering as such—it happens/gathers only in and
through itself. As such, it serves to give expression to something of the
topological character of situatedness to which I have already referred: situatedness is not grounded in anything other than situatedness itself,
moreover, situatedness is also constituted through the interrelating of the
elements that already belong to the situation.

The idea of situatedness as indeed a happening that is also a gathering
or belonging means that the elements that are gathered together in that
happening cannot be understood as elements that have somehow been
separated, but are now, in the happening of situatedness, simply returned
to their proper relation with one another. Instead, the happening of
belonging that is at issue here is indicative of the character of the "belonging" in question as a matter of the reciprocal determination of elements
within a single "structure." This idea may, at first encounter, seem a little
difficult to grasp—if the elements at issue here are not already differentiated, how can they be differentiated through their being related to one
another? Given Heidegger's use of the term *"Ereignis"* to connote both
gathering or belonging and happening, the point at issue can usefully be
illustrated, however, by looking to the way in which things that grow or
develop (things that themselves "happen"), whether these be a living
thing, a community, a musical improvisation, or even the writing (or
reading) of a book, possess a differentiated structure that arises only
through the process of growth or development as such. The differentiation
of one element is always dependent on the differentiation of other elements. Moreover, while one can take the thing at issue at a certain
"instant" and then analyze or dissect it into its apparently separate elements, treating each as if it had an identity of its own, any such analysis

is always somewhat artificial. This way of understanding in terms of the connectedness and differentiation that arises through growth or development applies, not only to the elements that make up a thing, but also to the thing as such—its own identity and unity is given only in and through the ongoing and reciprocal determination of the elements of which it is constituted. This means that one cannot grasp the thing other than in its constant and ongoing constitution—its identity and unity is thus not to be found at any statically conceived "instant" in that constitution.

What is at issue here, of course, is not just the conception of situatedness, but a conception of the nature of unity (which appears in Heidegger's emphasis on situatedness as a belonging, owning, or gathering), as well as a conception of differentiation. Indeed, on this account, the two notions are necessarily tied together—a point that is central to Heidegger's later discussions of the relation between identity and difference.[49] The idea of the hermeneutic circle in which understanding always relies on prior understanding—and in which the elements that make up a text can only be understood in relation to the unity of the text as a whole, while the unity of the text is only to be understood in terms of the elements that contribute to that unity—provides one important exemplification of the basic conception of unity that is at issue here. Similarly, the Aristotelian prioritization of living things as the primary instances of the really real, of substance or *ousia*, is indicative of the centrality of the idea of unity in the Aristotelian understanding of substance, but also of the way in which that unity is conceived precisely in terms of the unity of differentiated, but integrated elements (in Aristotle, one might argue that the unity at issue here is ultimately seen as teleological in character, although this requires an appropriate understanding of what "teleology" itself might be). It is a similar conception of unity that is in play throughout Heidegger's thinking, including the very early work, as well as *Being and Time* (although there, as we shall see, it also encounters some problems). Indeed, it is a conception of unity that is undoubtedly influenced by Aristotelian and medieval ideas concerning the "analogical" unity of being that appears explicitly in Heidegger's habilitation dissertation.[50] This conception of unity is also exemplified in the unity that pertains to place, and as such it underpins both my own and Heidegger's use of notions of topography or topology. The unity of *topos* is itself constituted through the interplay of the elements found within it, while those elements are themselves differentiated only in and through that topological play.[51]

The character of situatedness as a certain happening in which the elements that are disclosed within it are both differentiated and unified means

that any attempt to uncover the ground of situatedness can look only to
situatedness as such. Inasmuch as situatedness is understood in terms of
"facticity," then facticity turns out to be its own ground. Of course, as facticity was originally employed, in Fichte for example, facticity referred to
the irrationality and impenetrability of existence, to what we may understand precisely as its lack of ground (the German *"Grund"* means both
"reason" and "ground") or its resistance to grounding. Already, then, in
his insistence on the character of factical situatedness as a single "happening" in which we are brought into "belonging" with ourselves, with
things, and with the world, Heidegger has taken issue with the traditional
understanding of what it is to ground and what it is for something to be
grounded—although, in his early thinking, the real nature of ground has
still to be properly articulated, and, in *Being and Time*, the question of what
it is to ground constitutes a central problem that remains, for the most
part, implicit.

The concept of ground is one that Heidegger takes to be fundamental to
philosophy. He writes, for instance, in *Introduction to Metaphysics* in 1936
that "[P]hilosophy has constantly and always asked about the ground of
beings. With this question it had its inception, in this question it will find
its end, provided that it comes to an end in greatness and not in a pow-
erless decline."[52] The question of ground is also one to which he returns a
number of times—not only in *Introduction to Metaphysics*, but also, and
perhaps most directly, in the 1929 essay "On the Essence of Ground" (Das
Wesen des Grundes) and in the lectures from 1955–1956 published in 1957
under the title *Der Satz vom Grund* (The Principle of Reason). Although Heidegger does not deny the legitimacy of the question concerning ground,
he also maintains that the way the question has been addressed has always
been in terms that reflect the metaphysical tendency to look to understand
being in terms of some entity or feature of entities, to understand presence
or disclosedness in terms of some principle or structure that is apart from
it. As Joseph Fell comments:

The metaphysical tradition, then, has held that to know what-is as it really is—to
know beings in their Being—is to know their ground. This view, Heidegger thought,
was not altogether wrong; in fact . . . the phenomenological program presupposes
it. But the tradition has mistaken the nature of the ground. The answer to the question why there are beings at all is not a being, a highest or first being, but rather
the event or coming on of the clearing, not as a one-time beginning but as the
always-already unity of Dasein as the original thrown projection and articulation of
the ground of beings.[53]

The conception of ground to which Heidegger constantly refers us back, however, is a conception of ground that is closely tied to the conception of unity and differentiation as occurring together in a single happening/gathering. There is thus no "ground" other than this happening/ gathering as such, and no grounding that can do other than allow the disclosedness of this very happening/gathering as such. Fell explains this in terms of Heidegger's phenomenological background such that:

> for both [Husserl and Heidegger] the question of the "ground" (basis or source) of beings is a crucial one, and exploration of the nature of "ground" cannot be construed as a retreat by phenomenologists from their announced goal, to go back to "the things themselves" . . . When Heidegger insists that phenomenology must be phenomenological ontology, what he means is that phenomena, to be understood as what they are, must be understood from within *the original oneness of Being*, which is the prior ground of any distinction between ego and nonego, subject and object, or man and thing. To point to this original oneness is Heidegger's purpose, from early to late, and is his basic response to the "question of unity."⁵⁴

The "original oneness" to which Fell refers here is one that he takes Heidegger to find in the way in which being-there is the original and unitary place of being.⁵⁵ But as such a place, being-there does not stand apart from being, nor does it refer us to some ground that stands apart from it—being-there grounds in and through its own happening, its own gathering.

By the time Heidegger comes to *Being and Time*, this conception of ground, and of its relation to unity, has been significantly developed within the framework of the Kantian idea of the "transcendental." Indeed, as Heidegger later explained, the Kantian project provides a model for the attempt to understand the unitary character of being-there as that is worked out in *Being and Time*. Indeed, the very idea of fundamental ontology as an analysis of the structure of being-there is one that Heidegger refers back to Kant, and he does so with specific reference to the nonreductive character of that analysis, that is, the way in which it looks to articulate the already given unity of a differentiated structure:

> From this Kantian concept of analytic, it follows that it is a dissection [*Zergliederung*] of the faculty of understanding. The fundamental character of a dissection is not its reduction into elements, but the tracing back to a unity (synthesis) of the ontological possibility of the being of beings, or in the sense of Kant: [Back to synthesis] of the objectivity of objects of experience. . . . In the ontological sense, "the analytic" is not a reduction into elements, but the articulation of the [a priori] unity of a composite structure [*Strukturgefüge*]. This is also essential in my concept of the "analytic of Da-sein."⁵⁶

What Heidegger gives us here is thus a Kantian reading of the method of approach that aims to exhibit the already given unity of the differentiated structure that, in his earlier writing, he refers to in terms of the happening/gathering of experience, of world, of the "there." Yet although this concept of "analytic," and with it the idea of the "transcendental," can be seen as a development of the topological approach already adumbrated in Heidegger's early lectures and writings (and so as constituting a form of topology in itself), it also leads Heidegger to a way of articulating the structure that is at issue here in a way that gives rise to some difficulties. To a large extent, these difficulties relate to the way in which the concept of analytic is understood as a "tracing back to a unity," where that is taken to mean a tracing back to some primary element or structure on which other elements depend. The way this works out in *Being and Time* is in terms of a "tracing back" to temporality, and, notwithstanding the emphasis on resisting any reductive tendency here, the exhibiting of the dependence[57] of the structure of the "there," and so also of world, on the structure of temporality in its fundamental and originary character. As a result the topology that comes to appearance in *Being and Time* is a fundamentally temporal one—which does not mean that place is not at issue, but rather that place is itself understood as fundamentally temporal. In itself, this need not be a problem—place is indeed temporal—but it becomes problematic when the attempt is made to establish temporality alone as the ground for place. Place is temporal, but it is also spatial (and so also stands in an essential relation to body). Moreover, it is not that place is to be derived from temporality, instead temporality has to be itself understood in relation to the temporalizing/spatializing of the happening/gathering that is place.

3 The Ontology of Existence: Meaning and Temporality

In what manner space *is*, and whether a Being in general can be attributed to it, remains undecided.

—Martin Heidegger, "Art and Space"[1]

Heidegger's early thinking, as we have already seen, gives priority to the idea of situatedness. Rather than seeing the basic questions of philosophy as concerned with the uncovering of some basic principle or principles that underlie the being of each individual thing, Heidegger takes philosophy to be essentially concerned with the disclosing of that within which things can be the things that they are, within which they can stand in relation to other things, within which we find ourselves. The philosophical task, as Heidegger conceives it, then, turns out to be a matter of the uncovering of a certain place—although a place that is essentially unitary, dynamic, and constantly unfolding. Yet while Heidegger employs, even in his early thinking, a range of topological and sometimes even spatial ideas and images in the attempt to articulate the place at issue here—especially the idea of the "there"—he does not make the topological character of what is at issue explicit, and the ideas of place and space that appear implicated here receive very little direct attention as such. This is itself indicative of a basic difficulty inherent in Heidegger's project here: as the history of Western philosophy over much of the last two thousand years demonstrates, place has often been seen as a derivative and secondary concept, one that is properly to be understood in terms of space, while space itself is understood, particularly within the frame of modern thought, in terms of measurable extension; consequently, any analysis that gives priority to place (whether explicitly or not) would seem also to give priority to space understood as tied to such measurable extension, but, as becomes especially clear in *Being and Time*, such a notion would seem completely inadequate to understanding the situatedness that is the starting point for Heidegger's inquiry. How, then, to understand the topology that is at issue here?

The passage of Heidegger's thinking from at least 1919 and through much of the 1920s can be read as an attempt to articulate the essential sit-uatedness against which the question of being has to be understood, and yet to articulate that situatedness in a way that does not make it depen-dent upon some notion of measurable, homogenized, spatial extension. Already the dynamic character of situatedness as such, something captured in Heidegger's early talk of happening and "event" (*Ereignis*) may be taken to indicate that the situatedness at issue here is in some essential way tem-poral. Moreover, that situatedness is also a situatedness in which we are ourselves caught up, and within the Western philosophical tradition, espe-cially in the work of Christian thinkers such as Plotinus and Augustine, there is an important way of thinking that understands self and time to be bound together (an idea also present, significantly, in Schelling, and in whom can also be found an argument for the priority of time over space).[2] One can thus see a movement in Heidegger's early thinking that begins with what is fundamentally a question of topology, but in which that topology is increasingly interpreted in terms of temporality. Consequently, Heidegger declares at the very beginning of *Being and Time* that the aim of the work "is the Interpretation of *time* as the possible horizon for any understanding whatsoever of being"[3]—situatedness must be viewed, it seems, as fundamentally determined by, as "grounded in," temporality.

The prioritization of temporality in *Being and Time* means that spatial-ity cannot have a fundamental role in the structure of being-there, and inasmuch as it is temporality alone that is taken as determinative, so the same would seem to apply to the notion of place. Indeed, Heidegger's project in *Being and Time* would seem to be to show the way in which place and space are both, in a certain sense, dependent on time. Yet spatiality constantly intrudes into Heidegger's account, and Heidegger's explicit attempt to provide an argument for the secondary or "derivative" charac-ter of spatiality is a conspicuous failure—as Heidegger himself later admits.[4] In this respect, although the Heideggerian prioritization of temporality arises, in part, out of his recognition of the inadequacy of the traditional conception of spatiality in the understanding of situatedness (something Heidegger specifically criticizes in terms of the Cartesian ontology), it is most obviously in relation to spatiality that the attempted prioritization of temporality turns out to be problematic—and this is indeed a reflection of the ineliminability of spatiality, in some sense (although in just what sense remains to be determined), within the structure of topology. In this respect, when we come to *Being and Time*, even though place is still not directly taken up there, two key elements of place, namely space and time, do appear as central points of focus. The analysis of the topological character of *Being and Time* that is the task of this chapter will thus be largely directed at an investigation of Heidegger's treatment of these two concepts and their relation, but especially at the concept of spatiality.

3.1   The Idea of "Being-In"

Being and Time contains many elements of the preliminary analysis that we have already encountered in his earlier thinking. It begins with the question of being, but very quickly moves to demonstrate the way in which that question is already implicated with the question of the being of that mode of being that is being-there and with the character of its being as being-in-the-world. From a topological perspective, it is notable, however, that the substantive analysis of the division 1 of *Being and Time* begins with the problem of how to understand the notion of "being-in" (*In-Sein*) that is brought to the fore in the idea of being-there as a being "in" the world (and which already seems to be present in the very idea of "situatedness"). Indeed, in this respect, the fundamental orientation of *Being and Time* would seem, from the start, to be directed at the articulation of what is an essentially topological structure—the structure of just that mode of being that is constituted in terms of its "there." Such a topological orientation should be no surprise given the path along which Heidegger's thinking has already come. Yet in focusing on the "in" as a key element within that structure, it would also appear that Heidegger is taking up, right from the start, a concept that is indeed essentially *spatial*.

The idea of "being-in" is a notion we first understand in terms of the idea of "being-in something" as one thing is *contained* in something else. Heidegger notes, in section 12 of *Being and Time*, in which the issue of the nature of "being-in" is first broached, that the phrase "being in something":

designates the kind of Being which an entity has when it is "in" another one, as the water is "in" the glass, or the garment is "in" the cupboard. By this "in" we mean the relationship of Being which two entities have to each other with regard to their location in that space. Both water and glass, garment and cupboard, are "in" space and "at" a location, and both in the same way. This relationship of Being can be expanded: for instance, the bench is in the lecture-room, the lecture-room is in the university, the university is in the city, and so on, until we can say that the bench is in "world-space."[5]

Heidegger's words here echo comments that appear in the text of a lecture course he gave in the summer semester of 1925 in which he also looks to examine the character of "being-in":

When we then try to give intuitive demonstration to this "in," more accurately to the "something-in-something," we give examples like the water "in" the glass, the clothes "in" the closet, the desks "in" the classroom. By this we mean that one is spatially contained in another and refer to the relationship of being with regard to place and space of two entities which are themselves extended in space. Thus both the first (water) and the second (glass), wherein the first is, are "in" space; both have their place. Both are only "in" space and have no in-being . . . the desk in the class-room, the classroom in the university building, the building in the city of Marburg, Marburg in Hessen, in Germany, in Europe, on Earth, in a solar system, in world-space, in the world.[6]

It is worth noting, in both these passages, the appearance of a notion of place as referring to the location of a thing in space ("Both water and glass, garment and cupboard, are 'in' space and 'at' a location, and both in the same way"; "Thus both the first (water) and the second (glass), wherein the first is, are 'in' space; both have their place")—and this is indicative of the tendency, already noted, for Heidegger to talk of place for almost the whole of his early period, in ways that take it to be a matter of the spatial location of a thing. Moreover, the conception of "being-in" that Heidegger introduces here and that treats it as a matter of spatial containment appears very close to the concept of "being-in-a-place" that Aristotle explores in his discussion of *topos* in the *Physics*—although Heidegger nowhere makes this connection explicit[7]—a concept that was also a focus for much premodern discussion of space and place. Before we consider Heidegger's own account of this idea of containment, then, and his criticisms of it, it is worth reacquainting ourselves with some of the "history of place" that stands as the background to Heidegger's discussion.

Aristotle's treatment of *topos* is tied to the idea of *topos* as that which is the answer to the question "where"—consequently *topos* figures as one of the Aristotelian *Kategoriai* (which constitute both the different ways in which things can be spoken and certain basic ways in which things can be).[8] Here it seems as if Aristotle assumes an understanding of *topos* that would match the understanding of place as location, such that each thing has its own place within a world of such places, rather than as that open region within which things appear. Yet although Aristotle does indeed treat place in a way that seems to assimilate it to a notion of location, and his treating being-at-a-place as one of the nonsubstantial *Kategoriai* would also seem to indicate that place is only accidental to the being of the thing, he nevertheless also takes it to be a central concept in philosophical analysis, writing in *Physics* 4 of the importance of arriving at an understanding of place[9] and reiterating the Archtyan maxim that to be is to be somewhere.[10] Indeed, Heidegger himself recognizes the significance of the Aristotelian, and, more generally, the Greek understanding of place, as that which supports the being of the thing—"the place [*Platz*] pertains to the being itself. . . . every being has *its* place [*Ort*]. . . . *The place [Ort] is constitutive of the presence of the being*."[11] Notably, however, while the sense of place at issue is clearly more than the sense associated with mere location within a realm of spatial extension, still the way in which place might function as the open realm of gathered disclosure is not yet apparent. Place thus appears as a problematic notion, and appears to be recognized as such by Heidegger himself as he repeats Aristotle's own comment that "it is something great and very difficult to grasp place for what it is."[12]

In his own discussion in *Physics* 4, Aristotle criticizes and rejects a number of alternative accounts of the nature of *topos* as form, matter, and extension in order to arrive at his own characterization of the notion as "the first unchangeable limit of that which surrounds."[13] The "place" or *topos* of a thing is thus understood to be the inner surface of the body (where "body" here means simply the thing in its physical extendedness) within which that thing is enclosed—on this account the "place" of a rosebud contained within a glass paperweight is the inner surface of the glass that surrounds the enclosed flower. The implication of this account is that to be "in place" is always to be contained within an enclosing body, and Aristotle states this explicitly: "a body is in place," he says, "if, and only if, there is a body outside it which surrounds it."[14] Since Aristotle rejects the concept of void, almost everything is necessarily enclosed within something else. The only exception is the universe as a whole, which is literally "no-place" and which is therefore not contained within anything at all—a claim that gave rise to extended discussions among ancient and medieval writers concerning the possibility of something extending beyond the bounds of the universe. The Aristotelian characterization of place that understands the notion by means of the idea of containment within an enclosing body is echoed by Heidegger, not only in section 12, but also in section 21 of *Being and Time*, where he writes of the contrast between being-there and "a way of Being in space which we call 'insideness' [*Inwendigkeit*]."[15] "Insideness" is elucidated by reference to the way in which "an entity which is itself extended is closed round [*umschlossen*] by the extended boundaries of something that is likewise extended."[16] Here, particularly in the notion of being "closed around by . . . boundaries," there seems a clear echo of Aristotle's "unchangeable limit of that which surrounds."

In fact, while the Aristotelian characterization of *topos* certainly seems to play a part in Heidegger's thinking, it is not so much an Aristotelian as a Cartesian view of space that appears to dominate Heidegger's discussion. And Descartes's understanding of space, although historically continuous with that to be found in Aristotle and also dependent upon a concept of containment, is quite distinct from that which Aristotle proposes in the *Physics* and is in part developed in opposition to it. In *The Principles of Philosophy*, Descartes writes of the notions of *"l'éspace"* (space) and *"le lieu"* (which would seem to correspond to "place") that:

the extension in length, breadth and depth which constitutes a space is exactly the same as that which constitutes a body. . . . The terms "place" and "space," then, do not signify anything different from the body which is said to be in a place. . . . The difference between the terms "place" and "space" is that the former designates more explicitly the position, as opposed to the size or shape, while it is the size or shape that we are concentrating on when we talk of space.[17]

Whereas Aristotle treats *topos* as tied to the bounding inner surface of a container, Descartes takes *"l'éspace"* to be identical with the area or volume enclosed within the container and *"le lieu"* to be just a matter of the container's position, with both notions tied to the concept of an extended body. From the idea of space as tied to a particular body, it is easy to arrive at a more generalized notion of space as the extended realm within which all bodies can be contained. Albert Einstein talks in just this way of the development of the modern idea of space: the idea of an "independent (absolute) space, unlimited in extent, in which all material objects are contained" is arrived at by "natural extension" from the concept of the particular space that exists within any particular enclosing body.[18]

This Cartesian view of space is continuous with the Aristotelian in that it derives from a concept of space (and of place) that is tied to containment. But the Cartesian view is much more dependent on ideas deriving from the Greek atomists and Stoics than from Aristotle. Indeed, the Cartesian view of space is clearly descended from the idea of *kenon* or void that was especially important in providing the basis for a notion of space as undifferentiated and unlimited extension in writers from Philoponous to Giordano Bruno. The Cartesian view is also indebted to Platonic ideas of space. Plato's view of space—the view presented in the famous discussion of *chora* in the *Timaeus*—is explicitly criticized by Aristotle in the *Physics*. Aristotle takes it to be a view that reduces space or place to matter understood as pure extension.[19] The Platonic account of the *Chora* is notoriously obscure, but it involves a concept of the *Chora*—or Receptacle—as opening up a space into which qualities can be received so that particular things can come into being. The Receptacle is thus the "Nurse of Becoming."[20] The concept of space or place that is involved in this account—of space as the receptive and nurturing opening or "womb" in which things come to be—is one that is amenable to a more geometrical or mathematical account than the Aristotelian. And this is not surprising since Aristotle's concern, at least in the *Physics*,[21] is with place as it plays a role in change, especially motion, which he defines "in its most general and primary sense" as change of place,[22] while Plato is interested in the role of *chora* in generation, viewing the process of generation as itself governed by geometrical principles and forms. The space or place that is the *chora* is indeed a space of pure, featureless extension. For this reason, the Platonic account of space or place in the *Timaeus* can be seen as an ancestor to modern conceptions of space in a way that the Aristotelian notion cannot.[23] Thus, although, in *Introduction to Metaphysics*, Heidegger claims (perhaps somewhat ambiguously, given the difficulty in establishing exactly how either place or "*topos*" should be understood) that "The Greeks have no word for 'space' . . . for they do not experience the spatial according to *extensio* but instead according to place (*topos*),"[24] still he writes elsewhere that "Platonic philosophy—that is, the interpretation of Being as *idea*—prepared the transfiguration of place (*topos*) and of *chora*, the essence of which we have barely grasped, into 'space' as defined by extension."[25]

While Descartes distinguishes between "*l'éspace*" (space) and "*le lieu*" (place), using two distinct terms to do so, still it is clearly the notion of space that is the dominant term in his thinking. Only within an all-encompassing absolute space can the idea of place as simple position make sense. The move to a concept of space as tied to extension, and to measurable extension, and to a notion of place as a matter of position is thus directly connected with Descartes's development of the system of coordinate geometry in which space can indeed be presented as a realm of pure extension within which both the shape and size of bodies, and their locations can be simply plotted. The connection between the move toward a conception of space as pure extension and the mathematical understanding of the spatial are thus brought clearly into prominence in Descartes.

There is a great deal of the history of philosophy, then, behind these few comments with which Heidegger first introduces the problem of the nature of "being-in." When we return to those comments, and what follows, we find Heidegger giving his own elaboration of what is at stake in this "history of space" by looking to the way in which the understanding of space in terms of measurable extension brings with it a certain conception of the entities that are found "in" that space. Of things that have the character of "Being-in-something"—things that have the character of existing (or "being-contained") "in" space—Heidegger claims that they also possess a characteristic sameness: "All entities whose Being 'in' one another can thus be described have the same kind of Being—that of being-present-at-hand [*Vorhanden*]—as Things occurring 'within' the world."[26] We might say that grasping things as spatial in this sense—as having the character of "being-contained"—is to grasp those things as "objects" and so as "objective" (for this reason I will refer to the notion of space at issue here as "objective spatiality").[27]

The sense in which things-present-at-hand are "within" the world is just the sense in which one thing may be contained within another and in which all things may be said to be contained within the space of the world or, better, of the physical universe. And insofar as things are so contained, they may also be said to be located within the framework of a space that does not give priority to any one location or region within it, but in which all locations, as with all "things," are the same inasmuch as they stand within the same unitary, but also undifferentiated, "space." Being-in space, in this sense of being-contained or being-in-a-location, is thus a characteristic feature of the leveled-out mode of being that is being-present-at-hand (*Vorhandensein*). Moreover, Heidegger claims that being "in" space in this way—being merely present-at-hand—implies no real "encounter" between the things that are thereby "in" that space:

> when two things are present-at-hand together alongside one another, we are accustomed to express this by saying something like "The table stands 'by' ['*bei*'] the door or "The chair 'touches' ['*berührt*'] the wall." Taken strictly, "touching" is never what we are talking about in such cases, not because accurate re-examination will always eventually establish that there is a space between the chair and the wall, but because in principle the chair can never touch the wall, even if the space between them should be equal to zero. If the chair could touch the wall, this would presuppose that the wall is the sort of thing "for" which a chair would be *encounterable.* . . . When two entities are present-at-hand within the world, and furthermore are *worldless* in themselves, they can never touch each other nor can either of them "*be*" "*alongside*" the other.[28]

The things that are merely present-at-hand and so are simply "contained" "in" an extended space are thus not things that are properly "in" the world in virtue of themselves alone. The clear implication here is that the being "in" the world of such things must depend on something else that is "in" the world in a different way, that is not worldless, but "has" a world in virtue of itself. Indeed, Heidegger says just this: "An entity present-at-hand within the world can be touched by another entity only if by its very nature the latter entity has Being-in as it own kind of Being— only if, with its Being-There [*Da-sein*], something like the world is revealed to it."[29]

Being-there has a world in a way that merely present-at-hand things such as tables and chairs do not. And although Heidegger acknowledges that being-there can itself be understood as "present-at-hand" in the way in which tables and chairs are present-at-hand—as mere entities "in" space— he also makes clear that this is not a mode of being that properly belongs to being-there as such. Thus he comments that "even entities which are not worldless—Dasein itself for example—are present at hand 'in' the world, or, more exactly, *can* with some right and within certain limits be *taken* as merely present-at-hand. To do this, one must completely disregard or just not see the existential state of Being-in." That is, to view being-there as present-at-hand one must ignore or not see the way in which it has a "being-in" that is proper to it that is not the "being-in" associated with objective spatiality. Indeed, that being-there cannot be properly understood on the basis of spatiality viewed in terms of mere location, measurement, or extension is already evident as far back, for instance, as the lectures of 1919. There Heidegger denied that the concept of space as measurable extension was relevant to the sort of situatedness with which he was concerned:

In the course of a hike through the woods I come for the first time to Freiburg and ask, upon entering the city, "Which is the shortest way to the cathedral?" This spatial orientation has nothing to do with geometrical orientation as such. The distance to the cathedral is not a quantitative interval; proximity and distance are not a "how much"; the most convenient and shortest way is also not something quantitative, not merely extension as such.[30]

The relation between things understood in terms of "nearness" and "farness" is not to be understood on the basis of that which is measurable and quantifiable—on the basis, that is, of objective spatiality alone. Such a spatiality allows of no "nearness" or "farness" since within it all places are nothing more than "locations" that are related to one another by the same numerically given measures; all locations are the "same" because all stand within the "same" extended, quantitative frame. Within a space understood in this way, there can indeed be no proper relatedness. Consequently, the sense of "being-in" that is of most interest for the analysis in *Being and Time* and that is taken as proper to being-there is not to be understood in terms of "being-contained" *in* something or "being-in-a-location." As Heidegger writes, "Being-in . . . is a state of Dasein's Being; it is an existentiale. So one cannot think of it as the Being-present-at-hand of some corporeal Thing (such as a human body) 'in' an entity which is present-at-hand,"[31] and elsewhere he comments, "Dasein takes space in [*nimmt . . . Raum ein*]; this is to be understood literally. It is by no means just present-at-hand in a bit of space which its body fills up."[32]

3.2   The Nature of Dwelling

As the considerations adduced above already indicate, the discussion of "being-in" that occurs in section 12 leads fairly quickly to the conclusion that what is at stake in the idea of "being-in" as this relates to being-there is not a matter of spatial "containment" or "location" in the sense associated with objective spatiality. The question, however, is how to characterize the alternative mode of "being-in" that seems implied here. Heidegger's discussion of this matter, however, is highly condensed and summary in character, and he moves almost immediately from the claim that the being-in of being-there is not to be understood in terms of the spatiality of the present-at-hand to the claim that it is rather a matter of the being-in associated with that "within which" one lives or "resides." In a passage, some of the main elements of which reappear some twenty-seven years later (in "Building Dwelling Thinking"),[33] Heidegger looks to the etymology of the German "in" as providing an indication of the direction in which an adequate understanding of "being-in" must move. He writes:

"In" is derived from "*innan*"—"to reside," "*habitare*," "to dwell" [*sich aufhalten*]. "An" signifies "I am accustomed," "I am familiar with," "I look after something." It has the signification of "*colo*" in the senses of "*habito*" and "*diligo*." The entity to which Being-in in this signification belongs is one which we have characterized as that entity which in each case I myself am [*bin*]. The expression "*bin*" is connected with "*bei*," and so "*ich bin*" [I am] means in its turn "I reside" or "dwell alongside" the world, as that which is familiar to me in such and such a way. "Being" [*Sein*], as the infinitive of "*ich bin*" (that is to say when it is understood as an *existentiale*), signifies "to reside alongside . . . ," "to be familiar with. . . ." "*Being-in*" *is thus the formal existential expression for the Being of Dasein, which has Being-in-the-world as its essential state.*[34]

The "being-in" that is characteristic of the being of Dasein is thus distinguished from the being-in of mere spatial *location* or *containment* and is instead characterized as a "being-in" that is tied to "residing" or "dwelling." Such dwelling is taken to involve familiarity and a sense of "looking after" or "taking care" that presages Heidegger's discussion of care (*Sorge*) later in *Being and Time* as determinative of the structure of being-in-the-world. In fact, even here dwelling is understood, not as something in which Dasein may or may not engage, but as characterizing Dasein's very being—for Dasein to "*be*" is for Dasein to *dwell*. In fact, the etymology that Heidegger draws on here, while it introduces, but does not develop, the idea of dwelling, nevertheless seems to refer us back to the idea we encountered in Heidegger's earliest thinking, namely, the way in which our situatedness in the world is indeed something that cannot be separated from what we are and what is closest to us, from that which is most familiar and with which we are already engaged.

Having noted this, however, it also has to be said that it is all too easy to suppose that this passage tells us more than it actually does and to read it in a way that is already laden with an analysis that has still to be provided. It certainly tells us very little about the concepts to which it draws attention, and we still need to inquire into what it means to "be familiar with" and to "look after," what it means to "reside" and to "dwell." The concept of dwelling, in particular, will become a key concept in later Heidegger, and although one may well view Heidegger's connecting of dwelling with familiarity and "looking after" in this passage as given further elaboration through the analysis of care and temporality that appears later, still *Being and Time* gives little or no attention to an explicit analysis of dwelling as such, and the concept remains somewhat in the background. Nevertheless, putting the connection with care to one side, the idea of dwelling does appear elsewhere in *Being and Time* in ways that help to provide some sense of what Heidegger has in mind when he uses the notion even in his early thinking. Dwelling appears, for instance, in *Being and Time*, section 36, as an important contrastive notion in the discussion of curiosity:

curiosity is characterized by a specific way of *not tarrying* alongside what is closest. Consequently it does not seek the leisure of tarrying observantly, but rather seeks restlessness and the excitement of continual novelty and changing encounters. In not tarrying curiosity is concerned with the constant possibility of distraction. Curiosity has nothing to do with observing entities and marvelling at them— ϑαυμάζειν. To be amazed to the point of not understanding is something in which it has no interest. Rather it concerns itself with a kind of knowing but just in order to have known. But this *not tarrying* in the environment with which one concerns oneself, and this distraction by new possibilities, are constitutive items for curiosity; and upon these is founded the third essential characteristic of this phenomenon, which we call the character of "never dwelling anywhere" [*Aufen-thaltslosigkeit*]. Curiosity is everywhere and nowhere. This mode of Being-in-the-world reveals a new kind of Being of everyday Dasein—a kind in which Dasein is constantly uprooting itself.[35]

In taking the characteristic feature of curiosity as "never dwelling any-where" and as thereby revealing a kind of being in which being-there is "constantly uprooting itself," is "everywhere and nowhere" and continu-ally seeks "restlessness and the excitement of continual novelty and chang-ing encounters," Heidegger implicitly draws on the spatial and topological connotations associated with dwelling—of dwelling as always tied to a certain space and place. If curiosity is "everywhere and nowhere," dwelling is surely a "being-somewhere"; if curiosity is a continual "uprooting," then dwelling is surely a "putting down of roots"; and as curiosity involves dis-traction and novelty, the relation to things that is associated with dwelling is surely a relation of attentiveness and of familiarity—of "homeliness" we might say. We might even add that while curiosity remains removed from things, never properly attached to them, in dwelling we stay close to things and are connected to them.

In these respects dwelling involves what is, to use a form of words espe-cially significant in the Heideggerian context, a "bringing-close," a *nearing*, of what is otherwise apart from us.[36] The idea of such "nearing" turns out to be a central notion in Heidegger's later analysis of the existential spa-tiality that he claims is proper to being-there. "Nearing" is not just an over-coming of a purely objective *spatial* distance but also a "picking out" or a "bringing into salience" that overcomes the distance of inattention or "not-seeing." In this respect, it might be thought of as analogous with the cinematic technique in which a particular object or detail in a scene is brought forcefully to the attention of the viewer by a sudden zooming shot that bridges the distance between camera and thing seen. The cinematic technique is, indeed, a way of making evident through exaggeration and extremity of technique a phenomenon that we are already quite familiar with in terms of our ability to pick out and attend to particular things in the vast array of things presented to us in experience—it is an exaggerated presentation of a mundane form of intentionality. It is also a simplified way of picking up on what is essentially involved in the sort of situated-ness that was the focus for the discussion in the last chapter—the way in which such situatedness always involves an orientation to one's sur-roundings that consists in a particular configuration of those surroundings so that certain features emerge as more salient than others. The cinematic illustration is limited, however, in that it is indeed visual and homes in on one part of a certain visual field, whereas the "nearing" at issue here is not primarily visual at all, nor is it a matter of bringing close a *part* of some sensory field, whether visual or otherwise. Instead, the nearing at issue here involves the interplay of all our senses and typically focuses on things or aspects of things, on events or particular features of events. The cinematic example may also suggest that it is we who bring things close through some act of choice or decision—as the camera brings things close to it through the adjustment of its lens—for Heidegger, however, the nearing at issue here arises out of the way being-there already finds itself in a particular situation. The nearing of things thus occurs through the interplay between elements within being-there's existential situatedness.

Being-in appears, on the face of it, to be a spatial notion. But the relation of spatial containment that is usually taken to be at issue in "being-in" cannot be appropriate to the way being-there is in the world. Being-there is "in" the world, not through some relation of physical containment, but rather through "dwelling." It might seem, then, the obvious conclusion to draw here is that there are two senses of "being-in," one that is spatial and one that is not, and that only the latter sense is relevant to understanding the character of being-there as "in" the world. This is indeed the interpretation that, at least initially, Hubert Dreyfus seems to propose. Dreyfus distinguishes between two senses of "in": what he terms a spatial sense ("in the box") and an existential sense ("in the army," "in love"). The first use expresses inclusion, the second conveys involvement.[37] The sense of "being-in" that is characteristic of being-there can be seen, suggests Dreyfus, as a sense of "being-in" as "inhabiting," and he goes on:

When we inhabit something it is no longer an object for us but becomes part of us and pervades our relation to other objects in the world. Both Heidegger and Michael Polanyi call this way of being-in "dwelling." Polanyi points out that we dwell in our language; we feel at home in it and relate to objects and other people through it. Heidegger says the same for the world. Dwelling is Dasein's basic way of being-in-the-world.[38]

Dreyfus refers to the sense of "being-in" associated with inclusion or containment as the "objective, 'literal' sense of 'in.'"[39] This seems to suggest a contrast between spatiality, understood as a matter of containment or inclusion, and the dwelling associated with involvement that treats the latter as strictly speaking *nonspatial*. Dreyfus also writes, however, that although "Dasein is not in the world in the same way that an occurrent thing is in physical space," still this "is not to say that Dasein has no spatiality."[40] There is, then, a spatiality that Dreyfus takes to belong to being-there that is not identical with the spatiality of the physical, but is rather a form of spatiality that is "existential." The closeness of dwelling, the idea of dwelling as a putting down of roots and of a "being-somewhere," the connection of dwelling with "homeliness," are all suggestive of connections with spatiality. Consequently, we may well take the view that two distinct senses of spatiality are what is needed here, corresponding to the two senses of "being-in," rather than a spatial and a nonspatial sense of "being-in"— conceptions of spatiality that can be distinguished by reference to the notions of "inclusion" (or containment) and "involvement" (as in Dreyfus), or in talk of objective versus "existential" spatiality, or perhaps even by reference to a contrast between space, as tied to measurable extension, and space as tied to place, to that in which one dwells.

The idea that Heidegger does indeed distinguish between two senses of spatiality—the objective spatiality tied to extension and "containment," and the existential spatiality that is proper to being-there's own being-in-the-world and is tied to "involvement"—seems incontrovertible. Not only is the acceptance of such a distinction as present in Heidegger's text wide-spread within the current literature, but it also finds solid support in the way Heidegger himself approaches these matters, in *Being and Time*, as well as in his earlier thinking. Indeed, to repeat something of what I indicated in the introductory comments to this chapter above, we can summarize the underlying considerations here quite simply: if what is at issue is a certain sort of situatedness (a certain sort of "being in") that is associated with "being-there," then no conception of space as objective will be adequate to the understanding of that situatedness—objective space allows only for standardized "locations," not for situatedness as such; the result is that we cannot treat situatedness as based in the spatiality of measurable extendedness, and yet, since situatedness also has a spatiality of its own, we must distinguish between space understood in "objective" terms and an alternative conception of space, the nature of which still remains somewhat obscure, which we can refer to as "existential." Inasmuch as the question of situatedness and of the "there" that is at issue here can be understood as a question about the nature of a certain sort of "place," so the way spatiality arises as a problem here relates directly to the way in which, in spite of the traditional assimilation of place to space, no conception of space as objective can be adequate to the understanding of place—just as space, in this sense, does not allow for situatedness, it also does not allow for place properly understood. It seems, then, that we must distinguish between objective space, taken on its own, and the space associated with situatedness, the space associated with place.[41]

Yet although the distinction between objective and existential spatiality is one that seems clearly present in Heidegger and seems, indeed, to be required by the character of his argument, still the distinction also presents some serious difficulties. To a large extent, these difficulties are indicated by tensions and obscurities in the way Heidegger himself talks about spatiality. In this respect, Heidegger often seems to be pulled in two different directions: on the one hand, he recognizes the inevitability of spatiality as part of the structure of being-there and so insists on being-there as having spatiality proper to it, while, on the other, he constantly seeks to deemphasize the role of spatiality and to stress that it cannot be a primary notion in the analysis of being-there. This tension comes out at many places in his discussion, but it is particularly clear in his comments on the concept of world. Thus he writes that:

We shall seek the worldhood of the environment (environmentality) by going through an ontological Interpretation of those entities within-the-environment which are closest to us. The expression "environment" [Umwelt] contains in the "environ" [um] a suggestion of spatiality. Yet the "around" [Umherum] which is constitutive for the environment does not have a primarily spatial meaning. Instead the spatial character, which incontestably belongs to any environment, can be clarified only in terms of the structure of worldhood.[42]

Here it is not any one form of spatiality that is at issue, but, so it would seem, spatiality as such. Even the "aroundness" of environmentality, which itself seems to refer us back to the "in" of situatedness, appears not to be primarily spatial at all. Yet at the same time as Heidegger insists on "aroundness" as not primarily spatial, he also tells us that the interpretation to be attempted is aimed at "those entities . . . closest to us." While one can only assume (and there are of course good reasons for doing so) that the closeness at issue here must also be such that it "does not have a primarily spatial meaning," it is noteworthy that Heidegger here argues against the spatial understanding of "aroundness" in a way that nevertheless leaves the spatiality of "closeness" beside it and unremarked upon.

    Although, in this passage, Heidegger seems to suggest that environmentality is not spatial at all, such that one might conclude that perhaps being-there is not spatial either, he does, of course, talk elsewhere of a spatiality that is proper to being-there. Yet even Heidegger's acknowledgment of being-there's spatiality is always given with the qualification that such spatiality is not primary, but is itself possible "only on the basis of Being-in-the-world in general."[43] In this respect, being-there seems to have a "spatiality" of its own, and yet it also appears ambiguous as to whether the "spatiality" that belongs to it (the "in" as well as the "around") is really a form of spatiality at all. Indeed, the ambiguity here also seems to affect the sense in which the spatiality proper to being-there is indeed "not primary": as a mode of *being*, it is derivative of, and therefore secondary to, world-hood; but, inasmuch as Heidegger also seems to claim that it is not primarily spatial, so it would also seem to be derivative, as *spatial*, from the spatiality associated with containment. Some of the difficulty here is also apparent in the way Dreyfus presents the distinction between "inclusion" and "involvement." It is not at all clear, for instance, how far Dreyfus intends that distinction to be taken as properly a distinction between different modes of *spatiality*. Although he repeats Heidegger's own pronouncement that being-there does indeed have a spatiality of its own, at the same time, Dreyfus also writes that the sense of "in" that is associated with containment is the "objective," "literal" sense. The seeming implication is thus that the "in" of involvement and so also, one assumes, the spatiality associated with it, is not "literal," not "objective." Is the "in" of involvement then, only metaphorical? Is the spatiality associated with involvement and so the spatiality that belongs to being-there similarly metaphorical? Here it starts to look as if it really is the case that the sense in which the spatiality proper to being-there is a mode of spatiality is, in one sense, derivative of the literal, objective spatiality associated with "inclusion," while in another sense, it is also derivative of worldhood. The upshot would seem to be, however, that it is not properly a mode of spatiality at all.

That there is a real difficulty here can also be seen when we reflect back on the way in which the notion of containment is itself taken up in the Aristotelian account of *topos*. As we saw in the discussion above, although *topos* looks as if it is a notion tied to the location of a thing, such that each thing has its own location within the larger system of locations or "places" that is the world, the *topos* of a thing is also inextricably bound up with the being of the thing. As I noted above, Heidegger himself acknowledges this point, just as he also insists that the Greek concept of *topos* cannot be construed in terms of the modern concept of space as measurable extension. Yet while the Aristotelian notion of *topos*, in particular, is quite clearly a notion that involves the idea of one thing being "contained" in another (what Dreyfus refers to as "inclusion"), in *Being and Time*, Heidegger seems quite unequivocal in taking such a notion of containment as designating the mode of being-in that is associated with objective spatiality and so with measurable extension—the mode of being that we saw him explicitly refer to above as the "way of Being in space which we call 'insideness' [*Inwendigkeit*]"[44] and that stands in contrast to the being-in proper to being-

there. Once again, there seems a deep ambiguity in Heidegger's treatment of the concepts of spatiality, including the notion of containment,
at issue here.

Dreyfus himself comments that Heidegger's thinking about spatiality is
fundamentally confused,[45] but he views that confusion as arising elsewhere
than in relation to the distinction between objective and existential spatiality as such. Yet although the distinction between objective and existential spatiality may seem, initially, to be plausible, even persuasive, the
considerations set out above suggest that the distinction is itself problematic, and, if that is so, then the confusion in Heidegger's thinking about
spatiality must be present at the most basic level—at the level that concerns the very notion of spatiality as such. Indeed, Heidegger's account
seems to be faced with a dilemma that Heidegger himself seems never to
recognize or satisfactorily resolve.

If, on the one hand, we treat containment and involvement as each
giving rise to, or being associated with, distinct modes of spatiality, then
it seems inevitable to ask after the relation between the modes as well as
after that in virtue of which both containment and involvement are indeed
separate modes of spatiality as such. The difficulty will be to answer that
question without presupposing a more basic concept of spatiality that
encompasses both containment and involvement.[46] This is not because of
any "essentialist" assumption concerning spatiality, but simply because the
forms of spatiality that are supposedly being claimed as distinct here also
seem inextricably entangled—as is evident from the importance of the
concept of "containment," as well as notions of "aroundness," "closeness,"
"situatedness," and so on, irrespective of the form of spatiality that is supposedly at issue. We may well postulate distinct senses that belong to these
associated concepts corresponding to the different senses of spatiality,
but the question is whether or not it is, in fact, possible to distinguish different senses for all of these terms that retain the conceptual connections
that must obtain between them, and yet do so in a way that limits those
connections within the bounds of each supposedly distinct mode of spatiality. On the basis of the considerations set out above, this seems
unlikely—indeed, one might say that, in this respect, space resists the
attempt to separate it out into different conceptual spaces. Perhaps this
should also be seen as a reflection of the way in which both objective and
existential spatiality, however they may be distinguished, must nevertheless continue to relate to a space that is, in some sense, the "same" (as the
space in which I now move is the "same" space that is also laid out before
me in the form of the map by means of which I guide those movements).[47]

Inasmuch as they do relate to such a space, they cannot be wholly independent of one another.

If, on the other hand, we treat one or the other of containment or involvement as the primary mode of spatiality (perhaps as the only "literal" or "objective" sense, in the way Dreyfus suggests), then we face the difficulty of having to deny that the other is a mode of spatiality except as a secondary and derivative mode. But this would have the problematic consequence that it will not be possible to speak, for instance, of being-there as having a spatiality "of its own"—for if it is the case that the primary sense of spatiality is that of containment, while the sense of spatiality associated with being-there is that of involvement, then the spatiality of being-there would only be understandable on the basis of the primary sense associated with the spatiality of containment from which it derives, and so on the basis of something that is not proper to being-there at all. Indeed, such a conclusion may even be seen as reinforced by the claim concerning the ontologically derivative status of the spatiality of being-there in relation to worldhood. The difficulty that would follow, however, is that we would then have to acknowledge that, strictly speaking, being-there does not have a spatiality that is proper to it, that what appears as a mode of spatiality, namely existential spatiality, is only improperly characterized in that way, and that, if being-there is to be given an adequate account in terms proper to it, we must expunge from that account all spatial references and connotations. Although this seems a thoroughly problematic outcome and one that Heidegger never actually embraces, it seems, in many respects, to be closest to the path Heidegger's account actually follows.

It often seems to be assumed that the problem of spatiality, while no doubt important, does not lie at the heart of the problematic of *Being and Time.* Yet the dilemma that seems to attend Heidegger's treatment of spatiality appears to bring with it some quite drastic consequences for the project of fundamental ontology that *Being and Time* attempts. Indeed, not only is the issue of Heidegger's understanding of spatiality at issue here, but his understanding of the entire ontological structure, beginning with the structure of worldhood from which existential spatiality is supposed to be derived, also comes into question along with the very notion of derivation as such. Thus, if spatiality may have appeared to be peripheral, it now turns out to be absolutely central. But that should not be surprising since the way spatiality arises as a problem here is directly related to the way in which the project of fundamental ontology, as Heidegger pursues it in *Being and Time,* is essentially concerned with the articulation of a *topological* structure—with the fundamentally "situated" or "placed" character of being. Although such situatedness or "placing" is not to be understood in terms merely of spatial location, it nevertheless stands in an essential relation to the question of space and spatiality. Before we go further in exploring the issues at stake here, especially those concerning the derivative status of spatiality, including existential spatiality, we need first, however, to give some closer consideration to Heidegger's account of the structure of spatiality as it pertains, in his account, to the being of being-there.

3.3 The Structure of "World"

Although, as we have already briefly seen in the discussion above, Heidegger accepts that there is a mode of spatiality that belongs to being-there, he also claims that such existential spatiality "can be clarified only in terms of the structure of worldhood"[48] and "is possible *only on the basis of Being-in-the-world in general.*"[49] Thus the investigation of the nature of "being-in," which might seem initially to lead to the idea of spatiality, and so might be thought to lead on to the understanding of "being-in-the-world" as a matter of "being-in-space," actually leads Heidegger to the grounding of spatiality in the structure of worldhood. Consequently Heidegger concludes his discussion of "being-in" in section 12, after having considered being-there in its epistemic relation to its world as a secondary mode of "being-in-the-world," by indicating the need to turn to a closer investigation of "Being-in-the-world" itself—"Thus Being-in-the-world, as a basic state, must be Interpreted beforehand"[50]—and this leads Heidegger directly to an analysis of world itself. It is in the analysis of world, and the environmentality that belongs to it (which occupies division 1, chapter 2, sections 14–24), that Heidegger provides his account of the spatiality proper to being-there.

The starting point for the analysis of worldhood is the account of equipmentality—of "availability" or "readiness-to-hand" (*Zuhandenheit*).[51] That aspect of the world that is closest to us is the structure of equipment, of things ready for use, that immediately surrounds us, and this structure is one that is essentially ordered in terms of what such things are *for*—it is ordered teleologically. As Heidegger tells us in *The Basic Problems of Phenomenology* (lectures given in 1927):

We say that an equipmental contexture environs us. Each individual piece of equipment is by its nature *equipment-for*—for traveling, for writing, for flying. Each one has its immanent reference to that *for which* it is what it is. It is always something *for*, pointing to a *for-which*. The specific structure of equipment is constituted by a *contexture of the what-for, in-order-to*. Each particular equipmental thing has as such a specific reference to another particular equipmental thing. We can formulate this reference even more clearly. Every entity that we uncover *as* equipment has with it a *specific functionality*, *Bewandtnis* [an in-order-to-ness, a way of being functionally deployed].[52]

Heidegger thus understands things ready-to-hand as being ordered in relation to one another in a way that reflects their ordering within such a teleological or "referential" totality. Each thing thus has a "place" (*Platz*) within a "region" (*Gegend*)—the hammer has a place on the workbench or the tool-belt and a place where it belongs when being used (in my hand and positioned so as to enable, for instance, the driving home of a nail)—and in being so located it is also located with respect to other things—with respect to saw, drill, the box of nails, the timber. The region is the set of places that are implicated with one another by particular forms of involvement and activity in the world, and our grasp of those activities and of our concernful involvement with things is itself a grasp of a region—a grasp of the ordering of things and places—a grasp that Heidegger calls "circumspection" (*Umsicht*—almost literally a "seeing-around"). Moreover, not only do things such as the hammer and the nails have a "place," but places themselves are ordered in relation to this equipmental structure: "Thus the sun, whose light and warmth are in everyday use, has its own places—sunrise, midday, sunset, midnight. . . . The house has its sunny side and its shady side; the way in which it is divided up into rooms [*Räume*] is oriented to these, and so is the arrangement within them."[53] Even those things and places associated with life and death, the cemetery, for instance, are ordered within this structure. Thus, just as we found the present-at-hand to be associated with a certain form of spatiality—that of homogeneous, measurable extension—so too does there seem to be a distinctive form of spatiality associated with the ready-to-hand—a heterogeneous, but ordered spatiality of places and regions in which proximity and distance are based on relations in the context of activity or task, on relations given in terms of an essentially teleological structure (the structure of the "toward which" and "in order to").[54]

Existential spatiality, the spatiality that belongs to being-there as such, is clearly closely tied to the spatiality of the ready-to-hand, what we might call "equipmental spatiality," but equipmental spatiality is not alone sufficient for existential spatiality. The structure of equipmentality establishes, and indeed consists in, an ordering of things and thereby establishes a certain structure of relations in which things are brought into proximity with one another. However, that structure, although it consists in certain places and regions, does not, as such, establish anything as proximate to "being-there"—indeed, that structure does not itself bring any particular "there" with it. The structure of equipmentality is thus an ordering of things, but it does not place being-there in any particular situation within that ordering, while the "places" and "regions" that figure within it are places only in the sense of *locations*—locations for certain items of equipment, locations for certain activities or tasks, locations that direct activities in certain ways. In being an ordering of things and places that is not, of itself, tied to any particular "there," equipmental spatiality also has an essentially "public" or "intersubjective" character.

Although items of equipment can be crafted to individual needs and preferences, still even the most personalized item fits within a larger equipmental structure that is, at least in principle, accessible to all. Indeed, although Heidegger does not even allude to such an argument, it seems likely that the very possibility of something functioning equipmentally presupposes its being publicly accessible in its equipmental character. The reasons for this are analogous to those at work in Wittgenstein's so-called private language argument. Just as what makes an utterance meaningful is not some private entity to which it refers, but the way it connects up with other utterances (the role it plays in a larger system of utterances), so what makes some particular thing into a piece of equipment is not the way it relates to some "private' intention" or "purpose," but rather the way it connects up with other such things as part of a larger equipmental structure. Moreover, such a structure, like the system of utterances, will always be an intersubjective, publicly accessible structure, simply because it is a systematic structure. A set of elements constitutes a system by virtue of the connections that obtain between the elements of the system themselves. Thus, to take a linguistic example (and language provides a key illustration here, though not a unique one), "apple" refers to apples, not because I choose that it so refer, but because of the way the reference is determined by the word itself as the word is in turn determined as just that word "apple" by the system of language to which it belongs—a system of language that is given in the ongoing practice of linguistic usage.[55] Systematicity thus resides in the elements that make up the system rather than in any act or intention associated with such systematicity. In this sense systematicity is always "public," inasmuch as the system is itself "public." In discussions of language and especially in discussions of the "private language argument" and the problem of rule-following with which it is associated, this point is developed through consideration of the role of intersubjectivity in the possibility of meaning. Without the constant interplay between individuals, in which each adjusts to the other's linguistic behavior and in which each is sensitive to being corrected by the other, there can be no way in which to maintain any consistency of usage and therefore also consistency of meaning over time; consequently a language that was wholly based in an individual's "private" assigning of meanings to expressions in a way isolated from any broader "public" practice would not be capable of functioning as a language at all because there would be no way in which one could prevent those assignments shifting in ways that could not be kept track of by the individual concerned.

Of course, in terms of the equipmental structure that interests Heidegger, the public character of the equipmental "system" is also determined by the need for items of equipment to have a character that will allow them to function in certain specific ways. Thus no matter how intent we may be on assigning the equipmental character, for example, of "hammer" to a piece of string, the string will remain incapable of taking on that particular character. Items of equipment are oriented to particular uses and tasks to which they must themselves be adequate. Moreover, even though particular items of equipment may be crafted for individual use (perhaps my hammer is custom-made in weight, shape, and so forth to fit, not only my specific type of work, but also the contours of my hand and the strength of my arm), still those items are always available to be taken up by others with more or less facility. Tools that may be designed only to be able to be employed by one person in particular and that are made so through being keyed to a particular code, perhaps to a fingerprint, retinal image, or whatever, do not count against the point at issue here. It is not that such tools are properly "private" as such, but that they are simply "made private" through being "locked" away from the use of others—moreover, it is precisely because they could be used by others that such locking is required. The equipmental structure of the world is thus a necessarily public structure both in virtue of its systematic ordering and in virtue of the need for items of equipment to be geared to particular equipmental tasks. The space of equipment is thus also a necessarily public mode of spatiality, and thus it also directs attention to the way in which being-there is as much a being-with others (*Mitsein, Mitdasein*) as it is a being-amidst or being-alongside things (*Sein bei*).[56]

Heidegger's discussion of being-with others takes up an entire chapter of its own (division 1, chapter 4, sections 25–27), but what is particularly relevant to the present discussion is the way in which the character of being-there as always a "being-with" is itself closely tied to the way being-there finds itself engaged with things, places, and regions—the equipmentality of the world is always "public," but the public character of the world, that is, its intersubjectivity, is in turn tied to its spatiality as that is given in and through the ordering of things, places, and regions (indeed, this is so even in the case of language, which has its own spatialized, embodied form in utterance and text). The connection between spatiality and the intersubjective or "social" can be clearly seen in Heidegger's initial descriptions of the way in which our being-with-others (*Mitsein*) is already evident in our involvement with things as ready-to-hand. So, for instance:

> When . . . we walk along the edge of a field but "outside" it, the field shows itself as belonging to such-and-such a person, and decently kept up by him; the book we have used was bought at So-and-so's shop and given by such-and-such a person, and so forth. The boat anchored at the shore is assigned in its Being-in-itself to an acquaintance who undertakes voyages with it; but even if it is a "boat which is strange to us," it is still indicative of Others.[57]

Indeed, these comments echo earlier comments prior to *Being and Time*— for instance, in the 1923 lectures on facticity, from which I quoted in chapter 2 above, Heidegger writes "The dining-table at home is not a round top on a stand but a piece of furniture in a particular place, which itself has particular places at which particular others are seated everyday. The empty place directly appresents co-Dasein to me in terms of the absence of others."[58] Although the encounter with things is always within a framework in which others are also implied, the encounter with others is also an encounter with things. Indeed, one might say, in general, that it is only within the externality of space, as worked out in and through the things and places with which being-there is involved—the book, the table, the boat, the shop, the field, the shore—that we encounter other persons at all. And so, not only does the idea of things as ready-to-hand refer to an ordering of things and places and to a system of social interconnectedness, but it also indicates the way in which that social realm and our interactions within it are organized *in space* and, conversely (but significantly, given the derivative character of spatiality for Heidegger), the way in which the spatial also takes on a certain ordering in virtue of the social.[59] The realm of our involvement with others is thus a realm that is defined and marked out through our involvement with things and places, and so, while our involvement with things as ready-to-hand is also an involvement with others, our involvement with others is also an involvement with things. To be involved with others is, in this respect, to be engaged within the

organized structure of equipmentality—involvement with others is organized and oriented through this equipmental structure, which is also a
social structure. And to the extent that the ordering of the world of equipment is something laid out "in space," so too the ordering of the social is
a spatial ordering.

The spatial ordering of social life is not a merely contingent fact about
being-there. Although the point is not made in any explicit fashion, Heidegger offers ample evidence for the claim that social being is *necessarily*
spatial being. Essential to the grasp of properly social life is a grasp of the
very concept of otherness, and to grasp this is to grasp the very possibility of an existence that is both *similar* to my own existence and yet nevertheless *different* from it. It is only through the location of others in space,
and so also in relation to the things and places with which I am myself
located in that space, that I can grasp others as existing both outside and
yet alongside myself, as having a view on the world that is like my own
and yet a view that is not my own. In space I separate myself off from the
things and from those other persons that I encounter within the world.
The externality made possible by space is thus also the externality that is
implied in the very idea of the other—an externality given special emphasis by Bergson, in particular (though also, more recently, by Levinas). Since
the realm of others is indeed a realm that is, in a certain sense, "external
to" me, so it is also a realm that takes on a concrete form through the
ordering of space and the ordering of things and places in space. Indeed,
in the establishing of a form of social life is also established a form of
space.[60] The idea of the social as essentially constituted in space is a notion
that has taken on a highly developed form in much twentieth-century
thinking about social life that is exemplified in the work of Foucault and
also, though in a different and more developed fashion, of Lefebvre.[61]
Admittedly the idea can be seen as a way of taking up certain materialist
strains of thought, as are to be found, for instance, in Marx, but Marx does
not provide the framework within which the tight conceptual connection
between spatiality and sociality can be grasped so readily. Indeed, one
might take Marx to be largely insensitive to, or even uninterested in, the
ontological implications and nature of this connection. Through Heidegger we can see much more clearly how and why it is that *human* life might
necessarily be *social* life, and why social life is always *spatialized*. Society is
itself established and constituted through the organization of space, and
so is the sociality of being-there expressed in spatialized form, although,
it is the spatiality that consists in the ordering of things and places given
through the structure of world.

Heidegger's account of being-there as always social—of being-there as always "being-with"—indicates the way in which Heidegger takes issue with the predominantly solipsistic underpinning of many traditional ways of thinking of human being—especially those ways of understanding that are taken to have their origins in the internally centerd thinking exemplified in Descartes's *Meditations*. Just as being-there does not first find itself apart from the world, but finds itself only in and through the world, both self and world being given together, neither does being-there first find itself apart from others, but is instead always already there among others. Indeed, the way in which being-there is both a "being-with" others and a "being-alongside" things and places is indicated by the way in which these two modes of its being are themselves always entangled in the ways indicated above—in ways that are fundamentally geared to spatiality. Indeed, one can view the realm of spatiality, in a way that contrasts significantly with Heidegger's own emphasis on the absence of any "relatedness" with the space of mere "containment," as just that realm that makes for mutual differentiation between entities that nevertheless also stand in a mutual relation to one another. Without spatiality there can be no such differentiation or relatedness. Moreover, inasmuch as being-there's essentially social mode of being also implies that the meaningful character of the world is always a character articulated through that which is public and intersubjective—inasmuch as being-there understands its own being, as well as the being of others, of things, and of its world, in terms of possibilities, then those possibilities must themselves be drawn from the realm of the public and the intersubjective. Indeed, at this point the considerations that we saw to apply in the case of equipmentality, as well as in the case of language, and that indicate the necessarily spatialized character of the equipmental, must also apply to the structures on which understanding itself draws—and this is just what is evident, in fact, in the way the public character of the equipmental can be seen to be analogous to the public character of language. What is evident now, however, is that the public, intersubjective character of being-there as both a being-with and a being-alongside (and even as "being-understanding," which is essentially what is taken up in Heidegger's notion of "existence"—see the discussion in section 3.4 below) is, in addition, intimately and inextricably tied to being-there as "being-spatial"—although it is clear that, for Heidegger, such "spatiality" turns out to be grounded, at least in terms of the analysis of *Being and Time*, in something other than the spatial as such.

The way in which equipmental spatiality is a necessary element in being-there's being-in-the-world, while also being necessarily public, may be viewed, and seems to be so viewed by Heidegger, as itself bringing with it a tendency for being-there to understand itself in terms of the form of generalized anonymity that comes with being one among many—being one of the "they" (*das Man*). The possibility of such an "alienated", or what Heidegger terms "inauthentic" (*uneigentlich*), form of understanding[62] is at its most obvious in our use of systems of mass communication, transport, and entertainment—"In utilizing public means of transport and in making use of information services such as the newspaper, every Other is like the next"[63]—but it is a possibility that resides in all our activity insofar as such activity takes place within the realm of the ready-to-hand, which is also essentially the realm of the anonymous "they." Moreover, recognition of this point also enables us to see the way in which the structure of equip-mental space, in its public, spatial character, is itself capable of being rendered in terms that bring it very close to a leveled-out "objective" space—the sort of space, understood as a framework of multiple locations, to which Heidegger directs our attention in his preliminary discussion of the nature of being-in and the notion of "insideness." Thus we can already see how it is that the realm of the ready-to-hand may lend itself to appro-priation in terms of the present-at-hand—the realm of equipment, con-sidered aside from Dasein's involvement in it, can readily be transformed into an anonymous, mappable structure, available to all and belonging to none, almost identical with a mode of objective space. The way in which equipmental spatiality can be viewed in this way, may itself provide a reason for supposing that spatiality cannot be the primary notion in under-standing the proper nature of being-there—it certainly provides Heidegger with a reason for taking equipmental spatiality as a secondary concept.

Being-there finds itself "in" space, not through a grasp of objective spa-tiality, according to Heidegger, but rather through its active involvement in a complex and ordered structure of things, places, regions—and other persons. Indeed, it is being-there's involvement in such a structure, through its involvement in particular activities and tasks, that allows par-ticular things, places, and regions, and thereby also, it would seem, par-ticular persons, to become salient—my involvement in the task of fixing a chair brings chair, wood, nails, glue, hammer, and the rest into view in a way that fits with that task; it also brings into view the others with, in relation to, and for whom that task is performed. This is what I described earlier in talking of dwelling as associated with a "bringing-close" or "nearing" of things. In being situated we are also oriented in such a way that our surroundings configure themselves so as to bring certain elements into salience while others remain in the background. Thus, in working with hammer and nails to make a timber joint, what is brought close through my oriented activity is the joining of timber and the movement of nail into wood—brought closer even than the feel of wooden hammer handle in hand, of air in lungs, and of feet on ground. The specific spatiality that is at issue here is characterized by Heidegger in terms of the notions of "*Ent-fernung*," translated by Macquarrie and Robinson as "de-severance," and "*Ausrichtung*," which they translate as "directionality"— Dreyfus suggests the terms "dis-tance" for "*Ent-fernung*" and "orientation" for "*Ausrichtung*," and I shall employ these latter terms in the subsequent discussion here.[64] "Dis-tance" refers to the way in which specific things take on a certain relation to us from out of the larger structure in which they are situated—finding a word I need to check in my reading, I glance over at the bookshelf to find the dictionary, but discover I cannot quite reach it from my chair, and so it is brought close, even before I take it from the shelf, in a specific way that also allows its distance from me to be apparent. "Orientation" refers to the way in which, in being involved in a certain task, I find myself already situated in certain ways with respect to the things and places around me—in working at my desk, I have the computer in front of me, bookshelf to one side, a pad of paper to the right, a desk-lamp to the left, and so on. The dis-tance and orientation that are characteristic of being-there thus capture the way in which being-there is situated with respect to the ordering of things in the world as that ordering is focused around a particular "there" and so with respect to a particular configuration of that "there," a particular "nearing" of things in a specific activity or task.

Notice that both dis-tance and orientation are themselves directly related to the equipmental structure associated with the ready-to-hand. Consequently, inasmuch as being-there always finds itself engaged with things, so it always finds itself enmeshed with some equipmental structure, and so, given the configuration of things, places, and regions within that structure, being-there always finds itself oriented in a particular way with certain things, places, and regions standing out as salient for it. In this respect, the way being-there finds itself "in" the world is always on the basis of the interplay between equipmental spatiality and the more specific mode of existential spatiality associated with dis-tance and orientation. Thus, in finding myself seated at the dinner table, I already find myself situated within a certain region—to which belong cutlery, plates, chair, table, kitchen, and so forth—such that certain things and places "automatically" configure themselves in a certain way through my particular positioning within that structure—through my being seated for dinner. Of course, sometimes that engagement will falter or break down (I find I don't have a knife, there is something wrong with the food, perhaps there is a fire alarm), but while that engagement may be interrupted, it can always be reconfigured (a knife is brought from the kitchen, a decision is made to go out to a restaurant, responding to the threat of fire becomes the primary task—suddenly what is salient is the fire escape, the fire extinguisher, and the smell of smoke). The crucial point for the moment is the way in which the spatiality at issue here is constituted through both the active engagement that proceeds from my own being-there as itself a constant "being-engaged" as articulated spatially in terms of dis-tance and orientation and the field of engagement that is already laid out in advance through the equipmental configuration of things, places, and regions.

The structure of existential spatiality is crucially determined by the structure of activity, task, and purpose. Not only does this determine the ordering of things and places within the equipmental field—so that a hammer is situated in relation to nails and so on—but it also determines how that field will itself be configured in relation to a particular instance of being-there's engagement within it. Standing in the dining room with a paint brush, a tin of paint, and the furniture covered in protective sheets, a different set of things and places come to salience than when I am sitting at the table with spoon in hand and a plate of soup before me. Moreover, the way in which these different modes of engagement arise as different— so that, for instance, I do not try to eat the paint or paint with the soup— is not determined by the way these items stand in terms of the objective spatial relations they may have to one another, but rather through the way they are related temporally in terms of the activities, tasks, and ends that allow them to appear as the sorts of things they are—as soup for eating and paint for painting and so forth. Of course, this means that their appearing in this way is determined, not primarily by their equipmental relations as such, for those relations do not appear independently of the involvement of being-there, but rather through the way in which being-there relates to things in dis-tance and orientation, that is, through being-there's own existential spatiality. Thus Heidegger claims that "*Space is not in the subject, nor is the world in space. Space is rather 'in' the world, insofar as* space has been disclosed by that Being-in-the-world which is constitutive for Dasein."[65] Space is thus disclosed through the way in which being-there has an essential capacity to "give space" or "make room" (*Raum geben, Einräumen*), which is also a matter of letting entities within-the-world "be encountered in the way which is constitutive for Being-in-the-world," in "freeing the ready-to-hand for its spatiality."[66]

It is to this point that Dreyfus directs his claim concerning the "fundamentally confused" character of Heidegger's analysis of spatiality: Dreyfus claims that Heidegger fails to distinguish *public* space in which entities show up for human beings, from the centered spatiality of each *individual* human being."[67] More specifically, Dreyfus claims:

Heidegger fails to distinguish the general opening up of space as the field of presence (dis-stance) that is the condition for things being near and far, from Dasein's pragmatic bringing things near by taking them up and using them. Such pragmatic bringing near as Heidegger uses the term can only be near to *me*, it is not a dimension of public space.[68]

Dreyfus argues that the establishing of things as ordered within a spatial field in which they show up as near or far actually depends, as we have already seen in the discussion above, on the ordering of the public structure of equipmentality. Moreover, as Dreyfus reads him, Heidegger seems to remain unclear on this point, treating dis-tance as apparently a matter both of the field of presence given in equipmentality and of being-there's own capacity to "bring things near" through its active engagement in the world. As Dreyfus points out, this seems to threaten an incipient subjectivism in Heidegger's account since dis-tance appears to be something established by the being-there's individual activity rather than being already given in the public space of equipmentality. Moreover, if dis-tance and the field of spatiality is dependent on each individual being-there, then they must be primarily subjective structures, and their relation to the public realm would seem problematic.[69]

Yet although there is an important point to Dreyfus's criticism here, there is also a respect in which it does not get matters quite right. Yoko Arisaka takes issue with Dreyfus on the grounds that Dreyfus's emphasis on the need for existential spatiality to be understood in its publicness and not as something merely tied to individual activity threatens to turn existential spatiality into something indistinguishable from the leveled-out spatiality associated with merely occurrent entities ("world-space").[70] In fact, the problem at issue here is not one that affects Dreyfus's reading as such, but rather a point about the nature of spatiality—spatiality has a necessarily public character, and one of the difficulties in Heidegger's position is how to take account of that publicness. Moreover, when we consider the character of equipmental space, the problem is particularly acute since although the public space of equipmentality is supposedly a space ordered by places and regions in a way that the space of the merely occurrent is not, it is also a space that, in its public character, seems difficult to distinguish from the "objective" space in which entities can be arrayed in relation to one another (a requirement of their being ordered as part of a single region) in such a way that also makes them accessible from a multiplicity of positions within that space (the latter being a requirement of their publicness). The issue of the relation between objective spatiality and equipmental space is one to which I shall return (see sec. 3.6 below), but even if we leave aside the specific question as to how equipmental space stands in relation to objective space, there is still an issue to be explored regarding Dreyfus's claim that the Heideggerian account of spatiality is prone to subjectivism in virtue of its emphasis on dis-tance and orientation as structures tied to individual being-there.

As we have already seen, the structure of equipmentality does not itself determine any *particular* "positioning," any particular "there," within it—rather, given a certain positioning, the space of equipment emerges in relation to that "there" in a way that is already determined by the equipmental structure itself. The situation is somewhat analogous to the employment of a map. The map sets out a particular configuration of a public space, and yet it does not specify any particular position in the space thus mapped from which that configuration appears. To use the map, that is, for the configuration of space it represents to become apparent, one must occupy a position in the mapped space which can then be related back to the map itself so that the space, already set out in the map, becomes evident in one's surroundings. In the case of equipmental space, it is through being-there's having a certain positioning within that space that the ordering of equipmentality becomes salient to it in its activity. The structure of equipmentality is thus prior to any particular individual being-there since it is indeed a public structure, but it always emerges into salience in the particular activity of individual being-there. Its being public is not a matter of its standing in some relation to some generalized form of being-there, as if equipment was always already taken up by a "public" mode of being that was constantly engaged—being-there, in its generality, is no more capable of concrete engagement than the *concept* of being-there is capable of using a hammer. Without being-there in general, of course, there is no equipmentality—a workbench, for instance, with all its various tools in "place," but removed from the context of the being-there (in the sense of the human community) with whom it belongs, no longer carries any equipmental ordering. Yet for an equipmental structure to stand in proper relation to the being-there with whom it belongs is just for there to be a community of individuals who are themselves engaged within that equipmental structure. The opening up of what Dreyfus calls "the field of presence" thus has to be understood as based in *both* the prior, generalized equipmental ordering, given in terms of things, places, and regions (equipmental spatiality) *and* in the particular realization of that ordering through being-there's individual engagement within that ordering in terms of distance and orientation (existential spatiality).

The way in which both equipmental and existential spatiality are required here is not, in itself, a source of subjectivism in Heidegger's account. Indeed, as a general point, the involvement of what might be termed a "subjective" element within some larger structure need not itself determine that structure as subjective or as subjectively grounded.[71] A structure that comprises both subjective and objective elements, for instance, may turn out to be one in which both elements are reciprocally determined within that structure, in which case the structure as a whole can neither be construed as objective nor as subjective, or it might be a structure in which the determining role is taken by the objective element, in which case the structure would be construed as "objective." The real question concerns the priority, if any, assigned to the elements within the structure and so, in this case, whether or not existential spatiality is given priority over the equipmental. The claim, then, that there is an incipient subjectivism in Heidegger's account just in virtue of the way Heidegger treats the public spatiality of the world, articulated in terms of equipmentality, as requiring both equipmental and existential spatiality cannot be right. Nonetheless, Dreyfus in correct in asserting that there is a problem concerning the way Heidegger understands the relation between equipmental, public space and the existential space belonging to individual being-there. Part of the problem involves exactly how equipmental and existential spatiality are supposed to relate, as well as the difficulty, noted above, of the relation to objective spatiality (and here we will indeed have cause to return to some of Dreyfus's concerns, particularly as these relate to the role of embodiment in sec. 3.6 below), but what is also at issue is the way in which Heidegger appears to assign priority to existential over equipmental spatiality, and so to the "subjective" element over the "intersubjective," by arguing that the former is dependent on the latter. It is this prioritization that is the real source of difficulty. Indeed, it seems that in Heidegger we can discern a sequence of prioritizations and dependence relations: the spatiality of "involvement" is prioritized, in the being of being-there, over the spatiality of "containment"; within the structure of the spatiality of involvement, analyzed into equipmental and existential spatiality, the existential is prioritized over the equipmental; and finally, as we shall see in more detail shortly, Heidegger argues for the prioritization of temporality even with respect to existential spatiality, and, within the structure of temporality, for the prioritization of what he calls "originary temporality" over other such modes.[72]

The overall priority of temporality is already indicated by Heidegger's comment at the very beginning of *Being and Time* that the aim of the work is to interpret time as the horizon for being, but Heidegger also attempts to provide a specific argument for the supposedly "derivative" character of spatiality, including existential spatiality, in relation to temporality. The need for such an argument arises out of Heidegger's explicit recognition that the emergence of a mode of spatiality, "existential spatiality", as indeed belonging to being-there as such, and so appearing as a basic attribute of being-there, threatens to limit the existential-temporal analysis that is Heidegger's aim, such that "this entity which we call 'Dasein,' must be considered as 'temporal' and 'spatial' co-ordinately."[73] The specific argument that Heidegger provides for the prioritization of temporality over spatiality in section 70 is brief and highly condensed. Yet, in essence, it follows the same general line of argument that runs throughout *Being and Time* and that is particularly evident in the way Heidegger analyses the "involvement" of being-there in its world through the idea of care and his explication of the meaning of care itself in temporality: only temporality can provide the necessary unity and directionality that allows things, persons, places, and spaces to appear as significant, as meaningful, as mattering to us. Understanding the supposedly derivative (that is the "founded") character of spatiality within the structure of *Being and Time* thus requires that we give some attention to care and its analysis in terms of temporality; more generally, however, it requires that we examine more closely the way in which temporality is given priority over the various elements within the structure of being-there, including spatiality, and the way Heidegger understands the notion of priority (and the associated concept of "derivation" or "foundation") as such.

3.4   The Temporality of the "There"

In the accounts of equipmental and existential spatiality, and of being-with-others, Heidegger provides an analysis of both the "where" and the "who" of being-there. Moreover, as we have seen in the discussion above, these two aspects are connected since the way in which being-there with others is tied up with the way it encounters things, places, and regions in the space of the world. Nevertheless, the spatiality of the world and the spatiality that is proper to being-there is not the spatiality merely of the objective, the measurable, or the extended, but is rather tied to the ordering that comes from task and activity. Yet understanding the "where" and the "who" of being-there does not mean, according to Heidegger, that we have thereby arrived at a fundamental understanding of the "how" of being-there's being-in. The structures that determine being-there as "*there*," such that the world, both as a world of spatially ordered things and places and a world of others, can emerge into view, still need to be exhibited. The way in which being-there is there in its world, in its *there*, is what Heidegger refers to as "care" (*Sorge*). In the analysis of care (which encompasses, not only the section specifically titled "Care as the Being of Dasein," division 1, chapter 6, secs. 39–44, but also the preceding discussion in chapter 5, secs. 28–43), Heidegger provides what he regards as the real articulation of the sense of "being-in" as involvement that was already presaged in the initial discussion of "being-in" in terms of "dwelling" and of dwelling as connoting familiarity and a sense of "looking after" or "taking care."

Given that the analysis of care is supposed to provide an account, in fundamental existential-ontological terms, of the structure of involvement, and thus of the "there" of being-there, so that account must be of special significance for the inquiry into the topological character of Heidegger's thinking. Indeed, when one looks to the discussion of care with a topologically oriented gaze, one soon notices (as is the case throughout so much of *Being and Time*) the way in which ideas and images of space and place emerge in important ways throughout that discussion. Indeed, the way in which the issues at stake here are introduced is specifically in terms of a set of topological notions associated with the idea of the "there." Thus Heidegger writes that:

The entity which is essentially constituted by Being-in-the-world *is* itself in every case its "there." According to a familiar signification of the word, the "there" points to a "here" and a "yonder." . . . "Here" and "yonder" are possible only in a "there"— that is to say, only if there is an entity which has made a disclosure of spatiality as the Being of the "there." This entity carries in its ownmost Being the character of not being closed off. By reason of this disclosedness, this entity [*Dasein*], together with the Being-there [*Da-sein*] of the world, is "there" for itself. . . . By its very nature Dasein brings its "there" along with it. If it lacks its "there," it is not factically the entity which is essentially Dasein; indeed, it is not this entity at all. *Dasein is its disclosedness*.[74]

This passage makes clear the focus of the Heideggerian problematic on the "there," but it also highlights the way in which spatiality remains at issue in the discussion of the "there"—the "there" is the disclosure of a form of spatiality. The way in which spatiality appears here (and reappears throughout the discussion of the various structural elements at issue) is indicative of the fact that if Heidegger is indeed to arrive at a purely temporal interpretation of the "there," and even after the analysis of the "there" in terms of the structure of care, he will still need to deal with the apparent residue of spatiality that seems to be inextricably a part of it. Indeed, it is his explicit acknowledgment of this point in section 70 that leads to his attempt to demonstrate the derivative character of spatiality.

What is at issue in the discussion of care is thus the unity of being-there in its "there." In exhibiting that unity, being-there is also itself exhibited (in division 1, chapter 6, sec. 44) as essentially "disclosedness" or "revealedness" (*Erschlossenheit*): "disclosedness is that basic character of Dasein according to which it *is* its 'there.' Disclosedness is constituted by state-of-mind [affectedness], understanding, and discourse, and pertains equiprimordially to the world, to Being-in, and to the Self."[75] We may say that being-there is that mode of situatedness that allows things, places, and persons to be uncovered as what they are, and, as such, being-there is also shown to stand in an essential relation to truth, understood, in what Heidegger claims is the most primordial sense, as just such "uncoveredness" or "unconcealedness" (*Entdecktheit, Unverborgenheit*).[76] Significantly, exhibiting the character of being-there as a mode of disclosedness does not depend on the specific details of Heidegger's analysis of the unity of being-there in terms of care. In this respect, the fact that the discussion of disclosedness appears at the conclusion of the discussion of care is indicative only of the way disclosedness is tied to the unity of being-there. Indeed, in the development of Heidegger's thinking after *Being and Time*, the concept of disclosedness comes to occupy a central role, although the way in which it is articulated calls upon a somewhat different framework and employs a rather different vocabulary than that set out in the analysis of the care structure in *Being and Time*.

The idea of the unity of being-there as fundamentally constituted in terms of *care* as such is not made explicit by Heidegger until after the completion (in division 1, chapter 5) of the analysis of the elements that make up the "there" and that are referred to, with one exception, in the passage just quoted. Nevertheless, care is not something in addition to those elements, but is rather that which is articulated through them. As the two primary elements in the structure of care, "understanding" (*Verstehen*) and "affectedness" (*Befindlichkeit*—translated by Macquarrie and Robinson as "state-of-mind" and by Stambaugh as "attunement") together constitute the basic structure of the "there."[77] Understanding refers to the way in which the being of being-there is always given in terms of being-there's "projecting" (*Entwurf*) of its potentialities for being,[78] and as such understanding must itself be seen as having a certain priority within the structure of being-there's being since it is at the heart of the idea of "existence"—for being-there to exist is just for it to understand itself in terms of its possibilities for being.[79] Understanding is always accompanied by a mode of affectedness. Affectedness, which is also linked to the notion of "mood" or "attunement" (*Stimmung*), refers to being-there's finding itself already situated in the world in some determinate way.[80] It is in terms of the notion of affectedness that the concept of *facticity* makes its appearance in the framework of *Being and Time*. Understanding and affectedness are linked in that every projecting of possibility always arises on the basis of a situation in which being-there already finds itself in some determinate way. The structure of the "there" is given articulation through what Heidegger calls "discourse" (*Rede*)—discourse is that by which the world is differentiated, and the elements so differentiated are interrelated (hammers distinguished from nails, nails seen in terms of the way they can be used to fix timber, timber seen as cuts of oak, beech, or whatever). Although the discursive articulation of the world is not something that pertains only to linguistic items—discourse is the articulation of the world as such[81]—it is in language that discourse gets expressed.[82] There is also a fourth element here, falling (*Verfallen*), although it sometimes seems to stand in a somewhat equivocal relation to the other three and is noticeably absent from the list that appears in Heidegger's characterization of disclosedness I quoted above.[83] "Falling" names being-there's inevitable proneness to understanding itself inauthentically—in terms, for instance, of the anonymous "they." This complex of elements taken together is what Heidegger calls "care" and which manifests itself in relation to things as "concern," "*Besorge*," and to others as "solicitude," "*Fürsorge*."[84] "Care" is thus the name Heidegger gives to the structure of being-in-the-world understood as unified through the idea of being-there as that very being whose being matters to it—about which it *cares*.

In this latter respect, the account of being-there in terms of care returns us directly to Heidegger's initial characterization of being-there as that entity for which, "in its very Being, that Being is an issue for it."[85] Already, in that initial introduction of being-there, Heidegger says of being-there that it "always understands itself in terms of its existence—in terms of a possibility of itself."[86] In the discussion of care, Heidegger explicates the way in which being-there's being is an issue for it in terms of the way in which being-there is always "ahead of itself":

Dasein is an entity for which, in its Being, that Being is an issue. The phrase "is an issue" has been made plain in the state-of-being of understanding—of understanding as self-projective Being towards its ownmost potentiality-for-Being. This potentiality is that for the sake of which any Dasein is as it is. In each case Dasein has already compared itself, in its Being, with a possibility of itself . . . ontologically, Being towards one's ownmost potentiality-for-Being means that in each case Dasein is already *ahead* of itself in its Being. Dasein is always "beyond itself," not as a way of behaving towards other entities which it is not, but as Being for the potentiality-for-Being which it is itself. This structure, which belongs to the essential "is an issue," we shall denote as Dasein's "*Being-ahead-of-itself.*"[87]

Being there thus understands itself in terms of the projecting (*Entwurf*) of its own potentialities for being, and such "projecting" is at the heart of the idea of "understanding" as part of being-there's existential constitution. But this projecting, this "being-ahead-of-itself," is also an "already-being-in-the-world" (being-there's factical situatedness in which the world presents itself through affectedness) and a "being-amidst" (being-there's situatedness within the equipmental articulation of the public world). The single unitary structure of care, and of the being of being-there, is thus summarized as "ahead-of-itself-Being-already-in-(the world) as Being-alongside (entities encountered within the world)"[88]—and it is noteworthy that, even in this summary characterization of care, we continue to find (in the "in" and the "alongside") connotations of space and place. Although the character of being-there as projecting understanding has a certain priority in the structure of care, understanding cannot be separated from the way being-there already finds itself in terms of its "affectedness," as well as from the way its existence is structured in terms of discourse, and from its own tendency to falling. Yet the unity of care that is at issue here is not fully exhibited simply in the analysis of understanding, affectedness, discourse, and falling, for the question is how these elements are nevertheless unified as such. Care is the "formal existential totality of Dasein's ontological structural whole,"[89] but in what does the unity of this totality consist?

The answer, of course, is that the unity of care is to be found in temporality,[90] and the entire complex structure of care, and so also of the "there" and of "disclosedness," can thus be viewed as the articulation of being-there's fundamentally temporal mode of being (Heidegger's argument for this is complex and takes up most of division 2, especially chapters 1–4, sections 46–71). Crucial to the relation between care and temporality is the idea of care as an articulation of the being of being-there as essentially constituted in terms of being-there's own projective understanding of itself—its "being-ahead-of-itself." Being-there understands itself primarily in terms of what it can be, but is *not yet*. Already, then, in the very character of being-there's projective understanding, there is an obviously temporal orientation—one that is significantly futural. Yet in being "ahead-of-itself" in this way, being-there comes up against the possibility of its own end, namely, its own death. Yet death is not simply a possibility like others, it is that which constitutes the limit of being-there as such and so the possibility that is the limit of all being-there's possibilities. Moreover, death is being-there's "ownmost" possibility in the sense that being-there's death belongs to it alone—no one else can die our death for us. Heidegger thus characterizes being-there as "being-toward-death" (*Sein zum Tode*). Death is not, however, some event that still has to happen to being-there and to which being-there stands in a relation—it belongs to the very being of being-there, it is the "ownmost, nonrelational possibility" of being-there that cannot be outstripped.[91] The way in which being-there understands itself as being-toward-death Heidegger calls "anticipation." In anticipation (which is also associated with the mode of affectedness proper to it, namely, anxiety), being-there is forced to face up to the fact of its own being as belonging to it and thus to recognize the way in which it is already given over to a certain set of possibilities (the way it is itself "thrown") that it must take up as its own (for which it is itself responsible or "guilty"). The entire structure is one that Heidegger refers to as "anticipatory resoluteness," and it is in such resoluteness that being-there is itself disclosed in the determinacy and possibility of its "there" as articulated in its own particular "situation."[92]

The structure of anticipatory resoluteness underpins the structure of care—the way in which being-there's being is at issue for it is through anticipatory resoluteness, through the way in which its possibilities are shown as its own through its being-toward-death—but the structure of anticipatory resoluteness is also fundamentally temporal. In anticipating its "ownmost, distinctive possibility," as being-toward-death, anticipatory resoluteness lets that possibility "come toward it" (*zukommen*) and as such is essentially *futural* (the German word for "future" is "*Zukunft*," which Heidegger hyphenates as "*Zu-kunft*" to indicate the connection with "*zu-kommen*.")[93] Yet in understanding itself as already given over to certain determinate possibilities—it is constituted by "affectedness" and so also as "thrown"—and in taking up those possibilities as its own, being-there understands itself in terms of "having-been" (*Gewesen*) and so in terms of the past.⁹⁴ Of course, since "having-been" depends on being-there's grasp of itself in its possibilities, and so in terms of itself as "coming toward," so Heidegger writes that "'having been' arises, in a certain way, from the future."⁹⁵ As disclosive, anticipatory resoluteness allows the disclosure of being-there's own "situation" in such a way that being-there can be concerned with what is around it environmentally and so can act upon what is present to it. In this way, anticipatory resoluteness also makes things present and, in so doing, constitutes the present (*Gegenwart*).⁹⁶ Falling is not omitted from this structure since falling finds its own basis in "making present."⁹⁷ Thus, writes Heidegger, "Temporality makes possible the unity of existence, facticity, and falling, and in this way constitutes primordially the totality of the structure of care."⁹⁸

It is notable that the temporality that is at issue here, what Heidegger calls "originary temporality" (*ursprüngliche Zeitlichkeit*), and which is unified in terms of the "temporalizing" of temporality in the three "ecstases" of the future, the "having been," and the present, is not itself a structure that is temporal in the usual sense. Although the three ecstases carry within them notions of "before" and "after" (this is important since it is out of the unity of the ecstases, that is, out of originary temporality, that Heidegger derives the "ordinary" temporality that understands temporality as the succession of past, present, and future), they are not themselves successive: "Temporalizing does not signify that ecstases come in a 'succession.' The future is *not later* than having been, and having been is *not earlier* than the present. Temporality temporalizes itself as a future which makes present in the process of having been."⁹⁹ To understand the ecstases as indeed successive would be to treat care as something occurring "in time" and being-there as something present-at-hand.¹⁰⁰ Originary temporality is thus a more fundamental sense of temporality than is given in the notion of temporal succession, which means that temporal succession must indeed be a derivative of originary temporality. Originary temporality is that in which the entire structure of care and the "there"—the entire structure of "situatedness"—has its proper unity and "ground."

In essence, originary temporality is, as the meaning of care, the meaning of disclosedness—that which makes disclosedeness possible as its origin and unity. But in this respect, the character of originary temporality is directly tied to its character as the meaning of the "there"—as the meaning, we might say, of situatedness. This is something also indicated by the way the concept of "situation" emerges in the discussion of anticipatory resoluteness, but it comes out too in Heidegger's emphasis on the way in which authentic temporality is essentially *finite*.[101] The originary future does not extend endlessly ahead of us, but is rather, as Heidegger says, "closed off"[102] inasmuch as it is always turned in toward "having been" and "making present" (in this it also reflects the character of being-toward-death as not a relating to some event in the future, but an essential feature of our being as such). The finitude of originary temporality is, in this respect, directly tied to the way in which originary temporality is the opening up, the "making possible," of the "there" of being-there—as such it is constitutive of the "there." The "there" is an essentially topological concept, as are the notions of "situation" and situatedness also, and so we may say that, in the account of originary temporality as the meaning of care, Heidegger presents an understanding, an "interpretation," of place *as* time. Yet acknowledging the finitude of originary temporality itself and its character as constitutive of the "there," we may also say that originary temporality itself constitutes a certain "there," a certain *topos*, a certain "place"—one might thus also say that, in the account of temporality as the meaning of care, Heidegger provides an understanding of time as "place." Significantly, while Heidegger never comes close to saying that in *Being and Time*, this is almost exactly the reading he himself gives some fifteen years later. In his lectures on Parmenides in the winter semester of 1942–1943, he tells us that:

In *Being and Time*, time is experienced and named as fore-word for the word "of" Being. . . . "Time" understood in the Greek manner, χρόνος [*chronos*], corresponds in essence to τόπος [*topos*], which we erroneously translate as "space." Τόπος is place [*Ort*], and specifically that place to which something appertains, for example, fire and flame and air up, water and earth below. Just as τόπος orders the appurtenance of a being to its dwelling place, so χρόνος regulates the appurtenance of the appearing and disappearing to their destined "then" and "where." Therefore time is called μακρός [*machros*], "broad," in view of its capacity, indeterminable by man and always given the stamp of the current time, to release beings into appearance or hold them back.[103]

In juxtaposing time with place here, what is raised is the question as to whether time can itself properly function as that which provides the meaning of place, or whether, perhaps, the understanding of time that is at issue in the articulation of the "there," with all its associations to care, disclosedness, and situation, does not itself already draw upon a notion of place or of *topos*. Indeed, I would suggest that it is precisely this problem that underlies Heidegger's difficulties with the role of spatiality in the structure of being-there and the constant intrusion of spatial ideas and images into the analysis of that structure. We must, then, go back to the discussion of spatiality, and to Heidegger's attempted derivation of existential spatiality from originary temporality.

3.5 The Problem of Derivation

If Heidegger's account of the unity of care, and so also of disclosedness and the "there," in temporality is to be successful, then it is necessary, as I noted above, that the entire structure at issue be shown to be unified in this way—there must be no "residual" element that falls outside of the unifying power of time. This means that what we may call "ordinary" temporality, the temporality associated with being-there's ordinary experience of time in terms of the passing of time and of temporal succession, must be shown to derive from originary temporality.[104] Indeed, Heidegger argues that it can be so derived, and he attempts to show how time as ordinarily understood, namely, as a series of "present moments," a series of "nows," can itself be seen as arising from the character of originary temporality as the unity of coming-toward, having been, and making present, and, more particularly, from the "leveling down" of that structure into a series of sequential elements that essentially gives priority to "making present" (and thereby treats the past and future as merely the present that is gone by and the present that is to come).[105] The analysis of the derivation of ordinary temporality from originary temporality is the focus of the very final chapter of *Being and Time* in its published form (division 2, chapter 6, secs. 78–82),[106] and clearly it occupies an important place in the overall analysis. Yet it is not only ordinary temporality that must be shown to be a derivative of originary temporality if the analysis attempted in *Being and Time*—namely the interpretation of being as time—is to be successful; since Heidegger acknowledges that spatiality is itself a feature of being-there's mode of being, so too must spatiality also be shown to be so derived.

Heidegger explicitly addresses the issue concerning spatiality in one brief and highly condensed section (sec. 70), titled "The Temporality of the Spatiality that is characteristic of Dasein" (*Die Zeitlichkeit der daseinsmäßigen Räumlichkeit*), close to the very end of the discussion, in division 2, chapter 4, in which he sets out the temporal interpretation of the various elements of the care structure and of being-in-the-world as a whole. There he notes that:

Though the expression "temporality" does not signify what one understands by "time" when one talks about "space and time," nevertheless spatiality seems to make up another basic attribute of Dasein corresponding to temporality. Thus with Dasein's spatiality, existential-temporal analysis seems to come to a limit, so that this entity which we call "Dasein," must be considered as "temporal" "and also" as spatial co-ordinately. Has our existential-temporal analysis of Dasein thus been brought to a halt by that phenomenon with which we have become acquainted as the spatiality that is characteristic of Dasein, and which we have pointed out as belonging to Being-in-the-world?[107]

In response to this possibility, Heidegger reiterates the point that what is at issue is not whether or not being-there exists "in" space or even "in" time. Being-there is not to be understood in the manner of some present-at-hand entity. Being-there is "in" the world through its involvement, and such involvement has to be understood in terms of what Heidegger terms "care."

Existential spatiality is thus to be derived from the structure of care, and thence from temporality. Such "derivation," which is, of course, a form of "grounding," has a particular character, however, and so Heidegger notes that although "Dasein's specific spatiality must be grounded in temporality [*in der Zeitlichkeit gründen*]," nevertheless "the demonstration that this spatiality is existentially possible only through temporality, cannot aim either at deducing [*deduzieren*] space from time or at dissolving it into pure time."[108] "Grounding," or the derivation that comes from "grounding," as it applies to spatiality cannot be the same as "deduction" or "dissolution into," and by this is meant, presumably, that the grounding at issue is not a matter of the "reduction" of space to time (much the same point arose in Heidegger's comments on the notion of "analytic" to which I referred in sec. 2.4 above).[109] Grounding spatiality in temporality is, according to Heidegger, a matter of showing that spatiality is existentially possible only through temporality (*"daß diese Räumlichkeit existenzial nur durch die Zeitlichkeit möglich ist"*).[110] The reference to "existential" here has a specific sense in the language of *Being and Time*. It refers to the way in which being-there's being is determined by understanding and so by the potentialities for being that belong to it. Indeed, although Heidegger does not put matters thus here, talk of "existential possibility" is elsewhere taken to be what is involved in the idea of "meaning"—in which case the derivation of spatiality from temporality would also mean exhibiting temporality as the "meaning" of time. This is a point to which we shall return.

The derivative character of spatiality is, as Heidegger puts it, "indicated briefly" as follows:

Dasein's making room for itself is constituted by directionality [orientation] and deseverance [dis-tance]. How is anything of this sort existentially possible on the basis of Dasein's temporality? . . . To Dasein's making room for itself belongs the self-directive discovery of something like a region. By this expression what we have in mind in the first instance is the "whither" for the possible belonging-somewhere of equipment which is ready to hand environmentally and which can be placed. Whenever one comes across equipment, handles it, or moves it around or out of the way, some region has already been discovered. Concernful being-in-the-world is directional—self-directive. Belonging-somewhere has an essential relationship to involvement. It always Determines itself factically in terms of the involvement-context of the equipment with which one concerns oneself. Relationships of involvement are intelligible only within the horizon of a world that has already been disclosed. Their horizonal character, moreover, is what first makes possible the specific horizon of the "whither" of belonging-somewhere regionally. The self-directive discovery of a region is grounded in an ecstatically retentive awaiting of the "hither" and "thither" that are possible. Making room for oneself is a directional awaiting of a region, and as such it is equiprimordially a bringing-close (de-severing) of the ready-to-hand and the present-at-hand. Out of the region that has been discovered beforehand, concern comes back deseverently to that which is closest. Both bringing-close and the estimating and measurement of distances within that which has been de-severed and is present-at-hand within-the-world, are grounded in a making-present belonging to the unity of that temporality in which directionality too becomes possible. . . . *Only on the basis of its ecstatic-horizonal temporality is it possible for Dasein to break into space.*[111]

The argument here proceeds, first, on the basis of an assertion of the dependence of equipmental spatiality (being-there's "making room" for itself in the discovery of a region, and the relation and placement of equipment within that region) on existential spatiality (orientation and dis-tance). But it is then argued that the directionality that belongs to existential spatial-ity itself depends on the unitary structure of temporality that is constitu-tive of a world. It is temporality that provides what might be termed the "teleological" horizon within which being-there is able to relate itself to specific entities as near and far and to orient itself to the regional order-ing of equipment. Moreover, the spatiality of "nearness" ("bringing close") as well as of measurable distance are both made possible through the way in which presence is temporally determined.

The idea that the "directionality" belonging to existential spatiality arises out of temporality follows almost directly from the temporal analysis of the care-structure: the being of being-there is determined by its possibili-ties for being as given in understanding, which are themselves disclosed to being-there through its being already disposed toward the world in affectedness, and on the basis of which being-there finds itself amidst things and persons in the world; this structure is itself unified as the struc-ture of the coming-toward (future), having been (past), and making present (present); temporality is thus that which determines being-there in its there, and which allows being-there to find itself in space inasmuch as temporality brings with it a fundamental directness and orientation that is based in its own orientation toward its possibilities for being (existence) as these are already given to it (its facticity) and as they are articulated in the world that surrounds it (as articulated in discourse and as prone to falling). In the simplest terms possible, one might say that Heidegger's argument for the derivative character of spatiality is based in the idea that orientation is first and foremost a matter of being oriented toward that which one can be—toward a possibility of one's own—which is always an orientation that calls upon temporality. Thus I orient myself spatially in the workshop through grasping the structure of the workshop in terms of its "toward-which" as that which is meaningful to me[112]—in terms of what each tool is for, and in terms of the end that the workshop as a whole serves (being-a-carpenter, being-a-metalworker, being-a-"do-it-yourselfer," or whatever)—and this orientation is, in Heidegger's terms, fundamentally temporal (though not in the sense associated with "succession") through being always directed toward what can be, but is not yet (and so is indeed "teleological"). If I lack the necessary orientation such that I cannot grasp the structure of the workshop, then neither can I pick out particular items within the workshop in ways appropriate to those items, nor can I orient myself properly to the workshop as a whole.

   The idea that is at issue here can be summarized as the claim that spatial orientation is impossible without temporal orientation. Joseph Fell puts this point succinctly, although in a way that also indicates the way place, and not merely space, is implicated, when he writes that "Dasein is a locale within which beings are revealed and identified. This locale is fundamentally temporal. . . . Dasein is place and place is orientation."[113] Although the claim that orientation is dependent on time will turn out to be insufficient to establish the derivative character of space in the way Heidegger claims, it is nevertheless an idea that is, in itself, eminently plausible. Indeed, elsewhere I have argued that the structure of space and place necessarily implicates time through consideration, in the simplest and most basic case, of the character of the dimensionality that belongs to space as itself opened up *as dimensional* through movement.[114] The necessary connection between space, place, and time is a theme to which I shall return, but here, of course, Heidegger is not merely asserting that space requires temporality, since this could be so, and yet time might require spatiality also, and if that were to be the case, then the project of *Being and Time* would be compromised just as surely as if spatiality were independent of time. Heidegger is committed to arguing that spatiality is dependent on originary temporality, and so a "derivative" of it, without it being the case that originary temporality is similarly dependent on spatiality. The same point applies, of course, to all of the claims regarding derivation that appear throughout *Being and Time*. In every case, the derivation or dependence at issue must be asymmetrical—it must always lead us back to the unity of originary temporality, and only there. Thus William Blattner makes a very similar point to mine regarding the necessary asymmetrical character of derivation in relation to Heidegger's argument concerning the derivation of ordinary from originary temporality, distinguishing between two senses of derivation or dependence, namely, "simple dependence" in which two elements or structures mutually depend upon one another, and a form of asymmetrical or hierarchical dependence in which one element or structure explains the other.[115] A question thus emerges here about the nature of derivation in *Being and Time*, in relation both to the derivative status accorded to spatiality, in particular, and to the argument of *Being and Time* as a whole. Before we go on to consider the adequacy of Heidegger's argument for the derivative character of existential spatiality, it will thus be useful to investigate the concept of derivation itself.

Although some form of derivation does indeed play an important role in *Being and Time*, Heidegger nowhere offers a clear and explicit statement of what it is to derive one thing from another, and he refers to the structure whereby one thing is "grounded" in another on the basis of an exhibition of its "conditions of possibility" in terms that remain somewhat obscure.[116] In this respect, the idea of "ground" that we saw is so central to Heidegger's thinking, and is indeed central to *Being and Time*, is nevertheless also an idea that Heidegger does not articulate in any especially clear fashion. There is, moreover, no single term that Heidegger employs here: at various points he talks about one thing being "primary" (*primäre*), of having "precedence" or "priority" (*Vorrang*—literally, "fore-rank") in relation to another; of one thing being "derived from" (*abgeleitet*), "descended-from" (abkünftig), "arising out of" (*entspringt aus*) another; of one thing being "founded" (*fundiert*), or "grounded" (*gegründet*) in another; of one thing being "only possible through" (*nur möglich durch*) another; or of one thing being "constituted" (*konstituiert*) by or in relation to something else (and this list is by no means exhaustive). In the discussion of the derivative character of spatiality, Heidegger talks specifically of temporality as the foundation (*Fundierung*) and ground (*Grund*) for spatiality, as well as of spatiality as "existentially possible" only though temporality.[117]

Nevertheless, in spite of the lack of any explicit attention on Heidegger's part to distinguishing between these terms, it does seem as if some distinctions can be made. This is most obviously so in respect of the notion of "primacy" or "priority." While that *from which* something is derived, or *in which* it is "founded," will itself be "prior" or "primary" in respect of that which is so "derived" or "founded," not all cases of primacy will involve derivation or foundation. Thus, the future is primary with respect to the other temporal ecstases within the structure of originary temporality,[118] and so too is understanding prior within the structure of care, it is not the case that any relation of derivation or foundation applies—having been and making present are not derivable or founded in the coming toward, and affectedness, discourse, and falling are not derived from or founded in understanding. Talk specifically of "derivation" (as associated with *"ableiten"*), or "descent-from" (*abkünftig*) is also less common in *Being and Time* than, for instance, talk of "grounding" or "foundation," and is used specifically in reference to the relation between modes of time as they are "derivatives of" originary temporality.[119] This might be a reason to suppose that the notion of "derivation" (inasmuch as this is more closely tied to terms such as *"ableiten"* and *"abkünftig"*) is itself a more restricted notion, as used in *Being and Time*, than that of "grounding" or "foundation," even though it may be viewed as a *form* of "grounding" or "foundation."[120] Although there is nothing explicit to confirm this from Heidegger himself, the latter view might seem to be supported by the need, already noted above, for derivation as it operates in *Being and Time* to be hierarchical in character since this seems to be indicative of a specific form of grounding or foundation. Indeed, in spite of Heidegger's lack of attention to the matter, we can discern a number of distinctions that are relevant to understanding the nature of derivation and foundation both in general and as they apply in *Being and Time* in particular.

If we think of "derivation" and "foundation" as entailing forms of dependence between certain entities or structures (and there will be many different types of dependence that fall within these general forms—causal, explanatory, and so on), then we can immediately distinguish, along the lines suggested above, between dependence that is mutual or "reciprocal" (Blattner's "simple" dependence) and dependence that is asymmetrical or hierarchical. The hermeneutic circle, which I used in chapter 1 to illustrate the idea of unity that is at issue in much of Heidegger's thinking, also exemplifies the first of these forms of dependence. In its simplest formulation, in terms of the relation between whole and parts as these figure within textual interpretation, the understanding of a text as a whole depends on understanding each part of the text, while the understanding of each part of the text depends on the understanding of the whole. In the hermeneutic circle, then, we find a relation of mutual dependence between the whole and the parts—in addition, since understanding each of the parts is necessary for understanding the whole, and since understanding each of the parts is dependent on that holistic understanding, so we also have a relation of mutual dependence between the parts (the understanding of each part of the text is, indirectly, dependent on understanding every other part).[121] Perhaps the clearest example of hierarchical dependence, by contrast, is that of simple causal dependence. If the icing-up of the road causes the car to crash, then the relation between the two events that are the icing-up and the crashing can be seen as hierarchically related to one another—the crashing of the car is dependent on the icing-up of the road, but the icing-up of the road is not dependent on the crashing of the car. This example also indicates the way in which explanation often (though not always) involves relations of hierarchical dependence. Thus I may explain my purchase of a new computer by my need to have a better machine on which to carry out my research, but my purchase of a new computer does not, as such, explain my need to carry out research (which is not to say that we cannot imagine a case in which it did, but only that in this hypothetical case it does not).

One might try to explicate the relations of mutual and hierarchical dependence using the notion of necessary conditionality: if X is hierarchically dependent on Y, then Y will be necessary for X, but X will not be necessary for Y; if X is mutually dependent on Y, then X will be necessary for Y, and Y will also be necessary for X. In the case of the mutual dependence of parts on whole in the hermeneutic circle, then, the understanding of the parts is necessary for understanding the whole, and the understanding of the whole is necessary for understanding the parts; in the case of the hierarchical dependence exemplified in the causal relation between particular events, the one event, the icing-up of the road, is a necessary condition for the other event, the crashing of the car (notice that the relation of necessary conditionality is applied here only to those particular events). This may look like a simple and obvious way to characterize the two forms of dependence, but, in fact, it does very little to clarify matters and may actually lead to confusion. Indeed, one can already see difficulties beginning to emerge when one tries to extend the analysis to the explanatory example used above.

My need to do research may explain my computer purchase, but it does not do so through being a necessary condition for it (at least not without circumscribing the description of that purchase in some particular way)—

given certain background conditions, my need to do research is the sufficient condition for my purchase of the computer. Perhaps, then, we need
only to bring a notion of sufficient conditionality into the analysis. Certainly, the nature of conditionality is such that, if X is necessary for Y, then
Y will also be sufficient for X, and, consequently, we can view the idea of
mutual dependence as already including a notion of sufficiency within it.
The situation is less simple, however, when it comes to hierarchical dependence. Although Heidegger seems to view the hierarchical dependence that
is involved in his account as very much like the hierarchical dependence
involved in teleological explanation of the sort illustrated by the example
of the computer purchase (indeed Blattner terms his version of hierarchical dependence "explanatory dependence"), its characterization in terms
of sufficient conditionality alone is problematic since Heidegger aims to
exhibit a certain uniqueness in the dependence of the structure of being-
there on temporality—temporality is unique in being that on which being-
there is grounded, and so, whether or not it is sufficient, it is certainly
necessary for being-there. We might be tempted, then, to characterize hierarchical dependence as applying only in those cases where one element is
both a necessary *and* sufficient condition for another (thereby ruling out
as hierarchical cases of explanatory dependence such as that used above).
In such a case, however, the elements that are supposedly related as hierarchically dependent, one on the other, will always be found in combination, and so any attempt to exhibit such dependence will itself crucially
depend on finding a way to distinguish between the elements that picks
out the right sort of conditionality such that it will indeed yield the hierarchical dependence that is in question. Talk of conditionality as such,
then, or of necessity and sufficiency, will be much less important than
getting clear on the exact respect in which conditionality is supposed to
hold, and, as we shall see, this is certainly true of the way Heidegger
approaches matters in *Being and Time*.

The distinction between mutual and hierarchical dependence is evident
in the existing Heideggerian literature—for instance, it is a distinction
whose essential form is noted, as we saw above, by William Blattner. Moreover, there is also a form of mutual dependence that Heidegger himself
makes explicit in *Being and Time* and that has already appeared in some of
the passages quoted from Heidegger in the discussion so far, namely, the
notion of "equiprimordiality" or "equioriginality" (*Gleichursprünglichkeit*—
I will use the term "equiprimordiality" since this is the translation established by Macquarrie and Robinson).[122] Although the idea occurs at many

points throughout *Being and Time* (the index to *Being and Time* compiled by Hildegard Feick lists thirty occurrences),[123] Heidegger gives only one brief discussion of the notion as such. He writes:

If we inquire about Being-in as our theme, we cannot indeed consent to nullify the primordial character of this phenomenon by deriving [*Ableitung*] it from others— that is to say, by an inappropriate analysis, in the sense of a dissolving or a breaking up. But the fact that something primordial is underivable [*Unableitbarkeit*] does not rule out the possibility that a multiplicity of characteristics may be constitutive for it. The phenomenon of the *equiprimordiality* [*Ursprünglichkeit*] of constitutive items has often been disregarded in ontology, because of a methodological tendency to derive everything and anything from some simply "primal ground."[124]

Here what is at issue is the fact that "being-in" may be analyzed in terms of certain elements that are constitutive for it without those elements being taken as somehow more primordial or originary than "being-in" as such and without any suggestion that those elements are themselves to be viewed as more or less primordial in relation to each other. Elsewhere Heidegger uses "equiprimordiality" to describe the relation between, for instance, being-there's self-understanding of its own being and its understanding of being other than its own,[125] between "freeing a totality of involvements" and "letting something be involved at a region,"[126] between being-in-the-world, being-with, and "Dasein-with,"[127] and also, significantly, between the three ecstases of temporality. What these various uses indicate is that, at least as Heidegger sees it, the equiprimordiality of certain elements does not imply anything about whether the structure that they comprise is dependent, as a whole, on something else ("freeing a totality of involvements" and "letting something be involved at a region" may be equiprimordial, but they both seem to be dependent, according to *Being and Time*, on temporality, while there is nothing more primordial than the unity of the three ecstases of temporality).[128] Initially, then, if we are to keep to Heidegger's presentation, the equiprimordiality of the elements that are constitutive of a structure must instead be understood in terms of the way those elements, taken only in respect to one another, are equally basic to that structure—are equally primordial or originary in their relatedness.

The holding of such mutual dependence seems to apply to each of the structures that is exhibited at each stage of Heidegger's analysis of being-there. It certainly applies to the structure of care and to the structure of originary temporality. The equiprimordiality of constitutive elements does not, however, rule out the possibility that there may nevertheless exist some form of priority between those elements, and this is clearly exemplified with respect to the ecstases of temporality.[129] The future, having been, and the present each seem to depend upon one another, and the entire structure of originary temporality is constituted in terms of their interrelation, and yet, as I noted above, the first of these elements, the future, is clearly prior in relation to the others. As Heidegger writes:

The future has a priority [eine Vorrang hat] in the ecstatical unity of primordial and authentic [ursprünglichen und eigentlichen] temporality ... temporality does not first arise through a cumulative sequence of the ecstases, but in each case temporalizes itself in their equiprimordiality [Gleichursprünglichkeit]. But within this equiprimordiality, the modes of temporalizing are different.... *The primary phenomenon [primäre Phänomen] of primordial and authentic temporality is the future.* The priority of the future will vary according to the ways in which the temporalizing of inauthentic temporality itself is modified, but it will still come to the fore [zum Vorschein kommen] even in the derivative [abkünftigen] kind of "time."[130]

This passage is noteworthy, not only because of what it shows about the relation of equiprimordiality, but in confirming the point, already made above, that priority need not imply derivation—the priority of the future does not mean that the other ecstases are somehow derived from it. Yet at the same time as he asserts the ordered, and yet underived, character of the elements of originary temporality, Heidegger also refers to another "time" that is derived from such originary temporality. The relation between "derivative" time, which it seems must refer to "ordinary" temporality, and originary temporality would seem to be a relation of dependence, yet it seems clear that it must be a relation of hierarchical, rather than mutual, dependence. Indeed, in general it would seem, given Heidegger's stated intention of advancing a temporal "interpretation" of being-there, that although the "internal" relation between the elements of the various structures that are exhibited in the course of Heidegger's analysis, from existential spatiality through to originary temporality, is one of *mutual dependence* (expressed by Heidegger in terms of "equiprimordiality"), the relation between those structures as such is one of *hierarchical dependence*. The picture one gets, then, is a series of structures made up of mutually dependent elements, each structure being, in turn, hierarchically dependent on another such structure, until the analysis finally arrives at originary temporality.

One of the key questions here must be whether such a combination of mutual and hierarchical dependence is actually consistent—whether Heidegger is right to suppose that a structure of mutually dependent, that is, equiprimordial, elements can stand in a relation of hierarchical dependence to another structure. Before moving on to this question, however, which will also involve closer examination of the way in which Heidegger himself understands the hierarchical dependence at issue here, it is worth clarifying the relation between the notions of mutual and hierarchical dependence, and the ideas of derivation and grounding (or "foundation"). Although there is a sense in which mutual dependence will allow for a sense of derivation, in that any element will be able to be "derived" from the other elements, it is probably more useful to distinguish between the sense of "derivation" that applies here and what is surely the stronger sense of derivation that seems to apply in the case of hierarchical dependence (a difference that is reflected in talk of elements as "derivative"—a way of speaking that does not seem appropriate to apply to elements that are mutually, rather than hierarchically dependent). This seems all the more important if we are to maintain a distinction between the sense of "dependence," but surely not "derivation," that it seems must obtain between equiprimordial elements (such as that which obtains between the ecstases of originary temporality) and the sense of "dependence" that would appear to obtain in the case of hierarchically dependent elements or structures. From here on, I will thus use "derivation" to refer only to the dependence at issue in hierarchical dependence; I will, however, take "grounding" and "foundation" as more general terms that can apply to instances of both mutual and hierarchical dependence.[131] This latter point is important since it allows for the possibility that, even should the idea of hierarchical dependence be abandoned, this need not entail the abandonment of the idea of ground—and certainly, as should already be evident from the way this notion has entered into the discussion so far, the latter idea is a central one in Heidegger's thinking, well beyond the analysis advanced in *Being and Time*.

In the discussion of the nature of mutual and hierarchical dependence as these relate to the notion of conditionality, we reached the conclusion that conditionality was not, as such, of much help in elucidating the nature of the dependence that is at issue in Heidegger's discussion of the various structures of being-there and their relation. What is much more important is the exact respect in which the conditionality or dependence in question is supposed to hold. While this may not be entirely clear in the case of mutual dependence (although here, in fact, the notion of mutual necessary conditionality is probably adequate), there can be no doubt that in those instances in *Being and Time* where some form of hierarchical dependence is at issue, the relevant respect in which one thing is said to be dependent on another is in terms of *meaning*: X is thus hierarchically dependent on Y inasmuch as Y is the meaning of X, or, in terms

that Heidegger also employs, inasmuch as *Y* provides the conditions under
which *X* is meaningful or "intelligible." Indeed, this is just what would
seem to be indicated by Heidegger's own characterization of the project of
Being and Time as a matter of uncovering "the meaning [*Sinn*] of Being."
Not only does Heidegger characterize the aim of *Being and Time* as a whole
in terms of this idea of meaning, but he also uses that idea at a number of
points in his analysis in relation to specific structures that emerge as in
question within that analysis, including the analysis of the care structure—
temporality, in fact, is to be exhibited as the "ontological meaning" of
care.[132]

Heidegger writes that, in asking after meaning, "*we are asking what makes
possible the totality of the articulated structural whole of care, in the unity of its
articulation as we have unfolded it.*"[133] This comment connects up with Heidegger's earlier explication of meaning (*Sinn*) in the discussion of understanding. There he writes that: "Meaning is that wherein the intelligibility
[*Verständlichkeit*] of something maintains itself. . . . *Meaning is the "upon-
which" of a projection in terms of which something becomes intelligible as something.*"[134] To ask after meaning, in this sense, is to ask after the "conditions
of possibility" in which intelligibility finds its ground or origin—and here
the Kantian "transcendental" elements in Heidegger's approach are clearly
evident (as is the associated notion of the Kantian idea of "analytic").
Moreover, the way in which "projection" enters the picture here should
also indicate the way in which this account of "meaning" is tied back to
Heidegger's account of "existence." Existence is the mode of being proper
to being-there, and it is a mode of being in which the entity, namely being-
there, understands its being in terms of its own possibilities for being.[135]
Indeed, understanding is itself characterized in terms of the projection of
such possibilities.[136] The idea that the inquiry into "meaning" is a matter
of the inquiry into the "upon-which" of a projection thus entails, within
the framework of *Being and Time*, that the question of meaning is fundamentally "existential," and that the inquiry into meaning is an inquiry
into the existential conditions of the possibility of intelligibility. Talk of
"existential conditions of possibility" immediately suggests a connection
with the way in which Heidegger talks of the derivation of spatiality as a
matter of exhibiting the "existential possibility" of spatiality in temporality (although it is perhaps noteworthy that Heidegger does not refer to
such derivation in terms of exhibiting the "meaning" of spatiality). If what
is at issue is the "meaning" of care, however, then understanding the
meaning of care, understanding the conditions of its intelligibility, will be
a matter of articulating that single unified concept (the "upon-which" of

its projection) that enables us to explain the unity of care in its own differentiated, yet unified structure. In Heidegger's account, it is temporality that functions as the meaning of care in this sense, and thus the task of exhibiting the unity in which the possibility of care resides means exhibiting the intrinsic unity of temporality as such.

It is significant that Heidegger talks about the inquiry into meaning, and the grounding that it aims at achieving, in terms of a question of unity—in the case of the meaning of care, *"what makes possible the totality of the articulated structural whole of care, in the unity of its articulation."* I have already noted, in the discussion in section 2.4 above, the way in which the ideas of unity and ground belong together, and unity is certainly a central and explicit theme throughout *Being and Time*. Heidegger says, in the opening sentence of chapter 6, on "Care as the Being of Dasein," that "Being-in-the-world is a structure which is primordially and constantly *whole*,"[137] and the focus on unity is referred to repeatedly, both in that chapter and elsewhere, seeming constantly to drive the argument of *Being and Time* forward. The preoccupation with meaning is thus also a preoccupation with the explanation or articulation of unity—itself a version of the question of ground—and the question of the meaning of being can thus itself be understood as a question concerning the unity of being. That unity is indeed an issue here can be seen to derive from a number of considerations, but it is a theme already evident in the idea of situatedness that was encountered at the very start of this investigation. The disclosedness or "presencing" of things in their situatedness, and our own involvement in such situatedness, is indeed a gathering together of what is otherwise differentiated and separated. For there to be disclosedness, then, for there to be situatedness or a "there," is just for there to be a certain sort of unifying occurrence in which differentiation is also evident. This focus on unity can be discerned, not only in the originary idea of "disclosive situatedness" as such, but also in Heidegger's oft-repeated story concerning his supposed awakening to philosophy through the gift of Brentano's book on the equivocity of being in Aristotle.[138] Whether or not we take this story to be biographically accurate, what it indicates is the way in which the problem of unity, and significantly, as is very clear in the Aristotelian context, the problem of the irreducible complexity of that unity, is indeed a central theme throughout Heidegger's thinking. *Being and Time* aims to articulate the unity of being, understood through the idea of meaning as the condition of "existential possibility," and so to exhibit the possibility of being in its "there."

It is quite clear that the inquiry into meaning or unity is taken by Heidegger as establishing a hierarchical dependence between the elements or structures at issue—the inquiry into meaning or unity is supposed to exhibit temporality as the foundational structure for being-there as whole, and so as being that on which the other structures of being-there are dependent as unitary and meaningful, but in a way that does not permit any mutuality in the dependence at issue. This must be so in the case of existential spatiality and originary temporality, but it must also be true in the case of the care structure as well—indeed, as we have seen, Heidegger talks of the relation between temporality and care precisely in terms of the one as the "meaning" of the other. Already it should be evident that there is a certain tension here, since it suggests that the dependence at issue in the case of existential spatiality and ordinary temporality will be identical in its general character to the dependence that must also obtain between temporality and care. Indeed, this is just what was indicated in the picture I suggested above of being-there as constituted, in terms of the analysis of *Being and Time*, of a set of what may be termed "vertical" and "horizontal" dependencies—as a series of structures, each separately constituted in terms of a set of mutually dependent elements, that are themselves hierarchically dependent. But if it is the same general form of dependence that applies in all these cases, then it is hard to see why we should not regard the care structure as "derivative" in much the same way as are existential spatiality and ordinary temporality. More seriously, perhaps, it is hard to see why we should not also regard the structure of being-there in its entirety as similarly derivative. Indeed, if exhibiting the meaning or unity of one thing in something else is a matter of exhibiting a hierarchical dependence between the things at issue, then is not the entire project of *Being and Time* committed to a demonstration of a hierarchical dependence (with the implication of derivation that goes with this) between being-there and originary temporality, and, ultimately, between being and time?

The problem here seems largely to be a reflection of what we noted above, namely, the lack of clarity in the way in which notions of dependence, derivation, and so forth appear in *Being and Time*. While on the one hand it seems that one might expect certain differences in the nature of the dependencies and derivations to which Heidegger seems committed, there is very little explicit indication of what those differences might be or how they might be configured. Thus, one might expect Heidegger to view the relation between originary temporality and care somewhat differently from the way he views the relation between originary temporality and ordinary temporality, and certainly care is never referred to as a "derivative" (*abgeleitete, abkünftige*) structure in the way that ordinary temporality is so characterized, but the matter is never even addressed, let alone clarified. When it comes to spatiality, the title of the section in which the argument for the "derivative" character of spatiality appears ("The Temporality of the Spatiality that is characteristic of Dasein") and its appearance immediately following Heidegger's temporal interpretation of the various elements of care might lead one to suppose that the account of the temporality of spatiality is exactly parallel to the accounts he advances of the temporality of understanding, affectedness, and so on. Yet not only does Heidegger's talk of temporality as the "meaning" of care not seem to be replicated by any direct reference to temporality as the "meaning" of existential spatiality (although he does talk, as I noted above, of temporality as providing the "existential possibility" of spatiality, and this does suggest a connection back to the way Heidegger understands "meaning"), but the language of "ground" and "foundation" is much more prominent in the discussion of spatiality as it relates to temporality than it is in the discussion of the relation between temporality and the care structure (although it is not absent from the latter either). Moreover, one would expect the account of spatiality as "derivative" to be more closely related to the account of the derivative status of ordinary temporality— especially since there also seems to be a tendency on Heidegger's part to associate spatiality with "being-amidst" and "making present," and thence also with "falling." Indeed, Heidegger claims that the way in which spatial ideas and images appear to dominate language and conceptuality, something he acknowledges as evident in his own analysis, is itself a product of the tendency toward falling.[139] While care, along with originary temporality, is itself essentially "falling" (since this is one of its essential modes), neither care nor temporality are taken to be associated with "falling" in the way that spatiality and ordinary temporality are so associated.

In his introduction to the chapter in which temporal analysis of the care structure is set out, Heidegger writes:

Our preparatory analysis has made accessible a multiplicity of phenomena; and no matter how much we may concentrate on the foundational structural totality of care, these must not be allowed to vanish from our phenomenological purview. Far from excluding such a multiplicity, the *primordial* totality of Dasein's constitution *as articulated* demands it. The primordiality [*Ursprünglichkeit*] of a state of being does not coincide with the simplicity and uniqueness of an ultimate structural element. The ontological source of Dasein's Being is not "inferior" to what springs from it, but towers above it in power from the outset; in the field of ontology, any "springing-from" [*Entspringen*] is degeneration. If we penetrate to the "source" ontologically, we do not come to things which are ontically obvious for the "common understanding," but the questionable character of everything opens up for us.[140]

The idea that the inquiry into the primordial totality of being-there requires that we retain a sense of the differentiated structure of being-there is a crucial point here that should not be overlooked—it is a point that I have already remarked upon in terms of the idea that what is at issue in the question of the unity of care, and so too in the question of the unity of being-there, is the unification of the structure of care and of being-there in all of its complexity. The dependence of the unity of care or of being-there on originary temporality cannot, then, be such as to do away with its complexity or multiplicity—the unity that interests Heidegger is never the simple unity of singularity or homogeneity, but always presupposes the multiple, the heterogeneous, the differentiated. This is precisely what is reflected in Heidegger's employment of the notion of mutual dependence in terms of the "equiprimordiality of constitutive elements." In the above passage, however, Heidegger seems to insist both that the attempt to understand the foundational unity of care in temporality should not be taken to impugn the structural multiplicity of care and also that what is originary or "primordial" in the structure of being-there "towers above" what "derives" or "springs forth" from it, and that *anything* that does so "derive" is "degeneration"—although he emphasizes mutual dependence on the one hand, he also seems to refer us to a notion of hierarchical dependence on the other. Moreover, that notion of hierarchical dependence seems to be expressed in very strong terms—what is hierarchically dependent is also, in ontological terms, a *degeneration* from that on which it depends.

The tension between mutual and hierarchical dependence is particularly evident when we consider the way in which equiprimordial elements are supposed, in virtue of their mutual dependence, to be "constitutive" of the structure to which they belong—the mutual dependence of those elements provides an articulation of the "internal" unity of that structure. This clearly applies in the case of originary temporality—its unity does not consist in the unity of a single, simple element, but is rather a matter of the "temporalizing" of the temporal ecstases as they belong together. Yet this does not apply in the case of originary temporality alone. At each level of Heidegger's analysis at which a structure of equiprimordial elements is exhibited, at the level of equipmental and existential spatiality, at the level of being-with-others, at the level of care, we find structures that are constituted by the mutual dependence that obtains between the elements that make them up—and since each element is necessary for every other, so each element is also sufficient for every other, thus entailing a very strong sense in which those structures are "made up of" those equiprimordial elements. Drawing on the notion of unity, we may say that the unity of a structure that is constituted of equiprimordial elements must consist in the articulation of the mutual dependence between those elements as such. This immediately creates a difficulty for any claim to the effect that the unity of a structure made up of elements that are mutually dependent in this way is itself hierarchically dependent on ("grounded in," "explained by") some other structure. The difficulty is as follows: any structure that is constituted by a set of equiprimordial elements must find its proper unity in the articulated dependence that obtains between those equiprimordial elements—to exhibit the structure, and so to exhibit its unity, is just to exhibit that articulation—but in that case, no reference to any other structure can be relevant to explaining the proper unity of the original structure at issue here; consequently, if a structure exhibits mutual dependence, then it is, by that very fact, a structure that cannot be hierarchically dependent on another structure, at least not in terms of its own unity or "constitution."

It may well be possible that a particular structure, while constituted in terms of a set of equiprimordial elements, is itself part of a larger structure and so stands in a relation to other structures within that larger, more encompassing whole. A question can then be put concerning the nature of the relation between the original structure and any one of the other structures within which it is located, or, indeed, about the relation between the original structure and the larger whole to which it belongs. It may be that in some cases that relation will obtain as one of hierarchical dependence, but this will only be so where the form or mode of dependence involved in that relation is distinct from the form or mode that obtains among the equiprimordial elements that make up that original structure. So one might suppose, for instance, that a functioning human body is made up of a set of core elements that are equiprimordial in terms of their interrelation with one another and in terms of their role in the continued functioning of that body. However, their mutual functional dependence has no bearing on what we might take to be the hierarchical causal dependence that obtains between that body and the set of physical causes that brought it into existence, or between that body and other bodies as they might constitute part of a social, cultural, or symbolic system. For a structure of mutually dependent elements to be hierarchically dependent on another structure requires that the mode of hierarchical dependence is of a different kind to the mutual dependence that also obtains. The difficulty in *Being and Time* is that it is the same kind of dependence that is at issue in terms of the mutual dependence between the elements in, for instance, the structure of care, and in the hierarchical dependence between care and originary temporality. Indeed, if that were not so, then not only would the unity of originary temporality not operate to account for the unity of understanding, affectedness, discourse, and falling in care, but neither, ironically, would it be possible for Heidegger to arrive at the account of originary temporality on the basis of the account of the care structure—if they are to be hierarchically dependent, then care and temporality must constitute distinct unities, but then it will not be possible to take the structure of care as providing any necessary clue to the structure of temporality.

The ideas of mutual and hierarchical dependence thus turn out, at least in terms of the way they apply to Heidegger's analysis in *Being and Time*, to be in tension with one another. We have just seen the way in which that tension arises with respect to the way in which the unity, or "meaning," of the various structures that emerge in Heidegger's analysis cannot be explicated in terms of both mutually and hierarchically dependent structures. Yet there can be no choice here—it is not as if, acknowledging the difficulty, Heidegger could choose to abandon the idea of mutual dependence at work in the notion of equiprimordiality and choose instead to treat the entire analysis as one that exhibits a series of hierarchical dependencies. To begin with, this would result in an unacceptable simplification of the self-evidently complex structure that is being-there. However, it would also lead to exactly the position that Heidegger rules out according to which "the *primordial* totality of Dasein's constitution" would "coincide with the simplicity and uniqueness of an ultimate structural element." Indeed, on such an account it is hard to see how being-there could be understood as anything other than simple originary temporality in the self-sameness of its pure "temporalization." Once we accept the complexity of the structure of being-there and accept the necessity of maintaining a sense of that multiplicity, then we are forced to understand the unity of that structure—"the primordial totality of its constitution"—as obtaining in and through the articulation of the elements that make up that unity in their equiprimordiality, that is, in their mutual dependence.

Although any unity may be taken to require that some elements within that unity will have a certain primacy within the unified structure as a whole, such priority cannot be based on a relation of hierarchical dependence. If originary temporality plays a role in the unity of being-there, it cannot be as something apart from the structure of being-there as a whole, which means that it cannot stand in a relation of hierarchical dependence

to that unity—nor indeed to the other structures that are also a fundamental part of it. What is at issue in talk of unity here is precisely the unity
of an entity or structure, not as it might be imposed from without, but of
the entity or structure as such—of the unity that belongs to the entity as
such. In this respect, we may say that the real unity of a thing is to be
found in the internal articulation of the elements that make it up and in
their interrelation, rather than in anything that "imposes" unity from
"outside" (this is just what is expressed in the idea of equiprimordiality).
Indeed, any attempt to provide a principle of unity for some thing
(whether "entity" or "structure") that stands outside of that thing would
fail to address the unity of the thing in itself, or in Heideggerian terms, in
its own being. It is just this point that appears in Aristotle, for instance,
when he says that things that are one "by nature" (paradigmatically *living*
things) are more properly unitary than those things that are one "by art"
(things that are "*made*"),[141] and it relates directly to the point I made about
the nature of unity at the end of chapter 2—that the sort of unity that is
properly at issue in Heidegger"s thinking, though it may sometimes be
obscured, is just the sort of unity exemplified by dynamic, complex structures whose unity is always self-unifying. What this means, however, when
read back into the account of the relation between, for instance, care and
originary temporality, is that exhibiting the relations that make for unity
cannot, strictly speaking, be a matter of showing how one thing is unified
by another, nor of how one thing provides the condition of intelligibility
for another, but rather of showing how a single, differentiated entity or
structure, and therefore a structure of equiprimordial or mutually dependent elements, is nonetheless itself unified, and this unity must be exhibited through showing the exact character of the relations between the
equiprimordial elements. Reflecting on the way in which what is at issue
here is indeed the character of being-there as "primordially and constantly
whole," it is hard to see how matters could be otherwise.

    Indeed, if we take seriously Heidegger's talk of "meaning" and "inter-
pretation" as it appears in relation to the task of exhibiting the conditions
of possibility, and so the unity, that is at issue here, then an obvious conclusion to draw is that the nature of that unity, and so of the dependence
between the elements in which that unity is based, must be one of mutual
dependence of exactly the sort exemplified in the example I used above of
hermeneutic circularity. In the case of textual interpretation, one exhibits
the conditions of meaningfulness of the text through an articulation of
what might be called the "internal unity" of the text—by showing how
the text works together as a whole. Of course, the way this is done may be

characterized in terms of finding some principle of unity that unifies the text, as one might interpret Shakespeare's *Othello* as a play about the destructive effects of jealousy, but any such "principle" must properly belong to the text as such (and so must be related to the elements of that text—indeed it will only appear in the text as articulated through those concrete elements) or else risk being simply an "arbitrary" imposition. Moreover, while any principle that unifies in this way can be said to have a certain priority as that which enables the text to be understood "in its intelligibility," such priority will consist in the way in which that principle stands centrally within the structure of the text, and so in a relation to the text as a whole—it will not imply that the entire text can be "derived" from that principle, nor need it imply that the principle will be the only explanatory element at work in the text (indeed, any interesting text will almost always have a multiplicity of elements or principles that are constitutive for it). If the concept of jealousy is central to *Othello*, for instance, then we would expect it to be able to be worked out in relation to the key scenes, characters, and so on as they occur throughout the play, and not only with respect to a few scenes or some part of the work. In the case of the project of *Being and Time*, we can say that what Heidegger attempts in that work is indeed an "interpretation" of being, or particularly, given the truncated character of the work, of the being of the "there" that moves successively to uncover the structure of the "there" in a more originary and basic fashion. However, what is thereby uncovered is not anything other than the "there" as such, and the progressive uncovering of elements within the "there" does not entail the discovery of separate elements as such, but rather involves uncovering the internal articulation of the "there" in its unity, while the priority accorded to care and to temporality rests in the way in which those elements can be shown to stand in a central relation to the other elements of the structure.

Such an "interpretive" or "hermeneutic" account of what is involved in exhibiting the unity, meaning, or grounds of possibility of a structure is one that I have elsewhere developed as the basis for understanding the nature of so-called transcendental argument.[142] Indeed, it seems that most of the problems that are supposed to accrue to transcendental modes of proceeding derive from treating transcendental argument as based in the demonstration of a form of hierarchical rather than mutual dependence. In this respect, it is interesting to note the close similarity between a common criticism of transcendental modes of proceeding and a problem that also seems to affect Heidegger's position. Stephan Körner famously argues that transcendental arguments cannot succeed since they need to demonstrate, not only that a certain structure is necessary for the possibility of some other entity or structure (and so to demonstrate a form of hierarchical dependence), but also that the structure is uniquely required in this way.[143] In similar fashion, Heidegger's argument for the hierarchical dependence of the structures of being-there on originary temporality will be of no avail if that dependence is not unique to originary temporality—if, for instance, some other structure, say a mode of spatiality, is also necessary along with originary temporality. It seems that there is no way that Heidegger can rule this out, and so no way that he can demonstrate what we may call the unique hierarchical dependence of being-there on originary temporality. The problem does not arise, however, if transcendental "argument" is understood in the interpretive fashion I suggest here—in terms, that is, of mutual, rather than hierarchical dependence—since then the task is not one of demonstrating some unique form of dependence, but rather of exhibiting the interrelatedness, and so the unity, of a single, complex, and differentiated structure (moreover, given the nature of interpretative indeterminacy, there can be no unique way of exhibiting such interrelatedness).

Although Heidegger appears to have some sense of the way in which transcendental modes of proceeding do indeed involve a notion of mutual dependence, what we have seen in the discussion here is that he nevertheless retains a notion of hierarchical dependence—at least in *Being and Time*. One of the reasons for this, in Heidegger's case, is the need to prevent what appears to be the problematic intrusion of spatiality—which constantly pulls in the direction of objective spatiality, "containment," the present, and the present-at-hand—into the structure of being-there in a way that threatens to disrupt its unity, not only through turning it into some spatio-temporal "composite," but also through dispersing it into the leveled-out space of the present. The reliance on a notion of hierarchical dependence also seems tied up with what Stephan Käufer calls the desire for "systematicity,"[144] namely, the desire to achieve an account that will be as encompassing and powerful as possible through the complete unification of the domain in question, in this case, being-there, through a demonstration of the dependence of the entirety of that domain on a certain fundamental element within it. The desire for systematicity and the need for the exclusion of spatiality are clearly not unrelated here. Heidegger's move away from talk of the transcendental in his later thinking can, in this respect, be construed as arising out of an assumption that the transcendental is indeed tied to this sort of systematic enterprise and so also to the idea of hierarchical dependence (as we shall see in chapter 4 below, however, it is also tied up with the way Heidegger understands the transcendental in terms of a preoccupation with "transcendence"—although this too is not unconnected with the notion of hierarchical derivation). Of course, what I have also suggested, if only implicitly, is that the transcendental can be understood in a way that does not require such hierarchical dependence. Similarly, while Heidegger's use of the notion of meaning here would seem to be tied up with the idea of hierarchical dependence (exemplified in the way he characterizes the issue of meaning through the idea of exhibiting the conditions of meaningfulness), my own account of interpretive articulation in terms of the articulation of relations of mutual dependence suggests a way of thinking in terms of meaning that does not give rise to the problems that appear in *Being and Time*. Thus the shift away from meaning that one finds in Heidegger's later work (and associated with this, the shift away from the hermeneutical, including the shift away from talk even of the hermeneutic circle)[145] can be seen as largely a result of Heidegger's having associated the methodology of the hermeneutical, along with that of phenomenology and the transcendental, with the idea of hierarchical dependence. My account here can be taken as showing that there is a way of understanding all these notions that need not require such a problematic association.

If Heidegger is to establish the interpretation of being-there in terms of temporality at which he aims, then it seems that what he needs to do is to establish the hierarchical dependence of the entire differentiated structure of being-there on temporality. Heidegger is driven to this by the need to exhibit the unity of being-there in temporality, and yet trying to do this turns out not to be compatible with the multiplicity that also attaches to being-there and the mutual dependence that obtains among the multiple elements that make it up. The problem of deriving the existential spatiality proper to being-there thus turns out to be a particular instance of a more general problem of derivation in the analysis of *Being and Time* as a whole. However, at the same time, it is clear that the way spatiality stands as a problem for that analysis is also one of the reasons for Heidegger's employment of a notion of hierarchical, as well as mutual, dependence within the framework of his analysis. These considerations, while absolutely central, deal with the problem of "derivation" in a relatively general fashion, however, and it is important to draw the discussion of *Being and Time* directly back to the consideration of spatiality and so also of place and topology, as such. In this respect, it will be important to look once again at the specific argument Heidegger advances for the derivative character of spatiality (and in passing to also briefly consider the argument for the derivative character of ordinary temporality) and thereby explore in more detail the way in which spatiality emerges within the structure of being-there, particularly inasmuch as it disrupts the supposed priority of temporality.

3.6   The Necessity of Spatiality

Heidegger's analysis of the idea of "being-in" already gives rise to a distinction between two modes of spatiality corresponding to the ideas of "containment" and "involvement." Containment seems to be tied to a mode of spatiality that is extended, measurable, and tied to the notion of "objectivity"—a mode of "objective" spatiality. Involvement is tied to being-there as it "dwells" and so to a mode of spatiality that is orientated, directed, and that is directly related to being-there's own active engagement in the world. It is the latter of these two modes of spatiality—the spatiality of "involvement"—that Heidegger tells us is proper to being-there. Moreover, "involvement," since it is tied to the notions of "dwelling" and "world," clearly points toward a more fundamental analysis. The derivative or dependent character of spatiality is thus presaged close to the very beginning of Heidegger's analysis in *Being and Time* in the very distinction between containment and involvement. As that analysis develops, it becomes clear that there are, in fact, a number of dependence relations that obtain with respect to spatiality as it stands within the structure of being-there: one is the dependence of existential spatiality on care and so on temporality; another is the dependence of equipmental spatiality on existential spatiality; another, though it has not so far been properly addressed, is the dependence of objective spatiality on the spatiality of world. There is no "originary" spatiality that underpins this, however, since it is temporality that is the originary foundational structure here. In discussing the way Heidegger attempts to derive existential spatiality from temporality, I noted that what drives this argument is the idea that spatiality is a matter of *orientation*, but that orientation is essentially *temporal*. Indeed, the priority of temporality as orientation seems to be essentially what drives the entire structure of dependence relations. But the claim that temporality is what determines orientation is only partly correct—spatiality itself has a part to play here also, and in a way that cannot be derived from temporality.

In the discussion of equipmental and existential spatiality in section 3.3, I noted the way in which the "opening up" of spatiality involves both equipmental spatiality, as articulated through the prior, public ordering given in terms of things, places, and regions, and the existential spatiality that is involved in being-there's individual engagement within that ordering in terms of dis-tance and orientation. I also noted that part of the problem in Heidegger's own approach here is that he asserts a priority of the latter over the former, seeming to make equipmental spatiality dependent on existential spatiality. The dependence at issue can be understood as a matter of equipmental space only becoming properly equipmental inasmuch as it is related to being-there in its particular, individual activity; in addition, of course, the very ordering of equipmentality is dependent on the teleological ordering given in task and activity that is, in turn, related to being-there's own existential possibilities. Thus the ordering of a carpentry shop, for instance, is partly determined by the way in which the shop is geared to a way of being for being-there that is tied to a range of activities centered around woodworking, although such an equipmental ordering is realized only in and through being-there's own actual engagement within that region of activity. Yet if orientation is what is at issue here, and the claim is that such orientation arises through being-there's own being-directed-toward some possibility of its being (its being a carpenter, for instance), then neither can the ordering of equipmental spatiality nor the orientation of existential spatiality be explained independently of spatiality as such.

Part of what misleads us here, and part of what seems to mislead Heidegger, is actually tied to a feature that is central to Heidegger's own account of being-there, namely, the priority of the "toward which" (which is itself tied, of course, to the priority of understanding within the structure of care and of the future within the structure of temporality). In being engaged in some activity, we are typically always ahead of ourselves—it is the "toward which," the end to which we are directed, that always comes first. In Heidegger's analysis this feature of the phenomenology of activity is elevated to become the determinative consideration in the analysis of being-there's spatiality. Yet what this hides, or at least leads us to overlook, is the way in which our activity, and our orientation to things and places within that activity, is not merely determined by the end *to which* we are directed, but also by the structure of the spatiality *in which* that activity is situated. Thus, my being oriented toward the tools around me in the carpentry shop—the hammer, chisel, saw, drill, and so forth—is not only a matter of understanding what they are for, but also of understanding the spaces that they occupy, their own spatial configuration, and their relation to my body and its capacities. Being oriented to the hammer is a matter of knowing that it relates to me through the way the shaft fits to my hand

and to the action of my arm, in terms of how the swing of the hammer and the impact of the head exert a certain directed force. Knowing how to pick up a hammer and use it certainly depends on knowing what the hammer is to be used for and on having a use to which it is to be put, but knowing how to pick up a hammer also depends on knowing the space occupied by both hammer and one's own body—one picks up the hammer thus and so, one swings it in this way, one lets the hammer do the work . . . and so on. The orientation at issue here clearly is not independent of temporality, but neither is it explicable purely in terms of temporality. Moreover, without the sort of basic spatial orientation at issue here, no grasp of the temporal orientation involved in the structure of the "toward which" in task and activity can be possible. Fully to grasp the hammer as able to be used for hammering, for the joining of timber, for the making of a chair, or the building of a house, and so for a certain possibility of being-there, is also to grasp the way in which that hammer relates spatially to the one who wields the hammer and to the things around it—it is to understand both its spatial *and* its temporal "fit." Neither one of these can be explained in terms of the other, and yet each is indeed mutually dependent on the other.

The question of orientation that emerges here gives a special prominence to the issue of embodiment and is indicative of the way in which *spatial* orientation is always a matter of *bodily* orientation. Significantly, the place of the body in the analysis of *Being and Time* has long been recognized as a point of difficulty for Heidegger's analysis. Yet although Heidegger has sometimes been accused of neglecting or ignoring the body, it is quite clear that he recognizes its importance—he writes, for instance, that "[being-there's] bodily nature hides a whole problematic of its own, though we shall not treat it here,"[146] while in the lectures on logic given in 1928–1929 (in which Heidegger's thinking still remains largely within the frame of *Being and Time*), he seems to view being-there's bodily nature as essential to its thrownness: "Dasein is thrown, factical, thoroughly amidst nature through its bodiliness."[147]

The reason for the absence of an account of embodiment in *Being and Time* should be transparently clear once one understands the problematic of situatedness with which that work grapples. The problem of the body is directly tied to the problem of being-there's spatiality. Heidegger writes that "Dasein does not fill up a bit of space as a Real Thing or item of equipment would, so that the boundaries dividing it from the surrounding space would themselves just define that space spatially. Dasein takes space in. . . . It is by no means just present-at-hand at a position in space which its body fills up";[148] and again, "Neither may Dasein's spatiality be interpreted as an imperfection which adheres to existence by reason of the fatal 'linkage of the spirit to a body.' On the contrary, because Dasein is 'spiritual' [*geistig*], and only because of this, it can be spatial in a way that remains essentially impossible for any extended corporeal Thing."[149] The structure of hierarchical dependence that is central to the analysis of *Being and Time* and which points inexorably toward temporality seems to allow of only two possibilities in the analysis of being-there's embodiment: either being-there's having a body is a matter of its extended spatiality, which would mean that the being of being-there as embodied was no different from the being of present-at-hand objects, or else it must be understood as essentially determined by its being-in-the-world and so by its being-as-care and as temporal. Although Heidegger appears to recognize that there must be more to the analysis of the body than this contrast would suggest, there is surely little doubt that only the second of these options can be acceptable within the framework of *Being and Time*. Indeed, as the second of the two passages quoted above indicates, the being of being-there as embodied *and* as spatial is determined by its being as "spiritual" (the German "*geistig*" carries connotations of both spirit and mind), which in this case must surely mean, as "temporal."

If there is any sense in which the bodily being of being-there is spatial, then, it is in a sense that is secondary to temporality in much the same way as the various modes of spatiality are also secondary. For this reason, Heidegger is unable to give any central place in his analysis to embodiment—indeed, since he has already committed himself to the dependent character of extended spatiality from almost the beginning of his analysis, the body as such simply falls outside the frame of Heidegger's discussion.[150] Steven Crowell claims that Heidegger gives little attention to the body since his interest is in the structure of being-there in its unity as it is prior to the traditional distinction between body and mind;[151] Søren Overgaard argues that the body is problematic for Heidegger because of the way it threatens the unity of being-there.[152] Both these claims are correct, but they fail to make explicit the crucial point here, namely, that the body is secondary in the structure of being-there, while also presenting a problem for the unity of being-there, precisely because of the way it threatens to make being-there into something spatial. The real danger to unity, within the framework of *Being and Time*, is thus spatiality. Not only does the intrusion of spatiality threaten a bifurcation between the "bodily" and the "mental/spiritual," but spatiality also threatens the loss of any sense of the "there" in the stretched-out dimensionality of pure extendedness. Yet at the same time, this indicates the extent to which Heidegger himself remains in the grip of the understanding of spatiality and embodiment associated with traditional metaphysics, according to which embodiment is itself tied to the spatiality of objective extension and according to which "the body" is indeed something that can, in some sense, be set against the "mentality" or "spirituality" of being-there. For *Being and Time* properly to rethink the metaphysical understanding of being and of the relation of being to situatedness, it is necessary to rethink the structure of spatiality as such, and, although Heidegger may be said to reconceptualize spatiality in terms of existentiality and temporality, this constitutes less a rethinking of spatiality as such than its abandonment to the realm of the derivative and the secondary.

The problem that Heidegger's analysis faces, however, is that, as is already evident, there seem to be important features of being-there's being-in-the-world that cannot be explained independently of spatiality as such. Indeed, it turns out that orientation in space, and so to the things and places in one's environment, or within a spatial region, itself depends on the way spatiality is articulated in and through one's own body. This is a point made quite clearly by Kant, and, indeed, in this respect Kant proves himself often to be more attentive to issues of embodiment and spatiality than the early Heidegger. Kant argues in a number of places, in both his pre-Critical and his Critical writings, that orientation requires a grasp of differences that are represented in space and in one's own body. Thus Kant writes that:

To *orientate* oneself, in the proper sense of the word, means to use a given direction—and we divide the horizon into four of these—in order to find the others, and in particular that of *sunrise*. If I see the sun in the sky and know that it is now midday, I know how to find south, west, north, and east. For this purpose, however, I must necessarily be able to feel a difference within my own subject, namely that between my right and left hands. I call this a *feeling* because these two sides display no perceptible difference as far as external intuition is concerned.[153]

Heidegger, of course, is well aware of Kant's emphasis on orientation as tied to embodiment.[154] Yet he takes this to be a remnant of Kant's subjectivism, arguing that such orientation presupposes being-there's prior being-in-a-world, and so being already involved in an equipmental context (although it is in his consideration of just this issue that Heidegger is led to remark on the way in which being-there's "bodily nature hides a whole problematic of its own").[155] It thus appears that what Heidegger calls being-there's own bodily "spatialization" is not a matter of being-there having a body, but of being-there's being-in-the-world: "The directionality which belongs to dis-tance is founded upon Being-in-the-world. Left and right are not something 'subjective' for which the subject has a 'feeling'; they are directions of one's directedness into a world that is ready-to-hand already."[156] This is a point on which Dreyfus comments, noting that:

Heidegger . . . seems to hold that orientation is a result of the fact that not all equipment is accessible at the same time. I can turn to one thing or another but not both at once. These incompatible fields of action group simultaneously accessible things together in opposed regions called right/left, and also front/back. But still without the body there could be no account of why there are these regions. We would not be able to understand, for example, why the accessibility of right and left is not symmetrical, or why we must always "face" things in order to cope with them. On Heidegger's account these would just remain unexplained asymmetries in the practical field. This is not inconsistent, but it is unsatisfying.[157]

Dreyfus's criticism is strengthened, however, once one understands that the point of Kant's comment about the "feeling of a difference in my own *subject*" has not to do with any mere subjectivism, but rather with the way in which the grasp of space is fundamentally tied to the body.

Orientation depends on a grasp of simultaneously presented regions of space and of an ordering among those regions. Contrary to Heidegger's assumption, however, such ordering cannot be given in the regions themselves, and this is evident in the fact that the orientation of these regions in terms of "left/right," "front/back" will vary depending on individual location—the pure ordering as such must thus be an ordering derived from the located individual, and more particularly, from the way the individual body is itself positioned "in" space, and so with respect to its surroundings. Such ordering is, in the first-person terms Kant employs, an ordering "in my own subject." Consequently, my grasp of the different regions of space around me depends on my grasp of the directions given in and through the different parts of my own body—left side, right side, upper, lower. The ordering of the space the body is "in" is thus also an ordering of the space "of" the body, and the former is grasped through and by means of the latter. Thus Kant talks elsewhere of the way in which "no matter how well I know the order of the divisions of the horizon, I can only determine the regions in accordance with them if I am aware of whether the order progresses toward the right or the left hand."[158]

It is not merely that without reference to the body we could not *explain* the "asymmetries in the practical field" that go with the ordering of equipmental space in terms of "left/right," "front/back," but that without the body there can be no such ordering—and this is so for the simple reason that the ordering at issue here is precisely an ordering of space *in relation to* the body. Inasmuch as this ordering of space is itself a prerequisite of orientation as such, then embodiment is also a prerequisite for orientation—it is also, one might say, a prerequisite for being-in-the-world, although the dependence here is certain to be mutual (in this respect, it is worth noting the way in which, once again, Heidegger's commitment to hierarchical dependence plays a large part in the difficulties that arise here). The role played by the body is not something that can in any way be "derived from" the structure of equipmentality—nor from the structure of care or of originary temporality. And inasmuch as spatiality and embodiment are here seen to be tied together, so too does the underivability of spatiality also become evident. Indeed, the role of the body here is itself indicative, not of "corporeality" as some feature of our existence that could be set over against our "spirituality," but rather of "corporeality" as itself indicative of our fundamental spatiality—to be embodied is to exist in space. Moreover, such fundamental spatiality, although it may conflict with the absolute centrality of the temporal, need not imply any lack of unity in the being of being-there. Although fundamental, spatiality is essentially bound to temporality—something reflected in Heidegger's later talk of "time-space"[159]—and the unity of being-there is given, not through its determination by temporality alone, but through the complex and integral interplay between a number of key elements.

Yet if spatiality is indeed a fundamental element in the constitution of being-there, there is still a question as to what mode (or modes) of spatiality is at issue: is it the space of objectivity or something more like a notion of "existential" spatiality? Talk of the latter may be thought problematic since the notion of the existential seems to contain an ineliminable reference to the mode of being of being-there as founded in understanding, rather than in spatiality as such. Moreover, one might also suggest that bodily spatiality should itself be understood as a matter of location in an extended, and hence, objective space, and that such a subjective, or, perhaps better, embodied space must itself be explicated in terms of the objective space that might be claimed to underlie it. The possibility of such an inference is part of what leads to Heidegger's emphasis on existential spatiality as given through being-in-the-world, and so through the existential structure of being-there, rather than in any way determined by the body. Such an inference itself depends, however, on the assumption that spatiality is indeed to be understood as fundamentally objective spatiality, and there seems no independent consideration that would require such an assumption. Indeed, for the very reasons that make the idea of spatiality, understood in terms of an extended, measurable mode of dimensionality, inadequate to an understanding of place, so too must objective spatiality be inadequate to an understanding of embodiment or the spatiality with which it is bound up. Yet such an inference also depends on ignoring the way in which the bodily space that is at issue here is not a space that belongs to being-there merely in virtue of its being some "bit of space which its body fills up,"[160] but is instead a space that belongs to being-there in its bodily activity. Bodily space is always the space of *action*, and as such it cannot be construed in terms of objective space alone, and nor should it be construed as identical with the extent of the body as "physical."[161] It is this that underlies Heidegger's much later comment, in the 1969 Le Thor Seminar, that:

> We need to grasp the difference between "lived-body" and "body." For instance, when we step on a scale, we do not weigh our "lived-body" but merely the weight of our "body." Or further, the limit of the "lived-body" is not the limit of the "body." The limit of the body is the skin. The limit of the "lived-body" is more difficult to determine. It is not "world," but it is perhaps just as little "environment."[162]

This does not imply, moreover, that bodily spatiality is, after all, a derivative of temporality—the active body is the body as given in its activity, and therefore as temporal, but its temporality, while thereby necessary for its spatiality, does not determine or explain that spatiality.[163] Heidegger is thus quite correct in claiming that objective spatiality does not exhibit the kind of directionality that is a necessary element in the spatiality of being-there, but mistaken in assuming that this means that such directionality must be derived from temporality alone—the body has a directionality of its own that is given in its essential spatiality.

Recognition of the basic character of bodily spatiality does not mean, however, that objective spatiality is thereby shown to be irrelevant to understanding the structure of the spatiality proper to being-there. The idea of bodily space is of a mode of spatiality that is centered on the body (we may wish to call it a "subjective" space since we might also view it as centered on "the subject," but it is actually the body, indeed, the *active* body, rather than any abstract notion of "subjectivity" that is central here[164]); the idea of objective space is the idea of a space centered, not on the body, nor on any one thing, but rather on things or objects as they stand apart from any particular "body." Thus, while bodily space is always structured in terms of the relation to a body, and so has a clear center and directionality (minimally, the directionality of up/down, left/right, front/back, near/far), objective space lacks such a center, being instead made up of a multiplicity of equally "ranked" positions and has no such directionality, with relations between positions characterizable only in terms of a uniform metric. Objective space is thus characteristically public—centered neither on the "subject" nor on the body—and the public character of objective space—understood as the mode of spatiality that is centered on the multiplicity of things or objects—is itself a central element in the spatiality proper to equipment.

Heidegger, of course, presents equipmental spatiality as distinct from the spatiality of objectivity. Equipmental spatiality has an ordering, a directionality, that is based in task and activity, and as such it would seem to be quite distinct from the extended multiplicity of position that is given in objective spatiality. Yet there is a problem concealed in Heidegger's treatment of equipmental spatiality that has already emerged in the discussion in section 3.3 above. Dreyfus criticizes Heidegger's account of spatiality for failing to distinguish "*public* space in which entities show up for human beings, from the centered spatiality of each *individual* human being."[165] The way Dreyfus articulates this criticism is in terms of the way Heidegger makes the nearing of things that occurs in dis-tance dependent on being-there rather than on the structure of equipmental space as such. In discussing Dreyfus's criticism, I noted that Dreyfus's account appears to misunderstand the way in which Heidegger's account must take spatiality as dependent on both the prior, generalized equipmental ordering given in equipmental spatiality and the particular realization of that ordering through being-there's individual engagement within that ordering in terms of existential spatiality—the real problem arises because of Heidegger's prioritization within that overall structure of the dependence of equipmental spatiality on the existential. As it turns out, this prioritization, which seems to take the form of an implicit, but nevertheless somewhat opaque, hierarchical dependence, arises not only from the way in which existential spatiality "opens up" the field of spatiality through dis-tance and orientation, but also from the way in which the ordering of the equipmental, although not directly tied to any individual projection of possibilities, is nevertheless itself dependent on the general character of being-there as being in and through its projection of possibilities. The "toward-which" or "in-order-to" of the equipmental must thus be derivative of the "being-ahead-of-itself" of existentiality. At this point Dreyfus's criticism, particularly when formulated in the general terms Dreyfus first uses, comes back into the picture since it now seems as if Heidegger really does have a problem, not merely in distinguishing the "*public* space in which entities show up" from the "spatiality of each *individual* human being," but in explaining how one can be possible on the basis of the other—since that, in essence, is what the emphasis on the priority of existential spatiality actually amounts to.

The situation is complicated, however, by the problem that also emerged in section 3.3 above concerning the relation between equipmental and objective space—a problem that is really about how the public space of the equipmental should itself be understood. On the one hand, Heidegger wants to distinguish equipmental space from the space of objectivity, and yet, on the other hand, equipmental space must also be a public, inter-subjective space that is also, therefore, distinct from the individually centered spatiality of the existential. Not only is there a problem about how to explain equipmental, or, more generally, public space, on the basis of individual, existential space, but there is also a problem as to exactly what sort of space is actually in question when we look to explain equipmental space in this way. The idea of equipmental space turns out, in fact, to stand awkwardly between the public space of objectivity and the centered space of the individual. Although this point is perhaps not entirely clear in his discussion in *Being-in-the-World* (although it is a point of focus, as I noted above, for Arisaka's criticism of Dreyfus), Dreyfus does seem to give it some recognition in discussion elsewhere. In an essay on the concept of equipment in *Being and Time*, he suggests that the being of equipment in that work "hovers ambiguously between that of craftsmanship and technology"[166]—in spatial or topological terms, between that of the "localized" and the "de-localized"—and that "[b]y highlighting the interrelationship between all items of equipment and by defining equipment by its position in this referential totality, *Being and Time* denies localness."[167] The problem that is presented by equipmental spatiality is that it has to be a space that allows for two sorts of spatial relationship: first a relationship between a multiplicity of items; second a relationship between those items and a multiplicity of individuals. The first is necessary for the very structure of equipmentality as constituted in terms of an array of items; the second is necessary for the possibility of equipmentality as an essentially public, intersubjective structure. Both these features of the space at issue suggest that, in its general form, it must be structured in a way analogous to objective spatiality. Indeed, a space that is not "objective" would seem to lack the publicness as well as the multiple positionality that are necessary for equipmental space. Yet equipmental spatiality is also supposed to have an ordering that is based in the teleology of the "toward-which" and "in-order-to," and such an ordering would seem incompatible with objective spatiality—objective spatiality is not an ordered space; it has no directionality, no here and there, no near and far. Indeed, the "a directional" character of objective space is essential to its public character—objective space is just that space that is accessible from any and every location within it—and in this respect, the problem of objective spatiality that has emerged here is identical with the problem of how the public and the intersubjective can be made explicable within the framework of *Being and Time*.

If equipmental spatiality turns out to be more like a form of objective spatiality, then the question of how equipmental space can be dependent on individual "existential" space will be identical with the question how objective spatiality can be shown to be dependent on existential space. Of course, part of what has come into question in the discussion so far has been not only the nature of equipmental space as such, but also the nature of existential space, and what has become evident is the way in which existential, or at least, individual, space is actually underpinned by bodily space.[168] Consequently, what originally appears in Heidegger's analysis as a question of the relation between an equipmental space that is already understood as ordered and directional, albeit as also intersubjective, and an existential space that is determined by a similar ordering and directionality, albeit individually centered and based in temporality now appears as much closer to a question concerning the relation between two forms of spatiality, one of which is tied to the multiple positioning of things or objects, and so is essentially a form of objective spatiality, and the other of which is tied to the unique centering of the body, and so is identical with what I have termed "bodily" spatiality. The difficulty in making sense of Heidegger's account of spatiality and the difficulty in deriving the intersubjective space of equipmentality from the individually centered space of the existential is thus underlaid by the opacity and inadequacy of Heidegger's account of both equipmental and existential spatiality as such, as well as by Heidegger's failure to understand the relation between the different modes of spatiality.

Objective space, though having no directionality of its own, can nevertheless be grasped, and indeed can only be grasped, as we saw in the discussion above, through the way in which it is related to a particular bodily space. Objective space is rendered directional, or better, orientation within objective space becomes possible, only through its relatedness to the body as it is both objectively located and also actively engaged (indeed, this general idea was already adumbrated in the emphasis, in sec. 3.3 above, on the way the opening up of space requires *both* the equipmental *and* the existential). Objective space is thus made accessible—is "opened up"— through bodily space, and yet what is thereby made accessible is not a space that is only the space of the body, but rather a space that is, indeed, objective. In this respect, we may choose to regard both objective and bodily spatiality as having no independent status of their own, but as each being mutually dependent on the other and as together giving rise to spatiality in the full sense (the fact that objective space has no directionality while bodily space lacks real intersubjectivity should be taken as indicative of just the mutuality at issue here). Equipmental spatiality appears to have an awkward position in relation to the structure of spatiality that has come into view here since equipmental spatiality is actually an attempt to reify a mode of spatiality that comprises elements of both objective and bodily space and yet is also supposed to be distinct from each.

In fact, equipmental spatiality can be nothing other than the idea of objective spatiality as it is given through a directionality that enables that objective space to be related back to a particular bodily space. In this respect, it is worth returning to the example of map-based orientation that was used in the discussion of the relation between equipmental and existential space in section 3.3 above. Although different spaces may require modes of map-like representation, and no map can ever capture every aspect of the space it maps, nevertheless any and every space is also a mappable space. A map is always a representation, or, we might say, an *articulation*, of a space in terms that make that space accessible and navigable to anybody who can be located within it, and so its mappability is also indicative of the way in which spatiality always carries a certain necessary "publicness" with it—a publicness that consists in the way in which both "objective" and "bodily" space are always interconnected and mutually dependent. Thus, when I look around the workshop before me, I can see the various tools arrayed in their places and with respect to the tasks to be performed. I can draw a plan of the workshop, both in terms of the way the tools are physically located with respect to each other, or, though it will be more complicated, in terms of their task-based interrelation—a map that can be considered "objective." Yet just as the equipmental array does not emerge as equipment except insofar as the tools concerned are equipmentally employed in relation to a specific task, so no map functions as a representation or articulation of space unless someone can take the map, locate themselves within it, and thereby orient themselves to the features around them through the way those features then relate to parts of their body.[169] The space given in the map is, strictly speaking, not an independent mode of spatiality (though sometimes mappable space is thought of as an "allocentric" space[170]), rather the map represents a particular space, which may well be an objective space, in a form that enables a connection to bodily space. An analogous point holds for equipmental space, which is properly not an independent mode of spatiality, but rather an objective space as it is understood and articulated in relation to certain modes of activity, and, hence, to bodily space.

While it is somewhat to one side of the main discussion here, it is also worth noting that this latter point does not rely on any assumption to the effect that a mappable space is also thereby an objective space, although it is indeed often assumed that mappability and objectivity are coextensive terms. Although I think there is an important sense in which every mapping of space is itself an objective representation of space, not every mapped space is an objective space. If we draw up a schematic map of bodily space, for instance, in terms of an array of regions corresponding to up/down, left/right, front/back, near/far, then the map that is so produced will itself be "objective," and yet the space that it represents will not itself be an objective, but a bodily space—that is, a space that takes a body as its directional center. In general I would say that all representation is "objective" in that it re-presents in terms that do not themselves depend on any particular "subjective" position within the represented space, although any such representation always requires some subjective position in order to become accessible. The key point at issue in the discussion here is the interdependence of notions of objective and bodily spatiality, and the idea of equipmental space as not a sui generis concept of space at all, but rather an objective space in which things are configured in relation to one another, as well as in respect to a certain bodily space, and thence to a certain order of activity.

Heidegger treats, not only equipmental space, but also objective space, as secondary to existential space, or, more generally, to the existential-ontological structure of being-there. Indeed, in more specific terms, Heidegger presents objective space, and so the space of measurement, as coming into view through the breakdown in being-there's active engagement with its world that "releases" items of equipment from their equipmental context, allowing them to appear as detached "objects" within an "objective" space. When we grasp an item of equipment as merely an object, possessed of certain abstract properties, we grasp it as merely "present-at-hand," stripped of its readiness-for-use, appearing within a "leveled"-out homogenous space:

In the "physical" assertion that "the hammer is heavy" we *overlook* not only the tool-character of the entity we encounter, but also something that belongs to any ready-to-hand equipment: its place. Its place becomes a matter of indifference. This does not mean that what is present-at-hand loses its "location" altogether. But its place becomes a "spatio-temporal" position, a "world-point," which is in no-way distinguished from any other. This implies not only that the multiplicity of places of equipment ready-to-hand within the confines of the environment becomes modified to a pure multiplicity of positions, but that the entities of the environment are altogether *released from such confinement [entschränkt]*. The aggregate of the present-at-hand becomes the theme.[171]

This passage indicates the close relation between equipmental and objective space such that the one can be transformed into the other and can, in certain respects, be taken as itself illustrating something of what is at issue in the analysis set out above—in particular the way in which equipmental space can itself be understood as containing a mode of objective space within it. But, in this respect, inasmuch as it also presupposes the idea of the dependence of objective space on being-there's existential character, so it also exhibits some of the difficulty in the very idea of objective space as a dependent concept. If we "overlook" the tool-character of the hammer, we can only do so because we already have access to the idea of the hammer as something other than a tool. The present-at-hand, and the spatiality associated with it, is thus not generated or derived from the ready-to-hand, but must be already given along with it—objective spatiality is indeed already a part of the idea of the equipmental.

    Moreover, just as a grasp of spatiality, both bodily and objective, is necessary for engagement with things as tools, so, in this respect, is the present-at-hand itself necessary for the possibility of the ready-to-hand—using things as tools also means being able to grasp them as objects (though this need not mean grasping them in both modes at one and the same time, nor need it imply a capacity to articulate conceptually the different modes at issue here). Notice that this means that the idea of a hierarchical dependence between the ready-to-hand and the present-at-hand, or between the practical and theoretical, must turn out to be just as ill-founded as the other forms of hierarchical dependence that figure throughout *Being and Time*. At the same time, however, this does not reestablish the present-at-hand, or the "theoretical," as independent of the ready-to-hand—there will still be a dependence here, but a *mutual* dependence, and thus a dependence that does not allow either term to be treated apart from the other to which it is bound. Indeed, this point is an especially important one since often the attempt to demonstrate the hierarchical dependence of the theoretical on the practical is itself a response to the tendency to assume the reverse—to assume that the practical is hierarchically dependent on some form of the "theoretical." The problem is not the assertion of dependence as such, however, but the failure to recognize the mutuality of that dependence. Of course, even in the case of mutual dependence there may still be some form of prioritization possible (analogous to that which Heidegger continues to hold, even after *Being and Time*, with respect to temporality), but it cannot be one based in derivation or hierarchical dependence, and it must be established, if at all, through the detailed analysis of the particular connections that obtain between the elements at issue. One element may thereby be shown to be "prior" to others in the sense that it occupies a more central position (exhibits more connections with other elements) within the overall structure, but it will remain embedded in the dependence relations that are constitutive of that structure.

There is, however, a commonly accepted account of Heidegger's position as presented in *Being and Time* according to which one of its basic tenets is the primacy of practical engagement or "coping" over the theoretical, the prepositional, and the epistemic—which often seems to carry the hallmarks of a primacy based in some form of hierarchical dependence.[172] The very idea of a clear distinction between the practical and the theoretical, however, is something with respect to which we have reason to be suspicious. Such a distinction is tied to a particular conception of theory that is itself open to challenge on grounds that Heidegger himself suggests in *Being and Time*. There he emphasizes a form of mutual dependence as obtaining between "practice" and "theory" such that not only does "practice" have a "theoretical" attitude proper to it, but so too does "theory" have its own "practice":

Holding back from the use of equipment is so far from sheer "theory" that the kind of circumspection which "tarries" and considers, remains wholly in the grip of the ready-to-hand equipment with which one is concerned. "Practical" dealings have their own kind of sight ("theory"), theoretical research is not without a praxis of its own.[173]

As Joseph Rouse points out, however, Heidegger seems to have a very narrow conception of the nature of the "praxis" at issue here.[174] Moreover, Heidegger also holds that there is a radical changeover in the shift from our practical engagement to the "theoretical" and "detached" scientific attitude that is fundamentally geared to a certain mathematical mode of projection of the world—a mode of projection particularly evident in the mathematical-geometrical understanding of space. Yet one can recognize such a distinct mode of scientific understanding without any commitment to a general distinction of theory from practice (that distinction may be viewed as always a distinction that is sensitive to its context of application) or of the "detached" from the "engaged" and without abandoning the recognition that whatever is designated as "theoretical" always carries its own mode of "practice" with it (and vice versa). The point of emphasizing the priority of practice, or of what may be better understood as "engaged activity," should not be that there are two distinct modes of being in the world, one of which stands apart from, but as in some sense prior to, or the basis for, the other; the crucial point is rather that even the theoretical, which may attempt to present itself as based in a disengaged relation between "subject" and "object," is always already constituted in terms of a prior engagement between (a prior "belonging-together" of) the one who theorizes and that which provokes such theorization. Not even in the theoretical attitude do we find ourselves cut off from the world; it is rather that in the theoretical attitude both we and the world emerge in a different light, within a different "project."

This I take to be the real point of Heidegger's analysis even in *Being and Time*—not that the practical and the theoretical, or the detached and the engaged, constitute two separate and distinct ways of being-there, but that being-there is itself such as to support different possible modes of disclosure, and that those modes are always underlain by a more basic gatheredness of being-there and world. What I would add here, and what Heidegger seems not to make clear, is that, for the most part, these different modes of disclosure are themselves in constant interplay. There is no purely "detached" mode of world-disclosure and perhaps not even, at least for beings that are capable of a theoretical grasp at all, any purely "practical" mode either. Indeed, in this respect, those cases that are often cited as examples of pure immersion in the practical and the engaged—being "in the zone" as is said in sports[175]—actually constitute another mode of projection, and one in which, even if we accept that it involves no "theorization" in the activity, the activity is nevertheless embedded within a context from which "theorization" (in the form of rules, conventions, strategies, and so forth) is not absent.[176]

The difficulty in making sense of the supposed dependence of the objective on the nonobjective, on what we may term the "engaged," is a quite general one and arises as a direct consequence of the nature of the concepts at issue here. There is certainly a common tendency to treat objectivity, in whatever mode it is considered, as arising out of some process of disengagement, detachment, abstraction, or formalization.[177] Yet such processes cannot give rise to a notion of objectivity since they themselves already depend upon, and are themselves expressions of, the very notion at issue. Disengagement, detachment, abstraction, and formalization all presuppose a preexisting capacity for objective understanding that cannot itself be construed as reducible to, or derivable from, the understanding associated with engagement or attachment, with the concrete or the material as such. Objectivity is, in this respect, a distinct and sui generis concept. The "leveling" out of the array of places and regions through some form of disengagement from equipmental involvement, while it may capture an aspect of the phenomenology involved in our thinking about engagement and objectivity, is not itself possible without an independent and prior grasp of that leveled-out space as such, but that means that we cannot view such an objective space as explained by, or as hierarchically dependent on, the space of engagement. Instead, the two modes of spatiality at issue are always given together as part of a single spatiality—to grasp space as such is, indeed, to grasp it in both its engaged and objective aspects—and it is the way in which these two are given together, the way in which they are "equiprimordial," to use Heidegger's term, that gives rise to the impression that we can get one from the other since the one already presupposes the other, and vice versa.[178]

The idea of objective spatiality may be understood in terms of a multiplicity of locations in which no one location has priority over any other—as a simultaneity of "heres." Heidegger understands ordinary temporality in a similar fashion in terms of a multiplicity of temporal locations in which no single location has priority over any other—as a succession of "nows." If there is a difficulty in demonstrating the dependence of the objective on the engaged in relation to spatiality, then a similar difficulty can be expected to arise with respect to time also. Indeed, a very similar problem does arise with respect to Heidegger's attempt to show ordinary temporality as dependent on originary temporality. The problem, as William Blattner presents it, is that the sequentiality of ordinary temporality cannot be derived from originary temporality, which, as we have already seen, is not itself sequential. Blattner develops his own argument to this conclusion in considerable detail,[179] but the main point is that although originary temporality does carry within it a notion of ordering between future, past, and present, it does not carry an ordering that would explain the public sequentiality of ordinary temporality as it applies to events in general, and such sequentiality is itself a core element in Heidegger's account of ordinary temporality, and indeed, in our ordinary experience of time.[180]

Originary temporality carries nothing within it that would explain the sequential ordering of the entire range of diverse tasks and activities in which we are involved. This is evident even when we reflect on quite mundane tasks and the way events are ordered within that task: in making a chair, the task of making the chair as such may stand as that which is "ahead" of any particular task within the work undertaken, and it may also determine a general ordering of those tasks (the components of the chair, legs, seat, back, and so on will need to be constructed before the chair as a whole can be assembled), but there will always be many different ways in which the sequence of events that are involved in that making could be laid out (perhaps one works on the legs first or one might plane the timber for the seat). The mere fact that any "projection" of a certain set of possibilities presupposes, as the means by which those possibilities are achieved, a set of stages in the process of attempting to realize those possibilities (x is directed toward y, y is directed toward z, and so on) does not entail that any particular series of such stages must be gone through. But that means that no particular sequence is actually determined by the projection of some possibility or set of possibilities, and so nothing is determined in its sequentiality as such. Put more directly: the fact that what I am doing is making a chair does not explain why I plane the timber for the seat before shaping the timber for the legs, and so does not explain that particular sequence in which planing the seat and shaping the legs both stand. One might argue that the particular way in which tasks are sequentially related arises because of the way in which different projective possibilities overlap and need to be fitted in relation to one another, but the notion of fitting together here already presupposes the idea that they have to be fitted together *sequentially*, and so does not serve to explain the sequentiality as such. More fundamentally, we may say that the idea of a pure series of "nows" that need have no intrinsic relation to one another, an idea which is at the heart of ordinary temporality, is just the idea of objective time, but this notion cannot be derived from time understood as the temporalizing of future, having been, and the present. Just as sequentiality appears to constitute an independent feature of temporality that cannot be derived from originary temporality (even though it may be required for it in the sense that originary temporality necessarily works itself out in terms of ordinary temporality), so ordinary temporality is an independent mode of temporality that cannot be derived from any other such mode. In the most general terms, the leveled-out, nondirectional character of the objective cannot be derived from the centralized, directional character of the "engaged." Situatedness, however, and so the "there" of being, always encompasses both the objective and the engaged— and this is so with respect to both the spatial and the temporal. This does not mean that our situatedness in the world is, after all, a matter of our objective spatial locatedness. Rather our situatedness is constituted in such a way that it encompasses both an objective and an embodied spatiality.

As will become clearer in the discussion in subsequent chapters, both these modes of spatiality turn out to be necessary elements in the structure of situatedness, or better of place, but neither taken on its own is sufficient on which to base an understanding of place as such.[181]

Heidegger is right that one can only gain access to the objective, and so to the disengagement that goes with it, through the directional and the engaged, but he is wrong in thinking, as he did in *Being and Time*, that this means that the one is "derived from," or hierarchically dependent upon, the other. The opening up that is the opening up of the "there" is an opening in situatedness of that which goes beyond the particularity of the situation—which is why it is indeed an opening up of "world." The relation between the elements that are constitutive of that situatedness, and so of the "there" and the world into which it opens, is thus one of mutual, not hierarchical, dependence—of the gathering of a multiplicity of elements into a single heterogeneous, though nonetheless unified, structure. It is just this structure that is at issue in the notion of place or *topos*—a structure that is both temporal and spatial, that encompasses the objective and the "engaged," the finite and, in a certain sense, the infinite. The analysis that Heidegger provides in *Being and Time* is an attempt to gain insight into the structure of the happening of the "there" that is also a happening of world—it is an attempt to exhibit the proper "ground" of that happening. But the analysis is compromised by Heidegger's adoption of a particular conception of what it is to ground that takes such grounding to consist in the exhibiting of a transcendental structure of possibility (a structure of "meaning") understood in terms of the uncovering of a hierarchical structure of dependence leading back to an originary unity—that of originary time. If the notion of hierarchical dependence is perhaps the single most pervasive and problematic element in the analysis of *Being and Time*, then the shift away from that notion, and toward a clearer focus on dependence in mutuality, will be one of the main keys to Heidegger's thinking as it develops subsequently.

The problematic character of the attempt to ground in terms of exhibiting a structure of hierarchical dependence comes out in a particularly critical way when it comes to the account of spatiality since, on the one hand, it is spatiality that appears to pose the greatest threat to the unity of the "there," and so exhibiting the derivative character of spatiality turns out to be crucial, and yet, on the other hand, it also seems clear that spatiality must belong in a fundamental way to the structure of the "there" that runs counter to any such "derivation." Moreover, the problematic status of spatiality within the analysis of *Being and Time* is also closely bound up with the problem of showing how it is possible to explain the opening up of a public, intersubjective world on the basis of the projective activity of individual being-there. The problem here concerns what Dreyfus refers to as the "incipient subjectivism" that seems to afflict Heidegger's account of spatiality, although William Blattner also sees this as emerging in respect of Heidegger's account of time and as leading to his abandonment of the position set out in *Being and Time*.[182] In fact, the problem is a deep-seated one that, in its more general form, preoccupies Heidegger in the years after 1927—a problem that he comes to view as centered around the notion of transcendence and that leads to a shift away from the focus on being-there as that is understood in *Being and Time* and to a shift in the articulation of many key concepts in Heidegger's thinking, including that of world. This problem is not specific to either spatiality or temporality alone, but concerns the proper understanding of the relation between human being and the world, and of the nature of world, and disclosedness, as such. Indeed, one of the results of *Being and Time* (although it is also its starting point) can be seen as the exhibiting of the way in which the problem of being is inextricably bound up with the question of world and with the problematic character of the relation between the world and the human. It is, essentially, the problem of the finitude of being—of the happening of being and of world as always a happening in and through the specificity of the "there."

Yet although temporality and spatiality must both be seen to be at issue here, the way in which spatiality is implicated is, once again, of particular importance. If what is at issue is essentially a question of situatedness, of place, then place cannot be thought apart from space, just as it cannot be thought apart from time, and yet space, much more than time, seems to bring with it a mode of thinking that itself tends toward the directionless, the extended, the *placeless*. Thinking the proper relation between human being and the world, thinking the fundamental nature of the "there," means rethinking the relation between place and space, and the nature of space as such. *Being and Time* does not itself succeed in such a re-thinking, and, as we have already seen, one of the prime reasons for its failure is its reliance on an inappropriate conception of what it is to "ground," and particularly, its reliance on a notion of hierarchical dependence. The notion of ground is itself a notion that has topological connotations, but if one takes those connotations seriously, then one cannot think of grounding in hierarchical terms, but only in terms of the relations of mutuality that are themselves characteristic of relations within and between places. Here also is an indication of the centrality of ideas of place and space in the problem with which Heidegger is engaged. The question of being, then, which is also the question of place, requires us to address the relation between human beings and the world, and to do so in a way that also addresses the question of the nature of ground. In Heidegger's thinking after *Being and Time*, these issues—of ground, of the human relation to world, and of place—become central points of focus, and it is to that later thinking that I now turn.

4 The Turning of Thought: Truth and World

"Dasein" names that which is first of all to be experienced, and subsequently thought accordingly, as a place [*Stelle*]—namely as the locality [*Ortschaft*] of the truth of Being.
—Heidegger, "Introduction to 'What Is Metaphysics?' "[1]

The path from Heidegger's earliest thinking to *Being and Time* is essentially directed toward the attempt to articulate the fundamental idea of our being in the world as a matter of our being as "situated"—a matter of our being "there"—and of being as itself tied to just such situatedness. What characterizes *Being and Time* is the attempt to provide a detailed analysis of the structure of such "being-there" as a whole in its more particular character as temporal. It aims to do this, moreover, through a form of transcendental grounding that consists in exhibiting the hierarchical dependence of what appears, at first, to be an essentially spatial structure on the structure of world, on the structure of care, and so on originary temporality. This attempt turns out to be one that Heidegger cannot complete, but the reasons that underlie this lack of completion bring to light a number of issues important in Heidegger's rethinking of what is at stake here: above all, as noted at the end of the last chapter, notions of ground, world, the human relation to world, truth, and also, though still not in a properly thematic way, place.

Some of the works that appear in the period immediately following *Being and Time*, most notably the lectures of the *Basic Problems of Phenomenology* from 1927, and the *Kantbuch* of 1929 (*Kant and the Problem of Metaphysics*), include materials from the abandoned second part of *Being and Time* itself—particularly the critical engagement with (the "de-struction" or "dis-mantling" of) the history of ontology. Thus the lectures on phenomenology contain extensive discussions of Aristotle and Descartes, as well as Husserl. The *Kantbuch*, moreover, attempts to exhibit the Kantian transcendental project as a precursor to Heidegger's own transcendental-ontological analysis in *Being and Time*, both in terms of the Kantian project as attempting a "laying of the foundation" for metaphysics, and so as engaged in a certain sort of "grounding," and also, in the inquiry into such a ground, as essentially oriented toward the question of unity understood in terms of temporality. Heidegger's claim, significantly, is that Kant ultimately recoils from the nature of the ground that is opened up in this inquiry. The concern with ground is explicit in the 1929 essay "On the Essence of Ground," but it can also be seen as present in Heidegger's repeated attempts to formulate an account of the unity that is essential to that which in *Being and Time* he called "disclosedness," and which is itself understood as the essence of truth. Indeed, in the period after *Being and Time*, truth rather than meaning becomes a central concern, and the reason for this is closely tied to Heidegger's attempt to rearticulate the nature of the unity that is characteristic of the "there," as well as of world, in a way that refrains from treating that unity in a way that would allow it to be understood as something "projected" by, or grounded in, "being-there" (at least insofar as the latter is tied to a human mode of being). Being-there is seen as itself gathered into the unity of truth, rather than the unity of truth being something projected by, or on the basis of, "being-there."

Although Heidegger emphasized the way in which his thinking was always "on the way" rather than having "arrived," his work during the period from the time of the publication of *Being and Time* until at least 1936 has to be seen as having a quite specific *transitional* character as it moves from the thinking of *meaning* to the thinking, or re-thinking, of *place* (in fact, as I will suggest below, this transition should be seen as continuing past 1936 and into the 1940s). Moreover, this period also encompasses the time of Heidegger's political engagement and his entanglement with Nazism. However one interprets that engagement, there can be no doubt that it is an entanglement that, even during the 1930s, becomes a source of difficulty for Heidegger philosophically, politically, and personally. Not only does he resign the rectorate at Freiburg after only one year, but he is also forced to rethink what it was that prompted his engagement with Nazism in the first place, to rethink the terms of that engagement, to rethink whatever it was that he saw as the "inner truth and greatness" of the movement.[2] It is perhaps no surprise, given the emergence of the problematic character of *Being and Time* coupled with the failure of his political ambitions,[3] that the period should indeed have been a transitional one—a time of "turning" and of "return."

4.1 Turning and Return

The question of being that is taken to be at the heart of Heidegger's thinking is, as we saw in chapter 1, a question that properly emerges only in conjunction with the personal involvement of the philosopher in the question—thus the question of being is itself always entangled with the being of questioning as such. In this respect, the forgetfulness of being that Heidegger takes to be characteristic of the philosophical tradition, and which is itself an expression of a deeper and more pervasive forgetfulness that characterizes our ordinary lives, can be understood as a forgetfulness of the questionability of being, and so also a forgetfulness of the way in which being only arises as a question in conjunction with the recognition that what is in question here is also our own being. Such forgetfulness is, says Heidegger, "nothing accidental and temporary, but on the contrary is necessarily and constantly formed."[4] Overcoming such forgetfulness requires a recognition of the questionability of being, of the question of our prior entanglement with being, but also, from the very start, a recognition of the question of being as inevitably tied to the question of the "there." The overcoming of forgetfulness is, of course, a matter of remembering. As Joseph Fell puts it: " 'Remembering' (*Andenken*) is a reversal (*Kehre*) of the movement of 'forgetting' such that thought recovers itself as it really always already is—that is, as 'ruled' by being."[5] For thought to recover itself as "ruled by being" is to recover itself as already belonging to being, as already given over to the happening of world, of presence, of disclosedness. Recovery or remembering is thus always a returning, or turning back, to that which we already are—a turning back to that which is "originary," that to which we already belong, that which is our proper ground, that in which we already find ourselves. The reversal of forgetting is also a turning back to our proper place—and it is in just this sense that Heidegger will frequently, in his later writing, call upon the idea of the reversal of forgetfulness as a matter of "homecoming" (*Heimkunft*)— although, as a return to the questionability of being, such a homecoming is not a simple return to the familiar, but a turning back to that which is both closest to us and also furthest away, to that which is both familiar and yet also essentially "uncanny" (*unheimlich*).

The idea of thinking as a form of remembering, recovery, or returning is a theme that runs throughout Heidegger's thinking. It is embedded in Husserl's own phenomenological method and the slogan "Back to the things themselves" (*Zu den Sachen selbst*); it is a part of the hermeneutical idea of the recovery of meaning as a moving back to that in which meaning is grounded; it is evident in the Eckhartian idea of the soul's return to its place in God. But as with so many of Heidegger's key concepts, the idea of return or turning back does not admit of any single reading or interpretation. The idea of a return, a turning back to origin, that is at issue here is not the idea of something that is performed only once and then completed. It is instead a movement that is perpetual and constant—a movement essential to thinking and so also to philosophy (although it is unlikely to be given universal recognition as such). Yet we can understand the idea of a return that is at issue here in another way too—as the return that is performed, not merely in every act of thinking as we try to engage with the subject matter that drives the thought, nor in philosophical thinking as it attempts to engage with its own origin, but also in thinking as it tries to recover its own sense of origin and to rearticulate itself at certain crucial moments in its development. Thus we may come to a point at which, while our thought is always caught up in an attempt to recover its own origin, we also find ourselves forced to make a more self-conscious reorientation in our thinking, a more explicit "turning back."

Hannah Arendt once said of Heidegger's thought that it was always returning to its point of origin, continually beginning anew,[6] and this is true in both the senses at issue here. All of Heidegger's thinking can be construed, in the terms I have presented it here, as an attempt at a certain sort of recovery, retrieval, or remembrance—what is recovered is being's own questionability, as well as the "place" or "placedness" within which such questionability arises. This sense of "turning" refers to the character of Heidegger's thought as such, and to Heidegger's thought as it instantiates the turning movement of all thought, rather than to any particular turning that occurs at a point within the historical development of Heidegger's thinking. Yet there is also a sense in which Heidegger's thinking does indeed exhibit certain specific turnings within its own path. These turnings occur at many different stages on that path—for instance, in the shift away from logical inquiry and toward the hermeneutics of facticity in the period 1917–1919, in the shift toward the engagement with Aristotle, and then with Kant, in the mid-1920s, in the espousal of the language of "existence" prior to the publication of *Being and Time*. There is also, however, a more particular and significant turning that occurs in the 1930s that relates to the overall conception and understanding of Heidegger's thought as such. This turning relates directly to the turning that already appears in the plan of *Being and Time*—the "turning" from the temporality of being-there to the temporality of being that was supposed to have occurred in the shift from division 2 of part 1 to division 3, and thence to the completion of the work in part 2. Thus, in the "Letter on 'Humanism,'" written in response to a letter from Jean Beaufret in the autumn of 1946, and published in 1947, Heidegger comments that:

In the publication of *Being and Time* the third division of the first part, "Time and Being," was held back (cf. *Being and Time*, p. 39). Here everything is reversed [in terms of the "what" and "how" of that which is thought-worthy and of thinking]. The division in question was held back because thinking failed in the adequate saying [letting itself show] of this turning [*Kehre*] and did not succeed with the help of the language of metaphysics. The lecture "On the Essence of Truth," thought out and delivered in 1930 but not printed until 1943, provides a certain insight into the thinking of the turning from "Being and Time" to "Time and Being." This turning is not a change of standpoint [i.e., of the question of being] from *Being and Time*, but in it the thinking that was sought first arrives at the locality of the dimension out of which *Being and Time* is experienced, that is to say, experienced in the fundamental experience of the oblivion of being. [First edition, 1949: Forgottenness— λήθη concealing—withdrawal—expropriation: event of appropriation [*Ereignis*].][7]

The difficulties that arise in Heidegger's attempt to carry out the task originally envisaged in *Being and Time*—a task whose attempted completion itself stands as an instance of the constant turning of thought back to its origin—thus lead Heidegger to return to the task, and to rearticulate the matter at issue. As Heidegger emphasizes, this turning is not a change in standpoint, but rather what might be thought of as a "reorientation" that enables the proper recognition of the place, the locality, in which thinking already finds itself.

The "Letter on 'Humanism'" presents the turning as a movement in thinking, as a movement, not properly accomplished, within the structure of *Being and Time* and also as a movement, an event, in the course of Heidegger's own philosophical biography. In the last of these three senses, the turning refers to the shift in Heidegger's thinking that has its inception in 1930, with "On the Essence of Truth" (although Gadamer reports that already in 1928 Heidegger acknowledged that the terms of his thinking had begun to "slip"[8]), and that is often taken to reach its culmination in 1936 with the writing of the massive *Contributions to Philosophy* (which Heidegger finishes working on in 1938, but holds back from publication).[9] 1936 certainly marks an important point in the turning of Heidegger's thought—it marks, in particular, the appearance of the idea of the "event," the "*Ereignis*," that dominates Heidegger's later thinking (and that will be a starting point for the discussion in chapter 5 below)—but there is also a significant sense in which the mode of thinking that is opened up in the *Contributions* in 1936 does not become entirely clear until around 1946 with the "Letter on 'Humanism'" and the works that follow it, and in this respect it is significant that Heidegger publishes very little, although he is by no means inactive, in the ten-year period from 1936 to 1946. Thus one can also envisage the turning as actually comprising two movements, the first occurring between around 1930 and 1936, between "The Essence of Truth" and *Contributions*, and the second between 1936 and around 1946, between *Contributions* and the "Letter on 'Humanism.'"[10] The first period sees the working through of the problematic presented by *Being and Time*, and the second the articulation of the reoriented framework inaugurated in *Contributions*.

Thomas Sheehan has recently argued, however, that it is a mistake to identify the turning or "change" that occurs in Heidegger's thinking in the period after *Being and Time* and that seems to culminate in the *Contributions* with the "turning" or "return" that is at issue in the movement of thought itself (Sheehan distinguishes between the "change"—*die Wendung*—in Heidegger's own thinking and the Turning—*die Kehre*—of thinking as such).[11] As Sheehan bluntly puts it:

Interpretations of Heidegger often fail to distinguish between two very different matters—on the one hand "the turn" (*die Kehre*) and on the other "the change in Heidegger's thinking" (*die Wendung im Denken*), that is, the shift in the way Heidegger formulated and presented his philosophy beginning in the 1930s. Failure to make this distinction can be disastrous for understanding Heidegger.[12]

Although I think that there is some point to Sheehan's argument here, I nevertheless think that it oversimplifies matters, implying a more straight forward distraction than is actually warranted. The shift in Heidegger's thinking that occurs between 1930 and 1936, and is probably not really completed until 1946, can itself be understood as a singular instantiation, if in the mundane terms of a particular biography of thinking, of a movement of return that was always present in Heidegger's thinking and that is a feature of all thinking. But inasmuch as it is such an instantiation, so the turning in Heidegger's thinking cannot be wholly separated from the turning of thinking as such. In this sense, too, the turning of thought and the turning that occurs in Heidegger's thinking in the period of the 1930s (as well as the many other shifts that can be discerned along the way from the beginning to the end of Heidegger's philosophical career) cannot be entirely separated from the turning that is projected, but not completed, within the structure of *Being and Time*. Sheehan draws attention to Heidegger's own comment that "First and foremost the *Kehre* is not a process that took place in my thinking and questioning. It belongs, rather, to the very issue that is named by the titles 'Being and Time'/'Time and Being.' . . . The turn operates within the issue itself. It is not something that I did, nor does it pertain to my thinking only."[13] But even a comment such as this is not decisive in the way that Sheehan seems to suppose. Indeed, it seems that Heidegger's point here is to emphasize the priority of the turning as something that does not belong to his thinking *alone*, but to the issue for thinking as such, and this emphasis does not rule out, but actually implies, that the turning does indeed also belong to Heidegger's thinking—belongs to it, not as something Heidegger *does*, but as something that Heidegger's thought *undergoes*. Indeed, it is always important to attend to the polemical context of comments such as this, and so to the particular point that they might be intended to rebut[14]—in the case of the passage quoted, Heidegger's concern seems to be to reject the idea that the turning is something peculiar to his own philosophical biography, or that it is something he himself brought about.

As both a movement that is intrinsic to thinking as such, and as a movement evident in a particular way within Heidegger's own thought, the turning is an especially important idea for the understanding of topology and place. The task of topology is always directed at the recovery of that place in which we are already situated. Indeed, it is the fact of our situatedness that impels us toward such a recovery, that makes it possible, and that also determines the character of the articulation in which such a recovery must consist. In *Being and Time*, moreover, the "failure" of the turning, which is the "failure" of the work as a whole, is itself closely tied to the inadequacy of that work in its attempt to articulate the spatial and the topological as such. This is a large part of the point behind Joseph Fell's claim that the Heideggerian turning is itself "the 'turn' of space . . . 'into' place, which it originally and always is."[15] Moreover, this can be said to apply to the turning that was supposed to occur in *Being and Time*, to the historical turning in Heidegger's own thought, and to the turning in thinking itself—in each case the turning is a turning back from space to place, just as it is also a turning back to being. The full realization of this turning is something that we will not come to until chapter 5. For the moment the task is to arrive at a better understanding of the way the turning in Heidegger's thinking arises out of the difficulties encountered in *Being and Time* and the way this develops in the writings and lectures that follow, particularly those of the late 1920s and early to mid-1930s.

In this respect, it cannot be sufficient to characterize the turning in the general terms that are commonplace in so much of the literature or simply to describe the shift in Heidegger's thinking that is at issue. To say that the turning is indeed a turning "back" to being, or back to "place," does little to help understand what is really at issue here. What is required, in fact, is some account of what impels Heidegger's shift from the mode of philosophizing exemplified by *Being and Time* to the thinking that is inaugurated in *Contributions*. What is it in the "matter for thinking" and in Heidegger's own response to that matter that brings about this change? Any adequate answer to this question must take its cue from the way Heidegger himself characterizes the turning in general, as well as in the terms in which it might be applied to his own thought (for instance, in comments such as that which I quoted above from the "Letter on 'Humanism'"), and also from the difficulties that we have already identified as present in the argument of *Being and Time* itself. One would hope to find some convergence between these two sources, so that the difficulties we have encountered in *Being and Time* would turn out to connect up with the ideas that Heidegger also takes to be characteristic of the turning and that he identifies as elements in his own reorientation of his thinking. As we have already seen, two central concepts around which many of the difficulties of *Being and Time* cluster are those of ground and world—and both also implicate issues of space and place. The concept of world, and its articulation, is the primary focus for much of division 1, part 1. What became evident in the discussion in chapter 3 above, however, is the problematic character of the relation between being-there and world as that is set out in *Being and Time*—thus the character of being-in-the-world itself presents difficulties. But the difficulty does not merely concern how the structure of being-in-the-world, of being-there in relation to world, is to be described, but how that structure is to be understood as a whole, and this is just the problem of how the relation between being-there and world is to be grounded, that is, how its unity is to be explicated. These difficulties—of the relation between being-there and world; of the proper ground, and so the unity, of being-there and world—are issues that also turn out to be at stake in the way Heidegger understands the turning both as it applies to the matter for thinking and as it occurs in his own thinking. In the period from around 1928 and into the early 1930s, these difficulties emerge in terms of a preoccupation with the concept of world and the role of being-there in the "founding" of world that often appears in terms of a preoccupation with the idea of ground, and more specifically with the notion of "transcendence" as that which refers us to the ground, and so also to the unity, of being-there and world. Transcendence is a crucial notion in the reorientation in Heidegger's thinking that is the turning, but so too is the concept of truth. Indeed, what emerges in Heidegger's thinking in the early to mid-1930s is a turn toward the truth of being itself understood in terms of a "topological" happening of world that also grounds.

4.2   Transcendence and Subjectivity

One of the most obvious changes in Heidegger's thinking from *Being and Time* to the works that appear after 1936 involves a shift away from being-there as the primary focus of Heidegger's analysis. In *Contributions*, for instance, it is not being-there as it is thought primarily in connection with human being that commands Heidegger's attention, but a radically refor-mulated concept of being-there as the ground of the truth of being, and so as integrally bound up with the "Event," the *"Ereignis,"* to which human being is itself "appropriated," but which is certainly no merely human hap-pening.[16] This apparent shift away from the mode of being that is human being might be taken to suggest that the turning should be understood, even if only in part, as an attempt to overcome a problematic prioritiza-tion of human being within the project of *Being and Time*. This might seem to be confirmed by the way in which the problem of "subjectivity" often arises as a central concern in his discussions of the reasons for the breaking-off of the work that appeared in truncated form in 1926.

"Meaning" is the term that Heidegger uses to frame the question of being that is the main concern of *Being and Time*, but that term itself seems to lend itself to a subjectivist construal. In the 1969 Seminar in Le Thor, Hei-degger comments on this as follows:

> *Meaning* has a very precise signification in *Being and Time*, even if today it has become insufficient. What does "meaning of being" mean? This is understandable on the basis of the "project region" unfolded by the "understanding of being." "Understanding" [*Verständnis*], for its part, must be grasped in the original sense of "standing before" [*Vorstehen*]: residing before, holding oneself at an equal height with what one finds before oneself, and being strong enough to hold out. Here "meaning" is to be understood from "project," which is explained from "under-standing." What is inappropriate in this formulation of the question is that it makes it all too possible to understand the "project" as a human performance. Accordingly, project is then only taken to be a structure of subjectivity—which is how Sartre takes it, by basing himself upon Descartes. . . . In order to counter this mistaken concep-tion and to retain the meaning of "project" as it is to be taken (that of the opening disclosure), the thinking after *Being and Time* replaced the expression "meaning of being" with "truth of being."[17]

The connection between meaning, project, and understanding is one with which we have already met in the discussion of the nature of dependence or derivation in section 3.5 above. In the passage just quoted, Heidegger suggests that one of the problems, perhaps *the* problem, with *Being and Time* is the way in which the emphasis on "meaning," and so on "project," lends itself to what is an essentially subjectivist or voluntarist reading that would make the meaning of being something that was accomplished by human being-there. Significantly, Heidegger does not affirm that the position set out in *Being and Time* is subjectivist or voluntarist, merely that it makes such a reading "all too possible." The problem that Heidegger identifies here is one that can also be seen to arise, in more specific fashion, in terms of the way in which the account set out in *Being and Time* seems to make spatiality, for instance, dependent on the projective activity, ultimately grounded in temporality, of individual being-there. It also indicates the way in which the emphasis on meaning and projective understanding threatens to make problematic the relation between being-there and world. Inasmuch as the structure of world, at least as set out in part 1, division 1 of *Being and Time*, seems crucially to be determined by the structure of the "toward-which" or "in-order-to" of equipmental ordering, and as such, appears ultimately to depend upon a set of essentially human concerns, purposes, and interests, so the world itself begins to look like a "projection" of being-there's own existentiality.

That the relation between being-there, or more broadly, the human, and the world does indeed threaten to become a problem within the framework of *Being and Time* is explicitly recognized by Heidegger elsewhere. In the 1956 "Appendix" to "The Origin of the Work of Art," Heidegger notes an ambiguity in the way in which that essay refers to the "setting-to-work of truth," an ambiguity "in which it remains undetermined (though determin*able*) who or what does the 'setting,' and in what manner." Here, says Heidegger, "lies concealed *the relationship of being to human being*. This relationship is inadequately thought even in this presentation—a distressing difficulty that has been clear to me since *Being and Time*, and has since come under discussion in many presentations."[18] The rethinking of what Heidegger here calls "the relationship of being to human being" is central to the turning of the 1930s—and the above quotation from 1956 indicates the extent to which, as Heidegger saw it, that rethinking was not yet complete even in 1935–1936, during which the original lectures that make up "The Origin of the Work of Art" were first presented (in fact, the published text of "The Origin of the Work of Art" is that taken from three lectures given in Freiburg in November to December of 1936 at a time when Heidegger was already hard at work on *Contributions* in which the account of the relation at issue here was developed in a radically reconfigured form).[19] The problem is one that can be seen as an almost inevitable consequence of the way in which, from Heidegger's early thinking onward, the question of being is itself necessarily entangled with the nature of our own being as essentially questionable—indeed, it is only thus that the question of being emerges as a question—and this entanglement of human being with being itself is not something from which Heidegger ever resiles. The turning is a rethinking of the nature of that entanglement, but does not entail its rejection.[20]

As Heidegger indicates, the question concerning the relation between being and human being is one to which he returns in a number of places. Sometimes he does so, as in the passage from the "Appendix" to "The Origin of the Work of Art" or from the Le Thor Seminar, in ways that make explicit reference back to *Being and Time*, and on a number of occasions he talks about the matter, as he does in the Le Thor Seminar, as a problem concerning "subjectivism," "voluntarism," or "anthropomorphism." Thus, in a brief comment in *Contributions*, for instance, where the concept of being-there is itself rethought, Heidegger writes that "In *Being and Time* Da-sein still stands in the shadow of the 'anthropological,' the 'subjectivistic,' and the 'individualist,' etc."[21] In one of the Nietzsche lectures from 1940, Heidegger also writes of the way in which the lack of understanding with which he claims *Being and Time* was met is based in what he terms "our habituation, entrenched and ineradicable, to the modern mode of thought" according to which "man is thought as subject, and all reflections on him are understood to be anthropology," and yet he also acknowledges that among the reasons that *Being and Time* itself breaks off is that "the attempt and the path it chose confront the danger of unwillingly becoming merely another entrenchment of subjectivity."[22]

On the basis of such comments, as well as the evident shift in Heidegger's thinking away from the analysis of being-there, it is not surprising to find that the turning that occurs after *Being and Time* is indeed often interpreted in terms of a turning away from the supposed subjectivism of the earlier work. One example of such a reading is to be found in William Blattner's work, with which we already have some acquaintance from the discussions in chapter 3. Blattner argues that Heidegger did view *Being and Time* as subjectivist and that he took this as the main failing of the work. But Blattner also argues that the reason Heidegger originally judged such subjectivism to be problematic, and so turned away from the particular account set out in *Being and Time*, was that he recognized what Blattner terms "an argumentative failure" within that account—a failure that consists in the inability successfully to derive ordinary temporality from "originary temporality," that is, from the temporality that is tied to being-there's own ontological constitution.[23] To a large extent, this claim is forced upon Blattner by the fact that he reads *Being and Time* as articulating an ontologically idealist position according to which being is dependent upon human being, and he sees this position as based in what he terms Heidegger's "temporal idealism," the view "the doctrine, roughly, that time depends on the human 'subject,' Dasein."[24] On that basis, subjectivism could not as such be a reason for Heidegger's rejection of the position set out in *Being and Time* since *Being and Time* itself aims to articulate a form of subjectivism, namely, idealism. Consequently, Heidegger's dissatisfaction with what *Being and Time* attempts, at least initially, must be due to something that became apparent in the attempt itself. Blattner acknowledges that Heidegger may later have come to express this dissatisfaction differently, and, indeed, he takes Heidegger's later thought to be characterized by a "mysticism" that is antithetical to subjectivism,[25] but also claims that such later considerations cannot have been what originally turned Heidegger away from the philosophy of being as set out in *Being and Time*.

Although Blattner is not alone in seeing subjectivism as the core problem in *Being and Time*, his account is somewhat unusual in basing that claim on such a detailed working out of the nature of the subjectivism that is supposedly at issue. Moreover, Blattner's account is also significant in its recognition of the exegetical consequence that follows from the claim that *Being and Time* is subjectivist or idealist in character. If one accepts that Heidegger's later thinking is indeed antisubjectivist, then any interpretation of *Being and Time* as intentionally committed to some form of subjectivism ("idealism," "anthropologism," "voluntarism," or whatever) needs to explain why such subjectivism is abandoned, and that means showing that what goes wrong with the project of *Being and Time* is indeed tied up with its supposed subjectivism. In its simplest terms, the point is that if Heidegger was committed to a subjectivist philosophy in 1926, but espoused an antisubjectivist position in 1936, then the shift from the one position to the other cannot be explained simply by pointing to the subjectivist character of that earlier position. Blattner recognizes this, and so attempts to explain the shift in terms of a breakdown that Heidegger recognizes in his own analysis.

I am in agreement with Blattner in his diagnosis of a failure in terms of the argument that *Being and Time* sets out, but I differ in seeing the failure at issue as arising, not out of Heidegger's subjectivist commitments, but rather out of his inadequate articulation of the spatial and topological concepts that are necessarily at issue in the work, concepts that are tied to the original problem of situatedness, and out of his adoption of a particular methodological commitment that tries to combine both mutual and hierarchical modes of dependence, and so brings with it a problematic conception of what it is to unify and to ground. This means, however, that I do not see a commitment to subjectivism in *Being and Time* itself as the reason for Heidegger's dissatisfaction with that work. Indeed, it seems to me mistaken to treat *Being and Time* as "subjectivist." One reason for this arises out of reflection on the relation between being-there and being as that is understood in *Being and Time*. Blattner takes Heidegger's idealism to be expressed, in one form, in the comment in *Being and Time* section 43 in which Heidegger writes that "only as long as Dasein is (that is, only as long as an understanding of being is ontically possible), is 'there' Being ['*gibt es' Sein*]."[26] Blattner notes that Heidegger himself refers to this passage later in the "Letter on 'Humanism'" writing:

But does not *Being and Time* say on p. 212, where the "there is/it gives" comes to language, "Only as long as Dasein is, is there [*gibt es*] being"? To be sure. It means that only as long as the clearing of being propriates does being convey itself to human beings. But the fact that the *Da*, the clearing as the truth of being itself, propriates is the dispensation of being itself. This is the destiny of the clearing. But the sentence does not mean that the Dasein of the human being in the traditional sense of *existentia*, and thought in modern philosophy as the actuality of the *ego cogito*, is that entity through which being is first fashioned. The sentence does not say that being is the product of the human being.[27]

Although Blattner's main discussion of this passage focuses on the first three sentences, and so on Heidegger's shift to talk of the "clearing" of being,[28] Blattner also responds to Heidegger's antisubjectivist or anti-idealist comments in a lengthy note. There Blattner argues that, as a reading of *Being and Time*, Heidegger's gloss on the passage from section 43 "is highly implausible" on the grounds that "*it reverses the conditionality*" of the claim in question. Thus, while *Being and Time* has it that "only as long as Dasein is, is there being," the "Letter on Humanism" claims that "only as long as the clearing of being obtains, does being convey itself to Dasein."[29]

Certainly, a conditional of the form "*x* depends on *y*" expresses a different relation of dependence than does "*y* depends on *x*," but these two dependence relations need not be incompatible. Indeed, they would be so only if the relation being expressed was a relation of *hierarchical*, rather than *mutual*, dependence. Moreover, if we take such a relation of mutual dependence, or equiprimordiality, to be what underpins Heidegger's claim in the passage from *Being and Time* section 43 and is expressed in it (albeit somewhat ambiguously), then the passage from the "Letter on 'Human-ism'" can indeed be seen to clarify what is at issue in the original claim—it aims, in fact, at clarifying something that remains obscure in the idea of the equiprimordial structure that, in *Being and Time*, is the belonging together of being-there and being. To read *Being and Time* as subjectivist or idealist (whether in the specific manner advanced by Blattner or more generally) requires that one read that work as committed to an under-standing of the relation between being-there and being as one in which a hierarchical dependence obtains between being and being-there such that being-there has priority over being. Blattner may argue that the exhibiting of such hierarchical dependence is indeed one of the results of *Being and Time*;[30] I would suggest that, inasmuch as it can be taken to be a result of the analysis of the work, then it is a result that indicates, and is taken by Heidegger to indicate, the problematic character of that analysis. To suppose that being is hierarchically dependent on being-there is to suggest that being is not after all what is primordial here, at least not when it stands in relation to being-there, and this would seem to go against Heidegger's own emphasis on the primacy of the question of being as such (notice that such primacy does not rule out a mutual dependence between being and being-there, in which being would remain primordial, but pri-mordial in a way equal to being-there).

The way in which the relation between being and being-there emerges as a problem here runs through much of the analysis in *Being and Time* in more specific ways. Perhaps most significantly for the discussion of topology, it is what can be seen to underlie the problem that arose, in section 3.3 above, concerning the relation between the existential spa-tiality of being-there and the public spatiality associated with world—what Dreyfus refers to as an "incipient subjectivism" in Heidegger's account of spatiality. More broadly, it underlies the whole question of the relation between world and being-there—a question that can be understood as con-cerning the nature of the unity of being-in-the-world and that already emerges as an issue close to the very beginning of Heidegger's analysis in the question concerning the nature of "being-in." The way in which *Being and Time* approaches the question of being in terms of the question of the being of being-there is a key element in the structure of the work, and one that is well grounded in Heidegger's recognition of the primacy of ques-tionability in what is at issue, and so of the necessary entanglement of being-there with being. Yet the manner in which Heidegger develops the focus on being-there in his analysis also creates problems for that analysis because of the way it threatens to destabilize the proper relation between being-there and being in favor of being-there. This is, moreover, a problem that arises internally to *Being and Time* as such, and it is thus that Heidegger is forced to rethink the very framework within which *Being and Time* operates.

Such an account of what is at issue here seems fully in keeping with what Heidegger himself says quite consistently about *Being and Time* and the problems to which it gives rise. When Heidegger talks about subjectivism, of whatever form, in relation to the work, it is not in terms of the work being itself committed to subjectivism, but rather in terms of the way in which the work makes itself vulnerable to such subjectivism or to being understood in subjectivist terms—the way in which its mode of thinking brings with it, as Heidegger puts it in the Nietzsche lectures quoted above, "the danger of unwillingly becoming merely another entrenchment of subjectivity." Indeed, Heidegger frequently emphasizes the point that *Being and Time* is not subjectivist, but has indeed already left behind "all subjectivity of the human being as subject."[31] Moreover, Heidegger makes the same point about those other forms of subjectivism with which *Being and Time* is often taken to be implicated—"voluntarism," "anthropologism," and "anthropocentrism." Such charges were already being made against *Being and Time* very soon after its publication, and Heidegger takes issue with them at an equally early stage. Thus he writes in "On the Essence of Ground," from 1929, that:

As regards the reproach . . . of an "anthropocentric standpoint" in *Being and Time*, this objection that is now passed all too readily from hand to hand says nothing so long as one omits to think through the problem, the *entire thrust*, and the *goal* of the development of the problem of *Being and Time* and to comprehend how, precisely through the elaboration of the transcendence of Dasein, "the human being" comes into the "centre" in such a way that his nothingness amid beings as a whole can and must become a *problem* in the first place.[32]

Admittedly, comments such as this can also be interpreted so as to confirm a subjectivist element in Heidegger's thinking, yet not only does this mean ignoring the antagonism that Heidegger clearly expresses here, and elsewhere, toward "anthropocentrism," or more generally, "subjectivism," but it also seems to depend on already assuming a notion of subjectivity when that is just what is here in question. Indeed, the way in which *Being and Time* aims to render "human being," and with it subjectivity, as itself a problem is evident, in fact, whenever the issue of subjectivism or idealism arises within the context of *Being and Time* itself. Thus, of idealism, Heidegger writes:

If what the term "idealism" says, amounts to the understanding that Being can never be explained by entities but is already that which is "transcendental" for every entity, then "idealism" affords the only correct possibility for a philosophical problematic. If so, Aristotle was no less an idealist than Kant. But if "idealism" signifies tracing back every entity to a subject or consciousness whose sole distinguishing features are that it remains indefinite in its being and is best characterized negatively as "un-Thing-like," then this idealism is no less naïve in its method than the most grossly militant realism.[33]

Moreover, when later Heidegger inveighs against subjectivism and its variants, it is not on the basis of some vague "mystical" commitment at which he arrived after *Being and Time*,[34] but instead derives from the "topologism," itself a form of "nonsubjectivism"[35] that is already embedded in his thinking as early as 1919—and that incorporates the idea of a factical involvement of ourselves "in" the world that is prior to both subjectivity and objectivity. The problem is how to articulate this insight. What Heidegger comes to realize in the period after 1926 is that the particular mode of articulation that he adopts in *Being and Time* ends up threatening to lead him back into the very subjectivism (or we may equally say, "objectivism," since for Heidegger the one is not strictly thinkable without the other[36]) that his original starting point already showed to be inadequate.

Blattner's account of the way subjectivism supposedly arises as a problem in *Being and Time* focuses on the specific failure of the attempt to establish the ecstatic temporality of being-there as the ground for temporality as such. As Blattner acknowledges, however, nowhere does Heidegger himself indicate that this failure is the basis for his turning away from the approach set out in *Being and Time*. Indeed, while Heidegger later admits the mistaken character of his attempt to derive existential spatiality from temporality, he does not appear to give any explicit recognition to the particular "argumentative failure" identified by Blattner. The reason for this is simple: it is not the failure of an argument necessary to establish an idealist conclusion that leads Heidegger to abandon *Being and Time* as originally conceived, but rather a recognition of the inability of *Being and Time* adequately to provide an articulation of the topological structure that is its central concern—a structure that is neither "subjective" nor "objective" in any of the usual senses of those terms. In this respect, the focus for much of Heidegger's rethinking in the years immediately after *Being and Time* (certainly in the period until "The Essence of Truth" in 1930) is the idea of "transcendence" (and with it the idea of the "transcendental") that appears in the passages from "The Essence of Ground" and *Being and Time* quoted just above. In the engagement with this concept, Heidegger can be seen both to be taking up the problem of "subjectivism," or better, the "distressing difficulty" of the relation between being and human being, as well as the problem of the unity of being-in the-world as such, along with the methodological problem concerning dependence and derivation that I identified in chapter 3 as an underlying issue in the structure of *Being and Time* as a whole. In this latter respect, the problem of transcendence is identical with the question of "ground" as that question underlies the methodological problem of "dependence" as such. All of these problems, of course, are problems that we have seen to arise in a particularly pressing way in relation to the analysis of spatiality, and one of the reasons for this is that the problem of spatiality in *Being and Time* is, as we have seen in the discussion above, a critical point of focus for the problem of world and for the question of the unity of being-in-the-world.[37]

The concept of transcendence appears at a number of points in *Being and Time*, usually in conjunction with the concept of world, and although its significance may not be entirely clear from the way it is presented in that work as such, in "On the Essence of Ground" in 1929, Heidegger tells us that "what has been published so far of the investigations on 'Being and Time' has no other task than that of a concrete projection unveiling 'transcendence' (cf. secs. 12–83; especially sec. 69)."[38] Nevertheless, the concept of transcendence is not itself given any straightforward or explicit elucidation within *Being and Time*, and Heidegger seems to assume it to be already well understood, presumably on the basis of its existing usage within the philosophical tradition. Certainly the notion of transcendence clearly connects up with the idea, taken from medieval thought, of being as a "*transcendens*"—that is, as that which goes beyond any category or class and whose unity is not itself that of any such class, but is "analogical."[39] Transcendence thus characterizes being itself, such that "Being and the structure of Being lie beyond every entity and every possible character which an entity may possess. *Being is the transcendens pure and simple.*"[40] Moreover, transcendence also belongs to being-there just insofar as being-there is being-in-the-world.[41]

The closest Heidegger does come to an explicit elucidation of "transcendence" in *Being and Time* itself would seem to be in his discussion of "The Problem of the Transcendence of the World" in section 69, in chapter 4 of division 2 (the section he refers to in the passage from "On the Essence of Ground" quoted above). There he writes that:

Circumspective concern includes the understanding of a totality of involvements, and this understanding is based upon a prior understanding of the relationships of

the "in order-to," the "toward-which," and the "for-the-sake-of." The interconnection of these relationships has been exhibited . . . as significance. Their unity makes
up what we call the "world." The question arises of how anything like the world in
its unity with Dasein is ontologically possible. In what way must the world be, if
Dasein is to be able to exist as Being-in-the-World? . . . The significance relations
which determine the structure of the world are not a network of forms which a
worldless subject has laid over some kind of material. What is rather the case is that
factical Dasein, understanding itself and its world ecstatically in the unity of the
"there," comes back from these horizons to the entities encountered within them.
Coming back to these entities understandingly is the existential meaning of letting
them be encountered by making them present; that is why we call them entities
"within-the-world." The world is, as it were, already "further outside" than any
"Object" can ever be. The problem of transcendence cannot be brought round to
the question of how a subject comes out to an Object, where the aggregate of Objects
is identified with the idea of the world. Rather we must ask: what makes it ontologically possible for entities to be encountered within-in-the-world and Objectified
as so encountered? This can be answered by recourse to the transcendence of the
world—a transcendence with an ecstatic-horizonal foundation.[42]

The problem of transcendence concerns the unity of being-there and the
world. Transcendence, and the unity of being-in-the-world, is not to be
construed, however, in terms of a subject reaching out to an object that
stands apart from it, as if transcendence were essentially a form of self-
transcendence performed by the subject. Instead transcendence is identical with the opening up of the world, and so with the happening of
disclosedness in the "there," which is itself "ecstatic-horizonal" in character. Transcendence thus belongs to both being-there and to world, since it
names their unity (in "On the Essence of Ground," Heidegger claims, somewhat problematically as it turns out, that "world co-constitutes the unitary
structure of transcendence"[43]), and transcendence belongs, of course, to
being as well. One can already see, even in the dense, and somewhat
opaque, explication that Heidegger offers here, the way in which the
"problem" of transcendence encompasses the problem of subjectivity, and
so of the relation of being and human being. Moreover, the way in which
the idea of transcendence also refers back to a set of Aristotelian and
medieval ideas concerning unity and analogy is indicative of transcendence as connecting up with a certain conceptual framework, and so with
a set of background assumptions, that is determinative of the nature of
Heidegger's inquiry. Indeed, not only does the idea of transcendence refer
us directly to the problem of the unity of being-in-the-world (in much the
same way as the medieval idea of the "*transcendens*" refers us to the cate-
gorical unity of entities), but it also points toward a way of explicating the

structure of the unity that is at stake here in terms of the unifying of an otherwise differentiated structure through something like the structure of analogy itself—in this respect the idea of transcendence points us in the direction of Heidegger's appropriation, not only of Aristotle, but also of Kant and the Kantian idea of the transcendental.

The way in which transcendence figures in *Being and Time* without itself being a focus of explicit elucidation or interrogation changes quite dramatically in the works that follow in the late 1920s. Transcendence, along with the concept of world, is directly thematized in a number of works including "On the Essence of Ground" (written in 1928), *The Metaphysical Foundations of Logic* (lectures delivered in the summer semester, 1928), *The Fundamental Concepts of Metaphysics* (lectures delivered in the winter semester, 1929–1930), and in the *Kantbuch* (*Kant and the Problem of Metaphysics*) from 1929. In "On the Essence of Ground," Heidegger connects the idea of transcendence directly with the notion of subjectivity:

[Transcendence] belongs to human Dasein as the fundamental constitution of this being. . . . If one chooses the title of "subject" for that being that we ourselves in each case are and that we understand as "Dasein," then we may say that transcendence designates the essence of the subject, that it is the fundamental structure of subjectivity.[44]

Yet even in making this connection, it is quite clear that the concept of subjectivity is not to be merely assumed, but is itself part of what is brought into question. Thus Heidegger also writes that:

World belongs to a *relational* structure distinctive of Dasein as such, a structure that we called being-in-the-world. . . . How then is Dasein's relation to world to be determined? Since world is not a being, and supposedly belongs to Dasein, this relation is evidently not to be thought as a relation between Dasein as one being and world as another. Yet if this is the case, does not world then get taken into Dasein (the subject) and declared as something purely "subjective"? Yet the task is to gain, through an illumination of transcendence, one possibility for determining what is meant by "subject" and "subjective." In the end, the concept of world must be conceived in such a way that world is indeed subjective, i.e., belongs to Dasein, but precisely on this account does not fall, as a being, into the inner sphere of a "subjective" subject. For the same reason, however, world is not merely objective either, if "objective" means: belonging among beings as objects.[45]

Elsewhere in the same essay Heidegger provides a more direct characterization of transcendence than he offered anywhere in *Being and Time*. "Transcendence," he says, "means surpassing [*Übersteig*]," and he goes on:

Transcendence in the terminological sense to be clarified and demonstrated means something that properly pertains to *human Dasein* . . . it belongs to human Dasein as the *fundamental constitution of this being, one that occurs prior to all comportment.* . . . If one chooses the title of "subject" for that being that we ourselves in each case are and that we understand as "Dasein," then we may say that transcendence designates the essence of the subject, that it is the fundamental structure of subjectivity. . . . We name *world* that *toward which* Dasein as such transcends, and shall now determine transcendence as *being-in-the-world.*[46]

A similar conception is evident in *The Metaphysical Foundations of Logic* in a passage that echoes some of the ideas that appeared in the discussion of the problem of transcendence in *Being and Time*, although here too Heidegger's approach is somewhat clearer and more direct:

transcendence means the surpassing, the going beyond. . . . Transcendence is . . . the primordial constitution of the *subjectivity* of a subject. . . . To be a subject means to transcend. . . . Transcendence does not mean crossing a barrier that has fenced off the subject in an inner space. But what gets crossed over is the being itself that can become manifest to the subject on the very basis of the subject's transcendence. . . . Therefore, what Dasein surpasses in its transcendence is not a gap or barrier "between" itself and objects. But beings, among which Dasein factically is, get surpassed by Dasein . . . beings get surpassed and can subsequently become objects. . . . That "toward which" the subject, as subject, transcends is not an object, not at all this or that being. . . . That toward which the subject transcends is what we call world . . . because this primordial being of Dasein, as surpassing, crosses over to a world, we characterize the basic phenomenon of Dasein's transcendence with the expression being-in-the-world.[47]

The way in which Heidegger characterizes transcendence in these passages makes clear the close connection of the idea of transcendence with the idea of world—world is that toward which transcendence is directed (although world is not itself thereby transcended) as a "surpassing" of entities—as well as with the idea of the subject. Subjectivity is essentially transcendence, and transcendence is being-in-the-world.

As Heidegger employs the term, "transcendence" is also connected, as I indicated briefly above, with the Kantian idea of the transcendental. Indeed, Heidegger says of the "transcendental" that "this term names all that belongs to transcendence and bears its intrinsic possibility thanks to such transcendence."[48] Yet Heidegger's conjoining of the idea of "transcendence" with that of the "transcendental" also creates some complications here, as he himself acknowledges. These complications arise from the fact that transcendence has two different senses, the distinction between

which is essential in relation to the transcendental, especially in connection with the appearance of that term in Kant (and it is significant, perhaps,
that Heidegger only feels the need to inquire into these senses and to distinguish them, in the period after *Being and Time*, when transcendence
starts to become a problematic concept in his thinking). The first sense is
that outlined above—it refers to the way in which being-there transcends
beings in the direction of world (or, as Heidegger also puts it in the passage
I quote below, transcends objects in the direction of their objectness).[49]
The second is the sense involved in the idea of transcendence as that which
goes beyond, not objects, but beyond the world as such. This latter sense
of transcendence is involved in all those attempts that look to ground
being or the world in something that is transcendent of them. That which
is designated as transcendent in this second sense may also be said to be
itself transcendental inasmuch as that which transcends in this way is itself
traditionally taken to ground that which it transcends, in just the way that,
for example, the supersensible (God, the Ideas, or whatever) may be said
to ground, as well as to transcend, the sensible. There is thus a very close
relation between the concept of transcendence and the idea of ground, and
this is evident in Heidegger's discussion: "The question concerning the
essence of ground becomes the *problem of transcendence*."[50]

Heidegger's understanding of the question of ground here is itself determined, however, by his understanding of transcendence in the first rather
than the second of the two senses distinguished, and this is indicative of
the way in which Heidegger's thinking can be understood as a continuation of Kant's own radical reinterpretation of the notion of the transcendental to designate a mode of grounding in which the ground is not itself
"transcendent" of that which it grounds, although it is nevertheless the
condition of possibility for that which is grounded. Of course, this Kantian
understanding of the transcendental leads Kant himself to present his
notion of the "transcendental" as standing in clear opposition to the idea
of transcendence in the second of the two senses distinguished above.
Thus, as Heidegger notes in *The Principle of Reason*, "Kant names 'transcendent' that which lies beyond the limits of human experience, not
insofar as it surpasses objects in the direction of their objectness; rather
insofar as it surpasses objects along with their objectness—and this without
sufficient warrant, namely, without the possibility of being founded,"[51] and
in "On the Essence of Ground," Heidegger explicitly directs attention to
the way in which Kant uses the transcendental in opposition to the notion
of transcendence, telling us that "For Kant the transcendental has to do

with the 'possibility' of (that which makes possible) that knowledge which *does not illegitimately* 'soar beyond' our experience, i.e., is not 'transcendent,' but is experience itself."[52]

Although Heidegger acknowledges the opposition between the terms "transcendence" and "transcendental" in Kant, he also tends to treat the problem of "transcendence" as he understands it as underlying the Kantian inquiry. As a consequence, Kant's investigation of the ground and limit of experience (an investigation into that which both *grounds* the structure of experience and also exhibits as *ungrounded* the attempt to go beyond experience) is understood essentially an inquiry into the structure of transcendence.[53] In the context of Heidegger's thought, the concepts of both transcendence and the transcendental relate primarily to just such a "surpassing." The attempt to elucidate the structure of transcendence, which is also the essential structure of subjectivity, is the uncovering of the transcendental. In that elucidation, the ground of transcendence is exhibited, but so too is the ground of subjectivity. Thus Heidegger can talk of transcendence as grounded in the essential structure of being-there, while being-there is itself grounded in the structure of transcendence—the two amount to one and the same. Yet the elucidation of transcendence is also essentially a matter of the elucidation of the phenomenon of world, since, as Heidegger says, "[t]o transcendence there belongs world as that toward which surpassing occurs,"[54] and, indeed, it is characteristic of Heidegger's discussion of transcendence, whether in *Being and Time* or elsewhere, that those discussions also center on the problem of world. Thus, in "On the Essence of Ground," Heidegger tells us that what is attempted is "an interpretation of the *phenomenon of world*, which is to serve the illumination of transcendence as such."[55]

Given this understanding of transcendence, it is easy to see how it maps back onto the structure of *Being and Time*—although it also maps onto that structure in a way that connects up with virtually all of the key concepts in the work. Transcendence names the "surpassing" of entities by being-there in the direction of world—it is just that movement that Heidegger describes in terms of the way in which being-there "comes back" from the ecstatic horizon that is given in its understanding of itself and its world to the entities encountered within those horizons and so lets those entities be encountered "by making them present." In this respect, transcendence can also be said, within *Being and Time*, to be another name for the phenomenon of "disclosedness" that is the focus of section 44 ("Dasein, Disclosedness and Truth"). The transcendental names the proper structure of transcendence, that which belongs to it, and so to being-there, and can thus be said to name that which makes such transcendence possible. In *Being and Time*, ecstatic temporality is the ground of transcendence—that which transcendence properly *is*. Transcendence itself clearly stands in a close relation to the notion of "project," and so to the ideas of "meaning" and "understanding." The "surpassing in the direction of world" that is transcendence can be taken as identical with being-there's projective understanding by which the world is opened up as horizonal, and so as that "within which" entities appear—that "projection" of world is also the opening up of the context of significance or meaning that allows entities to show up as meaningful. In the late seminar on "On Time and Being," Heidegger characterizes the "transcendental" in terms that bring many of these notions together—as the summary of the seminar has it:

> *Being and Time* is the attempt to interpret Being in terms of the transcendental horizon of time. What does "transcendental" mean here? It does not mean the objectivity of an object of experience as constituted in consciousness, but rather the realm of projection for the determination of Being, that is, presencing as such, caught sight of from the opening up of human being (*Da-Sein*).[56]

The way Heidegger characterizes the transcendental in this late seminar, however, puts the emphasis on a reading of the transcendental, as well as on the notion of projection, that has a slightly different emphasis from that which is apparent in *Being and Time*, or in the works of the late 1920s. In the later characterization, the emphasis is on "the realm of projection for the determination of being . . . caught sight of from the opening up of human being" and this places the realm of projection at the center with human being as that from which that projection is now glimpsed. The realm of projection is not itself dependent upon human being in any direct way, even though human being may be implicated in it (as it must be if it is to be that from which the realm of projection is glimpsed). In the earlier work, however, the structure of transcendence appears with a slightly different emphasis that is also indicative of a problematic tendency or ambiguity in Heidegger's analysis—the later passage can be viewed, in fact, as an attempt to dispel that ambiguity in a manner very similar to that which is at issue in the passage from the "Letter on 'Humanism'" discussed in relation to Blattner above.

Understood as a surpassing by being-there in the direction of world, transcendence is already viewed as comprising two elements, being-there and world (although these are not distinct *entities*) and as belonging to both. The problem of transcendence is the belonging together of those elements—it concerns their proper unity. Transcendence is not only that which names the unity of being-there and world, however, but also refers to the essential ground of being-there. This need not in itself present a problem since what it amounts to is just the claim that being-there cannot be understood as something apart from world—being-there *is* being-in-the-world—and so long as this is kept in view, there is always the possibility of being able to give an account of the "ground" that is at issue here that remains oriented to the task of exhibiting a unity that is more primordial than any "subjectivity" or, indeed, any form of "objectness" (and so of giving an account that remains focused on the "realm of projection" as such). Yet there will nevertheless be a tendency, simply because of the way transcendence is configured as a "relation" between being-there and world, to look to ground that relation in one or another of the two poles of that relation, and since transcendence is explicitly characterized as a "surpassing" *by* being-there *in the direction of* world, it seems almost inevitable that it will lead to a conception of the grounding to be accomplished here as one that looks to find the ground of transcendence in being-there.

The idea of transcendence brings with it a tendency to understand the grounding of transcendence as something to be accomplished by looking to one of the elements within the structure of transcendence—that is, by looking to being-there—and this tendency parallels the way in which Heidegger's own attempt to ground the unity of being-in-the-world proceeds, in *Being and Time*, in a way that looks to unify, and so to "ground", the elements that are together constitutive of being-in-the-world by exhibiting their hierarchical dependence on that which is more primordial within that unity. Indeed, in general, Heidegger's manner of proceeding in *Being and Time* is "transcendental," which means that it looks to "ground" by exhibiting certain necessary "conditions of possibility"—the meaningfulness of entities is thus grounded in, and thereby shown to be possible on the basis of, the original projection of meaning in temporalized understanding. Inasmuch as the transcendental is thereby understood as a mode of grounding that grounds the unity of one structure in the more primordial unity of another, so the transcendental appears to exemplify a mode of grounding that is identical to that to which the structure of transcendence itself tends—and this is no surprise, of course, given the way in which, at least in Heidegger's account, transcendence and the transcendental are tied together. Indeed, Heidegger's explicit focus on the concept of transcendence in the period from 1928–1930 is carried out with almost constant reference to Kant's own thinking[57]—not surprisingly, Heidegger's move away from the concept of transcendence as a foundational element

in his thinking is thus also accompanied by a move away from the engagement with Kant. Heidegger later refers to this engagement with Kant as
constituting a refuge rather than "a permanent dwelling place" (the latter
phrase itself referring us back to Kant's own description of Humean skepticism). As Heidegger wrote in the preface to the republished edition of the
Kantbuch: "With *Being and Time* alone—: soon / clear that we did not enter
into / the real question. . . . A refuge—underway and / not new discov-
eries in Kant Philology."[58] Significantly, Heidegger's own reading of Kant
in the *Kantbuch* itself gives a central place to the concept of transcendence,
while it also aims to show how Kant recoiled from the grounding of such
transcendence in the transcendental imagination and so in the unitary
structure of time.[59]

Understanding the way in which Heidegger treats the transcendental as
configured in terms of the notion of transcendence (the transcendental is
that which concerns the structure or ground for transcendence) itself
enables us to see how the transcendental takes on the particular character
it does in *Being and Time* since, as I indicated briefly in chapter 3, transcendence may itself tend toward a conception of the grounding relation
in terms of hierarchical dependence.[60] If transcendence concerns the unity
of being-there and world, and that unity is seen to be grounded in the
unity of being-there (analogously to the way in which the unity of the
structures that make up being-there are themselves grounded in originary
temporality), then exhibiting the proper unity of being-there and world
can be taken to depend upon showing how that unity is necessarily and
uniquely determined by the unity of being-there as such, and so by the
unity of being-there in its essence, that is, as ecstatic temporality. If there
were no such relation of unique and necessary dependence between being-
there and world, then given that transcendence already posits these two,
albeit somewhat obscurely (since they do not relate as separate "beings"),
as standing apart from one another—something that seems to be implied
by the very idea of transcendence as a *surpassing*—the unity at issue would
be open to being understood as an arbitrary and accidental one and so as
a unity that need not even be said properly to belong to being-there and
world as such. The "problem" of transcendence is thus to show how it is
that being-there and world can be unified when they are already posited
as distinct, and this leads to the positing of a more primordial unity that
can only belong to being-there and whose "projection" is the opening up
of world.[61]

As we have already seen throughout much of the previous discussion,
Heidegger's thinking is essentially oriented to the problem of understanding

things as gathered into a certain sort of fundamental "relatedness" by means of which they are also "disclosed." Thus Heidegger's inquiry into being is always centrally concerned with the articulation of an essential *unity* that belongs to being or, as we shall see shortly, to the "truth" of being—it is just this unity that is itself at issue in the question of "ground." One of the underlying themes in Heidegger's work is the question as to how such unity is to be articulated and understood, and the "turning" that characterizes Heidegger's work as a whole, as well as being specific to the period after *Being and Time*, can be seen as a return to, and rethinking of, just this question of unity. This is so inasmuch as the turning is itself a certain constant "being-gathered" back into the original and originary unity of the truth of being, as well as in the way in which the idea of unity itself requires a constant rethinking and rearticulation. The notion of transcendence—of which Heidegger says in "On the Essence of Ground" that it "comprises an *exceptional domain* for the elaboration of all questions that concern beings as such, i.e., in their being"[62]—constitutes one form of such a rethinking and rearticulation, and yet it also turns out not to think the unity at issue here in a sufficiently fundamental manner. In *Contributions* Heidegger says that:

Even when "transcendence" is grasped differently than up to now, namely as *sur-passing* and not as the *super-sensible* as a being, even then this determination all too easily dissembles what is ownmost to Dasein. For, even in this way, transcendence still presupposes an *under and this-side* [*Unten und Diesseits*] and is in danger of still being misinterpreted after all as the action of an "I" and subject.[63]

Why is it a problem to presuppose "an under and this-side" as belonging to "what is ownmost to Dasein" or to take what is ownmost as "the action of an 'I' and a subject"? The reason is that what belongs to "what is ownmost" is that unity into which being-there is first gathered, and this unity is precisely that which comes prior to any "side," to any "action," to any "subject." Even when we try to keep to this conception of prior unity in our thinking of transcendence, as Heidegger surely does in *Being and Time*, still the very structure of the concept of transcendence itself will pull us toward a mode of thinking that threatens to obscure and cover over the original unity that is at issue here. The way in which this unity is made problematic when understood from the perspective of transcendence also seems to be something to which Heidegger draws attention in one of the marginal comments to the section on transcendence in "On the Essence of Ground." To a passage in which Heidegger discusses the occurrence that is the entry of beings into world and which is identical with "the existing of Dasein, which as existing transcends," Heidegger adds "But Dasein and beyng itself? Not yet thought, not until *Being and Time*, Part II. Da-sein belongs to beyng itself as the simple onefold of beings and being; the essence of the 'occurrence'—temporalizing of Temporality [*Temporalität*] as a preliminary name for the truth of beyng."[64]

It is the articulation of this "simple onefold of beings and being" that is the focus for much of Heidegger's later thinking, in which it is no longer a matter of understanding being-there's transcendence as such, but rather of grasping the way being-there already belongs to the truth of being. Indeed, in the later thinking, the emphasis on the simple onefold (which is sometimes also presented as a simple, a unitary, "twofold"[65]) of the happening of the truth of being goes so far as even to leave behind, in a certain fashion, the ontological difference between being and entities that figures so often in the writings of the 1930s.[66] The way in which this thinking focuses directly on the articulation of unity—although a unity that is itself always differentiated—is indicative of the way in which the idea of ground is itself clarified, and to some extent, transfigured, in the course of Heidegger's thinking. The idea of ground is always, in Heidegger, closely tied to the idea of unity—to ground is to exhibit the unity of that which is grounded—the unity at issue here is also a unity that is always differentiated. The question of ground is, one might say, the question of the essential unity of unity and of difference. Heidegger is sometimes led to take up this question of ground, particularly when it is understood in relation to the notions of transcendence and the transcendental, in ways that also seem to compromise the nature of the unity at issue here (whether through the implicit reliance on a notion of hierarchical dependence, or through a tendency toward subjectivism or idealism). Still, the question of ground as such is never relinquished, for the question of ground is the question of being. As Heidegger tells us in 1957: "Being and ground/reason belong together. Ground/reason receives its essence from its belonging together with being qua being. Put in the reverse, being reigns qua being from out of the essence of ground/reason."[67] As ground, being is not itself in need of ground, and so is neither grounded nor groundless.[68] It is, says Heidegger, like the rose of which Angelus Silesius says, it is "without why; it blooms because it blooms/It cares not for itself; asks not if it's seen."[69] This understanding of the intimacy of the relation between being and ground, as well as the understanding of ground that is implicated here, is also indicative of the intimate relation between being, ground, and place. To speak of ground is to speak of that on which one stands, that which preserves and sustains, which shelters and protects, and which does so in no generalized or abstract fashion, but in terms of my very being *in this place*—ground and the "there" are, as the analysis of *Being and Time* itself might be taken to show, one and the same. Moreover, the "there," the place, requires no such grounding of its own since it is ground, "placedness," as such.

The account that I have presented here concerning the problematic character of *Being and Time*, and the work immediately following it, as it is configured in relation to transcendence and the transcendental, is not intended to show that there is some simple "error" which vitiates the work, but rather to set out the way in which the concept of transcendence sets up an "instability" that is internal to the work itself and that makes the work vulnerable to certain sorts of misunderstandings and misconstruals of the issues at stake. This is, indeed, how Heidegger himself seems to present matters in his own comments on the earlier work—it is not that *Being and Time* represents a mistaken entry into the question of being, but that the manner in which it enters into that question predisposes it toward misunderstanding. Indeed, it is characteristic of the way in which later Heidegger views *Being and Time* that he consistently emphasizes the importance of the work as a necessary stage in thinking—it may be a *"Holzweg,"*[70] yet as he writes in the preface to the seventh edition (1953), "the road it has taken remains even today a necessary one, if our Dasein is to be stirred by the question of Being."[71] Some paths, it seems, may lead nowhere in particular (which is what a *"Holzweg"* does), but it may still be necessary to follow them. The mistake would be to remain stuck on such a path, and in this respect, it is very clear that the path of *Being and Time*, while necessary, remains only a stage on the way. The idea of transcendence (along with the associated notions of "meaning" and "projection") does indeed take up, and provide an articulation of, a central element in the phenomenon with which Heidegger is concerned, namely, the way in which situatedness always opens out into "world"—a phenomenon that is also at issue in the ontological difference that "obtains" between being and entities. Moreover, the attempt to understand what is at issue in the idea of such transcendence, to understand the proper unity of the "there," of "world," and so of "being," is by no means something to be accomplished easily, nor is the direction in which to proceed in pursuit of such an understanding already laid out in advance.

Although the account set out in *Being and Time* presents certain undeniable problems, it is nevertheless always possible to interpret that account in ways that reveal the essential concerns that it is designed to address, as well as the way in which, even if imperfectly and at times obscurely, it nevertheless continues to point toward the "same" unity of meaning, truth, and place that is already indicated in the hermeneutics of facticity in the early 1920s and that is rearticulated through the idea of the poetic saying of the Event in the later 1930s. In this respect, the underlying consistency of Heidegger's thinking is not undermined by the shifts in his thinking, nor by the uncertainties that thinking often displays, or even by the changes in vocabulary and style. Its underlying consistency resides in its engagement with the subject matter that calls it forth—with what I have argued can be understood as the attempt to "say" the place of thinking, which is also the place of the opening up of world, the place of the truth of being. Moreover, it is not that Heidegger first attempts this through a saying that grounds that place in the human, or in the subject, and then later attempts to ground it in the "Event." The entanglement of the human in the place at issue here is already part of the matter that demands to be thought—in this respect, "subjectivity" names a problem that never disappears from Heidegger's thought: the way in which human being is "claimed" by being—and the task is to find a mode of articulation that acknowledges that entanglement and yet does not mislead as to its nature. The period in Heidegger's thought from 1929–1930 onward marks the opening up of the attempt to achieve just such a mode of articulation—a mode of articulation that not only shifts away from the focus on transcendence, but which also moves away from talk of meaning to talk of the truth of being, and which also aims to re-think the idea of being-there as such.[72]

4.3   Being and Being-There

In the very late lectures on the principle of "reason" (*Grund*) from 1957—lectures that take up the same problem of reason or "ground" that is also the focus for the 1929 lecture "On the Essence of Ground"—Heidegger summarizes the manner of the human entanglement with being as follows:

We are the ones bestowed by and with the clearing and lighting of being in the *Geschick* of being. . . . But we do not just stand around in this clearing and lighting without being addressed [*unangesprochen*]; rather we stand in it as those who are claimed [*Anspruch*] by the being of beings. As the ones standing in the clearing and lighting of being we are the ones bestowed, the ones ushered into the time play-space. This means we are the ones engaged in and for this play-space, engaged in building on and giving shape to the clearing and lighting of being—in the broadest and multiple sense, in preserving it.[73]

Heidegger then immediately goes on to add that:

In the still cruder and more awkward language of the treatise *Being and Time* (1927) this means that the basic trait of Dasein, which is human being, is determined by the understanding of being. Here understanding of being never means that humans as subjects possess a subjective representation of being and that being is a mere representation. . . . Understanding of being means that according to their essential nature humans stand [*steht*] in the openness of the projection of being and suffer [*aussteht*] this understanding [*Verstehen*] so understood. When understanding of being is experienced and thought of in this way, the representation of humans as subjects is, to speak in line with Hegel, put aside. According to their essential nature, humans are thinking beings only insofar as they stand in a clearing and lighting of being.[74]

The way in which the question of being implicates human being is not a matter to be avoided. Not only can we not understand human being independently of the way human being is "addressed" or "claimed" by being, but being itself requires human being—human being is that which is engaged in the "building on and giving shape to," in "preserving," the clearing and lighting of being. This does not mean, however, that human being "produces" being or that being is "dependent" on human being in the way that implies the sort of ontological dependence associated with idealism or subjectivism. Indeed, as I indicated in the discussion above, the mere fact that a relation of dependence obtains between two terms does not imply that the one term can therefore be understood as ontologically more fundamental or more basic than the other: the dependence at issue may be one of "equiprimordiality"—a relation that is mutual not hierarchical.

Moreover, the precise nature of the dependence of being on human being is in terms of the manner of its "projection"—the "appearing," "disclosedness," or "presencing" of being is always in terms that relate to human being; yet the "fact" of that projection, which includes the projection of human being itself—the fact that "*there is*" [*es gibt*] being—is not itself anything that is, as such, dependent on the human. Julian Young puts this point by saying that:

What is subjective, human-being-dependent, therefore is not what our horizon of disclosure discloses . . . but rather the fact that *that particular feature rather than some other* . . . is disclosed. What is subjective . . . is not *what* we experience as characterizing reality but rather the *selection* we make from the infinite richness of attributes possessed by reality itself.[75]

Of course, talk of "selection" here may make it sound as if the nature of the "projection" or "disclosure" at issue is something we could choose, but for such choice to be possible we would already have to stand in some sense apart from that disclosure, whereas we are ourselves part of that very disclosure as such—what is determined is the manner of projection that encompasses the disclosure of our own being (as understanding always brings with it a particular mode of *self*-understanding). We might say, in fact, that the disclosure or disclosure of being is always a disclosure that determines the disclosure of being as a whole, and so is always a disclosure that occurs in relation to our being, not only inasmuch as we are already encompassed by being, but also inasmuch as it must be a disclosure into which we are able to enter as witnesses to and preservers of such disclosure. Furthermore, that we are indeed "preservers" here is indicative of the way the disclosure as such is not itself dependent on any act that we may perform, but as disclosure happens in a way beyond any "choice" or "action" on our part. The difficulty with *Being and Time*, and with the analysis of disclosure in terms of "transcendence," is that it encourages a tendency to overlook this latter aspect of the disclosure that is at issue here—it tends to place the emphasis on the manner of disclosure or projection (on what we might characterize in terms of "intelligibility"), and so on the way that is determined by being-there, rather than on the fact of disclosure as such. As we shall see in the discussion below, the turning can be construed as a turn toward just this aspect of disclosure—a turning toward that which itself remains "concealed" even in that primordial disclosure that is the disclosure of being.

In taking up the idea of disclosure, and with it the ideas of clearing and lighting that have begun to appear in the passages from Heidegger quoted above, in a more direct fashion, the thinking of being takes on a much more explicitly topological character. Disclosure always involves the opening up of a cleared "space" within which specific beings are able to come forth as what they are—a "space" that allows beings to be "freed up" so as to be the beings that they are and that also allows entrance to those to whom such beings are disclosed. Disclosure thus presupposes a certain cleared, opened *place*—a place that gives space to beings—and while that place must be configured in ways appropriate to such disclosure ("tuned" to it), the place is not thereby determined as such either by the beings disclosed or by those who witness such disclosure. In the same way, when I encounter another person, the possibility of such encounter depends on our coming into a common "proximity," into a common "place" in which we are both situated and within which we appear in ways that enable us to recognize one another. Although the place of the encounter is itself partly configured by the encounter, it is nevertheless within that common place that the encounter occurs and on the basis of which it "takes place"; and while the fact that we appear to one another in ways that enable our mutual recognition, and so appear in ways partly determined by the conditions such recognition requires, it is nevertheless we ourselves whom we each recognize and who participate in that recognition, not any "mere appearance." Of course, if we focus on such an encounter in terms that emphasize our own role in determining the nature of the encounter—on the way the encounter, and the place in which it occurs, is determined by what we bring to that encounter—then it may seem as if it is we who play the decisive role here. But this is already to shift the focus away from the place in which the encounter occurs and the mutuality of the encounter in that place; it is to focus on the encounter as something brought about, rather than something that happens; it is to underestimate the complexity of the interconnections that obtain in that encounter. The shift that occurs in Heidegger's thinking after *Being and Time* is a shift that aims at moving away from such a tendency, not because *Being and Time* is already given over to such a way of thinking, but because its manner of presenting matters does not do enough to rule it out.

Although he does not draw on quite the same set of ideas, Gadamer characterizes the shift in Heidegger's thinking from *Being and Time* to the later thought in terms that are nevertheless explicitly topological. Drawing attention to a marginal note in *Being and Time* in which Heidegger talks of "the place of the understanding of Being" [*Stätte des Seinsverständnisses*], Gadamer comments that with this expression:

> Heidegger wants to mediate between the older point of departure from Dasein (in which its being is at stake) and the new movement of thought of the "there" [*Da*] in which *das Sein* or Being forms a clearing. In the word place [*Stätte*] this latter emphasis comes to the fore: it is the scene of an event and not primarily the site of an activity by Dasein.[76]

I would take issue with this characterization on only two grounds (and they constitute differences in emphasis more than anything else): first, by insisting that the being of being-there, or at least, of human being, always remains at stake in the question of being—in the later thinking this is clearest in terms of the way in which human being is gathered into the place of the truth of being through their essential being as beings that can die, that is, as mortals (*die Sterblichen*); second, by emphasizing that this shift is *not* a shift in which place (itself better understood in terms of the German "*Ort*," which is indeed the term Heidegger himself comes to use, rather than *Stätte*) only first comes to appearance with this "new movement of thought." As I have argued at some length in the discussion above, being-there already implicates the idea of place—being-there is itself a "topos." The way Heidegger puts this in the passage that I quoted at the head of this chapter is such that "'Dasein' names that which is first of all to be experienced, and subsequently thought accordingly, as a place."[77] Yet in a marginal comment added to his copy of the essay, Heidegger writes "Inadequately said: the locality dwelt in by mortals, the mortal region of the locality." The point is not that being-there is not to be understood in terms of place, but, rather, that the understanding of being-there as "place" that was already present in *Being and Time* contained an ambiguity that allowed being-there to be taken as identical with the place that is really at issue here, as identical with the "place of the truth of being." Heidegger's marginal comment thus points to the same issue that lies at the heart of the problematic that has been the focus for the discussion immediately above: the "relation" *between* being-there *and* being (what might also be called the problem of the "between" or of the "and"). The shift from "the early point of departure" and "the new movement of thought" is thus, as Gadamer's own way of putting this may also be taken to suggest, a shift in the understanding of the place that is already at issue here—in my own terms, place is to be understood, not as a "site" projected by being-there, but as the "taking place" of place as such, a "taking place" into which being-there is itself gathered.

The shift away from transcendence as a founding notion in Heidegger's thinking and toward the more explicit "topology" which Gadamer's comments seem to invoke is closely tied to Heidegger's articulation or rearticulation of a number of key concepts, not only the concept of place, itself only implicit in much of Heidegger's earlier thought, but including also the concept of being-there, as well as that of world. The shift in Heidegger's thinking of being-there is particularly important, but also particularly complex—and it is a shift that is sometimes obscured by the fact that, even in his later thinking, Heidegger still occasionally uses the term "being-there" in ways that refer back to its usage in *Being and Time*. In part, the shift in the meaning of the term is one that takes us away from the individualistic connotations that appear (though somewhat equivocally) to be present in *Being and Time*—thus, in the early 1930s, for instance, being-there is more often referred to in terms of the being-there of a historical "people" (*Volk*), where "people" is itself understood in terms of the belonging-together of a human community, rather than in terms of the being-there that wields equipment. Yet while the term contains some ambiguity within it, being-there comes increasingly to refer, particularly in the late 1930s and the 1940s, not so much to that which each individual human being is, but rather to a mode of being that is "the ground of the future humanness that holds sway in the grounding";[78] to a mode of being "in" the "there" that no longer closes off its own character as such a mode; to a mode of being in which human being, and that of the world, is evident in the "there" in which it always already belongs. It is the turning back to such "being-there" that constitutes the "other beginning" to which Heidegger's later thinking looks,[79] and which is the happening of the "Event" (*Ereignis*), understood as that mode of world-disclosedness that constitutes the "coming-home," the "remembrance," of being. In this respect, "being-there," which is now regularly hyphenated in a way that emphasizes the "being" and the "there,"[80] seems to take on a much more obviously "topological" character. Thus, in *Contributions*, Heidegger writes that:

Da-sein is the turning point in the turning of Ereignis. . . . Da-sein is the *between* [*das Zwischen*] between man (as history-grounding) and gods (in their history). The between [*Zwischen*] [is] not one that first ensues from the relation of gods to humans, but rather that between [*Zwischen*] which above all grounds the time-space for the relation.[81]

It is significant that Heidegger emphasizes elsewhere in *Contributions* that the "between" that is at issue here is not to be understood in terms of transcendence, "[r]ather, it is the opposite: that open to which man belongs as the founder and preserver wherein as Da-sein he is propriated [*er-eignet*] by be-ing itself—be-ing that holds sway as nothing other than propriative event [*Ereignis*]."[82] In characterizing the between as "the opposite" to transcendence, Heidegger emphasizes the way in which the between is that to which the human is gathered and to which the human already properly belongs, rather than, as in the case of transcendence, that which is somehow gathered by, or in relation to, the human (as transcendence is a surpassing of entities by the "subject").

In *Contributions*, and other works from the same period (for instance, the lectures from 1937–1938, titled *Basic Questions of Philosophy*), being-there also refers to a mode of being "in" the "there" that is the proper "destiny" of human being:

Truth . . . is grounded as the ground through that which we call *Da-sein*, that which sustains man and is entrusted to him only rarely, as both donation and destiny, and only to those among men who are creative and are grounding. The "*Da*" [the "there"] refers to that clearing in which beings stand as a whole, in such a way that in this "*Da*" the Being [*Sein*] of open beings shows itself and at the same time withdraws. To be this "*Da*" is a destiny of man, in correspondence to which he grounds that which is itself the ground of the highest possibilities of his being.[83]

In these passages, the idea of being-there has been transformed into that which is a defining possibility of human being, which is its proper "destiny," which also makes possible human being as such, and yet which is not yet realized, but will only be realized by those "few, solitary, and uncanny ones" (as Heidegger says elsewhere[84]) who are yet to come. Much the same ideas reappear in Heidegger's very last seminar in 1973, and there Heidegger is specifically concerned to address the way in which the human belongs to what he terms the "clearing" [*Lichtung*] of being, rather than such a clearing being identical with or produced by the human:

To leave the region of consciousness and attain to that of Da-sein: and thus to see that, understood as Da-sein (that is, from the ek-static), the human only exists in coming from itself to that which is wholly other than itself, in coming to the clearing of being. This clearing . . . this freed dimension, is not the creation of man, it is not man. On the contrary, it is that which is assigned to him, since it is addressed to him: it is that which is destined to him.[85]

Here, as in the earlier lectures, Heidegger also emphasizes that the proper entry into the domain that is referred to as "Da-sein" is something for which thinking can only prepare—it is something still to be awaited.

The ideas of the "Event" (*Ereignis*), "the truth of being," and the "clearing" that appear in these passages (and related ideas such as that of "the Open"—*das Offene*) are all bound up with Heidegger's thinking as it develops in the period after 1930, and particularly, in the case of the "Event," with Heidegger's thinking as it develops from 1936 onward. Consequently, given that we have yet to embark fully on the elucidation of that later thinking, those ideas must remain, for the moment, somewhat enigmatic. What should already be quite clear, however, on the basis of what has been said so far—especially what was said toward the end of the last section (sec. 4.2) above—is the way in which Heidegger's re-thinking of being-there involves a move that de-emphasizes the role of human activity. The human is itself seen as gathered into the "there," into the "event," rather than being that which "performs" such a gathering. Much the same move is evident in Heidegger's rearticulation of the other concepts at stake here also, including, as we shall see, the concept of world. Rather than thinking world in terms of transcendence, and so as that in the direction of which being-there transcends or "surpasses" entities, world comes to be understood in terms of the gathering, and thereby also the disclosing, of things—by the time of "The Origin of the Work of Art," in 1935–1936, world is seen as that which is established through the happening of the truth of being as it occurs in and through the work of art and in which all things, including the human, are first gathered into relation with one another, and thereby come to "appearance."[86]

The concept of world is itself very much at stake in Heidegger's discussions in the late 1920s. That should not be surprising given the centrality of that concept, together with the notion of "environing world" or "environment" (*Umwelt*), throughout Heidegger's thinking, especially his early thinking—an indication of its importance is given in Heidegger's comment, appended as a note to the final sentence of section 14 of *Being and Time* (division 1, chapter 3), that the analysis of the environing world (*Umwelt*), and the associated hermeneutics of facticity, had been "presented repeatedly" in his lectures "since the winter semester of 1919–1920,"[87] while in the lectures making up *The Basic Problems of Phenomenology*, he notes that "The elucidation of the concept of world is one of the most central tasks of philosophy. The concept of world and the phenomenon it designates that has never yet been recognized in philosophy at all."[88] Moreover, as I noted above, the critical notion of transcendence, when it appears in *Being and Time* itself, is invariably employed as that which pertains to world, and, in similar fashion, the phenomenon of world is also specifically taken up in relation to transcendence in essays such as "On the Essence of Ground."

The centrality of world here should not be surprising: it follows from Heidegger's original and continuing focus on the fundamental philosophical question as that which concerns the appearing or presencing of things, including ourselves, within a structure of prior interrelatedness. In this respect, we may say that while things are disclosed to us, that disclosure always takes place within a larger structure in which we ourselves as well as the things are already given together—the disclosure of things *to* us is thus properly the occurrence of a more primordial disclosure in which we are disclosed along with other entities within the world as a whole. The phenomenon of the world thus appears as a primary issue that is inextricably bound to the idea of situatedness—situatedness is always an opening into world. The phenomenon of world is also closely tied to the ideas of "projection" and "disclosure." World is, we might say, the cleared, lighted realm that is opened up in the projection of the understanding of being and within which beings appear as the beings that they are. In *Being and Time*, the projection of understanding is the projection of meaning, and the opening up of world is essentially the happening of meaningfulness, significance, or "intelligibility"—an opening up that also seems to be accomplished through being-there.

The rethinking of world that accompanies Heidegger's thinking in the period after *Being and Time* is, in part, a rethinking of the role of being-there in relation to world, and, as such, it is pursued in relation to the idea of transcendence; at the same time, however, that thinking is also a rethinking of the concept of world as such. In the late 1920s, this rethinking moves to resituate the concept of world more directly in terms of the notion of transcendence, and also, as we shall see, freedom. But it also leads Heidegger to interrogate the way in which world, as the "cleared, lighted realm" within which beings come forth, stands in relation to that which is not disclosed, to the realm of concealment, to what he will also call "earth." The shift in focus that occurs here, one that we might think of in terms of a shift from "unconcealment" to "concealment" (or, at least, to unconcealment *and* concealment), also takes the form of a shift from "meaning" to "truth." It is in this shift that place, and with it topology, begins to emerge in a clearer and more articulated fashion.

4.4   Clearing and Earth

In a lecture course from the winter semester of 1929–1930, *The Fundamental Concepts of Metaphysics*, the world appears as a central focus for Heidegger's discussion. There Heidegger characterizes world as the "manifestness of beings as such as a whole"[89]—thereby placing the emphasis squarely on being as the unitary realm of the disclosedness of beings in a way that follows on from *Being and Time*.[90] Yet unlike *Being and Time*, these lectures also look to an exploration of world that encompasses more than either the analysis of equipmentality or of intersubjectivity. Indeed, Heidegger expresses some dissatisfaction with the focus on these aspects of the analysis of *Being and Time* in the reception of that work. Thus he writes that:

I attempted in *Being and Time* to provide a preliminary characterization of the *phenomenon of world* by interpreting *the way in which we at first and for the most part move about in our everyday world*. There I took my departure from what lies to hand in the everyday realm, from those things that we use and pursue. . . . In and through this initial characterization of the phenomenon of world the task is to press on and to point out the phenomenon of world as a problem. It never occurred to me, however, to try and claim or prove with this interpretation that the essence of man consists in the fact that he knows how to handle knives and forks or use the tram.[91]

Moreover, a similar emphasis on the preliminary character of the analysis of world of the sort set out in *Being and Time* already appears in the lectures on *The Metaphysical Foundations of Logic* from the summer semester of 1928:

> We cannot . . . understand world as the ontical context of useful items, the things of historical culture, in contradistinction to nature and the things of nature. Yet the analysis of useful items and their context nevertheless provides an approach and the means for first making visible the phenomenon of world. World is therefore not beings qua tools, as that with which humans have to deal, as if being-in-the-world meant to move among cultural items. Nor is world a multiplicity of human beings. Rather all these belong to what we call intra-worldly beings, yet they are not the world itself.[92]

The point is also repeated in "On the Essence of Ground" where Heidegger emphasizes the way in which the analysis of the environing world in terms of equipment has "the advantage, in terms of an *initial characterization* of the phenomenon of world, of leading over into an analysis of this phenomenon and of preparing the transcendental problem of world."[93] Much later, in his very last seminar in 1973, Heidegger returns to the same point, on the one hand reiterating the importance of the analysis of environing world as that is given in *Being and Time*, yet also stressing that in relation to the project of *Being and Time* (namely, "to raise anew the *question of the meaning of being*"), "the analysis of the worldhood of the world . . . is only the concrete way of approaching the project itself. As such the project includes this analysis as nothing more than a means, which remains subordinate in relation to the project."[94] The analysis of world as undertaken in *Being and Time* is thus to be understood only as a way of entering into the question of being as such, and so into the question of world, rather than as providing the definitive analysis of the structure of world. This does not mean that there are not aspects of that analysis that have a broader significance, but we should not expect the phenomenon of world to have been completely spelled out in the analysis of the equipmental or social being of being-there.

The investigation of the "ontical context of useful items" or of the relatedness among the "multiplicity of human being" as a means to approach the phenomenon of world may actually lead to the world being thought of as just an assemblage of such beings, and this would be seriously to misunderstand the phenomenon at issue. It is perhaps for this reason, and so to provide an alternative way into the problem, that the lectures that make up *The Fundamental Concepts of Metaphysics* approach the question of world through a contrastive examination of the relation to world of different beings—of the stone, the animal, and the human.[95] In "On the Essence of Ground," and the lectures that comprise *The Metaphysical Foundations of*

Logic, Heidegger adopts a "historical" approach, examining the way the phenomenon of world has been taken up by the Greeks, by medieval Christian thought, by modern, rationalist metaphysics, and by Kant. Not surprisingly, Heidegger takes the Greek understanding of world to be of particular significance:

> The Greek expression for "world" is κόσμος [*kosmos*]. And what does the term mean? Precisely not what is usually believed; it does not mean extant beings as such, heavenly bodies, the stars, the earth, even a particular being. Nor does κόσμος mean something like all beings together; it does not at all mean beings themselves and is not a name for them. κόσμος refers rather to "condition" [*Zustand*]; κόσμος is the term for the mode of being [*Weise zu sein*] not for beings themselves.... Beings themselves remain the same, while their total condition, their world, can differ; or, one can hold the view that the world of beings always remains the same. To express this mode of being we use (already in my Freiburg lectures) the verb "to world" [*welten*].[96]

Talk of the "worlding of the world" harks back directly, as Heidegger himself notes here, to the language employed in his thinking from the early 1920s, and it is a form of words that will also be important in his later thinking. It is indicative of a way of thinking the unity of world as one that is constituted in terms of the original and originary unity of world as such—a unity not "brought about" by anything other than world itself. Moreover, as this passage also makes clear, world is not to be understood as the totality of beings, but rather as the unitary mode of being to which beings belong. Later, in this same lecture, Heidegger will explicate this mode of being, namely the world, in terms of the transcendence of being-there, and thence as *freedom*.

World, which Heidegger asserts must always stand in an essential relation to the human,[97] arises out of being-there's projecting of possibilities in a way that determines being-there's own being while it also establishes the world within which being-there finds itself (this is essentially the same structure we encountered in the analysis of *Being and Time* in chapter 3 above). Heidegger takes such projecting, determining, and opening to be identical with freedom. The possibility of such freedom arises out of the way in which being-there's own being is at stake for it, and freedom consequently consists in being-there's necessary projecting of its own possibilities for being out of such questionability (a questionability that means that those possibilities are not simply determined in advance, even though such projecting is always a projecting out of a certain pregiven, "thrown" situatedness). Heidegger also takes such freedom to name the essence of ground since in the free projection of world, what is projected is that on the basis of which being-there comes to be what it is and on the basis of which all beings are disclosed. Since being and ground name the same (a claim, as I noted above, that remains consistent throughout Heidegger's thinking), so the ground of being-there is being-there's projection of world, and so of that in which itself and all other beings first come to appearance. Moreover, this convergence of ground, world, and freedom also turns out to implicate truth, and to do so in a way that crucially reorients the thinking that is underway here.

In *Being and Time*, section 44, Heidegger takes issue with the traditional understanding of truth as expressed in terms of three ideas: that truth is primarily located in relation to judgment or "assertion"; that truth is essentially a matter of agreement between judgment and its object (expressed in the Latin formula that characterizes truth as *"adaequatio intellectus et rei"*—adequation of intellect and thing[98]); and that the role of judgment and of agreement in the understanding of truth has an essentially Aristotelian provenance.[99] Against the idea that truth belongs primarily to the judgment, Heidegger argues that truth is located in relation to the entity, and more fundamentally, in relation to being-there; against the idea of truth as agreement, Heidegger advances a conception of truth as the original "uncoveredness" (*Entdecktheit*) of the entity by which the entity first shows itself as what it is and so as that with respect to which the judgment is or is not in agreement. Heidegger thus takes "being-true," in its primordial sense, not as the obtaining of an agreement between the judgment and its object (although this is *a* sense of truth, it is not the primordial sense[100]), but rather as the "being-uncovering" (*Entdeckend-sein*) of the entity that makes possible any such agreement.[101] "Being-true" is a matter of the "being-uncovered" of entities; the being of truth is the "being-uncovering" of being-there as such, whose own primordial mode of being is in the "there" of disclosedness. It is this disclosedness that Heidegger presents as the primordial phenomenon of truth.[102] Heidegger claims that this understanding of truth is already present in Greek thought and is contained in the Greek term, usually translated unproblemtically as "truth," namely *"aletheia."*[103] Consequently, the idea that truth is primarily a matter of the agreement between assertion and its object, and so is primarily located in relation to the assertion, is not an idea that is to be found in Greek thought, not even in Aristotle.[104] The claim that, as Heidegger puts it, "the assertion is the primary locus of truth" cannot be defended by reference to Aristotle, nor can it be defended by reference to the structure of truth as such. Indeed, in a significant turn of phrase, Heidegger says that the assertion is not the *"locus"* of truth, rather "assertion is grounded in Dasein's uncovering, or rather in its *disclosedness*. The most primordial 'truth' is the 'locus' of assertion."[105]

In "On the Essence of Ground," the question of ground is seen as directly related to the question of truth, and both are explicitly tied to the issue of transcendence as part of a single, tightly knit problematic:

[T]he essence of truth must be sought more originarily than the traditional characterization of truth in the sense of a property of assertions would admit. Yet if the essence of ground has an intrinsic relation to the essence of truth, then the *problem* of ground too can be housed only where the essence of truth draws its inner possibility, namely, in the essence of transcendence. The question concerning the essence of ground becomes the *problem of transcendence*.[106]

Truth is seen here, in similar fashion to *Being and Time*, to have its essence in something more fundamental than the accordance of an assertion or judgment with its object (a point to which I shall return shortly), and the idea of ground is also seen to be connected with this essence. Moreover, as in *Being and Time* too, the essence of truth, and of ground, is itself found in disclosedness, which here appears in terms of the idea of transcendence. The line of thought that proceeds further in "On the Essence of Ground," however, and that can also be discerned in the Logic lectures from 1928, takes the essence of ground, and so, presumably, the essence of truth with it, as well as the elucidation of transcendence, to come together in the concept of freedom: "[t]he essence of the finitude of Dasein is . . . unveiled in *transcendence as freedom for ground*."[107] In "On the Essence of Ground" we thus find an argument that moves from the question of ground, itself understood as implicated with the essence of truth, to the idea of transcendence, and thence to an understanding of ground as the freedom for ground revealed in transcendence. Significantly, in the work that Heidegger identifies as the point from which the turning in his thinking properly begins, "On the Essence of Truth," although the notion of transcendence has disappeared, freedom is explicitly identified as naming the essence of truth:

The essence of truth reveals itself as freedom. The latter is ek-sistent, disclosive letting beings be. Every mode of open comportment flourishes in letting beings be and in each case is a comportment to this or that being. As engagement in the disclosure of beings as a whole as such, freedom has already attuned all comportment to beings as a whole.[108]

"On the Essence of Truth" seems, then, to pick up on the analysis of "On the Essence of Ground," but in a way that has shed the focus on transcendence, as well as on meaning, and has moved truth to the very center of the picture.

The disclosure of the essence of truth as freedom appears in section 5 of Heidegger's discussion in "On the Essence of Truth." If we take the idea of freedom as it appears there as actually picking up on what was at issue, if somewhat problematically, in the notion of transcendence (something confirmed by the way Heidegger characterizes freedom here in terms of the "ek-static, disclosive letting beings be . . . engagement in the disclosure of beings as a whole as such"), then the shift that occurs in "On the Essence of Truth" from section 5, "The Essence of Truth" to section 6, "Untruth as concealing" is especially significant. In a marginal note appended to the very end of section 5, Heidegger writes "Between 5. and 6. the leap into the turning (whose essence unfolds in the event of appropriation [*Ereignis*])."[109] The "leap into the turning" is precisely located in the shift away from what in "On the Essence of Ground" was understood in terms of "transcendence," but in "On the Essence of Truth" is "freedom," and toward what Heidegger refers to here as "concealment." The turning, it thus appears, is the turning into what Heidegger calls the "mystery"—the mystery of concealing as that which is always conjoined with unconcealment. It is essentially a shift from a focus on world as the realm of cleared, open projection—as, to use the phrase from *The Fundamental Concepts of Metaphysics*, the "manifestness of beings as such as a whole"—to world as it stands in relation to the realm of that which is unmanifest, that which is concealed and impenetrable. It is a turn toward what Heidegger, by the mid-1930s, will come to call "earth" (*Erde*)—a term that first appears in in a significant way in the 1934–1935 lectures on Hölderlin.[110]

Heidegger's inquiry into truth represents a continuation of *Being and Time*'s focus on "meaning"—in both cases what is at issue is the disclosedness or "presencing" of beings, which in *Being and Time* is also understood in terms of projection, and, up until "On the Essence of Truth," in terms of transcendence. Already in *Being and Time*, it is evident that truth, disclosedness, stands in an essential relation to "untruth," to concealment. In similar fashion, projection, tied to existentiality and understanding, also stands in an essential relation to thrownness, to facticity, "state-of-mind," and mood. In *Being and Time*, however, the emphasis tends to be on the priority of disclosedness over concealment, of truth over untruth, of projection over thrownness. There is an important sense, of course, in which the way world is founded, in *Being and Time*, in the ecstatic unity of temporality implies that world, as meaningful, is founded on that which, although it is the "meaning" of the being of being-there, is not itself "meaningful"—originary temporality, and so the being of being-there, cannot be "uncovered" in the way that entities in the world can be "uncovered" since it is the ground of being-uncovering, of disclosedness. Yet this is not thematized in terms of an essential concealment at the heart of disclosedness. Indeed, inasmuch as world is seen as distinct from the ecstatic unity in which it is grounded, so *Being and Time* posits a separation of the unconcealment of world from the "concealment" of its ground, while, at the same time, concealment is not understood as playing a positive role in relation to disclosedness, but rather is treated, for the most part, in terms of the tendency to falling, and so to the covering up of the original disclosedness of things.[111]

The issues at stake here are worked out in various ways in Heidegger's thinking between 1927 and 1930, and not only in the explicit rethinking that is tied to the idea of truth. As I have already noted, this period is one in which Heidegger pays close attention to a reconsideration of the phenomenon of world, and in which the analysis of world in terms of equipmental or intersubjective engagement is, to a large extent, left behind (which is not to say that it is thereby abandoned, but that it is seen as providing only a preliminary way into what is at issue here).[112] This reconsideration of world proceeds, in part, through the more direct focus on transcendence, and on world as it is tied to such transcendence, that has already come to light as an important feature of Heidegger's thinking in the period immediately following *Being and Time*. Indeed, once one relinquishes the idea that what is at issue in the question of transcendence is the grounding of transcendence "in" human being and instead focuses on what is at issue as a gathering of being-there with world, then what emerges as the real issue here is nothing other than the simple happening of world as such. It is just this question of the happening of world that seems increasingly to move to the center of Heidegger's thinking in the period from 1928 to 1936. In conjunction with this move from transcendence to a more direct focus on world, however, there is also a move away from the idea of world as the realm of disclosedness or unconcealment alone to a thinking of world that also looks to world as it stands in relation to concealment, to what Heidegger refers, in "On the Essence of Truth," as the "mystery." By 1936 this will lead to the understanding of the happening of the world in terms of the revealing-concealing of the truth of being that is the happening of world as it contends with "earth," and thence in terms of the happening of the "Event." In the late 1920s, however, the rethinking of world is pursued in terms that are geared much more to themes already present in *Being and Time*, but which nevertheless pick up on elements that are suggestive of concealment rather than disclosedness—thus, in the period from 1928–1930, Heidegger gives particular attention to that which appears in *Being and Time* as the affective counterpart to "projective understanding" (existence), namely, thrownness or facticity, and particularly to the way in which such throwness is manifest in "state-of-mind" and mood (or "attunement").

In *Being and Time*, state-of-mind (*Befindlichkeit*) was already understood as that by which we first find ourselves in the world—as the structure of the German "*Befindlichkeit*" (deriving from the verb "*finden*," to find) itself suggests. State-of-mind and mood thus constitute our original "affected-ness" (or, as I noted above, our prior "situatedness") whereby we are already given over to the world in some way or another such that things can show as meaningful or significant.[113] For the most part, state-of-mind and mood reveal the world in ways that orient being-there in particular ways toward the world, and so underpin being-there's active engagement in the world, but in the case of one particular mood, namely anxiety, being-there is dis-oriented—the world is revealed, along with being-there's own being-in-the-world, in a way that is severed from the familiarity of the world's meaningfulness, and so as having no intrinsic meaningfulness of its own. Being-there is revealed as pure thrownness in the face of the "'nothing' of the world."[114] In *Being and Time*, the significance of anxiety lies in the way it is revelatory of the being of being-there as a whole, and so of the way in which it also reveals being-there in the authenticity of its own potentiality-for-being[115]—the significance of anxiety is thus in its revealing of being-there as thrown *projection*, and so in opening up being-there to a recognition of its own "responsibility" in relation to its being. In *The Fundamental Concepts of Metaphysics*, as well as in "What Is Meta-physics?," there is a similar concern with the basic role of state-of-mind or mood in the disclosure of world and, more particularly, with the revealing of the world and our being-in-the-world—with the emphasis now on its character as transcendence—through anxiety, and also boredom.

Yet while Heidegger's thinking in these works remains continuous with that of *Being and Time* and does indeed develop themes that, as we have seen, are already present in *Being and Time*, what becomes evident here is a deepened concern with the way in which such fundamental moods or "attunements" as boredom and anxiety open up the question of world as it is simply "given" and as it stands in relation to finitude and to ground. In *The Fundamental Concepts of Metaphysics*, finitude itself is explored through the notion of "solitude" (*Einsamkeit*), and the lectures take certain lines from Novalis as their starting point: "Philosophy is really homesick-ness, an urge to be at home everywhere. Where, then, are we going? Always to our home."[116] The question of solitude, and of finitude, is a question concerning how it is possible for us to find ourselves "at home" (*zu Hause*) in the world. This is not a question about how we stand in relation to the world understood as the ordering of things, or of human sociality, but rather how we stand in relation to our own being, and so to being as such. It is indeed a question of what might be called the proper "groundedness" (*Bodenständigkeit*)[117] of the world and of our being in it.[118] The world is thus first encountered, not in terms of the opening up of a realm of intelligibility, but rather in terms of our own inexplicable being given over to world and to a situatedness in the midst of beings—such inexplicability is part of the original meaning of "facticity" and indicates the way in which the question of finitude and of ground opens up, not in the direction of something that is a determinate ground, but rather in the direction of a "ground" that is "nothing" at all.

The focus on the "nothing" is, famously, the focus for much of Heidegger's thinking as set out in "What Is Metaphysics?" The question that is placed at the end of that essay as the guiding question of metaphysics—"Why are there beings at all, and why not far rather Nothing?"[119]—brings together the question of being with the question of ground, and in a way that also indicates the character of the metaphysical forgetting of being. Metaphysics looks to answer this question by reference to beings, and is thereby oblivious of being; in looking to answer the question by reference to beings, metaphysics is also oblivious of the nothing. The question of ground, when taken up metaphysically, thus turns us away from being and the nothing in the direction of beings—in the direction, that is, of that which is meaningful, that which is intelligible, that which is explicable—and so away from what is indeed at issue in the question of ground. If we turn back to what is at issue here, however, then we must turn back, not to what is meaningful, intelligible or explicable, but to being as the nothing, to ground as that which, in the language of *Introduction to Metaphysics*, is an absence of ground (*Abgrund*).[120] It is, moreover, in mood and attunement that this first occurs, and it is in moods such as anxiety (though not only this) that the encounter with the nothing also takes place:

Only because the nothing is manifest in the ground of Dasein can the total strangeness of beings overwhelm us. Only when the strangeness of beings oppresses us does it arouse and evoke wonder. Only on the ground of wonder—the manifestness of the nothing—does the "why?" loom before us. Only because the "why" is possible as such can we in a definite way inquire into grounds and ground things. Only because we can question and ground things is the destiny of our existence placed in the hands of the researcher.[121]

None of this, of course, is obviously incompatible with the account set out in *Being and Time*, but it does indicate a shift in the primary focus of Heidegger's thinking. Not only do the works in the late 1920s exhibit a shift away from the account of world as given in terms of being-there's engagement with things and with other persons, but they also exhibit a shift to a more sustained interrogation of the way in which the disclosedness of world is underpinned by the impenetrability of what we might call "ground," by the "nothingness" of being, and which is revealed in the affectivity of mood and attunement.

The idea of nature provides another point of focus for the increasing "intrusion" into Heidegger's thinking, from the late 1920s onward, of a certain impenetrable "ground" out of which world emerges, but to which world is intimately bound. Nature seems to appear in *Being and Time* largely through the absence of any proper discussion of it, and on the few occasions when it does appear, it is in a way that seems to leave the being of nature unexplained.[122] In a note appended to "On the Essence of Ground," Heidegger comments directly on this apparent "omission":

if nature is apparently missing—not only nature as an object of natural science, but also nature in an originary sense (cf. *Being and Time*, p. 65 below)—in this orientation of the analytic of Dasein, then there are reasons for this. The decisive reason lies in the fact that nature does not let itself be encountered either within the sphere of the environing world, nor in general primarily as something *toward which* we *comport* ourselves. Nature is originally manifest in Dasein through Dasein's existing as finding itself attuned *in the midst of* beings. But insofar as finding oneself [*Befindlichkeit*] (throwness) belongs to the essence of Dasein, and comes to be expressed in the unity of the full concept of *care*, it is only here that the *basis* for the *problem* of nature can first be attained.[123]

It is significant that nature is here referred to in specific relation to being-there's "finding itself attuned in the midst of beings" and to throwness. The question of nature is thus seen as directly connected with the way in which we find ourselves already given over to the world and to our own "affectedness" in being so given over. Indeed, Joseph Fell argues that it is in mood that nature itself is disclosed—focusing specifically on anxiety as the disclosure of nature, or an aspect of nature.[124] In his later thinking, Heidegger will explore the concept of nature through the Greek "*physis*," exhibiting "*physis*" as standing in intimate relation to "*aletheia*"—nature, in this primordial sense, itself appears as a mode of the concealing/revealing of being. Thus Heidegger says in *Basic Questions of Philosophy* (from 1937–1938) that "The fundamental character of φύσις [*physis*] is ἀλήθεια [*aletheia*], and φύσις, if it is to be understood in the Greek sense and not misinterpreted by later modes of thought, must be determined on the basis of ἀλήθεια."[125]

The way in which the various issues that come to light here connect to the question of world, transcendence, and the concealing-unconcealing of truth is somewhat tangled, and, in the period of the late 1920s, and even into the early 1930s, is not yet clearly worked out in Heidegger's thinking. Yet it should already be apparent that what emerges is a set of issues centered around the attempt, not only to think the happening of disclosedness, and so of world, in a way that would rule out any grounding of that happening in the human, but also to understand it in a way that encompasses the "mystery" of that happening, and so does not treat it merely as the happening of disclosedness, but also of that which is not disclosed, that which remains concealed or else appears *as* concealment.

The emphasis on concealment can be seen as itself tied to that to which I referred at the end of chapter 3 above in terms of the essential "finitude of being"—the character of the happening of being, and so of the opening up of world, as always tied to the happening of the "there." It is a happening both of disclosedness and the opening up of a free, "cleared" realm in which beings can take a stand, but the opening up of that realm is also a concealing that itself provides the ground on which such a stand is possible. This is most obviously so in the sense that, although disclosedness is always a disclosure of things *as what they are*, it is never a disclosure of things as *all that they are*. The appearing of something in the open space of disclosedness is nevertheless always an appearing within a certain "locale," a certain "situatedness," a certain "clearing"—like the open, but also *bounded* space of a forest clearing (*Lichtung*)—in which the thing appears in a particular way that leaves open, but thereby also conceals, other such ways of appearing. Consequently, Heidegger presents the concealing that occurs in disclosedness as a form of "sheltering" or "protecting"—in the remaining concealed of things even in their disclosedness, things remain as more than is given in any such disclosure—and so truth is presented as properly a "sheltering that clears [*lichtendes Bergen*]."[126]

Yet not only are things both revealed and concealed in the happening of world, the happening of disclosedness conceals itself in such disclosedness. This is an inevitable consequence of the fact that the happening of world is not a "happening" in the usual sense—it is not a happening like the happening that is my typing of these words, like the happening that is "today," like the happening that is the holding of a football match or a birthday party—and so it does not itself appear in the way of such "happenings." The "happening" of concealing-revealing thus "withdraws" in that concealing-revealing, and so is concealed, in much the same way as the appearing of an object within the field of vision is accompanied by the receding, the "withdrawal," of the horizon within which the object is situated. The concealing that occurs here is thus not the absolute concealing of absence or obliteration (the horizon is not absent in being withdrawn), but the concealing that occurs through the withdrawing of that within which things come forth into appearance—indeed, the dynamic of concealing-revealing as such is the same as this dynamic of withdrawing-coming forth.[127] As revealing is always a withdrawal, a concealing, so revealing is withdrawn, not just from appearance in the manner of some specific "thing," "entity," or "event," but from any sort of "grounding" also. The happening of disclosedness (and notice that as there is only one happening here that is both revealing and concealing, to refer to disclosedness is always also to refer to concealment) cannot be grounded in anything other than itself, and, in this respect, can even appear as a refusal of ground. It thus appears as "mysterious," as impenetrable, as once again a form of "concealing"—in lacking any "ground" (for it is itself "ground"), just as it lacks any "appearance" in the manner of the appearances that occur within it, the happening of disclosedness is "nothing." The character of truth as both concealing and revealing is captured in Heidegger's emphasis on the "privative" character of the Greek term "a-letheia"—unconcealment comes out of concealment, but always stands in a relation to it. Yet the privation at issue here is not the privation of diminution or loss, and in this sense is no "privation" at all. So Heidegger claims that: "Concealment deprives ἀλήθεια of disclosure yet does not render it στέρησις (privation); rather, concealment preserves what is most proper to ἀλήθεια as its own."[128] Concealment means that revealing (un-concealing—revealing out of concealment) does not appear in the manner of any usual appearance, it has no ground, no "horizon," with respect to which it stands, it always occurs with respect to the finite and the particular, and yet such revealing is not closed off by "privation," but is the opening up into the "excess" of world.

The turn to concealing as that out of which unconcealment emerges and in relation to which it stands is itself indicative of the topological orientation of Heidegger's thinking. Indeed, it is in the thinking of truth that Heidegger's thinking most properly becomes a topology, for the thinking of truth, or at least of truth as a "concealing-revealing," also brings with it a thinking of place. This should already be evident from the way in which the question of the happening of truth is tied to the issue of the finitude of being as elaborated immediately above—and particularly in the idea of truth as a "sheltering that clears" and the image of the "clearing" that comes with this—but it also comes to light when one considers more closely what might be involved in Heidegger's argument concerning the need for a more fundamental understanding of truth than that which takes truth to be "a property of assertions." As Heidegger puts matters in 1936–1937, if what we are concerned with is a statement such as "the stone is hard," and if the statement is supposed somehow to "conform to the object," then:

This being, the stone itself, must be accessible in advance: in order to present itself as a standard and measure for the conformity with it. In short, the being, in this case the thing, must be out in the open. Even more: not only must the stone itself—in order to remain with our example—be out in the open but so must the domain which the conformity with the thing has to traverse in order to read off from it, in the mode of representing, what characterizes the being in its being thus and so. Moreover, the human who is representing, and who in his representing conforms to the thing, must also be open. He must be open for what encounters him, so that it might encounter him. Finally, the person must be open to his fellows, so that, co-representing what is communicated to him in their assertions, he can, together with the others and out of a being-with them, conform to the same thing and be in agreement with them about the correctness of the representing. In the correctness of the representational assertion there holds sway consequently a four-fold openness: (1) of the thing, (2) of the region between thing and man, (3) of man himself with regard to the thing, and (4) of man to fellow man.[129]

Truth as correctness thus seems to presuppose a more fundamental mode of openness that pervades the entire realm in which statement, "object," and human beings are situated in relation to one another. This openness is what is already at issue in *Being and Time* in the original phenomenon of disclosedness, and so is approached through the ideas of "meaning," projection, and understanding, but which, in being approached this way, is thereby understood in terms of the primacy of unconcealment over concealment. Yet the thinking of truth in terms of the open, in terms of unhiddenness or unconcealment, is not a matter of viewing truth in terms of some open space that stands "between"—a "clearing" that merely stands "cleared." The openness at issue is always an openness of engagement or involvement. Yet this means that openness itself is always to be construed in terms of the *happening* of such openness and so in terms of the coming of unconcealment out of concealment.

Perhaps the simplest way to see this is by considering the way in which the opening up of a region occurs only through movement within that region. A space may thus be "open," and yet if there is no movement within it, nothing will emerge as standing within that space. Yet, in movement, things are never exhibited "all at once"; instead one grasps them in terms of changing aspects and perspectives. Indeed, it is through those changes that things are grasped as things. Moreover, grasping things as things through the constant changes in their position and the aspects presented also requires that we ourselves grasp our own situatedness in relation to the things grasped, and so that we grasp the character of the region as a region. What starts to emerge here is the way in which the appearing of things within an open region is always a matter of the dynamic articulation of the region and of the things within it. In terms of the "four-fold openness" by means of which Heidegger characterizes the open region he describes in the quotation above, this dynamic articulation occurs in relation to the thing, to thing in relation to "man," that is, to the human, to the human in relation to the thing, and to the human in relation to other humans. Understood as the articulation of a "region," the structure that Heidegger lays out here is thoroughly "topological," not only in the sense of topology that is specific to Heidegger, but also in a more mundane sense according to which topology is the method by which a region is mapped out through the interrelating of the elements within it (see sec. 1.3 above).

It is this "topological" conception of truth, in which the interplay of unconcealment and concealment in place first begins to come properly to light, that emerges for the first time in "On the Essence of Truth." Yet it reaches a particularly important point of development in the lectures given between November 1935 and December 1936, and first published in 1950 as "The Origin of the Work of Art" in the volume of essays titled *Holzwege* (literally "Woodpaths"—"paths, mostly overgrown, that come to an abrupt stop where the wood is untrodden").[130] Gadamer takes those lectures as marking a new direction in Heidegger's thinking, and as the major point of departure for his own work, which he characterizes as an attempt to adhere to, and to make accessible in a new way, the line of thinking that extends from there into Heidegger's later thought.[131]

Certainly, given what we have already seen in relation to the shift in Heidegger's thinking after *Being and Time*, "The Origin of the Work of Art" takes up many of the central themes that are at issue here, but it also makes clear Heidegger's increasing preoccupation with poetry, which Heidegger takes to be the essence of art in all its forms. Perhaps most significantly for the inquiry into place and topology, however, these lectures also give a central role to a mode of place. Although neither *"Ort"* nor *"Platz,"* nor even *"Raum"* play any significant role in the essay, Heidegger does employ the term "*Stätte*," and it is this that takes Edward Casey's attention in his discussion of the way place appears here: "The work of art is bound to be in place: place that, though framed, is not a mere position or site. . . . It is a *Stätte*, with all that this latter term implies of the continuous and settled—even of home."[132] Gadamer claims, however, that the real innovation in "The Origin of the Work of Art," from the perspective of the development of Heidegger's own thinking, is the introduction of the concept of "earth," which Gadamer claims Heidegger finds in poetry, and particularly in Hölderlin,[133] and which does indeed seem first to appear in the Hölderlin lectures that precede "The Origin of the Work of Art" in 1934–1935. Joseph Fell writes that "Earth is not a category, nor is it advanced by Heidegger as a speculative ground. It is intended concretely, as an experienced place. Here the philosophical term "ground" ceases to be metaphorical; its original, literal, root meaning is recalled."[134] It is indeed the appearance of this concept of "earth," both in the lectures on the work of art and in the early lectures on Hölderlin, that represents the introduction of a new direction in Heidegger's thinking that moves explicitly in the dimension of place.

The primary focus for "The Origin of the Work of Art" is the nature of the artwork, and yet it is not merely art that is at stake in the essay so much as the relation between art and truth, and so, also, the way in which art may function in relation to world. Indeed, Heidegger argues that the artwork is not to be construed in representational terms, but rather in the opening up or "clearing" of world as such. Heidegger takes as his central example here a Greek temple.

Of the temple Heidegger writes:

A building, a Greek temple, portrays nothing. It simply stands there in the middle of the rocky, fissured valley. The building encloses the figure of a god and within this concealment allows it to stand forth through the columned hall within the holy precinct. Through the temple, the god is present in the temple. . . . It is the temple work that first structures and simultaneously gathers around itself the unity of those paths and relations in which birth and death, disaster and blessing, victory and disgrace, endurance and decline acquire for the human being the shape of its destiny. The all-governing expanse of these open relations is the world of this historical people. . . . Standing there, the temple work opens up a world while, at the same time, setting this world back onto the earth which itself first comes forth as homeland [*heimatliche Grund*]. . . . Standing there, the temple first gives to things their look, and to men their outlook on themselves.[135]

Although there is, to my knowledge, no evidence of any cross-influence, something of the way Heidegger describes the working of art in the temple is echoed in Vincent Scully's famous and exhaustive study of Greek temple sites in his *The Earth, the Temple and the Gods* from 1962 (Heidegger's essay is, of course, much earlier than Scully's book, and while Scully undoubtedly came to be familiar with Heidegger's work later, there seems no evidence that it had an impact on his thinking here). Scully writes:

> The mountains and valleys of Greece were punctuated during antiquity by hard white forms, touched with bright colors, which stood in geometric contrast to the shapes of the earth. These were the temples of the gods . . . the temples were not normally intended to shelter men within their walls. Instead they housed the image of a god, immortal and therefore separate from men, and were themselves an image, in the landscape, of his qualities . . . the temples and the subsidiary buildings of their sanctuaries were so formed themselves and so placed in relation to the landscape and to each other as to enhance, develop, complement, and sometimes even to contradict, the basic meaning of what was felt in the land.[136]

The Greek temple, as Scully presents it, is not merely a building constructed for the practical purpose of providing a site for certain religious activities. Instead, the temple brings the gods into their proper place, in a way that locates them as separate from human beings, and yet also in the vicinity of human beings, and at the same time, brings the landscape—earth, sea, and sky—into view in relation to the god, and so also in relation to human beings themselves. The temple brings into view a "sacred" landscape, which is also a meaningful landscape, and it does so through the way in which it works in relation to the landscape in which it is situated—through the way it works to "enhance, develop, complement, and sometimes even to contradict" that landscape.

In Scully's account the landscape is established through, in part, the contradiction between the architectural feature placed within it and the landscape as such; in Heidegger, the opening up of world occurs through the "strife" (*polemos*) that occurs between world and earth as this strife is brought to occurrence in the site of the temple. In each case it is notable that what is established or opened up itself plays a central role in that establishing or opening up as such: the landscape is established through itself standing in tension with the temple; the world is opened up through the way it stands in conflict with the earth. The elements that are named here are thus brought into the open, are themselves disclosed, through the interplay that occurs between them. Inasmuch as the opening of world is that which allows for the disclosing of both earth and world, as well as the temple, so world also, in a certain sense, encompasses, "world," "earth," and temple "within it"—this means that we can speak, as does Heidegger, of the opening up of world as an opening up of both world and earth.

Moreover, as earth is disclosed in this opening or clearing of world as that which supports and grounds the temple as well as the world that opens up around it, so earth is also that which supports and grounds its own disclosedness as earth, and so supports and grounds its own character as concealing. The interplay of these elements means that there is no possibility of viewing them in a way that leaves them clearly and simply delineated with respect to one another or as they each stand in relation to the overall structure of the happening of the strife of earth and world—earth and world, while they constantly oppose one another, also constantly project into and around one another.

The strife between earth and world that Heidegger describes seems akin to that which the pre-Socratic Greek thinker Xenophanes seems to have envisaged, though in perhaps somewhat simpler terms, as obtaining between earth and sky: "Earth pushing upward, sky pushing down." As Mourelatos elucidates this fragment, and others related to it,[137] it is the strife between earth and sky that establishes the open plain that is the dwelling place for mortals, and the cosmology in which the fragment seems to be embedded suggests a dual axis—that which obtains between the up/down axis given in the upward press of earth and the downward press of sky, and which thereby also opens up the crosswise axis (north and south, east and west) of the plain on which humans act. The structure is constituted through the ongoing opposition of earth and sky, while the plain of human life is itself one of constant movement—a plain stretching out in all directions across which the heavenly bodies unceasingly pass. Although there seems no reason to suppose that the Xenophanes fragment played any role in the development of Heidegger's "twofold" of earth and world, the fragment does indicate something of the Greek character, and the broadly Greek provenance of the Heideggerian picture.[138] The Xenophanes fragment is also useful in providing an independent means to illuminate the idea of the "twofold" structure at issue here. Earth and sky are each determined in Xenophanes' account by their relation to each other—we might put this in terms of their opposition, but we can also describe it in terms of their essential belonging together in that opposition. It is, moreover, in this determination through such oppositional belonging that the "between" of human dwelling is opened up. Although it is world that is opened up in the happening of truth that occurs through the templework, and it is in the opening of the world that beings come into view, along with earth and world themselves, it is actually earth that seems to be given a certain primacy in Heidegger's description—a primacy that mirrors the primacy he gives in "On the Essence of Truth" to concealment over unconcealment, and that is itself indicated by the "privative" character of "aletheia." It is earth on which the temple, the artwork, rests, and earth that shelters and protects it.

It might be supposed that here, in this account of the "worlding of world" as it occurs in and through the work of art, and so as a working or happening in which even human being is itself first brought into view, not only do we have an account that begins to come closer to a true "topology of being," but we also have an account of the truth of being that allows us to understand its unitary character, and so also to understand the proper relation between being and human being. Yet as Heidegger himself admits in the 1956 "Appendix" to the essay, in the comment quoted in section 4.2 above, there is still an inadequacy in the way matters are presented here. In the "Appendix," Heidegger refers to two "ambiguities" in the essay:

On p. 49 an "essential ambiguity" is mentioned with respect to the definition of art as the "setting-to-work of truth." On the one hand, "truth" is the "subject," on the other the "object." *Both* characterizations remain "inappropriate." If truth is subject, then the definition "setting-to-work-of-truth" means the setting-*itself*-to-work of truth (compare p. 44 and p. 16). In this manner art is thought out of the Event. Being, however, is a call to man and cannot be without him. Accordingly, art is at the same time defined as the setting-to-work of truth, where truth *now* is "object" and art is human creating and preserving. Within the *human* relation lies the other ambiguity in the setting-to-work which, on p. 44, is identified as that between creation and preservation. According to pages 44 and 33, it is the art*work* and art*ist* that have a "special" relationship to the coming into being of art. In the label "setting-to-work of truth," in which it remains undetermined (though determin*able*) who or what does the "setting," and in what manner, lies concealed *the relationship of being to human being.* This relationship is inadequately thought even in this presentation—a distressing difficulty that has been clear to me since *Being and Time,* and has since come under discussion in many presentations. . . . The problematic issue that prevails here, then, comes to a head at the very place in the discussion where the essence of language and of poetry is touched upon, all this, again, only in reference to the belonging together of being and saying.[139]

Thus, for all the focus on truth and world here, the question of the relation between being and human being remains at issue. Indeed, the period from 1930 to 1935–1936 is one in which truth comes to the fore in Heidegger's thinking, but in which truth is still thought of in a way that allows it to be seen as founded in or by the activity of human being.[140] From 1936 on, however, Heidegger starts more directly to articulate the happening of truth as itself that which is primary here, and so as determinative of human being, rather than as "founded" in the human—it is this which is a crucial element in the thinking of the "Event" (*Ereignis*) that appears in 1936–1938.

4.5 Language and Metaphysics

In the essays and lectures from the period after the publication of *Being and Time* through to the writing of *Contributions*, from "What Is Metaphysics?" in 1928 through to *Introduction to Metaphysics* in 1936, Heidegger returns frequently to the question of the nature and origin, as well as the necessary forgetfulness, of metaphysical thinking. This is no mere accident, but is directly connected to Heidegger's own diagnosis of the difficulties that surround *Being and Time* as having their source in the way the work retains an essentially metaphysical approach to the question of being. In the "Letter on 'Humanism'" this criticism is directly connected with the idea that *Being and Time* operates within a framework centered on the idea of transcendence: "being is thought on the basis of beings, a consequence of the approach—at first unavoidable—within a metaphysics that is still dominant. Only from such a perspective does being show itself in and as transcending."[141] In this context, Heidegger repeats the crucial sentence from the Introduction to *Being and Time* in which he states that: "Being is the *transcendens* pure and simple,"[142] commenting that this statement "articulates in one simple sentence the way the essence of being hitherto has been cleared for the human being," and as such "remains indispensable for the prospective approach of thinking toward the question concerning the truth of being."[143] Yet he also adds, "[b]ut whether the definition of being as the *transcendens* pure and simple really does name the simple essence of the truth of being—this and this alone is the primary question for a thinking that attempts to think the truth of being."[144] In the introduction to "What Is Metaphysics?," Heidegger comments that "every philosophy that revolves around an indirect or direct representation of 'transcendence' remains of necessity essentially an ontology, whether it achieves a new foundation of ontology or whether it assures us that it repudiates ontology as a conceptual freezing of experience."[145] Thus, although Heidegger constantly insists on the radical character of *Being and Time* and on the necessity of the path it follows, it is nevertheless the case that he also views the focus on transcendence, with all that implies, as itself bringing an ontological or metaphysical orientation with it.

This conclusion is, however, one to which Heidegger comes only gradually. In 1928, while already engaged in the rearticulation of aspects of the analysis of *Being and Time*, he still holds to a metaphysical perspective, writing that: "Several times we mentioned how all these metaphysical, ontological statements are exposed to continual misunderstanding, are understood ontically and existentially. One main reason for this misunderstanding lies in not preserving the proper metaphysical horizon of the problem."[146] The continued preoccupation with transcendence in the period up until 1929–1930 is indicative of Heidegger's continued attempt to work from within metaphysics, even if it is a metaphysics that also requires a radical "dis-mantling." By the time of "On the Essence of Truth," given as a lecture and revised a number of times between 1930 and 1932 (and further revised prior its publication in 1943), the attempt to persevere within a metaphysical frame seems to have finally given way, even if that attempt is not fully carried through, and so Heidegger comments in the concluding "Note" to the text of the lecture (presumably written closer to 1943 than 1930) that:

The decisive question (in *Being and Time*, 1927) of the meaning, i.e., of the project-domain (see *Being and Time*, p. 151), i.e., of the openness, i.e., of the truth of Being and not merely of beings, remains intentionally undeveloped. Our thinking apparently remains on the path of metaphysics. Nevertheless, in its decisive steps, which lead from truth as correctness to ek-sistent freedom, and from the latter to truth as concealing and as errancy, it accomplishes a change in the questioning that belongs to the overcoming of metaphysics. The thinking attempted in the lecture comes to fulfillment in the essential experience that a nearness to the truth of Being is first prepared for historical human beings on the basis of the Da-sein into which human beings can enter. Every kind of anthropology and all subjectivity of the human being as subject is not merely left behind—as it was already in *Being and Time* . . . rather, the movement of the lecture is such that it sets out to think from this other ground [*Da-sein*]. The course of the questioning is intrinsically the path of a thinking that, instead of furnishing representations and concepts, experiences and tests itself as a transformation of its relatedness to Being.[147]

The shift that is indicated here is a shift away from the focus on the inquiry into the truth of being as that might be understood through the focus on the structure either of transcendence, or what is termed here "ek-static freedom," as given in being-there, and toward concealment, the "mystery," the "there" of being (*Da-sein*). The shift is thus a shift away from metaphysics (although it may seem, even in this lecture, as Heidegger acknowledges, to remain to some extent metaphysical), and it is also, therefore, an attempt to begin the task of finding a new path or "way" for thinking that no longer moves by means of "representations and concepts," but through its own experience and testing of itself in its relatedness to Being.

The exact character of the way of thinking that is indicated here is by no means clear from what Heidegger tells us in "On the Essence of Truth." Yet elsewhere Heidegger is emphatic that what is at issue is fundamentally a matter of *language*. Thus, in the Le Thor Seminar from 1969, we are told that:

The posing of the question of being *as* being in *Being and Time* amounts to such a transformation of the understanding of being that it at once calls for a renewal of language. But the language of *Being and Time*, says Heidegger, lacks assurance. For the most part, it still speaks in expressions borrowed from metaphysics and seeks to present what it wants to say with the help of new coinings, creating new words. . . . Heidegger now says . . . that through Hölderlin he came to understand how useless it is to coin new words; only after *Being and Time* was the necessity of a return to the essential simplicity of language clear to him.[148]

Similarly, in his response to Ernst Jünger in 1955, Heidegger emphasizes the quite general point that *"[t]he question concerning the essence of being dies off if it does not relinquish the language of metaphysics, because metaphysical representation prevents us from thinking the question concerning the essence of being."*[149] The difficulties that appear in Heidegger's thinking in *Being and Time*, and in the work immediately after, can thus be seen as arising out of Heidegger's appropriation of concepts and ways of proceeding from the existing tradition that are taken up because they seem to offer ways of articulating the original unity that is at issue, and yet those concepts and modes of proceeding also tend to carry with them tendencies and presuppositions that run counter to key aspects of Heidegger's project.[150] Much of Heidegger's thinking up until 1936 can be seen as an attempt to disentangle himself from such concepts and modes of thinking, and so from the metaphysical tradition to which they belong, and this means finding a path on which thinking may nevertheless continue—it also means finding a language appropriate to this new path.

The need for a renewal of language is consequently a theme that runs through much of Heidegger's later thinking—and not only is it present as an explicit theme, but it is also apparent in the very different character of Heidegger's work in the period from the mid-1930s onward (and especially in his postwar writings and lectures) compared to that of the 1920s, or even the early 1930s. The transformation or "renewal" that is indicated in "On the Essence of Truth" is thus a transformation or "renewal" of language, and the thinking that "experiences and tests itself as a transformation of its relatedness to Being" is a thinking that also stands in a transformed relation to language as such—a thinking that stands in an essential relation, as the reference to Hölderlin suggests, to the *poetic*. This shift takes two forms, both of which are, to some extent, already evident in "The Origin of the Work of Art": it is a shift in the character of Heidegger's own approach—a shift toward a mode of presentation that is concerned less to "explain" or "analyze" than to "describe" and evoke, and so employs a more "evocative" and descriptive language; it is also a shift toward a more developed under-standing of language that sees language as essentially bound up with the question of the truth, and the place, of being.

Language was already, of course, an important topic in *Being and Time*, where it appears in relation to "discourse" (*Rede*). Discourse is named along with understanding, state-of-mind, and falling as part of the essential struc-ture of disclosedness. Discourse is world-articulation, and though it does not stand in an exclusive relation to language, it is through language that discourse is expressed (see the discussion in section 3.4 above). Language takes on a much more central role, however, in Heidegger's thinking after *Being and Time*, in which it is essentially related to being (and also, as we shall see later, to place and space), in a manner that the earlier work seems not to envisage. Heidegger famously writes in the "Letter on 'Humanism'" that language is "the house of being,"[151] while in "The Origin of the Work of Art" he tells us:

Language is neither merely nor primarily the aural and written expression of what needs to be communicated. The conveying of overt and covert meanings is not what language, in the first instance, does. Rather, it brings beings as beings, for the first time, into the open. . . . Language, by naming beings for the first time, first brings beings to word and to appearance. . . . Poetry is the saying of the unconcealment of beings. . . . Language itself is poetry in the essential sense.[152]

What it is for language to be poetry is for it to stand in an essential relation to the concealment and unconcealment that we have already seen is the essence of truth and that is also tied to the happening of place. The role that language plays here is something that will be explored in more detail in the discussion in chapter 5 below (see especially section 5.4)—the crucial point for the moment is that it is indeed language as understood poetically, and so as essentially disclosive, that is, as tied to the happening of the truth or place of being, that lies at the heart of Heidegger's concern with language in the 1930s and beyond. It is this same conception of language that also underpins Heidegger's own more poetic thinking in the period from 1935 onward, and especially in the period after 1945.

This turn towards poetic language and poetic thinking is a turn away from metaphysics, and as such, it also comprises a shift away from any attempt to "ground" the "truth of being" (which includes the truth of our

own being) in terms that would "explain" or "analyze" it. Even the transcendental mode of proceeding that looks to the uncovering of a structure
of necessary conditions is no longer operative here—not merely because
of the disappearance of the language of "transcendence," but because the
very attempt to exhibit such conditionality, along with the distinction
between condition and conditioned, is now seen as problematic—indeed,
if we are to regard Heidegger's late thinking as in any sense "transcendental" (as he himself does not), then it must be in a sense that takes the
transcendental as another term for "topological" and does not tie the
transcendental to the exhibiting of "conditions" in any strong sense. As a
result, it would be a mistake to view Heidegger's thinking on language as
advancing any form of "philosophy of language"—rather, like the later
Wittgenstein, Heidegger provides no "theory" of language, although,
unlike Wittgenstein, he aims instead to exhibit language in its "essence"
(of course, what such talk of "essence" means for Heidegger is quite different from what Wittgenstein, or most readers of Wittgenstein, would take
it to mean). In "On the Essence of Truth," although it is still the case that
truth as unconcealment is seen as the necessary ground for truth as correctness, the articulation of truth as unconcealment is not itself undertaken by means of any analysis that neatly "unpacks" the ideas at
issue—there is no conditionality at work within the phenomenon of truth
as unconcealment, and the different concepts used to elucidate it are not
related in any analytically transparent fashion.

Even at this stage in Heidegger's thinking, then, a stage at which the
turning in his thought is only going through its first, if nonetheless significant, movement, the manner in which he proceeds is through a mode
of language that is itself essentially "disclosive" (and so also, in a certain
fundamental sense, "phenomenological"), and that thereby aims to exhibit
the phenomenon that is at issue through often overlapping and intersecting ideas and images. Gadamer said of Heidegger that he was a thinker
"who sees," and Gadamer goes on:

And this "seeing" occurs not only in momentary evocations in which a striking
word is found and an intuition flashes for a fleeting moment. The entire conceptual analysis is not presented as an argued progression from one concept to another;
rather the analysis is made by approaching the same "thing" from the most diverse
perspectives, thus giving the conceptual description the character of the plastic arts,
that is, the three-dimensionality of tangible reality.[153]

Although seemingly intended by Gadamer to characterize Heidegger's
thinking in general, this seems a particularly apt characterization of that

thinking as it develops during the 1930s and onward. Moreover, it also gives another sense to the way in which Heidegger's thinking is essentially "topological" since this "seeing" of things in the manner of "the plastic arts" is also a seeing of things as they stand in their located, embodied "concreteness." In this respect too, inasmuch as Heidegger remains concerned with a certain project of "grounding," the grounding that is attempted is, as we saw earlier, not the grounding in some underlying "reason" or "cause," but is rather the grounding that is given in and through the exhibiting of something in its gathered unity, in the place in which it properly stands.

The turn to the poetic in Heidegger's thinking is, in an important additional sense, a turn toward what he himself calls the "mythical." This is not only evident, however, in his later talk of the "gods" (itself drawn, not only from the Greeks, but more directly from Hölderlin), so much as in the way in which his thinking invariably comes to depend on the articulation of a complex structure of meaning as it is concentrated in a single idea, a single image, a single word.[154] Heidegger himself seems to present "myth" as standing in a direct relationship to the poetic through the way in which he views myth (μῦθος), as well as "ethos" (ἔπος),[155] as intimately tied to language as disclosive, that is, to language as *logos* (λόγος):

Μῦθος, ἔπος, and λόγος belong together essentially. "Myth" and "logos" appear in an erroneously much-discussed opposition only because they are the same in Greek poetry and thought. In the ambiguous and confusing title "mythology," the words μῦθος and λόγος are connected in such a way that both forfeit their primordial essence. To try to understand μῦθος with the help of "mythology" is a procedure equivalent to drawing water with the aid of a seive. When *we* use the expression "mythical," we shall think it in the sense just delimited: the "mythical"—the μῦθος-ical—is the disclosure and concealment contained in the disclosing-concealing word, which is the primordial appearance of the fundamental essence of Being itself. The terms death, night, day, the earth, and the span of the sky name essential modes of disclosure and concealment.[156]

This turn to the mythical is, no less than the turn to the poetic, not a turn to the arbitrary or the "irrational," but quite the contrary—it is a turn to that which is the proper essence of reason, to the essence of *logos*. It is a turn back to the original gathering and unconcealing of things that determines all "rationality" as such. Indeed, our being as rational creatures is nothing other than our being as entities that stand in an essential relation to the *logos* that is named here—as the original Greek has it, "*zoon logon echon*" (the living being with the logos). Understood as "mythical," Heidegger's thinking does not lose itself in the telling of impossible and fantastic stories, then, but instead turns back to our original experience of being and of truth, aiming to articulate that experience, to unfold the "story" that belongs to it in a way that allows it to be disclosed in its own terms.

Although "The Origin of the Work of Art" is notable for the way in which it gives center stage to art and poetry, and also, one might say, to a certain "*mythos*," Heidegger's turn toward the poetic had already become evident in the lecture series, given immediately following his resignation from the rectorate in 1934, on Hölderlin's hymns "The Rhine" and "Germania." These are Heidegger's first real and sustained engagements with poetry as part of his own path of thinking, and it is here too that the idea of *dwelling*, presaged in *Being and Time*, but in no way developed, reappears, in conjunction with the image of "earth," as well as with the idea of "*Heimat*," the "homeland"—the latter understood, "not as the mere place of birth, or as the simply familiar landscape, but rather *as the power of the earth*, on which man, each time according to his own historical Dasein, 'poetically dwells' ['In Lovely Blue . . .' VI, 25, v. 32]."[157] The turn toward the poetic is thus also, and not unexpectedly, a turn toward a more explicit thematization of place; a turn of which Stuart Elden writes that it "seems to be initiated in the lectures on Hölderlin, where Heidegger seems to designate 'space' as conforming to Cartesian notions, and to replace it with a more originary understanding of 'place.'"[158] Julian Young also gives a crucial role to Heidegger's engagement with Hölderlin, arguing that the critical shift in Heidegger's own thinking as it occurs in 1936–1938 corresponds to, and is driven by, a development in his reading of the poet.[159] Heidegger's engagement with Hölderlin continues up into the 1940s, and beyond, and is undoubtedly one of the crucial elements in the turning toward the later thought, especially in terms of the topological development of that thought. Indeed, in the *Der Spiegel* interview from 1966, Heidegger says of his thought in general that it "stands in a definitive relation to the poetry of Hölderlin."[160]

Heidegger's focus on Hölderlin in the period from the mid-1930s to the early 1940s is matched, however, by a similar preoccupation with the work of Friedrich Nietzsche—yet while Heidegger increasingly comes to identify his own thought with that of Hölderlin, he increasingly comes to define it in opposition to Nietzsche. In this respect, although one can see the shift in Heidegger's thinking having already begun in the late 1920s and early 1930s as a result of the particular "problem-dynamic" present in *Being and Time*, it is the engagement with Hölderlin and Nietzsche that is crucial to the formation of Heidegger's new mode of thinking that emerges from

1936 onward and reaches a fuller articulation in the period after 1945. Indeed, Heidegger regarded both these thinkers (and it is quite clear that Heidegger views Hölderlin as no less a thinker than Nietzsche) as standing in a similar, and equally critical, position in relation to the metaphysical history of Europe, and so too, of the West.

Inasmuch as Heidegger's "re-thinking" of *Being and Time* involves a "re-thinking" of metaphysics, so it also involves a "re-thinking" of Western thought, and of the thought of modernity, as it stands in relation to its history, which also means, if we take the analysis of *Being and Time* itself at all seriously, in relation to its future (moreover, although there is not the space to explore this here, it also implicates a rethinking of the political, and with it an implicit rethinking of Heidegger's own political entanglement of the 1930s).[161] Indeed, Heidegger claims that we find ourselves in a unique position in relation to the thought that is at issue here that forces us to reflect back on the originary beginning of that thought:

We must reflect on the first beginning of Western thought because we stand at its end. Our use of the word "end" is ambiguous here. On the one hand, it means we stand in the domain of that end which is the end *of* the first beginning. In this sense, end does not mean either the mere cessation or the waning of the power of the beginning. On the contrary, the end of a real and essential history can itself only be an essential one. . . . The greatness of the end consists not only in the essentiality of the closure of the great possibilities but also in the power to prepare a transition to something wholly other. At the same time, however, "end" refers to the running out and dissipation of all the effects of the previous history of Western thinking. That is, it refers to a confusion of the traditional basic positions, value concepts, and propositions in the usual interpretation of beings.[162]

Heidegger claims that it is Hölderlin and Nietzsche who "had the deepest experience" of the end of the West in this double sense, it is these two who:

could endure this experience and could transform it in their creative work only through their concomitant reflection on the beginning of Western history, on what for the Greeks was necessity. . . . That these two knew the Greek beginning, in a more original way than all previous ages, has its ground uniquely in the fact that they experienced for the first time the end of the West. . . . they themselves, in their existence and work, became the end, each of them in a different way.[163]

Heidegger rejects the then-current interpretation of both these thinkers,[164] looking to each of them as providing an indication of the tasks to which thinking must now attend. In the case of Nietzsche, this comes to mean, as Heidegger's reading develops over the 1930s and into the 1940s, the articulation of nihilism as the essential problem of modernity, particularly as that is expressed in Nietzsche's proclamation of the "death of god" and the recognition of the "will to power" as that which dominates modernity and is realized in the mode of disclosure associated with the technological—the mode of disclosure that Heidegger names *das Gestell*—"Enframing" or "the Framework." In the case of Hölderlin, this means looking, not only to the first beginning of thinking among the Greeks, but, as I noted above, to another beginning for thinking (although not a "second" beginning)—namely, the beginning associated with the happening of the Event as such—and so to a thinking that is still to come, but of which Hölderlin is himself the harbinger. It also means the articulation of the proper dwelling place of human beings, the dwelling place that is the "there" of being (the "being-there" that is "the turning point in the turning of *Ereignis*") and that is both a concealing or sheltering and a revealing or clearing. It is in returning to this dwelling-place, the place in which we already are and yet are not, that we come into the "being-there" that belongs to our "future humanness."

In the postscript to "What Is Metaphysics?," Heidegger says of the difference between thinking and poetry that "[t]he thinker says being. The poet names the holy."[165] In Nietzsche, Heidegger finds a saying of being, expressed in the ideas of the "death of god" and the "will to power," that identifies the understanding of being that is determinative for human being as it is in modernity; in Hölderlin, Heidegger finds a naming of the holy as that realm in which human being always dwells, and yet in which, in modernity, human being has yet to find itself. In Hölderlin and Nietzsche, then, we find the two who point the way into Heidegger's later thinking, just as they also point, in different ways, to the beginning—the "first" and the "other"—of all thinking. It is to Heidegger's later thought, already begun in 1936, but not properly opened up until at least 1945–1946, that we must now turn.

5 The Poetry That Thinks: Place and "Event"

The more I study nature around home, the more I am moved by it. The thunderstorm, perceived not only in its more extreme manifestations, but precisely as a power and feature among the various other forms of the sky, the light, active as a principle and resembling fate, working to impart national shape so that we might possess something sacred, the urgency of its comings and goings, the particular character of its forests, and the way in which the diversities of nature all converge in one area, so that all the holy places of the earth come together in a single place, and the philosophical light around my window—all this is now my joy. Let me not forget that I have come this far.
—Friedrich Hölderlin, letter (1802)[1]

Heidegger's thinking begins with the attempt to articulate the structure of a certain "place." The place at issue is not, however, any mere location in which entities are positioned, but rather the place in which we already find ourselves given over to the world and to our own existence within that world—the place that is, one might say, the place of the happening of being. In Heidegger's very earliest thinking, this "place" is one that seems to resist attempts at any analysis or articulation of its structure, and, indeed, its unitary character leads Heidegger early on to talk about the "place" that is at issue here in terms of a single, originary unfolding or happening—the happening happens (*es sich ereignet*), it worlds (*es weltet*), it gives (*es gibt*). Of course, Heidegger does not, at this early stage, himself refer to what is at issue here in terms of the idea of place—this is indeed my own interpretative gloss on the early thinking—and yet the way this originary happening is understood by Heidegger through the key notion of "being-there" certainly points toward place as already being at issue. The developed account at which Heidegger arrives in *Being and Time*, however, is one in which the "place" that is implicitly at issue in his investigations is articulated in terms of a structure that is specifically temporal. The idea of place as such has still not been directly thematized, and yet spatial and topological elements nevertheless run through the very heart of *Being and Time*. Indeed, the attempt to demonstrate the unity of the there in temporality itself seems to depend on a notion of temporality as itself a certain *topos*. Moreover, what seemed to be the decisive breakthrough of the project of fundamental ontology, the idea that the structure of the "there" and of "world" could be explained by reference to their essential temporality, actually turns out to be a source of failure.

This failure arises both out of the attempt to derive certain elements within the structure from others (an attempt that, although it arises out of the need to explain the unitary character of the structure, actually threatens to compromise that unity) and the associated idea of the projective character of that structure, and so as a structure that has its origin in the activity of that which is also the underlying structure of subjectivity. Thus the "transcendental" character of fundamental ontology—where "transcendental" refers us both to a notion of *projection* understood in terms of the transcendence by the finite existence that underlies subjectivity in the direction of the world in which entities themselves appear and to a notion of *derivation* that separates the ground from that which it grounds—turns out to be what is most problematic about such an ontology. In the face of that failure, Heidegger is forced to try to rethink his approach to the question of being that preoccupies him. Although, in the period immediately after *Being and Time*, he continues with the attempt to think the question of being through the idea of transcendence, and with particular emphasis on the idea of world, that attempt eventually gives way to a more direct focus on the idea of truth as "uncoveredness" or "disclosedness" that was already adumbrated in the earlier work. The shift at issue here is one that Heidegger himself describes in terms of a shift from understanding the question of being in terms of the question of *meaning* to the question of *truth*, and it is intended to lead toward a more direct account of the original happening of being that does not operate on the basis of any notion of "projection," nor, one might add, that depends on the idea of derivation that is itself tied up with the focus on meaning as that appears in *Being and Time*. Consequently, in "On the Essence of Truth," truth is understood in terms of freedom, a "letting be," that is not something that being-there does, but in which being-there is already taken up.

In contrast to the structure set out in *Being and Time*, in which meaning arises through the "temporalizing" of time that lies at the heart of what being-there itself is, in "On the Essence of Truth," truth arises through a simple letting be as such that does not arise on the basis of being-there (where being-there is still understood in terms of the essence of human being), but as that in which being-there is already implicated. By 1935, in "The Origin of the Work of Art," the structure of truth that is first elaborated in the 1930 essay is able to be elaborated from within a richer frame, one that now draws on the poetic language that Heidegger finds in Hölderlin, and which understands truth as arising out of the interplay between two main elements (already presaged in the earlier essay in terms of the interplay of truth and untruth): the concealing, the sheltering of earth (*Erde*) and the unconcealing, the clearing of world (*Welt*). For Gadamer, the account offered in "The Origin of the Work of Art" is the starting point for his own work, and also what he sees as the starting point for Heidegger's later thinking. But for Heidegger himself, the account that is elaborated there is still problematic, partly because it remains vulnerable to the misconstrual of truth in terms of correctness, and so to the obscuring of what is at issue as not a matter of correctness at all,[2] but rather the "happening" of a form of "disclosive belonging," and partly, though perhaps most importantly, because of the way it still retains a problematic ambiguity in its understanding of the relation between being and human being. It is the attempt to articulate the truth of being in a more direct fashion, and from which talk of truth itself eventually disappears, that, beginning in *Contributions to Philosophy* from 1936–1938 and continuing in the works that follow after it, enables the explicit thematization of the question at issue in terms of place—a thematization that finally comes more clearly into view in the thinking after 1945, but which, as I have indicated above, was already opened up with the inception of the turning in Heidegger's thinking that began in 1929–1930. Moreover, place does not supplant the previous two terms—the question of the place of being *is* the question of the truth of being which *is* the question of the meaning of being—but in arriving at a recognition of the way place is at issue here, so the understanding of the way these other terms are also at issue is transformed. The task now is to explore some of the basic elements of this account, and, in doing so, finally to arrive at the "topology" that, in Heidegger's own thinking, has so far been largely implicit.

5.1   The Moment of the "Event"

In a comment added to the 1949 "Letter on 'Humanism,'" Heidegger notes that "What is said here was not thought up when this letter was written, but is based on the course taken by a path that was begun in 1936, in the 'moment' of an attempt to say the truth of being in a simple manner."[3]

The attempt to which Heidegger refers here is the volume to which I have already referred a number of times in the discussion above, but which I have not discussed in any detail so far, namely, *Contributions to Philosophy* (*Beiträge zur Philosophie*). In both structure and style, *Contributions* is quite different from any of Heidegger's other works. It does not originate in a series of lectures or seminars, and although it was begun with the intention of being a work for publication, it never, on Heidegger's own admission, achieved the form necessary for a publishable work. Thus, while sometimes hailed as Heidegger's "most important work after *Being and Time*" (as it is described on the dust jacket on the Emad and Maly translation), *Contributions* nevertheless seems to have fallen short of Heidegger's intentions, and the work is perhaps best regarded as a sort of "sourcebook" for Heidegger's later thinking (in which the groundwork of that thinking is laid out all at once in a single "momentary" glance), rather than its definitive expression.

Although my discussion of Heidegger's later thinking will not focus on this work alone, *Contributions* nevertheless plays an important role in my account (as it must play an important role in any such account) of the development of Heidegger's thinking after *Being and Time*. The work contains many of the key notions that are articulated in that period, the most important of which is undoubtedly the idea that appears in the parenthetical addition to the title of the volume—*Contributions to Philosophy* (*vom Ereignis*). Ordinarily one might understand "*Vom Ereignis*" as "Of the Event" (and when I have referred to "*Ereignis*" in the discussion previously, I have also translated it as just "Event," although whether this translation is adequate is a matter I will discuss below), although the English translators of *Contributions* render it as "From Enowning." In his additional comments on "Letter on 'Humanism,'" Heidegger tells us that "'Ereignis' has been the guiding word of my thinking since 1936."[4] If Heidegger's later thinking can be characterized in terms of the shift to place, *topos*, that he himself identifies, then given the centrality of the "Event" in this later thinking, one would also expect to find place and "Event" linked together. Heidegger nowhere makes this link in direct and unambiguous terms, and yet there nevertheless seems to be ample evidence, if we care to reflect sufficiently on the matters at stake, to indicate that "Event" is itself topological in character—perhaps *the* topological concept in Heidegger's later thinking. In the same way as "presencing" never occurs in some indeterminate "nowhere," but is always an appearing in place, so too the Event is always a happening of place in place. In this respect, the topological

character of the Event is something already glimpsed in the preceding discussion, while Joseph Fell states quite directly that "Heidegger's terms
'Event' (*Ereignis*) and 'Place' (*Ort*) mean the same."[5] Before we can go any
further in the discussion here, however, we need to clarify the term itself—
what does "event" mean in Heidegger and how, if at all, should it be translated? Henri Birault points out that the German "*Ereignis*" contains at least
three elements: the idea of event or happening; of being proper to; and
the idea of seeing or appearing,[6] and a similar tripartite structure is also
noted by Thomas Sheehan.[7]

    The idea of *Ereignis* as event or happening, the first element, is something
given in the ordinary German usage of the term (although unlike the
English "event," which normally appears only as a noun, "*Ereignis*" has an
associated verb form, "*sich ereignen*," to happen or take place). The dynamic element in *Ereignis* is important inasmuch as it constitutes a move away
from the static idea of being as presence in the present that, according to
Heidegger, has dominated the philosophical thinking of the West since the
Greeks. It also indicates the way in which the unity that is a key element
in *Ereignis* is a unity that arises through the interaction of elements rather
than through their mere "standing near" to one another. The sense
of "belonging" or "being proper to" that is the second element
in "*Ereignis*" is the primary focus for the translation of "Ereignis" as "enowning." Along with those translations that draw on terms such as "appropriation" or "propriation" ("event of appropriation," "disclosure of
appropriation"), this rendering picks up, as noted above, on the way in
which "*Ereignis*" contains within it an echo of the German "*eigen*," meaning
"own." Ereignis is thus understood in terms of the "happening of belonging" in the sense of a gathering or bringing of things into what is their own.
The emphasis on "own" here immediately connects "*Ereignis*" with "*Eigen-
lichkeit*," "own-ness," or "authenticity," which is such a key notion in *Being
and Time*, but "*Ereignis*" does not refer to some mode of being that belongs
to being-there; instead what is at issue here is a certain sort of unifying of
elements in which things are brought into a unity to which they already
belong. The third element in "*Ereignis*" is the idea of "coming to sight,"
"being disclosed," "being made evident." Etymologically "*Ereignis*" has its
roots in the now somewhat archaic term "*eräugnen*" meaning to see or to
be evident. Once again this is suggestive of a connection back to *Being
and Time*—to the idea of the "moment of vision," *Augenblick*, in which
being-there grasps its existential situation. It also refers us to the notions
of disclosedness and of revealing/concealing that emerged most clearly in

the thinking of the 1930s (hence the translation as "disclosure of appropriation").

Although I doubt that most contemporary German speakers will hear all of these elements in the word (except perhaps when prompted to do so by Heidegger's own writings), Heidegger himself seems to have heard all three as included in *"Ereignis"*: the idea of event/happening, of gathering/belonging, and of disclosing/revealing. Through all of these three elements there is a persistent theme of unity from the unity of happening, to the unity of belonging, to the unity of disclosedness. Above all, then, *"Ereignis"* is the name for the particular sort of unifying and differentiating happening by which things come to presence, by which they come to be. Once we consider the term in this way, it becomes evident just why *"Ereignis"* could have such a key role for Heidegger: not only is it a name for a certain sort of unity, but it also serves to bring together most of the elements that are central to Heidegger's thinking, both early and late. The way in which these elements are combined in the one term also means that *"Ereignis"* connects up in significant ways with other terms such as "clearing," "the Open," *"aletheia,"* as well as "being" itself. *"Ereignis"* is thus a notion of originary gathering, which gathers together almost the entirety of Heidegger's thinking.

The way in which Heidegger uses *"Ereignis"* so as to combine the various elements at issue here makes the question of translation especially difficult. Heidegger himself viewed it as a singular term in his thinking akin to the Chinese *"Tao,"* and therefore a term that resists any attempt at translation. Certainly, there is no English word, or any simple English phrase, that will readily carry at once all of the elements that seem to be involved in Heidegger's use of the term, and certainly none that will also allow the sort of word play of which Heidegger is so fond. The translation of *"Ereignis"* as "enowning" that is employed by Emad and Maly, the translators of *Contributions*, certainly picks up on the idea of *"Ereignis"* as "gathering/belonging", and perhaps on the dynamism associated with *"Ereignis"* as "event/happening," but it fails completely to reflect the third element, the idea of "disclosing/revealing" that is implied in the connection with *"eräugnen"* (a connection that, oddly, Emad and Maly appear not to acknowledge).[8] Moreover, it also has to be recognized that, as a translation, "Enowning" has the major drawback that it is not a word drawn from current usage, but a neologism.[9] In this respect, the translation not only presents problems in terms of its adequacy in capturing the sense of the original term, but it also serves to reinforce the opacity and insularity of Heidegger's thinking as it has been carried into English.[10] Alternative translations that have previously been employed elsewhere tend to draw either on "event" or "appropriation" or "propriation." In his translations in *Poetry, Language, Thought*, for instance, Albert Hofstadter is explicit in noting the connection between "*ereignen*" and "*eräugnen*," as well as with "*eigen*,"[11] and the translation he proposes, noted above, is "disclosure of appropriation"—a translation he claims "has survived the critical scrutiny of Heidegger himself, as well as J. Glenn Gray and Hannah Arendt."[12] Julian Young and Kenneth Haynes, on the other hand, simply use "Event,"[13] while Joan Stambaugh renders it as "appropriation" or "event of appropriation."[14] Perhaps the underlying difficulty with "*Ereignis*" is that the term is used by Heidegger in an essentially poetic fashion—not only does it aim at evoking a single set of complex ideas and images all at once, but it is also employed in ways that constantly play on those ideas and images and on the connections that the etymology and sound of the word enables. Its translation therefore brings all of the difficulties that attend the translation of poetic works[15]—which means that to be absolutely true to Heidegger's own use of the term would require, not so much an effort of translation, as of new poetic creation.[16]

The question is: where does that leave the present undertaking so far as "*Ereignis*" is concerned? Since I have already signaled my commitment to trying to provide an account of Heidegger's thinking in English, simply retaining "*Ereignis*" untranslated, although attractive, since it would respect Heidegger's insistence on the word as a singular term in his thinking (a "*singulare tantum*"[17]), cannot really be an option. But neither "Enowning" nor the variations of "appropriation" and "propriation" seem to be particularly felicitous or helpful. As a result, I will follow what seems to have been the default practice (and which is the practice I have actually been following up until now anyway) of using the capitalized English "Event" on the grounds that this is indeed the rendering of "*Ereignis*" that is most commonly employed in German–English translation generally, while its capitalization gives some recognition to the singular character of the term in Heidegger. As I noted in the discussion of the translation of "*Dasein*," it is too much to expect of a translation that it will do all of the work of philosophical explication for us, and we should not assume that we understand what is involved in the idea of "Event" as used here any more than we already understand what is involved in "*Ereignis*" as used in the German. What I will do, however, is generally to gloss "Event" in ways that pick up on the ideas of happening, gathering/belonging, and revealing/disclosing that have already become evident in the discussion so far. One could say, then, that by the Event that is at issue here, I mean something like the "disclosive happening of belonging"[18] except that this sort of density of phraseology can itself easily become a barrier to understanding and has little meaning independently of its explication.

Understanding the Event in the way I have sketched here, however, still leaves an important ambiguity concerning the precise nature of the happening that is the Event. While on the one hand it is clear that this is no ordinary happening—just as being is not a being among other beings, so the Event is not an event among other events. Yet there is also a sense in which Heidegger talks of the Event as something that "happens" to us— something in which we are "taken up" and "transformed." Thus Julian Young talks of the Event as an "experience of 'transport and enchantment [*Entrückung und Berückung*].'"[19] In this respect, the Event seems to refer to something like the experience of this "disclosive happening." Such a reading is not at all incompatible with the understanding of the Event, and of what was discussed in the last chapter in terms of "the happening of truth," as the originary "happening" of the opening up of world that is the ground for the revealing of things as such. Indeed, to talk of an "experience" of the Event is to talk about just the possibility of a "grasping" of the Event—a "grasping" that is presupposed by the idea that there could be any articulation, any "saying," of the Event—whether by thinkers, poets, or anyone else. If the Event can be spoken, then it must, in some sense, also be able to be "experienced," it must, in some sense, itself be disclosed.

Here, then, we have two senses of the Event: as the original happening of disclosedness and as the disclosing of that original happening. There is perhaps a third sense, however, that should also be acknowledged and that is at issue in Heidegger's talk, already briefly noted in chapter 4 above (see sec. 4.5), concerning the "other beginning." In this sense, the Event refers us to a new mode of world-disclosure that will be the counter to the mode of disclosure that currently dominates—and which Heidegger associates with the technological—and that will allow disclosedness as such to come forth, a mode of disclosedness in which the world will appear as "wondrous" and "holy." Yet rather than think of this as properly a third sense to be added to the other two, it is perhaps better to think of the Event as comprising two aspects that themselves play out in two ways. Thus the Event comprises *both* the original happening of disclosedness as such *and* the disclosedness of that happening; it can be seen to occur at an individual level, and so in respect of the happening of world in respect of the happening of disclosedness as it occurs in relation to particular things and persons, *and* it can also be understood in world-disclosive terms as these relate to the character of the disclosedness that pervades and so also constitutes an era or a time (understood, not merely "historically," but "metaphysically"). For the most part, Heidegger does not himself clearly distinguish between these different aspects or "senses" of the Event, but they nevertheless seem implicit in, in fact required by, the way he speaks of what is at issue here. Moreover, it is characteristic of Heidegger's mode of proceeding to leave such "ambiguities" unspoken—to allow them to remain in his actual employment of language, in what I have termed its own "iridescence"—and my own talk of the Event in the discussion below will also, for the most part, retain a similarly implicit "ambiguity."

It might seem as if having arrived, in *Contributions*, at the idea of the Event—the idea of the "disclosive happening of belonging" in all its complexity—we have reached the point at which the nature of Heideggerian topology finally becomes evident. Yet the proper understanding of the idea of the Event itself depends on an understanding of topology and place. The task of elaborating that understanding is barely even begun in *Contributions*, and, indeed, the work seems not yet even to contain a clear conception of the way in which place is at issue here. This is one reason, although only one, for not taking *Contributions* as definitive of Heidegger's later thinking, but as instead representing what is perhaps the real starting point for that thinking. Julian Young argues, as I indicated briefly above, that more important than *Contributions* is Heidegger's Hölderlin interpretation as developed in the period from 1934 to 1945, and which Young sees as dividing essentially into two parts, with *Contributions* appearing in between.[20] Certainly it is in relation to Hölderlin, as I noted at the end of chapter 4 above, that Heidegger's thinking of place as well as space develops in a much more direct, clear, and explicit fashion and from which the thinking that appears in the very late work after 1945 seems to draw its strongest inspiration.[21] *Contributions* thus announces a new stage on Heidegger's way—the breakthrough in the turning back to the Event—but it by no means accomplishes the journey that is thereby opened up. Following that journey as it moves further will return us to a more detailed consideration of the character of place and space, as well as of the idea of dwelling that appeared in such an enigmatic fashion in *Being and Time*, while also opening up the question as to the way in which place emerges in the contemporary technological world.

5.2 The Happening of Place

Although it is in 1936, and the years following, that the idea of the Event comes to prominence in Heidegger's thinking, the idea also has a "prehistory" in Heidegger's earliest thought. That this is so is something that has come to light through Kisiel's important work on the genesis of *Being and Time* in the period from 1919–1926 and on which I drew in the discussion in chapter 2. The historical considerations adduced by Kisiel are significant since they show the way in which the idea of the Event is already nascent in Heidegger's thinking in the early 1920s, as well as indicating how that idea is closely tied to the initial problem of situatedness that was the starting point for Heidegger's thought. In that early work, especially the lectures given in the Emergency Semester of 1919, we find Heidegger using language very close to the language of 1936, the language of the happening of belonging as this applies to the relation between self and the life in which that self is caught up, thus: "Lived experience does not pass in front of me like a thing, but I appropriate [*er-eigne*] it to myself, and it appropriates itself [*es er-eignet sich*] according to its essence."[22] Here, of course, the focus on the individual self, as well as the use of the notion of "life," represents an important point of difference between the "event" to which our attention is directed here and the "Event" that is the focus of Heidegger's later thinking. The idea of the Event does not disappear with the development of *Being and Time*, but is rather taken up through the idea of originary temporality as the unifying structure at the heart of being-there.

In Heidegger's later thought, the Event is not a matter merely of *my* being taken up in the world, but rather of the unitary happening of world through the gathering of the basic elements that are constitutive of it (as we shall see in more detail below, these elements are finally named as mortals, gods, earth, and sky). Nevertheless, the basic structure that appears in 1919 is very close to that which reappears in 1936. Most importantly, it is a structure that presents the relation between the human, whether in my own self or in mortal being as such, as itself coming to be what it is through its being gathered into that to which it already belongs. To what extent that gathering is accomplished in a way that gives any priority to human being itself is perhaps still unclear in the 1919 account (although it is out of that account that *Being and Time*'s attempt to ground the gathering in the projective temporality of being-there will arise—as Kisiel's detailed study shows), although even in 1919 the character of the gathering in which I am already bound up would seem to be such that it already indicates a fundamental reciprocity between myself and the life that I live through, between myself and that with which I am already involved. It is thus that Heidegger can talk of the structure at issue here as one that is simply "given"—"it gives" (*es gibt*)—as "happening." The unity that is exemplified and articulated in this giving, this happening, is not a unity that can properly be dissolved into the elements involved in it, nor does it depend on anything that stands apart from those elements; it arises only in and through the gathering of the elements which are themselves determined as what they are in that gathering.

The historical considerations at issue here (and especially the fact that we can find precursors to the appearance of the Event in 1936 in Heidegger's earlier thought) are actually secondary, however, to the conceptual connections that independently obtain between the idea of the Event and the notions of place and topology as such. The point is not merely that in 1919 Heidegger was already thinking about the problem of situatedness in terms that draw upon notions of happening and gathering, and so on, terms that are at the core of the later notion of Event, but that the notions at issue here are themselves already bound together. The problem with which Heidegger grapples from early on is how to understand the way in which our own being is given to us, "happens," along with the giving of world. That this is indeed a happening, and a happening in which we find ourselves gathered to that to which we already belong (as we are gathered in to the life that we live), is given in the original "datum" that gives rise to our thinking and to which it must respond. The Event is thus the starting point for thinking, while also being that to which thinking has to "return." Moreover, the happening that is at issue here is not some abstract "occurrence," but a happening in which we are gathered in to the concreteness and particularity of the world and to our own lives. As such, the happening at issue is also essentially a "there-ing," a "near-ing," a "place-ing"—it is a happening of that open region, that place, in which we find ourselves, along with other persons and things, and to which we already belong. In returning to the original Event that is the happening of belonging, the happening of *being*, we also return to the original happening of place.

The idea of place that is invoked here is not, it should be stressed, the idea of that in which entities are merely "located"; rather, in the terms I used immediately above, place is that open, cleared, yet bounded region in which we find ourselves gathered together with other persons and things, and in which we are opened up to the world and the world to us. It is out of this place that space and time both emerge, and yet the place at issue here also has a dynamic character of its own—it is not merely the static appearance of a viewed locale or landscape, but is rather a unifying, gathered *regioning*—place is, in this sense, always a "taking place," a "happening" of place. It is this idea which I have argued has to be seen as already, in a certain sense, determining Heidegger's thinking from the start, and it is this idea which, as I have argued elsewhere on quite independent grounds, has to be viewed as having a central role in understanding both the world and our own being "in" it. Moreover, the idea of a certain singularity and unity in "structure" that is characteristic of the way the happening of world occurs in Heidegger's earliest thought, and comes more clearly to the fore in the later, exactly parallels the singularity and unity that is a crucial part of the idea of place as I have employed it here and elsewhere, and that is captured in the idea of topology (or my own notion, as deployed in *Place and Experience*, of topography). Topology is the attempt to articulate place, not by means of any derivation from an underlying principle or ground, but rather in terms of its own differentiated and yet unitary character. The idea of the Event is topological in just this sense, operating against any attempt at grounding the original happening of place that is the focus here in anything more basic, more primordial, more originary. It is at this point, of course, that the idea of the Event both as happening and as gathering/belonging is crucial. Just as place does not gather separate elements "in" place, but is itself the gathering of those elements (elements which are themselves brought to light only in the gathering), so neither is the Event itself something that stands apart from the gathering of the elements that are themselves brought to self-evidence through it.

The idea of the Event thus already moves within the ambit of a topological mode of proceeding, even if not recognized as such, almost from the start—and that is so whether we talk of Heidegger's thought, or of any attempt to understand the original happening of our "being in" the world. It is topological both in the way it necessarily invokes and depends upon a conception of place and the way in which it draws upon, indeed requires, a mode of proceeding that aims, not at the founding of some structure through exhibiting a relation of hierarchical dependence between the elements that make it up, but rather at a mapping out of the reciprocal interconnection, or "mutual dependence," of elements within the original happening that is at issue.

If this latter point is not clearly evident in Heidegger's thinking in 1919, then that may provide one explanation of how the 1919 account could lead on to the account presented in 1927 in *Being and Time*, in which the happening of the "there" is understood in terms of originary temporality. Indeed, the trajectory from 1919 to 1927 is one in which Heidegger seems increasingly to move toward a more "analytical" understanding of the structure of the original happening that is his starting point. This "analytical" trajectory arises, as we saw in chapters 3 and 4, out of a confluence of phenomenological, hermeneutical, and Kantian ideas: the focus on "transcendence" as a name for the structure that is at issue; the idea of the inquiry as one that aims to uncover certain structures of conditionality (akin to the Kantian "synthetic a priori") on which other structures hierarchically depend; the emphasis on the structure of world in terms of "meaning"; and the adoption of temporality as the key to unlocking the entire structure of "transcendence," of meaningfulness, and of world. The result is that in the period from 1919 to 1927, Heidegger seems to move to an account that looks increasingly to uncover something from which the structure given in the original happening of world can be *derived*, or in which it can be *founded*, rather than to articulate the unfolding of that structure as it happens in and of itself. It is in turning back to that original happening, as not merely a starting point, but as the endpoint also, that Heidegger arrives at the revelation of the Event, as the disclosive happening of belonging, in 1936.

Heidegger's own account of this trajectory, not only to 1927 but through to 1936, tends, as I noted in chapter 4, to focus on the way in which aspects of his thinking lent themselves to being understood in "subjectivistic" terms (Heidegger often prefers to remain ambiguous as to whether this tendency is one to which he himself succumbed), and this certainly captures a central element in the story I have sketched out. As he explains matters in the 1969 Seminar in Le Thor, the problem with the account proposed in *Being and Time* was that, through its focus on the problem of the meaning of being, and its understanding of meaning "on the basis of the 'project region' unfolded by the 'understanding of being,'" it tended toward an understanding of meaning as itself something accomplished by and through being-there—as, one might say, "a human performance"— and so "project is then taken to be a structure of subjectivity." Heidegger goes on:

In order to counter this mistaken conception and to retain the meaning of "project" as it is to be taken (that of the opening disclosure), the thinking after *Being and Time* replaced the expression "meaning of being" with "truth of being." And, in order to avoid any falsification of the sense of truth, in order to exclude its being understood as correctness, "truth of being" was explained by "location of being" [*Ortschaft*]— truth as the locality [*Örtlichkeit*] of being. This already presupposes, however, an understanding of the place-being of place. Hence the expression *topology of be-ing* [*Topologie des Seyns*].[23]

It is significant that, in this passage, Heidegger indicates the shift, not merely away from "meaning," but also from "truth"—a shift I have so far noted only in passing. Although, in the "Letter on 'Humanism,'" Heidegger still talks of "the truth of being,"[24] the focus on truth as such (that is on "*Wahrheit*") gradually disappears from his later thinking (it is barely in evidence at all in the postwar thinking), and Heidegger comes publicly to disavow the use of "truth" as a name for the happening of concealing-revealing that is referred to more originally as "*aletheia*" and that is also at issue in the Event.[25] In spite of the shifts in the way in which his thought is articulated, however, one of the clear points of emphasis in the passage just quoted is the way in which the focus of Heidegger's inquiry is taken always to remain on the original "opening disclosure" that I have argued is given in the happening of place itself. And that this does indeed refer us back to place seems to be confirmed by the fact that the path taken by Heidegger's own thinking is a returning to the place (*der Ort, die Ortschaft*) of being. Moreover, the shift from meaning to truth, to place cannot be understood in terms of the mere replacement of one idea or image by another—it is not that meaning, truth, and place, as Heidegger invokes these ideas here, involve different *questions*. There is only one question, the question of being, but it is a question that unfolds through the three words: meaning, truth, place.

Although each of the terms at issue here allows the same question of being to appear, the shift from meaning to truth is nevertheless decisive, even in the face of Heidegger's later abandonment of talk of "truth" here, in that it opens up the shift to a more direct appropriation of place, and it does so through the way in which the focus on truth itself allows a more direct appropriation of the "disclosive happening" of the "there" as that occurs in relation to things themselves, rather than as it might be thought to occur through human activity in relation to those things. In some respects, this focus on the happening that occurs in relation to the thing is clearer in Heidegger's earliest thinking, in the lectures from 1919 and the early 1920s, than it is in *Being and Time*, where there is undoubtedly a tendency for it to be somewhat obscured by the emphasis on uncovering the transcendental structure of being-there (understood as the mode of being of the human), but already, in "On the Essence of Truth," there is clearly a shift toward a more direct focus on the happening as it occurs in relation to things (albeit a happening in which human being is necessarily caught up). What is still not clear in "On the Essence of Truth" is the way in which this happening always occurs in relation to things in their particularity, and so also in relation to things in their own situatedness, their own "place." Indeed, as the focus on truth leads Heidegger to a closer interrogation of the nature of the thing, so it also leads him to a closer interrogation of the nature of place as such, and so to look more closely at that which is a constant theme in all his thinking whether presented in terms of "place" as such, or else in any of a number of other forms—"situatedness," "nearness," the "there."

The shift toward truth is thus a shift toward the more explicit thematization of "place" in large part because of the way it also constitutes a shift toward the more explicit thematization of the "thing." Thus it is in "The Origin of the Work of Art" that the "place-being of place" seems to come more properly into view, and it does so through the analysis of the happening of truth as this happens in and through the "thing" that is the work of art—and, more particularly, through the way in which the thing that is the artwork *works* as art (in this emphasis on the artwork as work, there is already a rearticulation of the "thing" as no merely present presence, but rather as a certain "happening," "gathering," or "working"). Although Heidegger still does not talk directly in terms of place or topology here, it is quite clear, as we saw in chapter 4, that the way in which truth happens, the way art, and so also truth, works, is through its concrete unfolding of a particular landscape or world that is itself opened up through the "standing-there" of the concrete work within that landscape: "A building, a Greek temple, portrays nothing. It simply stands there in the middle of the rocky, fissured valley. . . . Standing there, the temple-work opens up a world . . . the temple, in its standing there, first gives to things their look, and to men their outlook on themselves."[26] Moreover, as we also saw in the earlier discussion, Heidegger describes this happening in a way that attempts to delineate its structure, not through something that underlies it, but rather through the dynamic interrelating of the elements that make it up.

In "The Origin of the Work of Art," the elements that are invoked are those of earth and world. In the strife that is initiated between them in the standing forth of the artwork is to be found the happening of truth. In *Contributions*, however, Heidegger introduces, for the first time, what appears to be a fourfold structure—a structure comprising earth and world, as well as man and gods—and Heidegger presents this structure in terms of a simple diagram:[27]

$$
\text{man} \quad \begin{pmatrix} & \text{world} & \\ & \uparrow & \\ \leftarrow & \text{E} & \rightarrow \\ & \downarrow & \\ & \text{earth} & \end{pmatrix} \quad \text{gods} \quad \text{(there/here } [Da]\text{)}
$$

Essentially, however, this structure appears to be a modification of that which appears in "The Origin of the Work of Art." Indeed, one might argue that it is simply a version of that original structure with humans and gods now explicitly indicated as standing in a relation to the twofold of earth and world—a relation that is, of course, already implicit in the account in "The Origin of the Work of Art" since there the temple provided the focus, not only for the strife of earth and world, but for the relation of humans to gods also. At the center of this diagram, however, we find an "E," with arrows pointing out to each of the other four elements, and alongside it the parenthetical "(t/here [Da])." It seems reasonable to take the "E" to refer to "Ereignis," the Event, and the arrows to indicate the way in which those elements are brought into their own, brought to be what they are through the Event. The "t/here [Da]" seems to refer us to the structure as a whole—this is the "there/here." Heidegger's comments on this diagram are not at all clear, but it does seem that the diagram is intended to present the happening of the Event in terms of the way this arises as the happening of the "there/here" that is the ground for human being, even though it is only within that "here/there," and so in and through the Event, that humans are brought into belonging with gods, earth, and world, and so come to be as humans.

If this structure looks to be a modification of the twofold of earth and world from "The Origin of the Work of Art," it is also clearly a precursor of the fourfold (das Geviert—literally the "fouring" or "squaring"[28]) that comes to prominence, for the first time, in "The Thing," originally presented as a lecture in 1949 and 1950. Here too we find earth, although now set in contrast, not to world, but to sky, while gods and mortals belong just as fully in the "onefold fourfold"[29] that is named here—"earth and sky, gods and mortals dwell *together all at once*,"[30] and each of the elements "mirrors in its own way the presence of the others" at the same time as each also "reflects itself in its own way into its own."[31] If we take the diagram Heidegger provides in *Contributions* as our model, then that diagram would seem to require only some slight modifications to match the structure that is set out in "The Thing," namely, that "man" is replaced by "mortals" and "world" by "sky"; yet, in fact, the account set out in the "The Thing" involves a more subtle reconfiguration of the structure as a whole than would be accomplished merely by the substitution of terms.[32]

The diagram that is set out in *Contributions* understands the Event in terms of the happening of place—the happening of the "there/here [Da]." The same is also true, though evident in a different way, in "The Thing," in which the question of the thing is approached through the question of "nearness," a question that itself arises because of the apparent loss of nearness that occurs through the apparent abolishing of distance through the

impact of modern technology. In the face of that technology, everything
is rendered equally distant and equally close, which is to say that "everything gets lumped together into uniform distancelessness."[33] What is it
then, asks Heidegger, for something to be near to us? What is nearness?
"Nearness, it seems, cannot be encountered directly. We succeed in reaching it rather by attending to what is near. Near to us are what we usually
call things. But what is a thing?"[34] The way in which the question of nearness, and of the thing, are here tied together is indicative of the way in
which what is at issue in both the question of nearness and the question
of the thing is the question of the "there/here," of "place," for it is only
in relation to "there/here," only in relation to place, that anything can be
near or far. Moreover, not only does "The Thing" share the topological orientation that is evident in the diagram from *Contributions*, but just as that
diagram provides an articulation of the Event (*Ereignis*), so too does the
language of the Event also figure in the account of the fourfold in "The
Thing." Yet there is also a crucial difference between the two accounts: in
Contributions, as in "The Origin of the Work of Art," world stands over
against earth; in "The Thing," world is that which comes about in the happening of the fourfold—using the phrase that appears periodically
throughout Heidegger's thinking, the happening of the fourfold is also "the
worlding of world [*das Welten von Welt*]."[35] (Similarly, it is a "nearing of
nearness [*Nähern der Nähe*].")[36] Thus Heidegger writes that: "The fouring,
the unity of the four, presences as the appropriating [*ereignende*] mirror-
play of the betrothed, each to the other in simple oneness. The fouring
presences as the worlding of world. The mirror-play of world is the round
dance of appropriating [*Ereignens*]."[37]

It may well be that the model provided by Heidegger's original diagram
in *Contributions* is actually inadequate to capture the full complexity of the
structure that emerges in "The Thing"—inadequate to capture the dynamic
interplay between each of the four elements, as well as the way in which
what is at issue is a worlding of world no less than a happening of the
Event. Nevertheless, if we do remain with the model provided in *Contributions*, then it may serve to summarize some of the shift that occurs in
Heidegger's thinking of the happening of place, the happening of the
Event, between 1936–1938 and 1950, and it is certainly useful to see how
that model may be modified to incorporate some of the elements of the
later position. Remaining with that model, then, it seems that, in addition
to the change from "man" to "mortals" and from "world" to "sky," along
with the removal of the bracketing that marks off the earth–world/sky axis,
we also need to reposition "world," and this would seem to be best

achieved by placing "world" alongside what appeared in the original diagram as "there/here"—if we are to keep with the language of "The Thing," then perhaps "there/here" is also best replaced by "nearness"— with the resulting structure appearing as follows:

sky
↑
mortals ← E → gods (world—nearness)
↓
earth

As I have already indicated, this diagrammatic presentation is not entirely satisfactory if only because it suggests a much less complex structure than does Heidegger's actual account in "The Thing"—it certainly does not capture Heidegger's talk either of the "mirror-play" or of the "round dance" (perhaps this could be partly overcome by adding a set of arrows that move from each element to the other in a circle), nor the way in which what is pictured is a *worlding* of world as well as a *nearing* of nearness. Yet if we keep these qualifications in mind and compare this second diagram with that which Heidegger himself gives us in *Contributions*, it is clear that the one is a development out of the other even while there are obvious points in which the later picture diverges from the earlier.

There is, of course, one other element missing from both the original diagram and the modified version based upon the account in "The Thing": even if we assume that the diagram taken from *Contributions* does present a similar picture to that present in "The Origin of the Work of Art," still in neither the original nor in the modified version is there any indication of the way the gathering or happening at issue might require a point of focus in some particular "thing." Perhaps, if one wishes to maintain a certain distance between that which is presupposed by the diagram in *Contributions* and the account in "The Origin of the Work of Art," then one could take the point of focus as being given in the diagram from *Contributions* in terms of the "there/here," rather than in terms of any thing that might stand "there/here" (although then one might also need to acknowledge the way in which the account in "The Origin of the Work of Art" itself presents the artwork in terms of the way it establishes a certain "site"). Still, it seems more likely that any omission of the thing as that in and through which the happening of the Event occurs has more to do with Heidegger's own particular focus, characteristic of *Contributions* as a whole, on the articulation of the Event as such. Consequently, the fact that the original diagram seems to place the Event at the center (represented by the

"E") is not because the Event stands as the point of focus *instead of* the artwork (or any other thing), but rather marks the way in which it is in relation to the Event that the elements of world and earth, man and gods are gathered into their proper belonging-together (which is presumably also why the four arrows are directed outward from the "E"), and, in this respect, the diagram may well be better adapted to *Contributions* than to "The Thing" inasmuch as the latter is indeed focused on the thing rather than on the Event as such. The apparent omission of the thing from the structure that is pictured, whether in the original diagram or my revised version of it, should not be taken, then, to detract from the central role of the thing in the happening that is the Event.

Indeed, notwithstanding the shifts that occur throughout his thought (and not only in the turning of the 1930s) and the fact that the question of the thing comes more properly into focus in his thinking only with the shift from meaning to truth, and thence to place, the centrality of the thing is another of those themes, like that concerning the belonging together of unity and difference, that runs like a thread from the beginning to the end of Heidegger's thinking. If we glance back to the lectures on "The Hermeneutics of Facticity," for instance, in 1923, the attempt to understand the thing was already at work in Heidegger's discussion of the table in his family home, and in those early lectures Heidegger also talked of things having their own "there."[38] In *Being and Time*, the discussion of equipmentality and of the present-at-hand and the ready-to-hand can be seen as another attempt to take up the question of the thing, even if in somewhat different terms. Heidegger's final major engagement with Kant, from 1935, is entitled *What Is a Thing?* and it is only a very short time later that Heidegger delivered the lectures that make up "The Origin of the Work of Art." In the latter work, the inquiry into the artwork, and its relation to truth, is also, as we have seen, closely tied up with the question of the thing—indeed, much of the preliminary discussion is given over to the question concerning the nature of the thing—and the account that Heidegger gives of the working of art in terms of the happening of truth can itself be seen as giving insight into the nature, not only of the artwork, but of the thing as such (in opening up a world, the artwork also opens up a space in which things are able to come forth as what they are—are able to come into nearness).

Although "The Origin of the Work of Art" takes as its focus the extraordinary thing, namely, the artwork, and specifically the Greek temple (a focus in keeping with the dramatic character of the world-opening that Heidegger takes the artwork to bring about), "The Thing" returns to the more homely and mundane things that figure so prominently in the early lectures from 1919 and the early 1920s—if not to the same table, then to the jug that is placed upon it (and although these too can sometimes be artworks, it is not their being as artworks that is to the fore).[39] Certainly the discussion of the jug that we find in the essay of 1950 has many points of similarity with the discussion of the table in the lecture of 1923, and both works attempt to grapple with much the same fundamental issue— what I referred to in the first chapter in terms of "situatedness," and what we can now understand in terms of the happening of the happening of world, the happening of place, the happening of what Heidegger calls the Event. The difference between 1923 and 1950, however, is that by 1950 Heidegger has gained a much firmer command of the philosophical and poetic-ideographic structure within which the issues at stake have to be pursued—a firmer command, it might also be said, than he had even in 1936. The task now is to explore the structure at issue here in more detail— to look at the way in which the happening of place, the Event, is related to the opening of space, to the dwelling of mortals, and to explore in more detail the gathering that occurs in relation to the thing.

5.3 The Gathering in the Thing

"Near to us are what we call things," says Heidegger near the start of "The Thing," and then he immediately goes on to ask, "But what is a thing?"[40] In exploring the question that is raised here, Heidegger is very careful to separate the question of *thingness* from that of *objecthood*. And he does so, in part, by emphasizing that what is at issue in talk of the thing is not the way in which the thing stands over against us—in German the way in which it stands opposite (*steht gegenüber*) and which is captured in the German sense of object as "*Gegenstand*"—but rather the way in which the thing "stands forth" (*steht vor*). This "standing-forth," says Heidegger, has a twofold character: it stems from somewhere, and it stands forth "into the unconcealedness of what is already present."[41] Heidegger then goes on to argue that the thingness of the jug resides in its being as a jug, which means in the way it serves as a vessel, and as a vessel, the being of the jug consists in the holding and keeping of what is within it (in its *containing*), which is in turn determined by giving of what it contains, that is, by its "gushing," its pouring out of what is held within.[42] But in this outpouring, this giving of what it contains, the jug also gathers together earth and sky, mortals and gods:

The giving of the outpouring can be a drink. The outpouring gives water, it gives wine to drink. In the spring the rock dwells, and in the rock dwells the dark slumber of the earth, which receives the rain and dew of the sky. In the water of the spring dwells the marriage of sky and earth. It stays in the wine given by the fruit of the vine, the fruit in which the earth's nourishment and the sky's sun are betrothed to one another. But the gift of the outpouring is what makes the jug a jug. In the jugness of the jug, sky and earth dwell. The gift of the pouring out is a drink for mortals. It refreshes their leisure. It enlivens their conviviality. But the jug's gift is at times also given for consecration, then it does not still a thirst. It stills and elevates the celebration of the feast. The gift of the pouring now is neither given in an inn nor is the poured gift a drink for mortals. The outpouring is the libation poured out for the immortal gods. . . . In the gift of the outpouring earth and sky, divinities and mortals dwell *together all at once*. These four, at once because of what they themselves are, belong together. Preceding everything that is present, they are enfolded into a single fourfold.[43]

If the jug is that which is constituted through its holding and keeping, and so also its "outpouring," then that outpouring is what it is through the way in which it enfolds and is enfolded in the gathered unity of earth and sky, gods and mortals. Without these four, there is no outpouring as such, no giving of that which is a drink for mortals, which is a libation for the gods, which is the betrothal of sky and earth. But equally, it is only with respect to something like the outpouring of the jug, that these four are gathered together. Consequently, the jug as jug, the jug as thing, is what it is through the way in which it gathers the four together: "The jug's presencing is the pure, giving gathering of the onefold fourfold into a single while [*eine Weile*]."[44]

The way Heidegger describes the gathering that occurs in relation to the thing draws upon language that echoes language also present in his earlier writing. In "The Thing," Heidegger says that "The thing things. Thinging gathers. Appropriating the fourfold, it gathers the fourfold's stay, its while, into something that stays for a while [*dessen Weile in ein je Weiliges*]: into this thing, that thing."[45] In this talk of gathering the fourfold into "its while" and staying "for a while," Heidegger draws on a notion that was also used to refer to the facticity of being-there in "The Hermeneutics of Facticity": each being-there "is what it is directly and only through its having its own lingering 'there.'"[46] The "lingering" (*jeweiligen/Jeweiligkeit*) that is at issue here is the same "staying" (*weilen*) whether we talk of being-there or of the thing. In each case it is the "staying" that is the gathering of world and the opening of place. Yet, when we take such staying to be focused on the thing, rather than human being-there, we allow human being to appear as that which itself arises within this staying/lingering. The difficulty that arose in *Being and Time*, and that Heidegger claims remained at issue even in "The Origin of the Work of Art," namely, what is the relation between being and human being, is thus answered here through the showing of the way in which human or "mortal" being, already belongs within the single gathered unity that happens only in and through the thing. Human being is not the ground for such gathered unity even though human being is a necessary participant in such unity.

In this latter respect, the fact that the jug is made by human effort, and that its outpouring depends on human activity, does not imply that the jug's being as a jug is actually derivative of, or rests in, something merely human. Indeed, as soon as we ask ourselves what the "human" might mean here and start to reflect on the way the human itself already implicates those other elements that Heidegger here invokes, the earth, the sky and the divine—and thereby reflect on the way in which human being itself necessarily encompasses that which is other than the human—then we can begin to see that there is nothing that corresponds to the human that could serve as an independent basis or ground for the gathering that occurs in and through the thing. Indeed, inasmuch as the making of the jug comes out of the world and is not possible without it, so the jug as itself something *made* already presupposes, not merely the human, but the prior gathering of the human and the divine, the earthly and the heavenly. What occurs in the stilling/staying of the fourfold is the Event, the disclosive happening of belonging, and as such, the unity at issue in this gathering is one that can only be understood in terms of the unfolding of elements that already belong together and that cannot be understood in separation from one another.

Whereas the structure present in *Contributions* appeared as a modification of the twofold structure from "The Origin of the Work of Art," the fourfold that appears in "The Thing" is quite distinct. The pairing of earth and world is no longer the primary axis against which gods and man are set; instead there are two clear axes: earth/sky and gods/mortals. The elements that are thereby counterposed stand to one another, not in a relation of "strife" or opposition (which is how the relation between earth and world is presented in "The Origin of the Work of Art"), but rather in terms of their belonging to one another within the belonging together of the fourfold. This is an important point of difference since it picks up on a characteristic feature of the way Heidegger understands the Event as indeed a gathering of that which differs only in, and through, a prior belonging-together. In the Event, at least as it is worked out by the time of "The Thing," we find an interplay of belonging *and* differing rather than a play of difference (a strife or conflict). Moreover, rather than the openness of world being simply opposed to the concealedness of earth, world as opening/closing is itself that which arises out of the interplay of earth, sky, gods, and mortals, each of which can in themselves be seen to mirror the same interplay of opening and closing that is a feature of world as such.   ·

The fourfold that comes to the fore in "The Thing" appears in a number of Heidegger's important later essays, most famously perhaps, in "Building Dwelling Thinking" (1951), but also in "Language" (1950), ". . . Poetically Man Dwells . . ." (1951), "Hebel—Friend of the House" (1957), and "Hölderlin's Heaven and Earth" (1959). In "Building Dwelling Thinking," we find a similar focus to that which appears in "The Thing" on the way in which the gathering of the fourfold happens in and through a particular, thing—and once again it is a thing of the everyday, rather than necessarily a thing of art—in this case, a bridge:

The bridge swings over the stream "with ease and power." It does not just connect banks that are already there. The banks emerge as banks only as the bridge crosses the stream. . . . With the banks, the bridge brings to the stream the one and the other expanse of the landscape lying behind them. It brings stream and bank and land into each other's neighborhood. The bridge *gathers* the earth as landscape around the stream. . . . The bridge lets the stream run its course and at the same time grants their way to mortals so that they may come and go from shore to shore. . . . Always and ever differently the bridge escorts the lingering and hastening ways of men to and fro. . . . The bridge *gathers*, as a passage that crosses, before the divinities—whether we explicitly think of, and visibly *give thanks for*, their presence. . . . The bridge *gathers* to itself in *its own* way earth and sky, divinities and mortals.[47]

Here we see the gathering of earth, sky, gods, and mortals; the way they are gathered together is, once again, through the way in which the thing "works" in its essential character as a thing—in the case of the bridge, it is through the character of the bridge as "a passage that crosses." Such a "passage that crosses" can take many different forms—bridges can "lead" in many ways:

The city bridge leads from the precincts of the castle to the cathedral square; the river bridge near the country town brings wagons and horse teams to the surrounding villages. The old stone bridge's humble brook crossing gives to the harvest wagon its passage from the fields into the village and carries the lumber cart from the field path to the road. The highway bridge is tied into the network of long-distance traffic, paced as calculated for maximum yield.[48]

It is significant that Heidegger refers specifically to the modern highway bridge here since it indicates that even the particular mode of gathering and disclosedness that holds sway in our contemporary world (a mode of gathering that, as we shall see in sec. 5.5 below, is also deeply problematic) is nonetheless a mode by which the fourfold is indeed gathered. Yet whatever form is taken by the crossing passage of the bridge, and whatever forms of passage it enables, it is significant that the way in which the bridge works as a thing, which here means as something that gathers, is a matter of the way in which its being consists in a certain sort of working or happening, in the case of the bridge, as a crossing, an "over-passing."

The way in which the thing gathers is directly tied to its working in this way—the thing is that which already gathers the fourfold together in a particular fashion proper to the thing as such (and here is an echo of the idea of the Event as the happening of what is "proper to" or what already belongs). The gathering is thus not a result of some mere combination of statically present features or properties that belong to the thing, but a matter of how the thing itself "works," how it "things"—in its own way the thing gathers earth *and* sky, gods *and* mortals. The way all four of the elements of world are gathered together in and through the thing means that no one element can be taken to be the "source" or "ground" for the thing, and neither can "nature," which appears primarily in the form of earth and sky, be such a source or ground. Nature never gives us "things," and the thing does not belong to "nature" alone. We may be tempted to say that this is so because nature alone does not imply any connection with the fourfold, but this would be a mistake since nature is itself part of the fourfold in the form of earth and sky. It is only through the gathering of the fourfold in the thing that nature comes to salience as nature, just as it is only in the gathering of the fourfold in the thing that the human comes to salience also. In the same way, the things of nature, rock, tree, stream come to salience only as they are gathered into a fourfold that includes more than just the natural. This is why there are no things that emerge out of nature alone—all things, inasmuch as they are things, stand within the sway of the fourfold as it encompasses nature and the human, as it encompasses earth and sky, gods and mortals. For this reason we may say that the rock, the stream, and the tree are never "things" so long as they are thought of in a way that separates them from the mortal. To try to understand rock, stream, and tree as purely "natural" is thus to try to understand them as not "things" at all, and so to understand them in a way such that their being as rock, stream, and tree is never itself disclosed. Indeed, the very idea of nature as that which could be "pure" in this way and distinct from the human already runs counter to the way in which even nature emerges as nature, along with the human, only within the fourfold, and so only in relation to all four of the elements that are there gathered together.

The way in which nature stands in this way in relation to the fourfold means that the gathering that occurs in and through the thing cannot be viewed as a gathering that occurs only in and through "made" things as opposed to things "of nature." Certainly, the examples that we have looked at so far—the jug and the bridge, and if we regard it as capable of once functioning in a similar manner, the Greek temple—can all be taken as examples of things that arise through making rather than through nature. Yet not only is the distinction at issue here such that it does not mark off the "made" from the "natural" in any absolute fashion, but it seems that "natural" things can indeed gather in ways analogous to the "made"—and this is evident in Heidegger's own thinking as well as elsewhere.

In the reverie on the pathway through the fields (*der Feldweg*) that surrounds his family home of Meßkirch, Heidegger describes the way the path itself serves to gather the landscape in a certain way, but on that path there also stands an oak tree. The tree shelters a rough wooden bench and so enables rest as well as a place for reading and thought; it provides an occasion and stimulus for reminiscence and meditation, a reminder of past days and days to come; the oak provides occasional firewood from dropped or lopped branches; it reminds us of the provision of such things that the nearby forest offers; its bark can be used to make toy ships to be floated in the brook or the well and so enlivens childhood play; the hardness and scent of the tree speak "of the slowness and steadiness with which the tree grows."[49]

Another tree, from another place, illustrates a similar gathering. In his discussion of a painting by Pieter Brueghel the Elder (*The Harvesters*, 1565), the anthropologist Tim Ingold describes the way the tree that appears in the foreground of the painting gathers the landscape around it:

Rising from the spot where people are gathered for their repast is an old and gnarled pear-tree, which provides them with both shade from the sun, a back-rest and a prop for utensils. Being the month of August, the tree is in full leaf, and fruit is ripening on the branches. But this is not just *any* tree. For one thing, it draws the entire landscape around it into a unique focus; in other words by its presence it constitutes a particular place. The place was not there before the tree, but came into being with it. And for those who are gathered there, the prospect it affords, which is to be had nowhere else, is what gives it its particular character and identity. . . . In its present form, the tree embodies the entire history of its development from

Figure 5.1
"Oak Tree," photograph by Elsbeth Büchin. From Martin Heidegger, *Der Feldweg* (Frankfurt: Vittorio Klostermann, 1989), p. 10. Reprinted by kind permission of the publisher.

the moment it first took root. And that history consists in the unfolding of its relations with the manifold components of its environment, including the people who
have nurtured it, tilled the soil around it, pruned its branches, picked its fruit, and,
as at present, use it as something to lean against. The people, in other words, are as
much bound up in the life of the tree as the tree in the lives of the people.[50]

Do Heidegger's oak and Ingold's pear tree gather a world around them? Are
they things? Ingold explicitly compares the pear with the church that can
be glimpsed through the trees in Brueghel's painting. Of the church he
writes that: "Like the tree, the church by its very presence constitutes a
place, which owes its character to the unique way in which it draws in the
surrounding landscape."[51] Ingold does not deny that there are certain differences between tree and building, but he nevertheless also insists on the
close similarities between them inasmuch as both *gather*. Heidegger does
not directly address the question whether the oak tree on the path is a
thing, but it is clear that it also gathers, and as such we must surely regard
it too as a thing that "things."[52]

In their gathering, both oak and pear tree gather as things that arise from
nature, and yet their gathering is not merely "natural" such that it occurs
apart from the made. Instead their character as things is a testament to the
way in which the natural and the made grow together in and through
them. For this reason, there can be no basis for the idea of a simple and
sharp dichotomy between the natural and the made that could be applied
here or elsewhere. Indeed, if we turn our attention from the tree to the
jug, then we find that the character of the jug as "made" itself refers us to
the "natural." That from which the jug is made refers us back to that which
is not "made" at all, perhaps to the clay from which the jug was shaped,
while that which the jug gives in its "outpouring"—water, perhaps, or
wine—is itself given from nature as well as from the jug. But what if that
of which our jug is made is itself something made—if it is, say, plastic? In
that case, the jug may still pour what nature provides, but even if its material is not immediately evident as referring us back to something from
which it comes that is itself not made, it may still do so in other ways:
through its being as something that is specifically nonnatural, and so as
referring to the natural through its absence; or, perhaps, through the way
in which even its made materiality is based on something "natural"—as
the production of plastic is based on the petroleum that is mined from
beneath the surface of the earth and the vegetable matter from which that
is formed (or, more fundamentally, on carbon);[53] or else, we may say, to
the way in which any making already presupposes and depends upon a
"natural order" that, in a certain sense, enables such making.[54] The thing,

Figure 5.2

Pieter Brueghel, *The Harvesters*, 1565. Oil on wood. Reprinted by permission of the Metropolitan Museum of Art, New York.

then, is that which gathers through the way in which it already takes in both natural and made, earth and sky, gods and mortals, and so never appears *merely* as nature (though it may well be represented as such, as it were, "after the fact"), never merely as made—and it is just as possible for this to occur in relation to the tree as it is in relation to the jug.

The way in which the natural and the made, or, as we also say, the natural and the human, both stand in a relation to the thing within the gathering of the fourfold means that neither can be understood as more fundamental in that gathering. This means that we cannot properly think of "nature" or of the "human," just as we cannot think of the "gods" either, other than in terms of their essential belonging together. In one respect, this echoes Heidegger's famous claim that truth is always dependent on being-there such that nothing can be true outside of its relation to being-there,[55] but whereas in *Being and Time* it seemed that this could be treated in terms of the dependence of truth on the activity of being-there, as if truth were something being-there brought about, the situation in Heidegger's later thinking is that, if anything, being-there—if by this we understand the being of mortals—is something brought about in the happening of belonging that is the gathering of the fourfold. That nature and the human cannot be thought apart from one another does not imply that there is no sense to be given to the study of nature undertaken within the sciences as an attempt to understand nature "in itself." However, what it does mean is that we need to be careful to understand what the "in itself" might mean here—understanding nature "in itself" can never amount to understanding nature in a way that is independent of the human simply because all understanding, that is, all coming to appearance, is dependent on the happening of the fourfold—on the gathering together of the natural, the human, and the divine.[56] Inasmuch as nature comes to be what it is through being gathered into the fourfold, so nature proper is not constituted merely by the causal interaction of entities according to certain patterns of regularity describable in terms of "natural" laws. This is indeed the way in which nature properly comes to be represented within the enterprise that is natural science, but this enterprise is already a particular mode by which the world appears—one that we might argue itself arises out of the way in which certain experimental practices, and the things on which they depend, allow the world to be gathered and opened up in particular ways.

In this respect, the sort of gathering that occurs in the jug and the bridge ought also to occur in and through the experimental apparatus of science. What it is to be a thing is to gather, and the things that appear in laboratories and experimental sites—whether they be microscopes or particle accelerators—are no less things, and so no less capable of gathering, than are the things of ordinary life such as jugs and bridges. Of course, the way in which scientific practice and scientific things gather the world together is a different form of gathering from that which we see in the gathering of the jug, but it is a form of gathering nonetheless—the Event that is the happening of belonging thus occurs in the laboratory no less than it does on the country path. And just as the gathering that occurs in and through the village bridge is different from the gathering of the highway bridge, and yet both still gather, so is the gathering that occurs in and through the microscope or the particle accelerator different from the gathering that occurs in and through the homely bridge or jug as such, in spite of the fact that all gather the same fourfold. Moreover, the character of the world that is revealed and opened up in these different gatherings is itself different—the world as it is disclosed in the gathering that occurs in and through the experimental apparatus of the laboratory is quite different from that revealed through jug and bridge. In this respect, the revealing that occurs through the gathering that occurs in relation to the thing is such that it reveals the character of the thing itself, but in doing so it also reveals a particular configuration of the world and so reveals other things in a particular light also.

When the jug opens up the world through its "outpouring," what is opened up is the entirety of that to which the jug belongs: the kitchen in which the jug is kept, the shop from which it was bought, the character of its making, the mode of decoration that it bears, the cups and glasses into which it pours, the wine, the milk, the water that are poured from it, the occasions of its use, the needs to which it responds, the people that make use of it or who are served by it . . . and so on. Indeed, the way we might attempt to describe the character of the world as it comes to light around a particular jug, or any such thing, will echo the description we found Heidegger giving in the hermeneutics lectures of 1923 in his description of the table in the Heidegger family home. The opening up of the world in terms of that which comes to appearance in the outpouring of the jug, will, however, be different from the world as it comes to appearance around the scientific instrument. The same point applies, of course, to artworks—the opening of the world in the artwork will be different again from the opening of the world as it occurs in more mundane things or as it occurs in the things of scientific practice. Perhaps what marks out the artwork in particular, however, is that it gathers in a way that, in the case of some works, brings, not merely the elements of the fourfold, but the gathering of the fourfold itself, and its very mode of gathering, at least partially into view.

The focus on the way in which the world is disclosed in and through the concrete thing, as this is set out in Heidegger's later thinking, bears comparison with the account of the world as articulated through the structure of equipmentality in *Being and Time*. In the earlier work, the tool, through having a certain "location" (*Platz*) that situates it within an equipmental "region" (*Gegend*), is always implicated within a larger context of activity and involvement. The hammer refers us to the activity of hammering, to nails, timber, and so on. As an analysis of the structure of equipmentality, that is, of the being of the tool, this analysis is not superseded by the analysis in Heidegger's later work. But as an analysis of the structure of world, the structure given in equipmentality is inadequate— as Heidegger himself, in some of the comments we considered in chapter 4, might seem to suggest. To begin with, the thing is not simply *at* a location in the way that the tool appears to be (or at least not primarily so).[57] Indeed, the "thinging" of the thing is also a certain happening of place out of which the very possibility of location can then arise. To think of the thing as itself having a certain location presupposes that one has already stepped back from the thing as "thinging," and so as gathering a world, in order to view it simply as one "thing" located with respect to other similarly located "things" within a larger order of such locations. As we step back in this fashion, so too will the analysis Heidegger gives in *Being and Time* of both the ready-to-hand and the present-at-hand come to appear more applicable, since in stepping back and allowing the thing to appear as merely one thing among many, so too will the thing come to appear as something ready for use or present at hand (and so the possibility of the thing appearing as a mere object is also opened up). Yet such a mode of appearing is not appropriate to the thing as it gathers a world. This is because, as I have already indicated, and as we shall see in more detail below, the possibility of location is itself opened up through the opening up of world in relation to the thing, and also because the way the gathering that occurs in the thing is itself the happening of a certain sort of place—not the place of simple location, but the place of openness.

There is, of course, another significant difference between the account of the thing at issue here and that which is given of the structure of equipment in *Being and Time*: whereas in the earlier work the structure of equipmentality turns out to be dependent on the more fundamental structure of temporality, there is no such dependence that obtains between the gathering that occurs in and through the thing and any other "more primordial" element or structure—the gathering or happening of place in the thing is not to be "founded in" or "derived from" anything else. Indeed, even Heidegger's talk of the Event is not a reference to any founding structure, but rather a way of characterizing the very gathering of the fourfold as such. Yet it is nevertheless important to recognize that the idea of the Event does carry a certain "temporal" dimension with it—the Event is a "happening." In this respect, it is noteworthy that the passage I quoted above from Ingold, in which Ingold describes the gathering of the landscape in Brueghel's *The Harvesters*, arises in an essay titled "The Temporality of Landscape," and Ingold's description of the gathering that occurs there is also a description that makes essential reference to time and to history. Neither the temporal connotations of Heidegger's talk of the Event nor Ingold's emphasis on time and history should be taken to mean, however, that the gathering at issue here is one that occurs *in* time or that it is merely an evolutionary or historical process. Admittedly, in Ingold's case, there is a concern to counter a particular static conception of landscape that is also tied to certain forms of cultural and ideological analysis—Ingold wants to advance a conception of landscape that understands it dynamically and "ecologically." From a Heideggerian point of view, the gathering that occurs in relation to the thing, and to place, is not a gathering that occurs *in* time—time, as usually understood, arises out of such gathering in the same way as does space, in the ordinary sense, also. Nevertheless, the Heideggerian understanding of the gathering at issue here in terms of the Event that is the "disclosive happening of belonging" also emphasizes the dynamic character of that gathering—the unity that is at issue is a unity that arises through the constant interplay, the interarticulation, of the elements that make it up and in which those elements are themselves defined and differentiated. It is indeed just this originary differentiation and unification that Heidegger tried to articulate in *Being and Time* in terms of the temporalizing of temporality, but which in his later thinking becomes the happening of the Event. The "temporal" character of this happening refers us, not to something that occurs in time, but rather to the constantly unfolding character of the differentiation in unity and unity in differentiation that is characteristic of the original gathering of the fourfold. It is this that Heidegger also sometimes refers to in terms of the idea of "play" or *Spiel* (sometimes too as a "dance"—"*Reigen*," meaning a "round-dance" or "roundelay").[58] Something of this is also present in Gadamer's understanding of what we might call the "happening of understanding" as similarly "playful."[59]

The gathering of world that occurs in the "play" of elements that occurs in and through the thing is also a gathering of the thing itself, and in this respect the unity, and differentiation, of the thing cannot be completely separated from the unity, and differentiation, of world. Indeed, the character of the thing as having different "facets" that properly belong to it (such that the thing is itself revealed as what it is through any and all of those facets) is vital in the thing's gathering of the elements of world. To some extent, this is evident in Heidegger's presentation in "The Thing," through the way in which the different elements of the fourfold, earth and sky, gods and mortals, are each present in and disclosed through the character of the jug and the outpouring that belongs to it—in the wine or water that gushes from the jug and that arises out of the conjunction of nature's giving and mortals' effort, in the earthiness that holds the outpouring and from which the jug is molded by the potter, in the way the jug may serve the worship of the gods, or enable the gathering of mortals. In each of these ways, not only is the world invoked, gathered, and opened up, but so is the jug itself invoked, gathered, and its own complex being opened up also. Moreover, the gathering that is at issue here, whether considered in terms of the gathering of elements that themselves reflect the complex, yet unitary, character of the jug, or the complex unity of world, is not a gathering of otherwise separate elements—mortals, gods, earth, and sky are not first present as distinct entities that must then be brought, somehow, into a single unity, nor do the different facets that make up the being of the jug somehow first stand separate from one another, so that they must then be brought together. This latter point is perhaps best expressed by Heidegger's own emphasis on the gathering of the fourfold as a "mirror-play"—a play of reflections:

Earth and sky, divinities and mortals—being at one with one another of their own accord—belong together by way of the simpleness of the united fourfold. Each of the four mirrors in its own way the presence of the others. Each therewith reflects itself in its own way into its own, within the simpleness of the four. This mirroring does not portray a likeness. The mirroring, lightening each of the four, appropriates their own presencing into simple belonging to one another. Mirroring in this appropriating-lightening way, each of the four plays to each of the others. The appropriative mirroring sets each of the four free into its own, but it binds these free ones into the simplicity of their essential being toward one another.[60]

That the gathering of world, and so too the unity of the thing, is not something constituted out of distinct elements at all, but is that in and through which distinctness itself is established, is one of the fundamental and determining elements in Heidegger's thinking from the early emphasis on the idea of our prior belonging to world, through the idea of the equiprimordiality of the structures that make up being-in-the-world, and thence to the concept of the Event.

Heidegger's thinking is, in this latter respect, fundamentally holistic in its orientation. Yet the holism at issue here should not be construed merely in terms of the simple giving of precedence to the whole over the parts, but rather in the terms that were already indicated in the discussion of mutual dependence as illustrated through the example of hermeneutic circularity in section 3.5 above: the whole is understood as itself determined through the interplay of the parts that make it up, while those parts are in turn determined through their interplay with one another, and so also in relation to the whole. Such holism entails a necessarily dynamic conception of the unity of the whole as well as of the parts—a unity that is constantly being "worked out" or articulated in the interplay of elements. One further consequence of such holism is also a certain "indeterminacy" that pertains to the whole and to the parts since the unity that belongs to them is a unity that can never be given any complete determination or specification. That this is so follows from the thoroughly relational manner in which both whole and parts are determined. The mutuality that obtains between the parts, and between the parts and the whole, means that neither parts nor whole can be given any final or complete determination, since for such determination to occur would be for the structure to resolve into its parts, with the whole as merely the conjunction of those parts.[61] Such a "resolution" would seem, in fact, to be characteristic of holism as it is sometimes applied in a methodological or epistemological fashion alone—thus it may only be possible to develop an understanding of the elements that occur within some domain through articulating the relations between those elements, but once that articulation is complete, the understanding arrived at is taken as indicating the character of those elements as they are "in themselves." Heidegger, clearly, is no mere "epistemological" or "methodological" holist.

Inasmuch as the gathering of world is that by means of which all things, as well as the elements of the fourfold itself, appear *as that which they are*— the gathering of earth, sky, gods, and mortals is a *letting be* of earth as earth, sky as sky, gods as gods, and mortals as mortals; the gathering that occurs in and through the jug is a *letting be* of the jug as jug—so the gathering that occurs in the happening of place that is the Event is a gathering of that which already belongs with that to which it is gathered. This is one reason why Heidegger places so much emphasis on the echo of "own" (*eigen*) in the German word that is translated by "Event," the word, "*Ereignis*." Yet the fact that the way things show up within the fourfold is in terms of what they properly are does not mean, of course, that they show up as *all* that they *are*. That things do not show up in any such completely determinate or "transparent" fashion is, in fact, what we have just explored in terms of the necessary connection between "holism" and "indeterminacy." The point can also be put, in more Heideggerian language, in terms of the way in which all appearing is also an inevitable concealing—one sense of which is that no appearing can exhaust all of the possible modes of appearing that are proper to what appears. The way in which things "show up" in the gathering of the fourfold, then, is always in certain particular ways, and yet, even though there will always be other ways in which they can also "show up," the way in which they show up in any particular instance is nevertheless proper to the things as such. Thus the jug may show up as a jug in and through its role in dispensing water at a family meal, and in doing so things will be "lit up" in a way that is proper to that meal; the jug may also dispense wine at a religious ceremony, and there too, both the jug and the things around it will be disclosed in a way that is proper to that ceremony.

At this point a certain ambiguity becomes evident, if it were not so already, in talk of the "thing" as that which "shows up" or is revealed in different ways—an ambiguity that is crucial in understanding the role of "things" in the gathering of the fourfold and in understanding the essence of the "thing" as such. There seem, in fact, to be two ways in which things can "show up" in relation to the fourfold, and, together with this, two senses of "thing." The first is the way that seems most often what Heidegger has in mind—the way in which the thing shows up through its gathering of world. In this sense the thing is something that gathers, and it shows up in and through such gathering as it occurs in a particular way. In this sense of thing as gathering, and as showing up in its gathering, however, there is, in any particular gathering, only one thing (in Heidegger's examples, the jug or the bridge), and only one way the thing can be (as outpouring or as crossing passage). Yet clearly, the gathering that occurs in and around the "thing" in this sense is also a gathering of other "things" that must be understood as "things" in a slightly different sense—not as that which gathers, but rather as that which is gathered. Moreover, in recognizing that the thing gathers other things in and around it, so we also have to acknowledge, as I indicated above, that the thing that is now the focus of the gathering could itself be gathered in relation to some other such thing. Thus the bridge, as a passage that crosses, will gather other things around it in certain ways—these may include the vehicles that we use in passing over, the boats in which we sail underneath, the decoration with which it is sometimes adorned, or the statues or decorations that are placed there, the commerce and communication that it enables, and so on—but if we look to the gathering that occurs in relation to another thing that is also connected with the bridge, say the surveyor's theodolite as employed in the bridge's construction and maintenance, we can see that the bridge is itself gathered there, and gathered in a way different from the gathering that the bridge itself enables. As the bridge shows up in relation to the theodolite, it appears in terms of the instantiation of certain spatial and geometric properties in relation, not only to its internal structure, but to the way it fits into a larger mapping or plan. Thus while the "thing" will, as it gathers, have a particular being that is tied to that mode of gathering, it will also be capable of showing up in ways that are distinct from, even if related to, that mode of gathering. There are, then, two senses in which "things" can show up, and two senses in which things can be "things."

There is, however, more to be said here, since the fact that there is a unique way in which the thing gathers *in any particular gathering* need not mean that there are not *other* ways in which that thing can gather (thus the same thing may support more than one mode of gathering). This follows from the way in which the gathering that occurs in the thing is a matter of the way in which the gathering in the thing is not something accomplished only by the thing, but reflects the way in which the thing already belongs to a certain configuration of the world—the gathering of the world in the thing is both a coming to salience of the world in the thing and a coming to salience of the thing in the world. The character of the jug as jug depends on the way the world configures around it, just as the way world is configured depends on the configuration given in the being of the jug. The thing does not create the world, just as the world does not create the thing—there is, instead, a relation of reciprocity between thing and world, such that the thing allows the world to reveal itself in the interconnection of things, just as the world also enables the thing itself to be revealed through the way it stands within that set of interconnections.

We may, of course, be tempted by the thought that, since there do seem to be different ways in which things can reveal and be revealed, that in each revealing we actually have quite different and distinct things. Thus, instead of saying that the bridge shows up both as it is part of the world of passage and movement, and as it may be part of a world of planning and construction, we may wish to say that there are simply different entities, different things here. This sort of conclusion has often been associated with "perspectivism" or "relativism." But such a conclusion is unwarranted since it fails to acknowledge the way in which the different ways in which things can show up, both in terms of the different gatherings they may enable and the different ways in which they may themselves be gathered, are themselves gathered or brought together in the thing *as* thing. This is something that may be obscured by Heidegger's focus, in "The Thing," on the way in which the being of the jug, and so its thingness, resides in its "outpouring." But the jug is a thing, not in virtue of its particular mode of thingness (though this is important to the manner in which it gathers in any particular case), but in virtue of the way it both gathers and thereby brings other things, as well as the elements of the fourfold, into the differentiated unity of the world and the way in which it is itself gathered, in multiple ways, into that differentiated unity of the world through the gathering enacted in other such things.

The way in which each and every thing is constituted as the nexus for a complex and ongoing folding and unfolding, gathering and being gathered, is crucial if we are to understand the way in which the world is itself constituted in terms of what Heidegger refers to as "the Open" (*das Offene*). The gathering of the fourfold is the happening of the Open. The Open does not admit of any simple characterization, just as the world does not do so either. The Open is that region that allows things, nature, the gods, and mortals to come forth and is that which Heidegger also refers to in terms of the "free" and the "cleared." In the 1930s, this is the focus for Heidegger's thinking of truth, and while this focus does not disappear, the emphasis on truth, as we have already seen, does—what is at issue is "the Open," the "clearing" (Lichtung) as such. In "The End of Philosophy and the Task of Thinking," Heidegger develops this image of the "clearing" in some detail:

The forest clearing (opening) [*Lichtung*] is experienced in contrast to dense forest, called "density" [*Dickung*] in older language. The substantive "opening" goes back to the verb "to open." The adjective *licht* "open" is the same word as "light." To open something means: To make something light, free and open, e.g., to make the forest free of trees at one place. The openness thus originating is the clearing. What is light in the sense of being free and open has nothing in common with the adjective "light," meaning "bright"—neither linguistically nor factually. This is to be observed for the difference between openness and light. Still, it is possible that a factual relation between the two exists. Light can stream into the clearing, into its openness, and let brightness play with darkness in it. But light never first creates openness. Rather, light presupposes openness. However, the clearing, the opening, is not only free for brightness and darkness, but also for resonance and echo, for sounding and diminishing of sound. The clearing is the opening for everything that is present and absent. . . . we may suggest that the day will come when we will not shun the question whether the opening, the free open, may not be that within which alone pure space and ecstatic time and everything present and absent in them have the place which gathers and protects everything.[62]

The Open, the clearing, is thus also a lighting, not on the basis of any etymological connection, but in virtue of the way the clearing allows light to "stream in," and so allows for the play of light and of darkness, just as it also allows for the play of sound and of presence and absence. The Open is, moreover, the *place* that gathers as it also protects or shelters, and in this it is identical with the happening of "truth" as concealing–revealing, as "*aletheia*" that emerged in chapter 4 above (see especially sec. 4.3). What is evident here is the way that concealing-revealing works in relation to the thing and the open region (the "clearing," the "Open") within which the thing appears and that it also opens up.

Just as the forest clearing is the clearing of a particular place out of the density of the forest, so the Open always emerges through a particular happening of world in and around the thing. In this respect, one of the core ideas in Heidegger's thinking is to show how what we may call "situatedness" or locality (here understood in terms of the nearness of the thing) is not that which prevents or blocks the opening up of world, but is rather that through which it occurs (in chapters 3 and 4 I talked about this in terms of the "finitude of being"). But that means that the happening of the thing is itself always an opening up into things, and so into the world, that is not restricted to the particular mode by means of which it occurs— it is not restricted to just one mode of appearing, but is always an opening into multiple such modes. The opening up of the world through the outpouring of the jug, while it is a distinctive mode of opening—as is true of all and every opening—is not thereby cut off from other possible openings. So far as the thing is concerned, it is the multiplicity of relations in which it is enmeshed that enable it to function as the focal point for such opening. Heidegger's emphasis on the happening of disclosedness or "opening" as always a concealing *and* revealing, a sheltering *and* clearing, is one of the ways in which he tries to express the arising of openness in the happening of the local, the situated, the placed—in the happening of the individual "thing." Such happening is always particular (or, as one may also say, "singular"), and as such it allows things to come forth because of the way it gives things a particular look and salience. Nothing could otherwise come forth at all. Yet in coming forth, what also happens is the opening up of other possible modes of salience. The happening that occurs in the happening of the world is thus a constant play of revealing and concealing, in which the thing as thing, is disclosed—and in which the disclosedness of the thing as thing never means a restriction to just one mode of disclosure, but allows for the possibility of other aspects or "perspectives" being constantly opened up. To use a metaphor that I employed in talking of Heidegger's use of language, what occurs in the happening of world is an "iridescence" in which things constantly shine out in different ways—the sort of iridescence that also characterizes the appearing of things in the play of brightness and shadow within the forest clearing.

What emerges here is a certain irresolvable ambiguity that pertains to the idea of the thing and that can be seen as a version of what I referred to above as the inevitable "indeterminacy" that is associated with holism. The thing is always that which gathers in a distinctive way, and yet it is also such that it goes beyond what is given in that mode of gathering alone. Both world and thing carry this same ambiguity—world and thing always occur in particular ways or modes, and yet, inasmuch as they truly are a happening of openness, so they are also always more than is given in any particular such mode. There is thus an "excess" that belongs to the thing and to the world—an excess that belongs to being as such and that is experienced in what the Greeks referred to by "*thauma*" and "*thaumazein*" and we call "wonder" (though it seems that such "wonder" is no longer available to us as something to be experienced in the manner of the Greeks).[63] In the Le Thor seminar, in which he addresses the happening of the fourfold in the gathering of the thing in terms of the happening of unconcealment, the happening of "*physis*," Heidegger claims that what is at issue in this happening is:

the *overabundance*, the *excess* of what presences. Here one should recall the anecdote of Thales: he is that person so struck by the overabundance of the world of stars that he was compelled to direct his gaze towards the heavens alone. In the Greek climate, the human is so overwhelmed by the presencing of what presences, that he is compelled to the question concerning what presences as what presences. The Greeks name the relation to this thrust of presence θαυμάζειν.[64]

The gathering of the fourfold in the thing is not a gathering that is to be understood in terms of any single such gathering, nor are things opened up in that gathering in only a single way. As it is indeed a world that opens up around the place that belongs to the thing, so what is opened up is the richness and inexhaustibility of being—a richness that goes beyond any being or collection of beings, a richness that cannot be "explained" in terms of any mere connection between beings,[65] a richness in the face of which, so long as we are not blind to it, we are given over to wonder.[66]

This brings me to a crucial, but, it seems to me, often overlooked point. The "excess," the "iridescence," that belongs to things, indeed, to being as such, is indicative of the way in which neither beings nor being can be reduced to any mere static "presentness." This is a point that should already be familiar from *Being and Time*, of course, but what does it mean for beings "not to be" in this way? *Being and Time* also emphasizes the character of human being as that mode of being for whom its own being is always already in question, and this is no less true of human being as it appears in Heidegger's later thinking—the being of mortals is just that mode of being that exists in the shadow of its own nonbeing and whose being is therefore always an issue for it. Yet what relevance does this have for the understanding of being as such? Throughout Heidegger's thinking, whether in *Being and Time* or elsewhere, human being is understood as inextricably linked to the world in which it finds itself, and so also to the beings in whose midst it dwells. The question of human being and the question of being are thus not two questions that happen to be linked, but one and the same question. Consequently, the "questionability" of human being must imply an essential questionability in respect of being also. What it is to be, what it is to come to presence, what it is to be gathered into the disclosedness of belonging, is *to come into question*—it is for things to appear in the vulnerability of their being.

The presencing or disclosing of things is thus not a "settling" or "final determination" of them in their being, nor is it the prevailing of being as some determinate and determinative principle or power, but is rather an opening up of being, and so of any and every being, in the unity of its multiple possibilities. The place of being, then, is also the essential place of questioning. The danger of metaphysics is that, insofar as it acknowledges such questioning, it sees it only in terms of the specific question that calls for a specific answer—that calls for explanation or resolution. But the questionability of being is not a questionability of this sort at all. It is the questionability that consists in the constant disclosing of things in one way and another, that opens up things in the difference of what they are, that opens up the mirror-play of the fourfold. The questionability of being is the open, the cleared, the free dimension within which things are gathered and thereby also "let be." The turn back to being, back to place, back to the Event, is thus also a turning back to the essential questionability of being, the essential questionability of place—a questionability that was prefigured in Heidegger's very early recognition of the way in which, in our own existence, we already find ourselves given over to a world and yet are called upon to act in relation to that world.

5.4   The Opening of Space

The gathering of the fourfold that is also the putting of things into the open "space" of questionability is not some abstract relating of generalized features of the world; it occurs always and only in and through the particular thing that gathers—whether that be jug or bridge, tree or path— and so also through the particular ways in which the elements of the fourfold are themselves brought to appearance—through the particular manner in which earth grounds and supports and sky spans and opens, through the particular "look" imparted by the gods, through the particular mode of building of mortals. As such, this "disclosive gathering of belonging" always "takes place" in place and always in a particular place as in a particular thing. The manner in which place is at issue here is evident in "The Thing" through the way in which the essay thematizes, not just the thing, but also nearness. The question concerning the thing is, as we saw above, a way of taking up the question of nearness. In the account of the fourfold that appears in "The Thing," then, we also have an account that can be seen as an account of the happening of place and of the structure of place as such. Yet the question of nearness itself arises in "The Thing" in relation to the apparent abolition of distance by contemporary technology; it begins, in fact, with an observation concerning time and space—"All distances in time and space are shrinking."[67] But how does space relate to nearness, to the thing—how does it relate to place as this figures in Heidegger's later thinking? In what sense, if any, is the dimension of questionability that is opened up in the gathering of the fourfold itself properly to be understood as a "space"?

In chapter 1, I noted that although place and space are distinct, they also have to be seen as standing in a close relation to each other (as place also stands to time)—although the exact nature of this relation is still to be clarified, still it is clear that place always requires "room," it always opens out "into" space. Moreover, we have also seen already, in the discussion of *Being and Time* in particular, the way in which space itself arises as a problem for Heidegger. Indeed, even in the development of the later thinking that is focused on the Event, space still seems to appear as problematic: on the one hand, space seems constantly to emerge as a feature of the opening that is the Event—as a feature in the happening of place—and yet, on the other hand, it seems that opening cannot be merely spatial. The problem here is one that Heidegger notes explicitly in his *Parmenides* lectures from the winter semester of 1942–1943. Addressing the question of the "open" as it appears in Rilke's poetry, but also as it relates to his own thinking, Heidegger comments:

> According to the obvious meaning, when we think of the "open," we think of something opened versus something closed. And what is open and opened is "a space." The open refers to the essential domain of space even if we think of it as what has been brought into the light, in the sense of the disclosed and unconcealed. On the path of the thinking that thinks ἀλήθεια in its essence we will arrive at the point at which we will have to ask about the relation between the unconcealed and space. Must we think the unconcealed on the basis of the essence of what is spatial, or is what is spatial and all space founded in the essence of ἀλήθεια as primordially experienced? In any case, the open refers to what is spatial.[68]

The question that Heidegger puts here might seem, however, to be one that he had already addressed at a slightly earlier point in the lectures. Acknowledging the connection between the open and spatiality, he immediately emphasizes that "the open in the sense of the essence of ἀλήθεια does not mean either space or time as usually intended, nor their unity, space-time, because all that already had to borrow its openness from the openness holding sway in the essence of disclosedness."[69] The earlier passage still leaves open, however, the question concerning "the relation between the unconcealed and space" inasmuch as it is decisive only in ruling out the understanding of the open on the basis of "space or time as usually intended," and what this means, as Heidegger himself makes clear, is the understanding of space and time in the sense of "the 'extended' or in the sense of the 'free' as commonly understood,"[70] which is to say, in the sense of the simultaneously extended and the merely successive, or their combination. But if we look to understand space and time in a more fundamental sense—on the basis of their essence—what then is the connection with unconcealment, with the open?

One of the difficulties in addressing this question in relation to Heidegger's own texts is that it often seems as if the question of space, and to some extent even the question of time, is not a question that ever seems to be properly resolved in his thinking—and this is so, not merely in the sense that every question that concerns Heidegger always remains "in question," and so is never resolved in a way that could lead to the cessation of questioning, but in the sense that the very question itself seems to remain difficult and opaque. In this respect, the emergence of space as a problematic notion in *Being and Time* is not only indicative of certain difficulties pertaining to that work alone, but of a difficulty that persists in the idea of space as such. Thus Heidegger's very last published piece, the short experiment on "Art and Space" that was produced in conjunction with the sculptor Eduardo Chillida, seems still to remain unsure as to exactly how the character of space, in its essence, should be thought. Yet what nevertheless does emerge clearly in all of Heidegger's later thinking concerning space, and is itself tied to the way space is related to the clearing and the open, is the character of space as opened up through place.

This latter relation is made clearly evident in a passage from "Building Dwelling Thinking" that is part of one of the few continuously sustained accounts of space as its stands in relation to place anywhere in Heidegger's work:

The bridge is a place [*ein Ort*]. As such a thing, it allows a space [*einen Raum*] into which earth and heaven, divinities and mortals are admitted. The space allowed by the bridge contains many locations [*Plätze*] variously near or far from the bridge. These locations, however, may be treated as mere positions [*Stellen*] between which there lies a measurable distance; a distance, in Greek *stadion*, always has room made for it, and indeed by bare positions. The space that is thus made by positions is space of a peculiar sort. As distance or "stadion" it is what the same word, *stadion*, means in Latin, a *spatium*, an intervening space or interval. Thus nearness and remoteness between men and things can become mere distance, mere intervals of intervening space. In a space that is represented purely as *spatium*, the bridge now appears as a mere something at some position, which can be occupied at any time by something else or replaced by a mere marker. What is more, the mere dimensions of height, breadth, and depth can be abstracted from space as intervals. What is so abstracted we represent as the pure manifold of the three dimensions. Yet the room made by this manifold is also no longer determined by distances; it is no longer a *spatium*, but now no more than *extensio*—extension. But from space as extension a further abstraction can be made, to analytic-algebraic relations. What these relations make room for is the possibility of the purely mathematical construction of manifolds with an arbitrary number of dimensions. The space provided for in this mathematical manner may be called "space," the "one" space as such. But in this sense "the" space, "space," contains no spaces [*Räume*] and no location [*Plätze*]. We never find in it any places [*Orte*], that is, things of the kind the bridge is.[71]

This passage is particularly important for the way in which it presents a transition between what we might view as a number of different senses or "modes" of space. Heidegger begins with a claim to the effect that the thing, in this case the bridge, is a location or place—a point that also appears in "Art and Space."[72] It is because it is a place that it allows a space to appear, and it does so, as Heidegger makes clear in an important passage just prior to the one quoted here, through the way in which place establishes a certain limit or "boundary":

> *Raum* [Space] means a place cleared or freed for settlement and lodging. A space is something that has been made room for, something that is cleared and free, namely within a boundary [*Grenze*], Greek *peras*. A boundary is not that at which something stops but, as the Greeks recognized, the boundary is that from which something *begins its presencing*. That is why the concept is that of *horismos*, that is, the horizon, the boundary. Space is in essence that for which room has been made, that which is let into its bounds. . . . *Accordingly, spaces* [*die Räume*] *receive their being* [*ihr Wesen*] *from places* [*aus Orten*] *and not from "space"* [dem Raum].[73]

The employment of the notion of horizon here, in relation to space as that which is determined within the horizon and the horizon as determined by place, echoes the often implicit, and sometimes explicit, employment of ideas and images of horizonality throughout his thinking. Here, the space that Heidegger describes as immediately opened up in and through the establishing of boundedess in relation to place is itself that which allows room for the elements of the fourfold. The space that is at issue is thus the between, the open distance that allows the elements of the fourfold to be differentiated—much like the "open" that was also at issue in the passage that I quoted from the *Parmenides* lectures above—the space between earth and sky, between gods and mortals. This is not merely a space of difference, but also a *real* space—it is the space in which we ourselves live and move, the space across which we glance when we look up from earth to sky, the space we cross, but that also remains, when we approach the figure of the god. It is this sense of space, a rich and complex sense that encompasses space as both objective and bodily, which emerged at the end of our discussion of *Being and Time* (in sec. 3.6 above). The space at issue here allows also for particular places in the sense of locations, but in opening up in this way, another sense of space also emerges in a way that is not discontinuous with the previous sense, and yet can also be distinguished from it—the sense of space as that within which various places can be "located" or "contained." This sense of space already moves us in the direction of the leveled–out sense of space as measurable extension—the space of the merely "present."

What Heidegger delineates in this passage, then, is not merely the way space stands in relation to place, but also the way space and place both ramify into a number of different aspects. We thus see how the proper dimensionality that belongs to space, and that is evident in the way space stands "between" things, thereby enabling them to stand in relation to one another, is transformed into the space that allows for multiple "places," as well as into the space of distance or "interval" that is subject to quantifiable determination. Yet it is equally clear that these are all modifications or transformations of space as such. The space that is quantifiably determinable, the space of *spatium* and *extensio*, is itself a space that emerges from out of the single, complex opening of space that is the happening of place in the gathering of the world in and through the thing. Similarly, the place that belongs to the thing can be grasped both as that primordial happening of place that opens up the very possibility of space as well as of particular places, and also as itself a particular place that is opened up in that happening. Just as the gathering of world that occurs in the Event is a gathering of the elements that make up world (of the things that are evident within the world, and of the thing as such), so we can see, in the way place opens into space, into places and spaces, into extension and location, the way in which place and space themselves comprise a certain gathering and opening of what is proper to them—a gathering and opening of a multiplicity of aspects. The mistake in the reading of place as mere location, then, or of space as mere extension, is not that location and extension are not proper to place and space, but that they reveal only a part of what is gathered or "appropriated" in them. Place is location, but also more than that; space is extension, but it is not that alone.

In its essential sense—the sense in which space is revealed in its original and originary "happening"—space is the "spacing" that is first at play in the unifying and differentiating of the elements of the fourfold and of the things that are brought to appearance in the clearing that is thereby opened up. The clearing is indeed "spatial" in this primordial sense. Of course, the clearing clears, "space" opens up, both in the sense that the clearing enables the elements of the fourfold to stand apart from one another (while they are also brought together) and in the sense that it enables the thing to stand out from the world (thereby allowing the disclosedness of world and thing together). The clearing that occurs in and through the thing clears a space in the midst of beings in such a way that beings can appear as the things they are—a space is thereby cleared in the midst of beings that "gives room" for being as such. In this respect, the clearing that occurs in the gathering of the fourfold is also a happening of difference—not only the difference between the elements of the fourfold, or between thing and world, but also of the difference between being and beings. In a lecture course from 1941, *Basic Concepts*, Heidegger refers to the difference or distinction between being and beings as that in which we have our "domain of residence,"[74] going on to say that:

The distinction between beings and being holds the differentia apart from one another, and this apartness is in itself an extension and an expanse that we must recognize as the space of all spaces—so far as we may still use this name "space" at all here, which indeed means only a certain type of apartness.[75]

What this passage leaves unclear is whether the term "space" as used here is indeed merely a way to refer to a "type of apartness" or whether all apartness might not itself be something that is essentially "spatial." I will return to this point in a moment, but first I want to note another feature of Heidegger's discussion in this passage. Irrespective of whether we consider the "dimension" that is referred to here in spatial terms, it is notable that it is the *spatial*, and not the temporal, that opens up out of that dimension. By contrast, when we come to discuss the other axis of the fourfold, that of gods and mortals, we shall see that the dimension in which they stand is not spatial, nor does it give rise to the spatial in any direct way. Instead it refers us primarily to historicality, to birth and death, to destiny and fate—in short, to the *temporal*. Moreover, just as earth and sky can be seen to be evident in and through bodily exertion and movement—through the upward glance of the eye from horizon to zenith, the leap of the body or the sweep of the limbs in and through air, the flow of water against skin or the falling of rain on the face, the weight and resistance of rock and soil as one works a stretch of ground—so this would seem to reinforce the idea of a special connection between the earth-sky axis and the spatial.[76] The possibility is thereby opened up that the twin axes of gods and mortals, earth and sky, should be understood as, to some extent, mirroring the twin axes of space and time that together make up what Heidegger calls "time-space" (*Zeit-Raum*). In opening up this possibility, however, there can be no suggestion that the earth-sky axis does not also implicate the temporal, or the gods-mortals axis the spatial—the way in which each axis relates to the spatial and the temporal will nevertheless differ according to the differing character of earth and sky, gods and mortals, and the relation between them.

The dimension that spans earth and sky may thus be seen as opening, in a way particular to that dimension, into the spatial. Yet it may nevertheless be argued that the focus on earth and sky here all too readily misleads—it lends itself too easily to literal construal in spatial terms. The dimension that stands between being and beings certainly cannot be construed in that way, and to do so, it may be argued, is completely to misunderstand the nature of the "apartness" at issue here. Being does not stand in contrast to beings as one being stands to another—and it is surely only in the latter case that talk of "space" could even be considered as having any possible application. This is not, however, entirely correct. The difference between being and beings is certainly not like any difference that obtains between beings, but it is very like the difference that obtains between world and thing, or between the clearing as such and that which is evident in such clearing. In this respect, talk of the apartness that prevails between being and beings can also be taken as referring to an apartness that is between the prevailing of a certain "space," a certain "openness," a certain "dimension" or, we might say, a "region," as such. Indeed, if we recall the understanding of space that is also implicit in the passage from *Basic Questions of Philosophy* to which I referred in chapter 4 above (sec. 4.3), in which Heidegger explicates the "fourfold" that pertains to the happening of "truth" (in terms of the openness that relates to the thing, to the thing and the human, to the human as it relates to the thing, and to the human in relation to the human), then it seems that "space" also plays a role in the very topology of "truth" as such. It is not that space stands between world, or being, and beings, as if each stood on one side of a room, but rather that the opening up of space differentiates between being and beings in the way the opening up of space differentiates between horizon and that which is located within that space—although, when we talk in this way in relation to "being" or "world," the opening up of difference is perhaps best understood in terms of the way the space that is opened up "stands between" the opening and that which appears within it.

In ". . . Poetically Man Dwells . . ." (a lecture written contemporaneously with "Building Dwelling Thinking" and first given in 1951), Heidegger also briefly addresses the question of the spatiality of what he there refers to specifically as "the dimension" that spans, not the "space" between being and beings, but between earth and sky—and so presumably refers to the open realm of the clearing that unfolds in the happening of the fourfold:

The upward glance spans the between of earth and sky. This between is measured out for the dwelling of man. We now call the span thus meted out the dimension. This dimension does not arise from the fact that earth and sky are turned toward one another. Rather, their facing each other depends on the dimension. Nor is the dimension a stretch of space as ordinarily understood; for everything spatial, as something for which space is made, is already in need of the dimension, that is, into which it is admitted.[77]

At first sight it might seem that this settles the question of the spatiality of the "dimension"—the dimension is *not* spatial—until we notice that even here Heidegger only says that it is not "a stretch of space as ordinarily understood." Certainly the "dimension" at issue here is not primarily temporal, and it seems that it must stand in some relation to the spatial, even if that relation remains unclear. I will return to this question in a moment, but I want first to give some consideration to the way in which the dimension to which Heidegger draws attention here is explicitly understood in terms of the span between earth and sky—the span that is encompassed in a "glance."

Elsewhere, in one of the *Zollikon Seminars*, Heidegger discusses the character of a space as that through which something (a table) can show itself to someone and into which a wall could be put so as to block such showing:

> the spatiality of this space consists of its being pervious, its being open, and its being a free [realm]. In contrast, the openness itself is not something spatial. The open, the free, is that which appears and shows itself in its own way. . . . The open, the free [realm]—that which is translucent [*das Durchscheinende*] is not grounded on what is in space. It is the other way around: What is in space is grounded on the open and on the free.[78]

Here it seems that Heidegger is indeed straightforwardly prioritizing the open over the spatial, making the point that the openness of a space is not itself something spatial. Yet the issue is still somewhat muddied by the fact that Heidegger refers to "the spatiality of *this* space" (but what space is at issue here?—is it the same as space as "ordinarily understood?"), while that in which the open is said *not* to be grounded is "what is in space" rather than space as such. Moreover, even if we take Heidegger seemingly at his word, then how are the open and the "free" (as Heidegger means them here) to be understood without relying on *some* notion of the spatial? And what is the spatial such that its openness is not something spatial? If by space, we mean, in fact, the realm of material extendedness, then it does make sense to claim that the openness of that realm is not to be construed on the basis of such material extendedness; but, if we think of space differently, then this is not so obvious. Moreover, it would be a mistake to suppose that we already know what space is, for what is itself at issue in this discussion is indeed the essence of space and of the spatial as such.

Certainly Heidegger seems himself to advance a way of thinking of space that is more fundamental than the "usual" understanding—a way of understanding that seems evident in "Building Dwelling Thinking" and that also seems to be envisaged as a possibility in "Art and Space." In the latter essay, Heidegger asks "how can we find the special character of space?" and he replies:

There is an emergency path which, to be sure, is a narrow and precarious one. Let us try to listen to language. Whereof does it speak in the word "space"? Clearing-away [*Räumen*] is uttered therein. This means: to clear out [*roden*], to free from wilderness. Clearing-away brings for the free, the openness for man's settling and dwelling. When thought in its own special character, clearing-away is the release of places toward which the fate of dwelling man turns in the preserve of the home or in the brokenness of homelessness or in complete indifference to the two. Clearing-away is release of the places at which a god appears, the places from which the gods have disappeared, the places at which the appearance of the godly tarries long. In each case, clearing-away brings forth locality preparing for dwelling. Secular spaces are always the privation of often very remote sacred spaces. Clearing-way is release of places.[79]

Here it seems that space is understood in its most basic sense as "clearing-away" (*Räumen*), and so in a sense that appears very close to the notion of the opening up of dimension or apartness—the freeing or opening up of "room"—that is at issue in the passages from the 1941 lecture and the 1951 essay, as well as being similar to the original sense of space that is also evident in "Building Dwelling Thinking." Indeed, much the same understanding of space as "making room" or "clearing away" also appears in the extended, if somewhat unsatisfactory,[80] discussion of space in the *Zollikon Seminars*.[81] There Heidegger talks of space as "free" and is then asked whether this "free" space is "the same space as the space of this room." Heidegger answers: "The room belongs to it. Once more you see that language is wiser than we think. 'Space' comes from 'making space' [for]. . . ."[82] The space of the room (the space, perhaps, into which one can put a wall) belongs to the free space of "making space," of "making room," of "clearing-away." Although Heidegger leaves the question open, it seems increasingly as if space, in its essence, is another name for the open and the free—space is a form of opening. Perhaps the reason for Heidegger's frequent tendency to invoke space, and then to dismiss it, as he appears to do in the passages from *Basic Concepts*, ". . . Poetically Man Dwells . . . ," and elsewhere, indicates the way in which Heidegger's main concern is often to preempt any tendency to understand the "apartness" or "dimension" about which those passages speak in terms of the usual conception of space as tied to material extendedness alone. Yet these passages, when looked at in conjunction with other passages in which space also figures, suggest that Heidegger's own talk of space, at least in his later thinking, oscillates between this narrower conception and the richer understanding of space that I sketched above, an understanding of space that is indeed associated with the original opening up of world and of place.

At the same time, however, it should also be acknowledged that even if thought in this more fundamental fashion, Heidegger still sees space as opened up *through* the happening of *place*. Thus, although in "Art and Space," Heidegger looks first to the way places are "released" through the opening up of space, he also goes on to ask whether space is not also first determined in relation to the original gathering of place:

> The question comes up: Are places first and only the result and issue of making-room? Or does making-room take its special character from the reign of gathering places? If this proves right, then we would have to search for the special character of clearing-away in the grounding of locality, and we would have to meditate on locality as the interplay of places. We would have then to take heed that and how this play receives its reference to the belonging together of things from the region's free expanse. We would have to learn to recognize that things themselves are places and do not merely belong to a place.[83]

It seems clear that in putting this in the form of a question, Heidegger's aim is to raise as questionable the usual prioritization of space over place—even when space is thought more fundamentally in terms of "making room" or "clearing-away." In doing this, he also indicates a very similar way of understanding the relation between place and space to that which is set out in "Building Dwelling Thinking"—place, or the gathering of places in a region, is what determines the opening up of space. The way this opening up of space through place occurs is not through place somehow first appearing and space then being disclosed as a consequence; instead, place allows space to appear in much the same way as the placing of a single object into the midst of an otherwise flat and empty plane immediately configures that plane around the object—rather than a single undifferentiated "space," space now appears as that "in which" the object is located and as constituted in terms of different spaces that stand in relation to the object. The way in which, in this fashion, the discussion in "Art and Space" allows for the possibility that the "clearing-away" of space may be first determined by "the reign of gathering places" seems to confirm the account set out in "Building Dwelling Thinking" according to which the opening of space arises out of the gathering of place—the gathering of place may already include space since space opens out of it (much as the placing of a landmark within an empty plane already presupposes or "includes" that plane, even while it opens it up), but that gathering of place cannot itself be understood in purely spatial terms. Perhaps this may also play a role, at least in some cases, in explaining Heidegger's tendency to deny that the original opening up of dimensionality, of "apartness," or of world is itself "spatial"—that original opening is, instead, properly "topological."

Of course, the opening up of space, whether it arises out of place or not, is not something that occurs "in" space any more than the happening of the Event is something that occurs "in" time. To put matters in a way that runs the risk of opacity through sheer density of image and idea: the opening up of space *is* the spatializing of space as the happening of the Event *is* the temporalizing of time—which is to say that time and space themselves first appear in and through the Event, the thing, the place. One might argue, as Heidegger himself does,[84] that the opening of space is in a certain way secondary to the opening up of time here, but this is so only in the sense that there is a form of priority that obtains between the gathering or unifying of the fourfold and its differentiation, and this corresponds to a certain difference in the relation between unity and differentiation in respect of time and space themselves. One might say that time is the fundamental principle of unity, while space is the fundamental principle of differentiation so that, in one sense at least, time gathers what space sets apart.[85]

The role of space in the differentiation of the elements and the things that are gathered together in the happening of world and of place is already indicated by the role space plays, quite independently of the Heideggerian account, in the possibility of an objective world of things as this is worked out in Kantian and more recent post-Kantian philosophy. Indeed, one can see in the Kantian distinction of time and space as, respectively, the forms of "inner" and "outer" sense (the use of a pair of spatial terms in the making of this distinction is itself significant) something of the way in which each relates more primarily to unity and to differentiation. Moreover, it is also quite clear the way in which, in Kant, spatiality plays a central role in the constitution of objects and in the distinction between objects, including the distinction between objects and the self. Only within a unity and encompassing space can things be present in a way such that they can stand as distinct from one another or from ourselves.[86] Within twentieth-century Anglo-American thought, this same point is developed by Strawson in his *Individuals*,[87] and the idea has also been taken up in the work of a number of contemporary philosophers.[88] Once again, however, it is important to stress that the space that is at issue here cannot be merely the space of measurable extension, but is rather the space that allows for movement and a sense of embodiment, as well as a sense of extendedness and dimensionality. It is not the space of objectivity alone, then, but the space that "gives room," the space of the free and the open.

If space is that which stands "between" things and between the basic elements of world, then space is also that which can be traversed. Indeed, there is an essential connection between space and movement—whether it is the movement of bodily passage across or through, or the movement given in the glance of the eye, the sweep of the hand, the rise and fall of sound. The space that first opens up in and around the place of the thing is thus a space of movement and activity rather than a space of static "pre-sentness." Indeed, Heidegger's account of the way in which things thing, world worlds, the fourfold "rings" constantly presents that happening in terms of the way in which the thing itself "works" as a thing—much as in "The Origin of the Work of Art" the emphasis is on the artwork as a work, not as a mere object. Consequently, it is in the jug's outpouring that the essence of the jug as a thing is made evident and in its outpouring that the fourfold is gathered around it; it is in the bridge as a "crossing passage" that it gathers earth and sky, gods and mortals together; it is through its sheltering, steady growth that the oak tree gathers the world of Heidegger's *Meßkirch*. Although the space differentiates, the unity of the space is itself given through the unity of the activity and movement that occurs within it.

Inasmuch as space gives room for a multiplicity of places to emerge within it, so the way the unity of places is given in space is through the movements that connect those places, and thus also through the passages and pathways that connect them. In this respect, we can understand the interconnectedness of places as also an articulation of the unity of a space, though we may also say that, inasmuch as the space that contains places within it can be understood as having something of the being of a place itself—of the sort of place we call a "locality" or "region" (in Heidegger's German, not so much a "*Gegend*," the term referring to a localized ordering of equipment, as an "*Ortschaft*"). As we have already seen, place itself gathers, but the gathering of places, and so the gathering of places in space, is itself something that occurs by means of the pathway. Thus Heidegger can write of place, or of the Greek *topos*, in a way that indicates both its character as a gathering together of that which already belongs, as well as of the gathering of places as a region, locality, or "district" through the paths that go between them:

Τόπος is the Greek for "place," although not as mere position in a manifold of points, everywhere homogeneous. The essence of the place consists in holding gathered, as the present "where," the circumference of what is in its nexus, what pertains to it and is "of" it, of the place. The place is the originally gathering holding of what belongs together and is thus for the most part a manifold of places reciprocally related by belonging together, which we call a settlement or a district [Ortschaft]. In the extended domain of the district there are thus roads, passages, and paths. A δαιμόνιος Τόπος [daimonios topos] is an "uncanny district." That now means: a "where" in whose squares and alleys the uncanny shines explicitly and the essence of Being comes to presence in an eminent sense.[89]

The character of place as both a gathering and as itself gathered, as well as the way the gathering of places occurs through the pathways between places, indicates the way in which place, out of which space is itself opened up, is also that which calls upon space in its own articulation and its own gatheredness. The idea of places as themselves gathered, although it does not figure in any significant way in "Building Dwelling Thinking," does appear as a theme in "Art and Space"—indeed, it constitutes a significant point of difference between the accounts in the two essays that has so far gone unremarked. In "Art and Space," the emphasis is on the settled local-ity—"die Ortschaft"—rather than the solitary place, and on the belonging together of things, rather than on the gathering that occurs in the single thing. In this way, the account that is suggested in "Art and Space" con-tains an important recognition of the way in which places themselves always implicate, and are implicated by, other such places; the way in which, as we saw in the discussion above, things constantly light up, and are lit up by, other things; the way in which the Event is not some simple coming to presentness, but a constant presencing, gathering, disclosing.

Space and place thus stand in an essential relation to one another—albeit a relation that cannot be given any simple or unequivocal characteriza-tion. Moreover, both also stand in an important and essential relation to language. This is so in at least two respects: first in the character of place and language as "gathering," and, second, in the character of language and space as both "differentiating" or "dif-fering"—although as space and place themselves belong together, so too does such gathering and differing. In considering Heidegger's thinking about language, however (and this applies, as I have noted earlier, to Heidegger's later thinking in general), there is no attempt to provide any sort of "explanation" or "analysis." Indeed, neither is there anything like an inquiry into the transcendental conditions of language, or into language as it might itself figure as such a condition (at least not in the strict sense according to which such condi-tionality implies a relation according to which the condition is necessary and sufficient for that which is conditioned), but there is an attempt to "disclose" the originary character of language, to exhibit language, or to "evoke" it in its fundamental relatedness to world and to being. World itself is no mere assemblage of entities, but is rather a gathered unity in which things find themselves brought together with one another while they are also disclosed in their difference—"language" is a key word that names this happening of unifying and differing. For this reason, language is understood in only a secondary fashion when it is thought primarily in terms of the many forms of language that we refer to as "English," "German," "Greek," "Arabic," "Chinese," and so forth. Language belongs first and foremost, according to Heidegger, to being and is thus not something "produced by" or "at the disposal of" humans—"language" he says "is the language of being, as clouds are the clouds of the sky."[90] It is thus that Heidegger talks of language as, in its essence, "not the utterance of an organism"[91]—it is the original and originary articulation of being as such that speaks in and through each and every human language.

If language is the original articulation that belongs to being, then language must also be understood in terms of the original opening of being in its difference. In the 1950 essay "Language" Heidegger writes of the role of language as the "happening or occurring of the dif-ference for world and things"—a dif-ference that occurs in the intimacy that also obtains between the two:

The intimacy of world and thing is not a fusion. Intimacy obtains only where the intimate—world and thing—divides itself cleanly and remains separated. In the midst of the two, in the between of world and thing. . . . division prevails: a dif-ference. The intimacy of world and thing is present in the separation of the between; it is present in the dif-ference. . . . The dif-ference carries out world in its worlding, carries out things in their thinging. . . . The dif-ference is neither distinction nor relation. The dif-ference is, at most, dimension for world and thing. . . . Language speaks. Its speaking bids the dif-ference to come which expropriates world and things into the simple onefold of their intimacy.[92]

The image of language as a mode of dimensionality, as that which holds apart, is also suggestive of language as that through which one can move. Indeed, this is clearly suggested by the image of language as the "house" of being, a phrase that Heidegger explains in terms that explicitly present language as something like a dimension or region (a "precinct") in and through which we move:

Language is the precinct [templum], i.e., the house of being. The essence of language is neither exhausted in reference, nor is it only a matter of signs and ciphers. Since language is the house of being, we therefore arrive at beings by constantly going through this house. If we go to the fountain, if we go through the woods, we are already going through the word "fountain," through the word "wood," even if we are not saying these words aloud or have any thoughts about language. . . . All beings . . . each in its own way, are (as beings) in the precinct of language. That is why only *in this precinct,* if anywhere, can the reversal from the region of objects and their representation into the innermost of the heart's space be realized.[93]

That language is the house, or the "precinct," of being means not only that language is that in which being itself resides, and so is also articulated in the manner in which that house or precinct is articulated, but that being is that which, in the form of language, is also a dwelling-place. The dimensionality of language is the dimensionality of being—the dimensionality of world. Inasmuch as that dimensionality is also necessarily spatialized (although it is not only that since its very spatialization also involves time), so language is inextricably bound up with the unifying and dif-fering of things and of world that occurs in and through the opening up of space understood as that complex dimensionality that itself allows for the grasp of the sensuous, the bodily, the extended, and even the measurable. Heidegger thus draws on ideas and images of spatiality in his articulation of the relation between language and being, but, perhaps more significantly, his characterization of language is itself presented in terms that mirror the character of space as that in which the "differing" of being occurs.

One may object here that Heidegger's use of spatial images to describe the originary character of language is merely figurative, and at most, perhaps, is indicative of the fundamental role of spatial or bodily imagery in all our thinking.[94] Yet Heidegger specifically rules out any merely "figurative" interpretation of the phrase "the house of being"—"talk about the house of being is not the transfer of the image 'house' onto being."[95] This does not, it seems to me, imply any suspicion of the figurative as such in favor of the literal, but rather a rejection of any simple contrast between the figurative and the literal—a rejection of the idea that we already understand what is at issue in this contrast, or that we already know what things are such that we can indeed already differentiate that which is properly "figurative" from that which is "literal."[96] Language is itself "spatialized," not only through the way in which it relates to the opening up of difference and the between, but also through the way language always takes the form of *inscription*—an inscription that occurs no less in the spoken than in the written word. Inscription is the spatializing of language, and as such, is the appearing of language in the world, and yet such inscription is also essential to the happening of language. As inscription, language allows for the re-presenting of the world and of the things within it, and that re-presenting is itself necessary for the opening up of the between that allows world and thing to come into their own. The between is as much the between that lies between word and thing as between thing and world;

moreover, it is also the between that lies between the concreteness of the inscribed word—the sounding or the script—and the generality of its sense:

A word of language sounds and resounds in the voice, is clear and bright in the typeface. Voice and script are indeed sensuous, yet always within them a meaning [*Sinn*] is told and appears. As sensuous meaning, the word traverses the expanse of the leeway between earth and sky. Language holds open the realm in which man, upon the earth and beneath the sky, inhabits the house of the world.[97]

The between of language is thus multiple: not only is language the house of being, the region of being's dif-fering, but language is that which holds open the realm in which the house of the world is inhabited.

In talking of language as the "house of being," language is already spoken of in a way that takes language to be, in some sense, a place or "topos," and, as such, language does not only allow the prevailing of difference, it also gathers and unifies. Indeed, in chapter 1, I noted the way in which the use of place-related terms that have linguistic connotations—the use of "topic" in English or of "*Erörterung*" in German, both of which involve the "gathering" of elements in language (within a text or discussion)—can be seen as indicative of an essential connection between language and place. The poet William Wordsworth took place and language to be intimately connected in the form of the poetic, and especially through the naming of places—which naming is also, of course, a form of gathering.[98] The encounter with place in its determinacy and distinctness is invariably an encounter with the place that is inseparable from the naming of that place. In this latter respect, the giving of a name to newly discovered places is not only a matter of geographical, topographical, or navigational convenience, but relates directly to the way in which the naming marks the emergence of the place as a place—moreover, names themselves have the capacity to "conjure" the places to which they belong (even though the way they may bring those places to appearance may be in a way that does not always square with the places as such). Moreover, in the naming of things as such, what is "named" a thing is also "placed" or "situated" in relation to other things. Indeed, if, as Heidegger claims in the passage I quoted from his discussion of the Greek "*topos*" above, the essence of place consists "in holding gathered . . . ," then this is something that the place shares in common with the word, and with language, for language too is a gathering, and the word is that which gathers.[99] It is as a gathering in place that language is the house of being, but it is through naming, through the way the word calls up the thing, and the place with it, that language is also a happening of place and place a happening of language.

5.5   The Dwelling of Mortals

One of the central problems in Heidegger's thinking from the 1920s through into the 1930s was, as we saw above, the problem of the relation between being and human being. Thus, at various points, Heidegger criticizes his thinking, especially as set out in *Being and Time*, but also, as we saw, in "The Origin of the Work of Art," for a tendency to allow being to be construed as if it were somehow a result of human being or activity, as if it were grounded in something human. The way in which Heidegger places the thing at the center of the gathering of the fourfold, however, and the way in which mortals are themselves gathered in and through the thing ought to indicate that there can no longer be any possibility of think- ing of the gathering of the fourfold as something that is accomplished by, or grounded in, the human. Indeed, once we recognize the way in which the question of being and of human being are bound up in questionabil- ity, then it becomes very clear how this cannot be a matter to be decided only by, or in relation to, the human. Yet this still leaves much to be said about the manner in which human being, the being of mortals, is indeed gathered into the essential questioning of being, into the happening of the fourfold. Moreover, the fact that mortals do indeed stand in a relation to that happening in a way that other beings, such as the stone, the tree, and the animal, do not still leaves considerable scope for misunderstanding. A crucial question, then, concerns the exact mode of belonging to the fourfold that is proper to mortals—a question that also concerns the original determination, the "essence," of mortal being.

The question of "essence" is usually understood in terms of what prop- erly belongs to a thing, but for Heidegger it is that to which the thing itself properly belongs rather than what belongs to it, that is the real domain of the question of "essence." Already, in putting matters in this way, the ques- tion of essence starts to appear "topologically," that is, as a question that concerns a certain "place" or *topos*—to determine that to which a thing properly belongs is also to determine its proper place or *topos*. In this respect, it is notable that much of Heidegger's discussion of the "essence" of human being, or in the terms of the fourfold, of the being of mortals, is in terms of the proper "home," "abode," or "residence"[100]—this is why Heidegger's work so often comes, as I have already noted, to thematize ideas and images of homeland (or *"Heimat"*), "homecoming" (*Heimkunft*), and the "homely" (*heimlich*), as well as of the "unhomely" or "uncanny" (*unheimlich*),[101] and of "homelessness" (*Heimatlosigkeit*)—a thematization that is to be understood in terms of a preoccupation with the proper belonging that determines us in our very being. When Heidegger comes to name the character of mortal belonging to the fourfold, then, he does so in a way that draws on a similarly topological idea and image of belonging, one already familiar from *Being and Time*, namely, "dwelling" (in contemporary German, "*Wohnen*").

In "Building Dwelling Thinking," Heidegger approaches the character of such dwelling through the way in which human being also involves productive activity or "building" (*Bauen*), exploring the connections at issue, in part, by recourse to some of the same linguistic considerations that also appeared in his discussion of "being-in" in section 12 of *Being and Time*, but that are here augmented by a much richer set of explicitly topological considerations that cluster around the old word for building *and* dwelling, "*buan*":

What, then, does *Bauen*, building, *mean*? The Old English and High German word for building, *buan*, means to dwell. This signifies: to remain, to stay in a place. The real meaning of the verb *bauen*, namely, to dwell, has been lost to us. But a covert trace of it has been preserved in the German word, *Nachbar*, neighbour. The neighbour is in Old English the *neahgebur*; *neah*, near, and *gebur*, dweller. The Nachbar is the *Neahgebur*, the near-dweller, he who dwells nearby. The verbs *buri*, *büren*, *beuren*, *beuron*, all signify dwelling, the abode, the place of dwelling. Now to be sure the old word *buan* not only tells us that *bauen*, to build, is really to dwell; it also gives us a clue as to how we have to think about the dwelling it signifies. . . . Where the word *bauen* still speaks in its original sense it also says *how far* the nature of dwelling reaches. That is, *bauen*, *buan*, *bhu*, *beo* are our word *bin* in the versions: *ich bin*, I am, *du bist*, you are, the imperative form *bis*, be. What then does *ich bin* mean? The old word *bauen*, to which the *bin* belongs, answers: *ich bin*, *du bist* mean: I dwell, you dwell. The way in which you are and I am, the manner in which we humans *are* on the earth, is *Buan*, dwelling. To be a human being means to be on the earth as a mortal. It means to dwell. The old word *bauen*, which says that man *is* insofar as he *dwells*, this word *bauen* however *also* means at the same time to cherish and protect, to preserve and care for.[102]

To dwell is to remain, to stay in a place (and here we may recall the idea of curiosity, in the way it appears in *Being and Time*, as characterized by a mode of being that consists in "not tarrying," in constant "uprooting"), and so the question of dwelling also becomes a question concerning what it means to remain, to stay (indeed, Heidegger also notes the way the Old Saxon "*wuon*" and the Gothic "*wunian*" echo in the contemporary word "*Wohnen*," "to remain, to stay in a place").[103] Moreover, the question of dwelling is not merely a question concerning one among a number of other aspects of human being, but instead dwelling reaches so far as to

encompass the nature of human being as such—to say that "I am" is to
say that I dwell. To be human, then, "to be on the earth as a mortal," is
to remain, to stay, to be in a certain relation to a place—moreover, as such,
it is also, as we might already surmise from the discussion of space and
place in the previous section, to stand in a certain relation to space:

> When we speak of man and space [*Raum*], it sounds as though man stood on one
> side, space on the other. Yet space is not something that faces man. It is neither an
> external object nor an inner experience. . . . Spaces open up by the fact that they are
> let into the dwelling of man. To say that mortals *are* is to say that *in dwelling* they
> persist through spaces by virtue of their stay among things and locations [*Dingen
> und Orten*]. . . . Man's relation to places [*Orten*], and through places to spaces, inheres
> in his dwelling. The relationship between man and space is none other than
> dwelling, strictly thought and spoken.[104]

The claim that the relation between man and space is given in and through
dwelling might appear as a repetition of the claim in *Being and Time*, partly
elaborated through some of the same etymological considerations that we
have seen appear in "Building Dwelling Thinking," that the "being-in" of
human being is indeed a matter of human residing or dwelling,[105] yet in
Being and Time, of course, "dwelling" was set in contrast to spatial being,
whereas here dwelling and spatiality are themselves intimately linked.
Moreover, whereas space is seen to be opened up through dwelling, and
so through place, in a way that may appear reminiscent of the opening up
of space through the activity of being-there in relation to the structure of
equipment, here the opening up of space occurs through mortal dwelling,
but such dwelling is not something merely accomplished by mortals, being
determined, instead, by the overall structure of the gathering of the fourfold in its unity. Nevertheless, dwelling also refers to a certain mode of
comportment on the part of mortals: "to remain, to stay in a place" is thus
"to cherish and protect, to preserve and care for." Heidegger goes on to
identify such protecting and preserving in terms of being "at peace" (something he takes from the Gothic "*wunian*") and such being at peace is itself
a preserving, a sparing from harm, a freeing (a freeing that is surely closely
akin to the freedom that, in "On the Essence of Truth," was revealed as
"letting beings be").[106] "*The fundamental character of dwelling*," then, says
Heidegger "*is this sparing and preserving*,"[107] and to spare and preserve means
"to take under our care, to look after."[108] The connection between dwelling
and "looking after" or "caring for" suggests another reference back to the
early appearance of dwelling in *Being and Time* and its connection with
"looking after,"[109] but what is now seen to be looked after, to be cared for,

is that of which *Being and Time* showed no inkling, namely, the fourfold itself—the "simple oneness" of earth, sky, mortals, and gods.

Inasmuch as the fourfold is gathered always in relation to the thing, so the character of dwelling as a looking after—as a preserving, sparing, and freeing—is also a looking after things. The fourfold is itself preserved and spared through the preserving and sparing of the thing. Such preserving and sparing is not, however, a matter of our withdrawing from things. This is, indeed, already evident in Heidegger's talk of "letting be" in the 1930 essay "On the Essence of Truth." There Heidegger says that "to let beings be . . . does not refer to neglect and indifference but rather the opposite. To let be is to engage oneself with beings."[110] Nevertheless, in this essay the tendency is still to understand such "letting be" as something that is up to human being—it is a matter for human will and decision. One of the shifts, as we saw above, in Heidegger's thinking during the 1930s, is a shift away from the understanding of disclosedness or presencing (the happening of the truth of being) as something that happens on the basis of human will or decision. Talk of "sparing and preserving" thus refers us to a mode of human being that is itself determined by the particular way in which human being is gathered into the fourfold by the fourfold as such. Strictly speaking, then, we might say that "sparing and preserving," and so "letting be," is something that occurs in and through the particular manner in which the fourfold is gathered, although it will always appear as a "sparing and preserving" that works through the mode of human being since "sparing and preserving" is what is proper to human dwelling. "Sparing and preserving" will thus appear as something of which human beings are themselves capable.

Keeping in mind the essential connection between being and questionability that has already emerged, we may also say that to spare and preserve must be to allow beings to remain in their questionability. Of course, this means that metaphysics, insofar as it remains oblivious to being (such oblivion lying, according to Heidegger, at the very heart of metaphysics[111]), and so also to questionability, must inevitably be associated with a failure properly to dwell—a failure to spare and preserve. Certainly, in its insistence on understanding being and beings in terms of that which is merely present, and so in terms of certain determinate features or aspects of beings, metaphysics would seem not to "let be" at all, but rather to attempt to constrain, control, and de-limit being—metaphysics, as a mode of philosophy, may begin in wonder, as the Greeks claim and Heidegger affirms,[112] but it ends by turning that wonder into nothing more than curiosity and the thing into a mere "object." Inasmuch as metaphysics is

incapable of dwelling, so metaphysics turns out to constitute itself as essentially a mode of "homelessness."[113] This emerges as an important element
in Heidegger's diagnosis of the essential plight of the contemporary
world—our world is one in which homelessness prevails because of the
manner of revealing that metaphysics brings with it. This is an issue to
which we will have to return later, however, since the main concern for
the moment must be a clearer understanding of the nature of human
dwelling as such.

   To spare and preserve is to "let be," but not through a withdrawal so
much as a certain mode of engagement, and in "Building Dwelling Thinking," the manner in which human beings are engaged with things and in
the world is through that by which the idea of dwelling is itself introduced,
namely, "building." Building is the activity that produces, that brings
things forth, either through cultivation or through construction. Building
brings forth the temple, the bridge, presumably, if in a slightly different
form, it is also responsible for the jug (although in "Building Dwelling
Thinking," Heidegger's focus is primarily on the building associated with
the construction of dwellings). All human being involves building, and so
stands in an important relation to the Greek *"techne,"* itself understood by
Heidegger in terms of the disclosing or "letting-appear" that lies behind
our word "technology."[114] Yet the productive activity of building is not
simply identical with technology, with any technique, nor with any technical enterprise such as architecture or engineering.[115] Building is that
mode of productive activity that articulates the world in a way that allows
for human dwelling. But this means that building must be understood as
arising on the basis of dwelling rather than being that on which dwelling
is itself based. Thus Heidegger writes that "Only if we are capable of
dwelling, only then can we build."[116] Building is the productive activity
through which human beings make a place for themselves in the world
and so by means of which their own dwelling is articulated. The building
that is undertaken on the basis of our proper dwelling is a building that
allows for such dwelling and so allows for the gathering of the fourfold—
it is a building that itself spares and preserves through allowing human
beings to engage with things in a way that reflects the unitary and differing character of things. True building produces things that allow the world,
and the things that make up the world to come forth in their abundance
and multiplicity—true building produces, as it also works in relation to,
"things"; true building makes for, as it also arises in, places.

   If the building that arises out of dwelling spares and preserves, and in
so doing allows things to come forth as things, and so also allows the world

to come forth as world, then building must also work in such a way that
it allows the different elements of the fourfold to gather together in a way
that allows them properly to appear. This means allowing earth and sky to
appear as earth and sky, as the giving, grounding, opening of nature; allowing the gods to appears as gods, whether in their shining presence or the
darkening of their absence; and it also means allowing mortals to appear
as mortals, as beings who always stand in the shadow of their own
nothingness.

Understanding the nature of dwelling, and so also of building, is thus
to grasp the nature of the fourfold in all its dimensions, but it is especially
to grasp the nature of the fourfold as it is configured in relation to the
being of mortals, and so to their being as mortal. In "The Thing," Heidegger writes:

The mortals are human beings. They are called mortals because they can die. To die
means to be capable of death. Only man dies. The animal perishes. It has death
neither ahead of itself nor behind it. Death is the shrine of Nothing, that is, of that
which in every respect is never something that merely exists, but which nevertheless presences, even as the mystery of Being itself. As the shrine of Nothing, death
harbors within itself the presencing of Being. As the shrine of Nothing, death is the
shelter of Being. We now call mortals mortals—not because their earthly life comes
to an end, but because they are capable of death as death. Mortals are who they are,
as mortals, present in the shelter of Being. They are the presencing relation to Being
as Being.[117]

To dwell is, in this respect, to be capable of death as death. The death that
is at issue here, however, is not merely a matter of inevitable physical
extinction, but is rather a matter of the way in which our own being is
constantly at issue for us. To be mortal is always to be given over to
care for one's being, and so also for the things and the world with which
that being is inextricably bound up; it is to be constantly faced by the
fragility, the vulnerability, and the essential "temporality" of that about
which we care and to which we are committed. In this respect, death colors
the very stuff of our lives inasmuch as those lives are made up, not of what
is eternal and abstract, but of that which is concrete, particular, and also
transitory: this person, this community, this place, these things, perhaps
even this particular feeling, glimpse, or moment. In this respect, the way
in which death functions as a condition for the possibility of individual
existence, as a condition for the possibility of a self, is not through its
functioning as a future endpoint, but rather through the way in which our
own being-in-the-world is constituted in terms of a specific and yet ever-
changing situatedness. When we consider the sparing and preserving that

is proper to dwelling in connection with the mortal character of human being, such sparing and preserving takes on an additional meaning—it is to respond to our own lives and that which is bound up with them in a way that attends to the finite, the fragile, and the interconnected character of those lives, as well as of the world in which they are lived. Recognizing our being as mortals, then, is not a matter simply of facing up to the fact that we die, but more significantly, it means recognizing the way in which we are already given over to the world, to the fourfold that also encompasses the gods, earth, and sky, to the gathering of the fourfold in relation to the thing that is also the happening of place. Indeed, inasmuch as the recognition of our being as mortal is a matter of recognizing the way our being is inevitably bound to the concrete and the particular, so it is also a recognition of the character of our being as inevitably bound to place.

Mortals are, says Heidegger, "the presencing relation to Being as Being." This presencing relation is evident in the mortal character of human being since the character of being as a constant unfolding of beings into the free and the open, of beings into the full questionability of their being, is also the unfolding of mortal being as that which is itself in question, as that which itself stands out into "the nothing," into the free space of cleared, iridescent appearing. Joseph Fell writes that:

If I acknowledge death as a dark limit to my understanding, I am thrown back on the wonder of a lighted world—the wonder that there are beings at all. Only if I acknowledge this essential limit can I find my time and my world as a wondrous gift—which means as a place in which significance wondrously inheres.[118]

Death marks a limit to our being as mortals, but not as a mere stopping point for our lives. Here Heidegger's recurrent emphasis on limit as essentially "horizonal" comes into view once more—death is the limit that opens up the "space" within which our lives can be lived. Death is that mystery beyond which we cannot think (to imagine the world after our death is to try to bear witness to a world from which we are also essentially excluded), but which forces us back to focus on the life that, so long as we are, always lies before us, that always remains in question, that is always demanding of our care. In this way the "dark limit" of death does indeed "light up" the world within which our lives are lived. The "presencing relation to Being of Being" is thus the "reflection" of being back into being, into the happening of world that occurs through the happening of mortal being in its being gathered, and so itself is brought to presence in the gathering of the fourfold.

In the fourfold, of course, it is not just mortals who come to presence, but earth, sky, and gods. Earth and sky are manifest in all the variety and power of nature—in the span and openness of the sky, the shifting patterns of climate and season, the support and concealment of earth, the growth and fecundity of living things, the surging energy of the ocean, even the vigor and energy of bodily life and movement—and both earth and sky can be seen to reflect the mortal character of human being, not only in the way our mortality may be seen to reflect our dependence on the natural world, but, perhaps more importantly, in the changing and interdependent character of the natural world as such, as well as its cycles of growth, decay, and regeneration. It is the gods, however, who stand in a more direct and very particular relation to mortals and, indeed, to mortals in their being *as mortals*. Yet of the four elements that make up the fourfold, it is also the gods who clearly present the greatest difficulty for contemporary readers—here Heidegger is often taken to be at his most obviously mystical and obscure. Part of the difficulty resides in the common tendency to think of the gods in religious terms, but Heidegger clearly does not intend them that way; a greater difficulty arises from the widespread inability, nowadays, to give any sense or meaning at all to that which seems to go "beyond" the natural, although here too it must be said that Heidegger's gods should not be construed as "supernatural" in any of the usual ways.

Much of Heidegger's thinking about the gods is determined by Greek thought and experience, particularly as he takes it to be mediated by Hölderlin, and in the *Parmenides* lectures, Heidegger offers a warning that is relevant, not only to his reading of the Greeks, but also to his understanding of the fourfold. "The Greek gods," he says "are not 'personalities' or 'persons' that dominate being; they are Being itself as looking into beings," and he adds that, "we are thinking the essence of the Greek gods more originarily if we call them the attuning ones."[119] Something of this same conception of the gods as "attuning" is also evident in a work with which Heidegger seems to have had some acquaintance, Walter Otto's *Homeric Gods*, first published in German in 1929.[120] Otto talks of the Greek gods as "worlds"—under the sway of each god things are differently configured in their entirety in terms of the essential attribute of the god, in the case of Aphrodite, for instance, in terms of the power of sensual beauty and erotic love, in the case of Ares, in terms of military prowess and war, in the case of Apollo, as lit up in order and harmony. As Otto writes: "A god is always a totality, a whole world in its completion. . . . None of them merely represents a single virtue, and none of them is found merely in *one* direction of vividly moving life; each of them fills up the whole extent of human life with their particular spirit—forms it and illuminates it."[121] As the gods are the "attuning ones," so they are the lighting up of the world— they are the shining into the world of the world in its differentiated and differentiating gatheredness ("Being itself as looking into beings").

Although the fourfold is that gathering of all four elements that make it up—earth, sky, gods, and mortals—the elements that comprise each axis of the fourfold also stand in a special relation to one another. Thus earth stands in a special relation to sky, and gods stand in a special relation to mortals. The mortals are those who are both the witnesses to the happening of world (those to whom the world is disclosed) and the guardians (those who "preserve and spare") of that happening. The gods are the appearing of the gathered unity of the world in the world, and, as such, the gods announce the happening of world, are the "messengers" of that happening;[122] they beckon mortals toward their proper task in witnessing and guarding that happening. As the appearing of the happening of being, the gods are those under whose sway and in whose dispensation all human life is lived—they announce the proper destinings that govern the world and the affairs of mortals within it. It is in relation to the gods that human beings are thus able to grasp their own being as mortal. It is also in relation to the gods that human beings are able to grasp their being as implicated in being in a way that goes beyond any individual human life. In this latter respect, it is only in relation to the gods that the human belonging-together in community is possible. It is the gods that make for the possibility of the common "*ethos*" that is the being of such community.

It is because the gods, as they appear here, stand in such an essential relation to the appearing of the happening of world in its gatheredness that Heidegger can talk of the world as a "holy" (*heilig*) place and of the happening of world as a happening of "the holy" (*das Heilige*)—of that which is also properly "whole" or "hale," as well as capable of "healing" (the associated German terms, "*heil*," "*heilen*," and "*heilig*" carry all of these connotations).[123] For the world to appear as holy is just for it to appear as a happening of disclosedness, as a concealing and revealing, as, indeed, a happening of "place." It is also for this reason that the "holiday," the day of celebration (*Feiertag*)—itself the focus for one of the poems from Hölderlin ("Wie wenn am Feiertag") to which Heidegger pays special attention—takes on a central importance in Heidegger's later thinking. The holiday, the festival, is no mere "diversion" from work, an interruption in our normal routine. Instead, says Heidegger, the celebration of the holiday is "a becoming-free for the unaccustomed element of the day which, in

distinction to the dull and gloom of the everyday, is what is clear. . . . The
festive character of the festival has its determinate ground in the *holy* . . .
the festival is the primal event [*Ereignis*] of the greeting, in which *the holy*
greets, and in the greeting appears."[124] Here the festival takes on the role
that, in "The Origin of the Work of Art," Heidegger ascribed to the artwork.
Indeed, Gadamer takes the festival as itself illustrative of the nature of the
artwork, emphasizing, like Heidegger, the character of the festival as no
mere "break from work," but also describing the way in which it constitutes the opening up of a different "time" in which celebration gathers
human beings in community.[125] The festival, the "holy day," would then
be that which is not only the happening of the belonging-together of
world, but also the happening of the belonging-together of the human, all
of which occurs in the sight of the gods. The festival is thus the appearing of the *Ereignis*, not merely as it is tied to individual experience, but as
it is determinative and disclosive of historical human being as such as it
stands always in relation to the holy.[126]

Inasmuch as what becomes evident in the festival is the proper *"ethos"*
of human being—that which determines human being as a whole and as
it is a belonging-together with the human—so the festival is also the bringing to light of the nature of human dwelling. Indeed, Heidegger points out
that:

ἦθος [*ethos*] means abode, dwelling place. The word names the open region in which
the human being dwells. The open region of his abode allows what pertains to the
essence of the human being, and what in thus arriving resides in nearness to him,
to appear. The abode of the human being contains and preserves the advent of what
belongs to the human being in his essence. According to Heraclitus's phrase this is
δαίμων [*daimon*], the god. . . . The human being dwells, insofar as he is a human
being, in the nearness of god.[127]

Insofar as the festival is that in which the *ethos* of human being is brought
to light, it is also the bringing to light of the proper dwelling place of
human being, and hence the proper relation of human being in nearness
to god and to the holy.

In the line that Heidegger cites from Hölderlin, human beings dwell
"poetically," and, as Heidegger explicates this, it means always to dwell in
proper "measure"—not a measure given in mere calculation, or in that
which is calculable, but rather in relation to that which determines human
being, that in relation to which it is disclosed as what it is.[128] To dwell is
always to dwell poetically, which means that it is always a matter of being
in relation to the fourfold that "spares and preserves." Those things that
are the product of human dwelling as it occurs through building—the

bridge, the jug, the temple, even the tree whose growth is watched and tended—are things that themselves allow and preserve the gathering of the fourfold in and through them. Thus Heidegger writes that: "To preserve the fourfold, to save the earth, to receive the sky, to await the divinities, to escort the mortals—this fourfold preserving is the simple nature, the presencing, of dwelling."[129] To preserve the fourfold is, in essence, to allow the fourfold its character as a gathering of difference in the unity that belongs to it; it is to allow things to appear in both their disclosedness and their concealment, in terms of their finitude, their boundedness, and their "excess." As such, to dwell is also to stand in a relation to the question of being, understood now in terms of the essential belonging of being to questionability. What threatens dwelling is, indeed, the loss of such questionability, the loss of concealment, the loss of finitude and boundedness—the loss, one might say, of the nearness to the holy, of a proper "*ethos*," of a proper place.

In the "Letter on 'Humanism,'" Heidegger responds to a question concerning the apparent absence of an explicit attempt in his thinking to address the matter of "ethics" by explicitly pointing to the connection, noted just above, between "ethics" and "ethos," and he goes on: "If the name 'ethics,' in keeping with the basic meaning of the word ἦθος, should now say that ethics ponders the abode of the human being, then that thinking which thinks the truth of being as the primordial element of the human being, as one who eksists, is in itself originary ethics."[130] If Heidegger does not appropriate this term to his own thinking, it is because he remains concerned that, along with the language of "metaphysics" and "ontology," talk of "ethics" will not be rethought in the terms that are proper to what is at issue, but will simply continue to be read "according to the established terminology in its customary meaning."[131] With this latter qualification in mind, there is indeed an essentially "ethical" orientation to Heidegger's thinking, but the "ethics" at issue is not one that consists in the establishment of certain rules for conduct or in the uncovering of certain basic ethical "principles." It is instead the "ethics" that speaks of the need to respond to the proper "*ethos*" of human being—an ethics that is given essentially in the form of dwelling. Such an ethics is also, of course, a poetics—it is an attending to the proper abode of human being as it stands within the compass of earth and sky, of gods and mortals—as such it is also essentially "*topoetic*." Yet it is the very possibility of such dwelling—and so of a properly "ethical" mode of human being—that Heidegger claims is threatened by the character of the revealing that prevails in the contemporary world and that is essentially tied to technology.

5.6 The Questioning of Technology

The essay that first introduces Heidegger's fully developed account of the fourfold, "The Thing," was first given as a lecture in conjunction with three other lectures in Bremen in 1949 under the titles "The Thing" ("Das Ding"), "The Framework" ("Das Ge-stell"), "The Danger" ("Die Gefahr"), and "The Turning" ("Die Kehre")[132] and that were the basis for the essays later published as "The Thing," "The Turning" and "The Question Concerning Technology."[133] The discussion of the thing is thus already situated in relation to a question about technology and the character of the contemporary world, and this is clearly reflected in the way that discussion begins with a comment on the apparent transformation of space and time in the face of modern technology. Here is the relevant passage from "The Thing" in its entirety:

> All distances in time and space are shrinking. Man now reaches overnight, by plane, places which formerly took weeks and months of travel. He now receives instant information, by radio, of events which he formerly learned about only years later, if at all. The germination and growth of plants, which remained hidden throughout the seasons, is now exhibited publicly in a minute, on film. Distant sites of the most ancient cultures are shown on film as if they stood this very moment amidst today's street traffic. Moreover, the film attests to what it shows by presenting also the camera and its operators at work. The peak of this abolition of every possibility of remoteness is reached by television, which will soon pervade and dominate the whole machinery of communication. Man puts the longest distances behind him in the shortest time. He puts the greatest distances behind himself and thus puts everything before himself at the shortest range. Yet the frantic abolition of all distances brings no nearness; for nearness does not consist in shortness of distance. What is least remote from us in point of distance, by virtue of its picture on film or its sound on the radio, can remain far from us. What is incalculably far from us in point of distance can be near to us. Short distance is not in itself nearness. Nor is great distance remoteness.[134]

Of all the ways in which modern technology has brought about a transformation in the world and our experience of it, it is in our relation to space—and thereby also time—that its effects have been most striking and pervasive. Indeed, technological development has often taken as its icons images of speed and power that are representative of precisely the technological mastery of space—the locomotive, the airplane, the automobile. Moreover, many of the technologies that have been most significant in their impact on everyday life have been those that enable the overcoming of distance through new forms, not only of transportation, but of communication as well. In 1950, Heidegger took television to represent what he there called "the peak of this abolition of every possibility of remoteness." The further development of telecommunication, computer, and telerobotic technologies, and especially their combination from the 1990s onward in the internet has achieved an even more radical abolition of "remoteness," allowing us not merely to see and hear, but also to act in relation to things far removed from us in physical space.

Yet what is most striking about Heidegger's approach to this characteristic phenomenon of contemporary life—a phenomenon often referred to as "time-space compression"—is that his account of this phenomenon, although it begins with a claim concerning the apparent abolition of distance, ends with what might appear a quite contrary conclusion concerning the apparent disappearance of nearness. In the modern world, it seems, not only is nothing at a distance anymore, but neither is anything brought close—"everything is equally near and equally far . . . everything gets lumped together into uniform distancelessness"[135]—a comment echoed, with respect to television, by Jerzy Kosinski in *Being There*, "Everything on TV was tangled and mixed and yet smoothed out: night and day, big and small, tough and brittle, soft and rough, hot and cold, near and far."[136] In this abolition of both nearness and distance, Heidegger argues, the thing as thing also disappears—"The failure of nearness to materialize in consequence of the abolition of all distances has brought the distanceless to dominance. In the default of nearness the thing remains annihilated as a thing."[137] Moreover, the default of nearness and the annihilation of the thing must also mean, if we take seriously Heidegger's account of the relation between the happening of the fourfold and the thing, the loss of the world. Indeed, one of the most important themes, perhaps *the* most important theme, in Heidegger's later thinking is his account of the contemporary world as suffering from an "oblivion of being" that is directly tied to the dominance of the technological—we live, he says, in a "desolate time," a time of destitution, a time of the "world's night."[138]

This contemporary destitution is not a matter of some merely contingent combination of circumstances, but is rather something "metaphysical." It is, in Heidegger's analysis, a matter of our almost complete forgetfulness of being. Such forgetfulness is precisely that which characterizes the essence of metaphysics,[139] and it is also that which underpins nihilism. "The essence of nihilism," says Heidegger, "resides in the oblivion of being,"[140] and so "the essential locale of nihilism shows itself to be the source of metaphysics . . . metaphysics . . . shelters nihilism within it."[141] Our contemporary world is characterized by such "nihilism"—a nihilism that may even be evident in the assertion of "values" (rather than in their apparent "rejection") since, according to Heidegger, the preoccupation with "value" *as* "value" is itself a symptom of the loss of what is valued.[142] Inasmuch as the nihilism of metaphysics is forgetfulness of being, so such nihilism, and metaphysics with it, also consists in a failure of questioning. This is not a failure in the asking of questions since metaphysics clearly has no difficulty in doing that, nor in providing answers; the failure is instead the much more fundamental one to which I drew attention at the end of sec. 5.2 above, the failure to attend to the questionability that consists in the opening up of things in the difference of what they are—the questionability that is also a "letting beings be." Consequently, Heidegger says that, "If we try to determine the present situation of man on earth metaphysically—thus not historiographically and not in terms of world-view—then it must be said that man is beginning to enter the age of the total unquestionableness of all things and of all contrivances."[143] Inasmuch as it is the age of the failure of questioning, then, as I noted earlier, this is also the age in which homelessness has come to prevail as the almost universal condition for human being. Such homelessness is manifest in a failure on the part of mortals to grasp their own being as mortals, and, linked to this, a loss of any sense of the holy or a proper connection to the gods—as Hölderlin puts it, "the gods have fled," and their shrines and temples are empty.[144]

   The metaphysical nihilism that lies at the heart of this destitution is essentially tied to the technological character of the contemporary world. Indeed, Heidegger sees technology as itself metaphysically determined—its essence is given in the metaphysical appropriation of being that Heidegger names "*das Gestell.*" In ordinary German, "*das Gestell*" means a rack or a stand that is used to keep things together—say books or bottles of wine—it can also mean a frame or framework on which something hangs or that gives it its shape—as does the frame of an umbrella; "*stellen,*" from which the term is derived, means "to set" or "to put in place," and "*stellen*" is itself related to "*vorstellen,*" often translated as "to represent," but also as "to imagine," and to "*herstellen,*" meaning "to produce." In keeping with the common tendency to translate Heidegger's own terms, which, in his later thinking especially, are almost always drawn from ordinary German (even if they stretch the ordinary meanings of those terms), by means of English neologisms, "*das Gestell*" has often been referred to as "Enframing" (this is the translation employed by William Lovitt in his translation of "The Question Concerning Technology").[145] Rather than "Enframing," however, I will simply use "the Framework" (keeping the definite article since the Framework does indeed refer to something quite specific).

The distinction between technology and the essence of technology is a critical one in Heidegger's thinking. It means that Heidegger's critique of technology cannot be viewed as an attack on any particular instance of technology as such—although such instances may well be used to illustrate general features of technology's essence. It also means that the fact that human beings have made use of a range of technologies and technological devices throughout history cannot, in itself, be taken to count against Heidegger's claim that the contemporary world is characterized by the dominance of the technological (one might say that although, in the past, technological devices appeared within the world, the world did not itself appear as technological). Furthermore, Heidegger is not recommending the abandonment of any particular technological device or system. The problem of technology is not to be found in any of the particular deliverances of technology, but rather in that out of which technology itself comes and which determines it, that which is its essence: the Framework. The Framework is no device or mechanism, but is itself a mode of presencing or disclosedness. As such, it is less evident in particular technological devices such as the computer or the genetically modified organism as in much broader features of the contemporary world. The most obvious such feature is undoubtedly to be seen in the treatment of the natural world as a source of "raw material" for human production and as open to human manipulation and control, but it is also elsewhere: in the rise of generalized notions of efficiency and flexibility in organizational structure and planning; in the tendency to take as the primary determinant of all social interactions the abstract and rational decision making of individual actors; in the application of the rationality of the market to all domains of action; in the prioritization of quantitative indicators, often purely numerical or financial, in assessments of that which is "qualitative"—including human well-being; in the idea of the world as a single "globalized" network that transcends the boundaries of place and space.[146] The Framework thus refers to a mode that allows the world and the beings within it to appear only insofar as they are available to an all-encompassing ordering, calculating, and controlling. It is a mode of revealing that allows beings to appear, not as things, nor even as objects, but as "Bestand"—as that which is available for sale ("stock"), or which is held "in reserve"—most broadly, that which is ready as "resource."

Inasmuch as something is usually understood as a resource in relation to some other productive activity—as timber may be a resource for furniture production—so one might be led to understand Heidegger's account of technology on the model of Being and Time's account of the ordering of equipment in the context of work—in both cases, it would seem, things appear in terms of a larger system of instrumental relations. The ordering of the technological is all encompassing, however, in a way that the ordering of equipment is not; the technological organizes itself, not in terms of the places and regions that characterize the equipmental, but instead as a single leveled-out and interconnected "space" in which everything is reduced to the "same." Moreover, while the equipmental stands always in relation to what is an essentially human projection, and so to human ends, the technological has no ends as such other than the ordering of things as available, as orderable, as resource. As Heidegger writes, "Everywhere everything is ordered to stand by, to be immediately at hand, indeed to stand there just so that it may be on call for a further ordering."[147] This ordering is also essentially tied to the measurable and the calculable so that, in the ordering of things as resource, the technological "brings all beings into the business of calculation, which dominates most fiercely precisely where numbers are not needed."[148] The compass of the technological is so wide that even the human falls within it and is taken up as another resource to be transformed, stored, deployed, calculated, consumed—"The current talk about human resources, about the supply of patients for a clinic, gives evidence of this."[149] Technology is thus not something that stands at the disposal of humans, nor is technology to be understood merely as a form of instrumentalism, instead, as it is determined by the Framework, technology appropriates everything to a single ordered totality. The metaphysical disclosure of things as "objects" itself gives way to the technological ordering of things as resource so that "today there are no longer objects (no beings, insofar as these would stand against a subject taking them into view)—there are now only resources [*Bestand*] (beings that are held in readiness for being consumed)."[150] There are thus no limits to technological ordering, nothing that stands outside its compass, nothing that is not taken into its global calculation.

Heidegger's characterization of the nature of technology seems to describe a phenomenon very similar to that which is described by Ludwig Clauss in his 1932 book, *Die nordische Seele* (to which I referred in chapter 1 above—see sec. 1.2). But whereas Heidegger is critical of this phenomenon, Clauss extols it as one of the strengths of the "Nordic" soul and style. According to Clauss:

[The Nordic soul] . . . aims to penetrate simply everything, and accordingly, to integrate it into its style and subject it to its law. Everything that has not yet been grasped and stamped by it, stretches out before it as a new land—its new land— which must be discovered, explored, put under cultivation, and hence conquered. In the last analysis it will recognize only the limits of the possible as its own limits.

It may even happen that at this point it will fall ill and will try to ignore all limitations—a characteristically Nordic illness.[151]

This impetus to control and to encompass—to encompass even the entire globe, so that Clauss can write that "The Nordic soul, needful of space, had no choice but to recast the whole world in accordance with its image and inner landscape"[152]—seems almost exactly the impetus that sustains the reign of the technological—of the "Framework." To quote from Clauss once more: "To assert that the world becomes Nordic means that countless hidden values are being opened up and made useful and productive— mines of iron ore, oil wells, water power, as well as animal and man power; they are useful in the Nordic sense, they become material to be formed by Nordic hands."[153] Of course, Heidegger does not regard technology as specifically Nordic, it has its origins in Greek thought,[154] although Heidegger sometimes also characterizes contemporary technological dominance in terms of the dominance of "Americanism."[155]

These passages from Clauss indicate the extent to which Heidegger's thinking about technology can be seen to reflect, and presumably to draw upon, themes and ideas that were already common in the period prior to the Second World War,[156] no less than in the period after, but they also indicate the way in which the theme of technology could be seen as connected with central elements of National Socialist ideology. In this respect, Heidegger's critique of technology can be seen as constituting an implicit critique of a certain understanding of Nazism, particularly inasmuch as that critique itself develops, in Heidegger's thinking, out of his engagement with Nietzsche, with the idea of the "will to power," and so with metaphysical "nihilism." Indeed, Heidegger himself seems to have viewed his own thinking of technology as closely tied to his engagement with Nazism, both in terms of that which drew him to it—something reflected in his infamous comment concerning the "inner truth and greatness of this movement [namely, the encounter between technology and modern humanity]"[157]—and that which was also associated with his later "critique" of the movement, particularly as he claimed that to have been developed through his engagement with Nietzsche.[158]

The question of the extent to which Heidegger's critique of technology can indeed be understood as also a critique of Nazism, and how adequate it is as such a critique, is a complex question and not one that I can adequately deal with here. However, there are some points that should be noted in this regard. There can be little doubt that Heidegger did indeed see his critique of technology as also constituting a critique of Nazism. In addition, it is also clear that a proper understanding of Nazism is

impossible without an appreciation of its specifically "modern" character—
not only in terms of its reliance on "modern" technologies, such as mass
propaganda and information, and bureaucratic forms of organization and
control, but also in terms of its attempt to realize a certain modern technology of the state and the nation as such.[159] Yet, in addition, Nazism
contains significant antimodernist, and what may even be viewed as
"antitechnological," elements, as well as elements that have little or
nothing to do with the modern or the technological as such. Thus Nazism
(and this also seems true of fascism generally) seems to have been configured around an opportunistic and brutalist approach to power—an
approach in which the personal ambitions of individuals loom large—that
is not especially modern or technological in character at all; both Nazism
and fascism were driven by objectives that have actually little to do with
the smooth ordering that technology aims to accomplish (though seldom
achieves), but rather consist in the attempt simply to order by an act of
individual will alone and through the enforcement of individual
command, with the result that the Nazi and fascist state often exhibits an
arbitrary and "irrational" character. Moreover, modern technological organization is primarily geared toward productive activity, and yet one of the
features of Nazism that makes it most horrifying is its willingness to engage
in organized and willful destruction (something not disconnected with its
character as arising out of, and partially determined by, a set of personal
ambitions and characteristics).

     This latter point becomes of particular importance in relation to Hei-
degger's famous, indeed notorious comment, that "agriculture is now a
motorised food-industry—in essence the same as the manufacturing of
corpses in gas chambers and extermination camps."[160] Putting other considerations aside (and there are certainly a number of important considerations at issue here), this passage seems to involve a misunderstanding of
Heidegger's own account of the technological. The "production" of corpses
in the ovens of Auschwitz and elsewhere is only a nightmarish parody of
production. In the sense relevant to the productive activity of technology,
there was nothing "produced" in the "extermination camps"—nothing
that could be taken up (except incidentally) into the ordering of production, transformation, and consumption that is characteristic of technological ordering. Indeed, even in terms of the ordering of technology alone,
Auschwitz, along with the many other places like it, constitutes a "blind
alley," an all-too literal "dead-end"—a point at which the ordering of technology simply ceases. Even from the perspective of the "Framework," then,
the Holocaust constitutes an absence of meaning rather than any fulfill-

ment of technological "essence."[161] Heidegger's mistaken reading of the Holocaust is itself indicative of his tendency to think of Nazism, and its actions, in terms of an idealized conception of the movement that fails to take account of its actual character. Thus, in 1933, he saw Nazism as the possible site for a decisive countermovement to nihilism; in 1950, he saw Nazism as the site for the realization of the essence of nihilism in the form of technological dominance. In both cases, Heidegger seems to have projected his own thinking onto the historical phenomena in a way that paid all too little attention to those phenomena as such.[162]

Irrespective of the role of National Socialism in his critique of technology, however, the engagement with Nietzsche provides an important point of reference for the development of Heidegger's thinking in relation to technology.[163] I noted at the end of chapter 4 the central role played by Nietzsche, along with Hölderlin in the turning of Heidegger's thinking in the 1920s, and Nietzsche's importance here is in the way he shows us the character of our own thinking as arising out of Greek thought, and as it stands in relation to what Nietzsche proclaims to be the death of God. In Heidegger's reading of Nietzsche, the death of God appears to have two aspects: on the one hand it accurately depicts our own situation in the loss of any transcendent source of value (and in this respect can be seen to express something close to what Heidegger also articulates in terms of the "ungroundedness" of being); on the other hand, it also signifies the advent of nihilism (apparent in the idea, not merely of the denial of value, but even, as I indicated above, of a "crisis" of value), which we have already seen Heidegger understands in terms of the "oblivion of being." It is in this latter sense that the death of God refers us to the same event that appears in Hölderlin as the "flight of the gods," the loss of the holy, which also marks the "destitution" of our times.

In its doing away with any transcendent source of value, the death of God opens up the possibility of a complete revaluation of values that overcomes the previous "metaphysics of value"—it is this revaluation that occurs in the appearance of the will to power as "the principle of the dispensation of value."[164] In Nietzsche, "value" does not merely refer to that which human beings assess as valuable, but rather that on the basis of which any stand in relation to things is possible. Thus "value" itself stands in direct relation to what Heidegger understands as "truth," and Nietzsche's placing of value under the determination of the will to power means the placing of the happening of "truth," the happening of being, under its sway also. Thus Heidegger asserts that "being has become value. . . . And yet, by being appreciated as a value, being is deprecated as a mere

condition set by the will to power itself."[165] Inasmuch as Nietzsche proclaims the rule of the will to power, so he attempts to overcome nihilism,
and yet in doing so he also remains caught within nihilism and within
metaphysics. Indeed, Heidegger claims that "[t]he value-thinking of the
metaphysics of the will to power is deadly in an extreme sense because it
does not permit being itself to come into the dawning, i.e., the vitality, of
its essence."[166] As the herald of the death of God and the triumph of the
will to power, Nietzsche also appears as the herald of the age of technological nihilism—the will to power is the drive for complete mastery over
all things, in which everything is taken up in representation, production,
exploitation.[167] As a consequence, Heidegger emphasizes Nietzsche's
importance as having "heard a calling that demands that human beings
prepare for assuming domination over the earth. He saw and understood
the erupting struggle for domination."[168] Of course, in this struggle, the
very essence of human being is itself at stake, and thus, although it may
appear as a struggle in which human beings are called to exert mastery, in
fact, it is the domination of the will to power, of the technological drive
to mastery as such, which is at issue here.

The drive for mastery and control that characterizes the technological is
evident in the idea of "total mobilization" that was already present in the
work of Ernst Jünger in the 1930s and in Jünger's claim that the figure of
the "worker" presents a new "*Gestalt*" that shapes the contemporary world
as a whole.[169] Indeed, this idea is one Heidegger also finds in Nietzsche.
Writing in reference to Nietzsche's talk of "workers," "soldiers," and
"socialism" in certain passages from *The Will to Power*,[170] Heidegger
comments that:

> The names "worker" and "soldier" are thus metaphysical titles and name the form
> of the human fulfillment of the being of beings, now become manifest, which Niet-
> zsche presciently grasped as the "will to power" . . . the names "worker," "soldier,"
> and "socialism" are already titles for the leading representatives of the main forms
> in which the will to power will be enacted![171]

The appearance of "the worker" as the name for the "human fulfillment
of the being of beings" is indicative of the way in which human being is
now almost entirely taken up in terms of the capacity for "production"
(and therefore also, one might say, for "consumption")—in terms of what
can also be understood as a form of "materialism," although it is a materialism understood as the metaphysical determination "according to which
every being appears as the material of labor," and so, says Heidegger, "[t]he
essence of materialism is concealed in the essence of technology."[172]

"Labor" or "work" can, of course, be taken to be a characteristic feature of human existence—something apparent in the way human dwelling always occurs through what Heidegger calls "building" (which he characterizes in "Building Dwelling Thinking" in terms of a mode of "productive activity").[173] In this respect, it may be supposed, in keeping with the comments from Heidegger quoted here, that the technological is continuous with the work-oriented character of human being.[174] Yet the domain of the technological is not the domain of mere "work" nor is the technological identical with productive activity as such. The technological is an ordering of things that allows things to appear such that they can be taken up into the framework of production, calculation, transformation, consumption. Within this ordering, work takes on the form of "production-consumption"—the dominance of the "worker" is the dominance of this mode of work as *the* mode of human work and, also, of human being.

In this respect, when understood in relation to work, Heidegger's account of technology can be said to direct attention to a shift in the character of work that is more explicitly taken up, though in different terms, by Hannah Arendt. Within the modern world, Arendt argues, "work," which she takes to be the mode of production geared to the making of enduring things for further use (a mode of production that might be taken to overlap with Heidegger's "building"), has been transformed into "labor," which Arendt views as the mode of production that generates things for immediate consumption ("using up").[175] All activities of "work," all activities of production, thereby appear solely in terms of the manufacture of commodities for consumption. Even the individual worker is taken up into this cycle of production and consumption, and so even the worker is assimilated to something to be consumed, to be "used up"—in the terms of the contemporary "efficiency-driven" workplace, this means as something that must be flexible and adjustable to meet the demands of business and "the market." Moreover, as the worker is transformed into something *consumable*, so does the consumer take on the character of *producer*: the act of consumption is itself productive—thus, economic activity is itself measured, in part, by consumer spending, and consumption becomes a mode of productive labor—while consumption is itself something produced by means of advertising and other "promotional" activity. Albert Borgmann points out, independently of Arendt's analysis, that one of the effects of technology in everyday life is, not only a transformation of things into commodities, but a conceptualization of human life itself around notions of desire and the satisfaction of desire through consumption[176]—life, as one recent columnist has it, becomes "shopping"[177]—moreover, the concepts of "desire" and "satisfaction" that appear here are themselves framed in terms of the market, the customer, the "end-user," while they also become commodities to be produced, sold, acquired.[178]

As technological ordering extends even to encompass the basic character of human life, so Heidegger writes of the danger of technology as consisting in just the possibility "that all revealing will be consumed by ordering and that everything will present itself only in the unconcealedness of available resource [Bestand]."[179] The exact nature of this danger— why and how technology threatens in this way—is something that requires more detailed consideration, but it is important to recognize, first, the way in which Heidegger's comment here indicates that, although technology threatens revealing, it is indeed, as I indicated earlier, also a mode of revealing in itself—it is just that mode in which everything appears only as resource and in which revealing or disclosedness appears only as ordering. The character of the Framework as such a mode of revealing is also suggested by the way in which, in the passage describing the bridge from "Building Dwelling Thinking" (the passage discussed in sec. 5.3 above), Heidegger included the modern highway bridge among the different ways in which a bridge may gather—in its case gathering things through tying them "into the network of long-distance traffic, paced as calculated for maximum yield."[180] In this example, the way in which the revealing accomplished through the highway bridge is indeed within the frame of the technological is also exhibited through its gathering of things in terms of a "network" of traffic "calculated" for maximization of "yield," of "production." The gathering of things in the thing—of which the gathering in the highway bridge is supposed to be one example—is also, of course, what Heidegger takes to be an instance of the Event, but in that case it would seem that the Event takes place even in the happening of technological gathering that occurs, as one example, in the highway bridge. In fact, elsewhere Heidegger talks about the Event in direct relation to the essence of technology that is the Framework. Thus, in the Le Thor Seminar, we find a remark according to which "the Framework [Gestell] is, as it were, the photographic negative of the Event [Ereignis],"[181] and similarly, in the "Summary of a Seminar" from On Time and Being, it is said that the Framework [Gestell] "offers a double aspect, one might say, a Janus head. It can be understood as a kind of continuation of the will to will, thus as an extreme formation of Being. At the same time, however, it is a first form of the Event [Ereignis] itself."[182] As a form of the Event, whether understood as the Event of a personal "experience," of the "other beginning," or of the everyday happening of world, it is clear that the Framework must be a form of the "disclosive gathering of belonging," but if it is that, then how and why is it such a danger? And how can the ordering of technology threaten to "consume" all revealing, to "consume," presumably, the Event as such?

What technology and the Framework threaten is the transformation of revealing, and so the gathering of the Event that is the happening of the fourfold, into nothing more than ordering, and so allowing a mode of appearance to all and everything that is only that of "resource." The threat that is posed here is particular to technology and the Framework. Consequently, it must be the case that other modes of revealing, and we know that Heidegger thinks there are such, do not pose such a threat—do not transform revealing into ordering, do not reveal things only as resource. Indeed, Heidegger's characterization of the nature of revealing, of the Event, and of the gathering of the fourfold takes such revealing to be a "letting be" of things; understood in relation to dwelling, it is a "sparing and preserving," a "caring for"; in terms of the concealing–revealing of *aletheia*, it is a "sheltering" that also "clears." These various characterizations are all directed at the idea that what occurs in the revealing of things is both a coming to presence of things in a particular way that is proper to the thing, and yet, in such coming to presence, the thing is also "preserved" in its being as that which goes beyond what comes to presence in that revealing. The thing is revealed, but it is also, in being preserved and "sheltered," concealed. Meanwhile, in such revealing, the happening of revealing, the happening of being, itself withdraws, and so maintains itself as different from the thing that comes forth into presence. In the mode of revealing that is the technological, however, the thing appears only as resource, while revealing as such is almost completely obliterated—the technological does not present itself as one mode of revealing among others, and so does not present itself as a mode of revealing at all, but instead appears as simply that which enables things to be grasped as what they are and as all that they are.

There is, of course, a sense in which every mode of revealing obscures its own character as revealing, while also obscuring other possible modes of revealing at the same time, but the way this occurs in relation to technology as compared with other such modes is rather different—and this is the crucial point.[183] The revealing of things within a particular mode of what we may term "the holy," whereby things show up in terms of, for instance, their relation to the God of the medieval Christian world, certainly blocks out other modes of revealing. One cannot properly grasp the world as revealed in the latter way and yet also be open to the revealing of the world that occurs through modern technology—things will simply show up differently in each case, and although one may be able to conceptualize these different modes of revealing, they will be accessible as such conceptualizations rather than as real happenings of the world. Yet there is also a crucial difference between these modes of revealing that goes beyond the mere fact that they each reveal differently.

The mode of revealing of the holy that occurs in medieval Christendom is a mode of revealing that opens up a world that is truly heterogeneous. It is heterogeneous in that it encompasses many different places that are so distinct from one another as not to be equally accessible from one another—this is true, not only of the "hierarchical" organization of the world into the realms of the sacred and profane, the divine and the earthly (and the infernal), but also of the differentiation evident in the earth as such, its separation into the center (the holy city itself) and the periphery (the outer reaches of the earth), in the ordering of places among the various spheres that make up the heavens, and the "natural places" relating to the basic elements that govern the movements of ordinary bodies. It is also heterogeneous in that it recognizes, even if it battles against, the presence within it of other modes of revealing as truly "other"—the presence within it of other modes of being, the pagan, the infidel, even, perhaps, the "demonic." Its heterogeneity is evident too in the impossibility of the world, even in its character as "created," being completely fathomed through reason.[184]

In contrast, the mode of technological revealing that dominates our contemporary world opens up a world that is homogeneous in almost every respect that the holy world of medieval Christendom was heterogeneous: the world that is opened up in technology encompasses no "places" other than as locations in place (which does not mean that there are no "places," only that they do not appear as such[185]), and all are equally accessible such that there is no "differentiation" of places and spaces corresponding to that between sacred and profane, center and periphery, divine and human, between the natural places of the elements; there is no "other" that stands in contrast to it. Indeed, even pretechnological peoples and cultures are understood as having a rudimentary technology that just happens to be not as developed as our own, and nothing is taken to stand outside of the capacity of technology to fathom and to harness—there is only the ever-onward press of the expansion of knowledge and capacity that recognizes no limits to its knowledge and capacity as such.[186] In this respect, opposition to technology can only appear, from the perspective of technology itself, as irrational, misguided, even nonsensical since technology just is the rational "knowing" that underpins the productive activity—the "work"—in which we are always, to some extent, engaged. The university professor who takes issue with the imposition of a new system of academic "accountability," supposedly geared to ensuring more "effective" use of resources and "higher quality" outcomes, is thereby seen merely as defending the inefficiencies and inequities of an outdated system; the environmentalist who argues for the preservation of old-growth forests, in the face of their obvious value in providing employment and a means of economic growth, is seen as given over to a naive and imprachcal romanticism; the urban preservationist who campaigns against the demolition of old inner-city neighborhoods to make way for high-rise commercial premises simply does not understand the need to stimulate inner-city development and growth.

The revealing that occurs in technology thus presents itself as, one might say, completely "neutral" and as geared simply to dealing with things "objectively," although here, given that even objectivity is replaced by the being of "resource," that means something more like "pragmatically" or "instrumentally" (but without any sense of an "end" which they can be said instrumentally to serve). It is the apparent "neutrality" of technology and its inability to recognize any mode of questioning that is not itself framed from within technology as such that is part of what leads Heidegger to talk of ours as "the age of the complete questionlessness of the essential"[187] and of "the total unquestionableness of all things and of all contrivances."[188] The inability of technology even to represent to itself the possibility of its own questionability is itself a reflection of the inability of technology to allow itself to appear as a mode of revealing—technology is always disguised and incapable of grasping its own essence.[189] It is indicative also of the reign of technology as consisting in the oblivion of being—a time in which "modern man is a slave to the forgetfulness of being."[190] The question of *being* cannot emerge as a question within a technological frame because *technology* cannot emerge as a question. In this respect, we are brought right back to the original claim in *Being and Time* that ties the question of being to the being of questionability—and to Heidegger's constant insistence that the remembrance of being, the turning back to being, is always a turning back to questionability. Such questionability is also evident in the character of the concealing-revealing that occurs in the gathering of the thing as a "sheltering" or a "preserving" of the thing as more than is given in any single mode of such gathering, and so of the possibility always of questioning that mode of gathering and the revealing that occurs in and through it.

Technological revealing thus has a special character in both covering over its own being as a mode of revealing and in covering over the being of things in their complexity and richness. Technology presents itself as essentially a mode of pure transparency, but in being just this, it is also essentially obscuring. When Heidegger talks about the "violence" of technology, what is at issue is just the way in which technology refuses, through its denial of itself as a mode of revealing, to allow other modes of revealing to be evident along with it, and the way in which it refuses to allow things to appear other than in the mode of resource alone—technology is violent through its imposition onto the world, and onto things, of a single mode of revealing and of presencing. The violence of technology, in this respect, is quite compatible with technology's own presentation of itself as gentle and attentive. Thus, if we look to the technological transformation of modern work, we can see the gradual disappearance of the wearing and wearying conditions, not only of the early industrial era, but also of preindustrial agrarian production, and the development of what may appear to be much less physically demanding, and less "violent" modes of work. The violence of technology lies in the demands it places on things, and so also on human beings, in terms of their being; it is not primarily a violence done to things in terms of physical or even psychological harm, at least not as we usually understand it (in this respect, the violence of the technological world is quite different from the violence to be found in the world of medieval Christendom). Yet equally, the violence of technology in relation to being can have more straightforwardly violent consequences, and it is just those consequences that can be seen all around us from increasing environmental degradation to the destruction of species and their habitats, to the devastation of human communities, to the loss of a sense of significance and meaning in individual human life.

In describing the contrast between the mode of revealing evident in contemporary technology and the mode that might be taken to be found in medieval Christendom, one of the key points of contrast was in relation to the way space and place appear within those two modes. In fact, given the character of revealing, and of the Event, as itself topological in character and as standing, therefore, in an essential relation to place and space, as well as time, then one would expect that place and space would take on a particular character in relation to technological revealing. More radically, perhaps, one might even argue that the character of technology is such that, within its frame, place no longer has any significance. Certainly, as we saw in chapter 1, the latter conclusion appears as an element in some common critiques of the Heideggerian emphasis on place such as that advanced, for instance, by Neil Leach (see sec. 1.2 above). The considerations that have been explored in these pages, however, suggest that, inasmuch as all revealing is bound to place, so the particular mode of revealing that occurs in technology must also be so bound. What technology does, however, is to hide its own character as a mode of revealing, and, in so doing, it hides its own place-bound character while also transforming and, indeed, obscuring place as such. In this respect, understanding the problematic character of technology and the "danger" it presents necessarily involves understanding the way technology reveals works in relation to place and in relation to space and time, and, of course, this is just the point at which my discussion of the technological began—through Heidegger's consideration of technology as it relates to the thing. What is at issue there is the way in which technology changes our relation to things through its effect in the transformation of nearness and distance—technology, says Heidegger, prevents things from appearing as things, and it does this through its abolition of distance, and so also of nearness.

The technological ordering of the world operates, in fact, through a certain form of "spatialization" of the world and everything within it. In this respect, the prominence of the technologies of transport and communication, particularly in the historically early stages of modernity, is indicative of the close connection between technology and the manipulation of space—something evident too in the preeminence of architecture within the development of "modernism" as a mode of thought and practice. At a more fundamental level, the fact that such a connection should obtain can itself be seen as a reflection of the character of disclosedness as essentially topological in character, and so as always occurring in and through place, and whereby place itself shows up in ways that are themselves dependent on the mode of disclosedness at issue. As a consequence, place "shows up" within technological modernity as nothing other than spatial "position" (which means that "place" as such does not appear at all), while things appear as nothing more than nodes within a uniform and extended spatial array. Thus, if the Event is to be understood, as Joseph Fell suggests, as "the 'turn' of space . . . 'into' place, which it originally and always is,"[191] then we can view the Framework as the "turning" of place "into" space—and so of the covering up of the place out of which space itself emerges. The way this operates within technological ordering has two aspects to it: first, technological revealing gives priority to a specific aspect of spatiality over other such aspects, as well as over both place and time, namely, to space as homogeneous extension; second, technological revealing presents this transformed spatiality as that which is determinative of the world as such—the world just *is* the spatial, and things are nothing other than as they are given in and through such spatiality.

Historically, the emergence of modern technology occurs in close conjunction with the development of the distinctive understanding of spatiality that we have already encountered at a number of points in the preceding pages and according to which space appears as homogeneous, measurable extension, often articulated through the notion of the coordinate system or grid. With this understanding of space goes a reduction of place to simple location (often a mere "point") or leveled-down "site." Although this conception of space has its origins in Greek thought, particularly in early atomistic thinking, it is with modern philosophers such as Galileo, Descartes, Leibniz, and later Newton, that it reaches its clearest formulation. Space is the neutral container, everywhere the same, in which bodies and the elements of bodies move and interact according to uniform geometrical and mathematical patterns. The changed view of space and place that came with the scientific revolution of the sixteenth and seventeenth centuries was not, however, merely a *consequence* of the shift toward the modern "scientific" understanding of the world, but was itself crucial in making that shift possible. Thus, the change from Ptolemaic to Copernican thinking, and the move, as Koyré puts it, from the "closed world to the infinite universe"[192] lay at the very heart of the new science that took matter and motion, quantity and number, extension and infinity as its determining ideas.

While space was itself understood, on this view, according to notions of uniform, quantifiable extension, it also provided the necessary framework within which geometrical and mathematical principles could be applied universally. Even though contemporary physics understands space differently from the way in which it was viewed by Newton (notably in its shift away from Euclidean geometry and its adoption of a "field" or "continuum" view), the crucial elements in the modern view of space that were decisive in underpinning the rise of modern science remain. Space is understood as that universal structure describable in terms of uniform, mathematical principles by means of which all other entities can be located. If space is now understood as necessarily conjoined with time, then time itself is understood in a way that assimilates it to space—as another dimension of the so-called block universe, in which location can be plotted according to both temporal and spatial axes. Henri Bergson famously talked of the modern tendency toward a "spatialized" view of time.[193] But such spatialization is merely indicative of the more widespread tendency to think of all things in the formal, quantifiable, uniform terms associated with the modern view of space. It is this view, of course, with which Heidegger grapples in *Being and Time*—the modern, "Cartesian" ontology of the world in which things are understood in terms of present-at-hand "objects" of knowledge is itself based on an essentially spatialized mode of understanding. Inasmuch as Heidegger claims that modern science is itself driven by a technological imperative—a consequence of Heidegger's view of technology as indeed a mode of world-disclosure (and so no mere "application" of the deliverances of science)[194]—so the development of this understanding of space can be seen as driven by a technological ordering that aims to bring things within a single, uniform framework within which they can be produced, transformed, and controlled, within which "anything can take the place of anything else."[195] If space is understood in this manner, then space, and so also time and place, becomes immediately amenable to the manipulation that occurs through the ability to operate directly upon such space. Moreover, inasmuch as technological ordering is given over to such manipulation and control, so the appearance of the world as available to such manipulation is also the appearance of the world as spatial.

Significantly, although the spatialization of the world that occurs here is a covering over of place, and of space and time, as anything other than homogeneous extendedness, it also turns out to involve a certain disappearance of space. Distance, whether the distance of the small or of the great, no longer appears in the way that it did previously—it becomes something entirely taken up in the operation of technology and its calculations. At the present time, this reduction or abolition of distance is evident at its most dramatic and most commonplace in relation to media and computer technology. Seated before my computer, I may find that something physically far removed from me is actually closer, through its electronic accessibility, than something in my immediate environment— an electronic text held on a Web server two thousand miles away may actually be closer than the hard copy of the same text that sits on the shelf in the next room. The result of this covering over of the difference between near and far is a corresponding obliteration of the difference between things and of the differences in the spatial ordering of things, not merely in my immediate vicinity, but throughout the world as a whole. Given the role of space in the differentiation of things and of world that was explored in the section immediately above, then the near-obliteration of distance means the near-obliteration of the differentiation between things that allows them to appear as properly distinct from one another. Difference becomes simply a matter of difference in spatial positioning and in the way in which items connect up within the overall structure of such positionings. One way of describing the disappearance of things that occurs here is to say that things are increasingly replaced by images and *representations* (*Vorstellungen*)[196] of things (that is, by things as they are removed from their original place—transformed and re-presented from within a particular "frame") except that even the idea of representation still refers us to something represented. Within the mode of revealing that emerges here, however, there are only representations, and so they cease to appear even as representations—as Heidegger puts it, there are not even any objects, only resources.

One of the most obvious consequences of the technological disruption in spatial and topological ordering is a disruption in our sense of location— our "sense of place"—a disruption that occurs through new technological devices such as the computer, internet, aircraft, automobile, and telephone, as well as through the technology associated with new new modes of organization and spatial configuration such as are to be found in the shopping mall, the airport, the highway, even, to some extent, the suburb. These new devices and new modes of organization offer greater convenience, comfort, and efficiency—events across the world are now as "close" as our television screen, friends and relatives separated from us by thousands of miles are as "near" as the telephone, we can access almost any product we might want from the same retail complex (and catch a movie at the same time). Of course, we often tend to think of the technological changes that result in these new possibilities, not as changes in ourselves, but rather as changes in the opportunities, commodities, and services available to us—indeed, that way of thinking is itself encouraged by the conception of ourselves as "consumers" of these various forms of technology. Yet, in fact, technological changes are not changes in something separate from us, but instead constitute changes in the modes by which our own being is disclosed—changes in the ways in which we encounter ourselves and others, and in the character of such encounter. Technology transforms, for instance, even the character of social role and function—important elements in the constitution of social identity—through breaking down the boundaries that restrict access to different social contexts and locations. As Joshua Meyrowitz writes, "We still live in and interact in segregated physical locales. But television and other electronic media have broken the age-old connection between *where* we are and what we know and experience. Children may still be sheltered at home, but television now takes them across the globe before parents give them permission to cross the street."[197] Meyrowitz goes on to point out that the effect of these changes is both an increasing homogeneity of behavior and attitude across society—such that divisions of class, gender, age, and so forth lose much of their signifi-cance—as well as an increasing heterogeneity of options available to indi-viduals. The technology of the mobile phone, and the various forms of communication and information devices now being linked to it, has brought about an acceleration of the phenomenon Meyrovich describes. The mobile phone connects each individual directly into the network of communication, information, access, and availability, and it can do so in a way that shows no regard for the differences between the life of work and home or of public and private.

The changes that Meyrovich identifies in terms of the way technology changes the character of social relations constitute, however, only one of a much broader set of transformations that technological ordering brings about. Not only does it change the way human identity is constituted, as well as the character of human belonging-together, but it also cuts us off from things and from the world, no longer allowing earth and sky, gods and mortals to appear as such. Our experience of the world may come to focus on a much narrower or segregated range of sensory and interactive modalities—in the case of the television and the computer, primarily those of sound and vision rather than of the engagement of the body in its entirety—and thus one no longer "sees" the sky or "touches" the earth. We no longer encounter things in their complexity—in their being revealed and concealed, in the "iridescence" of their being—and neither do we encounter our own being as it stands in relation to the fourfold, in its character as standing before the gods, as standing always in the face of death, of nothingness. Technological ordering thus involves, as Heidegger puts it in "The Thing," a loss of "nearness" to things in the rise of a "uniform distancelessness," a loss of nearness, and so also of "place," and an essential "homelessness." From the perspective of the mode of techno-logical revealing itself, that mode of revealing appears as no "revealing" at all, but as merely the world in its transparent simplicity, stripped of the coverings of superstition and irrationality. Inasmuch as technology appears as no mode of appearance at all, so there is no thematization of technol-ogy itself—there is no mode of revealing that is technological and neither is there any "essence" to technology.[198] This means also that technology cannot envisage any limit to the mode of ordering that it imposes—it cannot, in fact, even envisage its own ordering as an ordering.

Moreover, in its blindness to its own limits, technology cannot grasp the possibility of its own *failure* or its own predilection to failure. Technology thus presents itself as a source of solutions rather than of problems, and technological development appears as a steady progression—a process of "continuous improvement," as the language of "quality management" would have it. Yet as technological systems become more complex, the failure of those systems becomes an increasing problem. The simpler the technology, the more easily can breakdowns within that technology be coped with—the more complex the technology, the more even small failures give rise to difficulties. At the same time, the increasing complexity of technological systems—their very character, in fact, in drawing more and more elements into their sway—also increases the possibilities for failure, often requiring the development of new technologies designed to deal specifically with such possibilities. This is not to say that technology is unsuccessful, but that its success is always faltering and always brings new problems, new difficulties, in its train. Yet technology hides its own failing character, in this regard, both viewing its failures as an indication of the need for greater technological perfection, of a more encompassing grasp of the elements that comprise the technological system, and also shifting the focus of the "problem space" in which it operates, so that technological success is always measured with respect to just those aspects in relation to which technology is successful, while neglecting or ignoring those aspects in relation to which it fails.[199] The dominance of the technological is thus best understood in terms of the dominance of the *drive toward* a total ordering rather than the *achievement* of any such ordering— it is only in technology's own self-presentation that such a total ordering, such totalized control, ever appears as even a possibility, and that it does so appear is itself part of technology's own self-disguising character.[200] Ironically, perhaps, Heidegger himself seems sometimes to be blinded by this aspect of technology's self-image, often talking as if the total ordering envisaged by technology were indeed something that might someday be realized. Yet the fact that technology constantly drives toward what it cannot realize is part of the problematic and self-deceptive character of technology as such—it is crucial to technology's own inability to recognize the limitation that is intrinsic to it.[201]

The concept of limit that appears here is an important one. The limit or bound of a thing, as with the limit or bound of a space, is not that at which the thing or the space merely comes to a halt, but is rather that which allows the thing or space to appear as what it is. This is one reason why we can say that, from a Heideggerian viewpoint, the technological world contains no spaces, even space becomes a problematic notion since there is no place from which a limit on such a space could be determined, and so no space as such. This absence of limit is something that another critic of modernity, although one who comes from a very different cultural and political perspective, Albert Camus, also identifies with the character of the modern world—a world he sees as "European" in contrast to "Greek." Camus writes:

Greek thought was always based on the idea of limits. Nothing was carried to extremes, neither religion nor reason, because Greek thought denied nothing, neither reason nor religion. It gave everything its share, balancing light with shade. But the Europe we know, eager for the conquest of totality, is the daughter of excess. We deny beauty, as we deny everything that we do not extol. And, even though we do it in diverse ways, we extol one thing and one alone: a future world in which reason will reign supreme. In our madness, we push back the eternal limits, and at once dark Furies swoop down upon us to destroy. Nemesis, goddess of moderation, not of vengeance, is watching. She chastises, ruthlessly, all those who go beyond the limit. . . . It is by acknowledging our ignorance, refusing to be fanatics, recognizing the world's limits and man's, through the faces of those we love, in short, by means of beauty, that is how we shall rejoin the Greeks.[202]

The inability to grasp limit is, for Camus, at its most essential in its inability to recognize beauty, which means to recognize the transient, the vulnerable, and the fragile as that which is nevertheless the most worthy. Indeed, Camus's reference to beauty here is suggestive of what Heidegger, following Hölderlin, calls the "holy"—the way in which we, the moderns, have "exiled" beauty, as Camus puts it, is the analogue to the loss of the gods and of the holy in Heidegger and in Heidegger's reading of Hölderlin. In calling for a return to beauty and to the Greeks, Camus calls for something that appears very like what appears in Heidegger as the "other beginning" of the turning back to being that occurs in the disclosive gathering of belonging that is the Event—a turning in which we regain a proper relatedness to the world and ourselves, in which we recognize the proper place, and so the boundaries, of our dwelling. This turning is not a move to another world, not a move away from the place in which we already find ourselves, but a recognition of our being in that very place where we already are—"It is indeed my life that I am staking here, a life that tastes of warm stone, that is full of the sighs of the sea and the rising song of the crickets."[203] Thus Heidegger also tells us that the problem is not that we need to be somewhere other than where we are, but that, as our dwelling is determined by the technological, so "we do not reside sufficiently as yet where in reality [eigentlich] we already are."[204] This lies at the very heart of the problematic character of technology—not only does it cover over what it itself is, but it also displaces us from the place we nevertheless cannot leave.

On this matter, although Heidegger emphasizes that any "re-turning" from the obliteration and forgetfulness that is so characteristic of technological modernity cannot be accomplished by mere human "decision" or "action" (and is, indeed, something that can only be "awaited"), such a "re-turning," which is the turning of the Event, must involve a recovery of a sense of human dwelling, a recovery, one might say, of a sense of place, a recovery of the proper space within which disclosedness in the sense at issue is possible. Thus Heidegger writes that: "Unless man first establishes himself beforehand in the space proper to his essence and there takes up his dwelling, he will not be capable of anything essential within the destining now holding sway."[205] Yet how is such a return to dwelling—such a turning back to the happening of disclosedness—possible at all? What can any individual do in the face of the "destitution" that technology appears to bring with it?

The Event, it will be recalled, is both a happening of disclosedness and a disclosedness of that happening. It is the happening of that disclosedness in a way that is determinative of an entire era—as "world-historical"—but it is also the happening of that disclosedness as it occurs in relation to the particular thing and the individual person. As a turning in world-historical disclosure, the Event is something that can only be awaited, that cannot be directly brought about, any more than one can directly bring about any hoped for world-historical change. Here Heidegger need not be viewed as any more nor less pessimistic than, for instance, Karl Popper in his rejection of social engineering—the point is that there is no "technology" to be applied to bring about the turning, and certainly there is no technology that can be used to overcome technology as such. Yet the "awaiting" of the world-historical turning may take many forms, and it seems there is no reason why it cannot be awaited through activism, even political activism, so long as it is wary of itself being taken up into the technological mode of revealing against which it also struggles, and so long as it is aware of its own limits, and even its likely failure—such "activism" must, in this sense, always be guided by a recognition of the "poetic."[206] As it may occur in an individual life, however, and so as it concerns our own comportment toward the world and toward things, the Event need not only be awaited. Indeed, we can each cultivate a mode of being that constitutes a "turning back" to being, that is a "remembrance," that is a mode of dwelling. For us, of course, the question is how to achieve this in the face of the contemporary dominance of technology.

Heidegger does not respond to this latter question by urging the abandonment of technology[207]—but instead suggests that what must be done is to adopt a way of being with technology that does not give in to its domination:

We can use technical devices as they ought to be used, and also let them alone as something which does not affect our real and inner core. We can affirm the unavoidable use of technical devices, and also deny them the right to dominate us, and so to warp, confuse, and lay waste our nature. But will not saying yes and no this way to technical devices make our relation to technology ambivalent and insecure? On the contrary! Our relation to technology will become wonderfully simple and relaxed. We let technical devices enter our daily life, and at the same time leave them outside, that is, let them alone, as things which are nothing absolute but remain dependent upon something higher. I would call this comportment toward technology which expresses "yes" and at the same time "no," by an old word, *releasement toward things* [*Gelassenheit*].[208]

"*Gelassenheit*," in ordinary German, carries connotations of "composure" and "tranquility"; in the sense of "releasement toward things" that Heidegger employs it, a sense deriving from Meister Eckhart, it signifies a way of being in relation to technology that does not allow technology to dominate us, but leaves us, and so also things, free in relation to it. Such "releasement" depends, as Heidegger indicates here, on technological devices being placed in such a way that they are seen "as nothing absolute but . . . dependent on something higher"—that is, it requires such things to be seen in the light of a mode of revealing that is not simply that of the technological as such. The mode of revealing that is at issue here is surely that of "poetic dwelling" that is attuned to the Event as such, and so to the gathering of the fourfold, and thereby allows the "letting be" even of technology and its devices. Such a mode of comportment would certainly not relinquish technology, then, but would allow the technological to appear as itself a mode of revealing, and yet without things being thereby revealed only as resource. The comportment that goes with releasement is one that we can each cultivate ourselves—and it is, indeed, a comportment that should not be unfamiliar—but individual comportment will not itself rescue the world from its current "destitution." Moreover, such comportment will have to maintain itself in the face of the challenging of technology—a challenging from which, as technology pervades more and more aspects of our lives (the mobile phone being perhaps the most pervasive of its contemporary forms), it is increasingly hard to stand aside.

The possibility of a mode of revealing that would allow even the technological to appear as such is not, of course, new or unprecedented—as I suggested above, the very idea of being able to develop the sort of analysis of the technological that Heidegger proposes implies that the obscuring character of technological revealing cannot be so complete that it prevents *any* alternative revealing of things; moreover, we know that, even in the most technologically oriented parts of the contemporary world, it is still possible to find things revealed other than just as resource or commodity—sometimes through art, sometimes through the persistence of tradition, sometimes through sheer human eccentricity, sometimes through breakdown and failure. The ordering of the technological must always operate within the limits that are intrinsic to it, even though it may itself be incapable of representing those limits to itself. If we take seriously the idea of the technological as a certain reconfiguration of the topological in favor of a form of the spatial, then we must recognize that such a reconfiguration can never do away with the topological for the simple reason that all revealing occurs in and through place (to provide the very simplest of illustrations here, the Internet may abolish distance, but it can do so only on the basis of our own prior and embodied engagement with a particular computer, screen, and keyboard—and with much more besides). In this respect, even the technological can be understood, as it is a mode of revealing, as also constituting a certain *topos* and as accompanied by its own characteristic formation of places (albeit places that typically appear as "nonplaces"—as homogenous, arbitrary "locations" within an essentially spatialized world). Here, of course, is the tension that resides within the technological: the more the technological covers over its own character as a mode of revealing, and so as itself constitutive of a certain place and placing, the more it misunderstands and misrepresents its own character and the more it opens up the possibility of its own breakdown. The technological impulse toward a complete ordering of the world is thus at odds with the very character of the technological as a mode of revealing, as a form of the Event, as a happening of place, and it is this that sustains Heidegger's hope for "the other beginning." Moreover, so far as the comportment that goes with releasement is concerned, it must itself be a comportment attentive, not only to the Event, but also to the Event *as a happening of place*—perhaps as the maintaining of a certain "sense of place." Even in the face of technological ordering, then, place endures—both individually and "historically"—and so, in that endurance, does the possibility for another mode of revealing to come forth endure also.

The character of the Event, whether in relation to an individual life or the happening of world history, is the opening up of the world in its disclosedness and its concealment. It is essentially an opening up of things in their "excess" and their finitude. As such, it is also an opening up of the world and of things in their essential questionability. The Event, in contrast to the Framework, is thus in no way a "violent" mode of revealing, but allows things to come forth in their difference and unity, in their distance and their nearness. Unlike the Framework, the Event allows the fourfold to appear in terms of the mirroring interplay, the "round-dance," of the elements that are brought to appearance within it. Unlike the Framework, the Event is no domination either of human being or of world, and, in this sense, the Event must be a turning away from all modes of "decisionism" or "authoritarianism." This must apply as much in the domain of the political as elsewhere—indeed, the contemporary holding sway of the technological is itself a form of "authoritarianism," a "tyranny," that is as antithetical to, and destructive, of the "human," and of human community, as it is of the things of "nature."[209] In this respect, it is notable that Camus's condemnation of the drive for mastery that characterizes the "European" and the "modern" is closely allied with his own commitment to a politics of "moderation" that is essentially attentive to the fragility and vulnerability of individual human life and that is also committed to a form of "democratic" or "dialogic" politics. So long as democracy is understood as a mode of politics that is fundamentally tied to contestation as well as to negotiation—to the limitation *and* dispersal of power, to power as inevitable *and* constantly failing—then it would seem that it would also be in a turning to some form of "democracy" that the turning of the Event would itself be manifest.[210] On this basis, Heidegger's seeming antidemocratic disposition, which appears evident even in the *Der Spiegel* interview in 1966, and which also stands in marked contrast to Camus's politics (as well as to that of Heidegger's student, Hannah Arendt, whose thinking converges, in many respects, with that of Camus[211]), would appear to be inconsistent with his own articulation of the Event as it stands against the disguised authoritarianism of the technological.[212]

6 Conclusion: Returning to Place

"To convalesce" [*genesen*] is the same as the Greek *néomai, nostos*. This means "to return home"; nostalgia is the aching for home, homesickness. The convalescent is the man who collects himself to return home, that is to turn in, into his own destiny. The convalescent is on the road to himself, so that he can say to himself who he is.
—Heidegger, "Who Is Nietszche's Zarathustra?"[1]

In the previous pages we have traversed almost the entirety of Heidegger's thinking from what Kisiel calls the "breakthrough" lectures of 1919 through to the very last seminar in 1972. Along this fifty-three-year path there are many twists and turns, many shifts in direction and orientation. Yet what seems to remain consistent throughout is the attempt to articulate what might be thought of as a certain experience or insight that essentially concerns the "situated," or better the "placed," character of being, and of our own being, so much so that we may describe the thinking that is associated with the name "Heidegger" as a thinking that does indeed consist, as he himself claimed, in an attempt to "say" the place of being—as a *topology* of being. Having set out, in as much detail as is possible within what has already been a fairly long, and sometimes arduous, journey, the way in which that attempt works itself out across the span of Heidegger's thinking, all that remains are some more general considerations about the nature of the topology that is at issue here.

6.1 The Recovery of Place

The idea of topology as such appears only quite late and rarely in Heidegger's thinking. Yet a topological approach can be seen to underlie much of Heidegger's work both early and late. In spite of the shifts in his thinking that occur between the 1910s and 1950s, all of his work can be seen as an attempt to articulate, that is to "say," the unitary place in which things come to presence and in which they come to be. The place at issue here (which appears in various guises as the *"Da"* of Dasein, as the clearing, *die Lichtung*, that is the happening of the truth of being, as the gathering of the fourfold in the *Ereignis*) is itself constituted only through the interrelations between the originary and mutually dependent ("equiprimordial") elements that themselves appear within it. In *Being and Time* those elements are delineated through the analysis of being-in-the-world and unified in the structure of care and temporality; in "The Origin of the Work of Art," they are seen in terms of the originary strife between earth and world; in late essays such as "The Thing," they are articulated though the mirroring "dance" of earth and sky, gods and mortals that is the gathering of world.

Heidegger's thinking thus begins with what is, in a certain sense, the simplest and most everyday of phenomena—the everyday fact of the constant and ongoing encounter that is the world, an encounter with which we are inextricably bound up, an encounter in which things, persons, and our own selves come to light. This encounter is not something that first occurs in some inner space within our skulls, nor in some purely mental realm apart from the world as such (as if we could make sense of the inner in separation from the outer, as if we already knew what the "mental" itself is); it is not something that occurs in a purely external realm of cause and materiality (as if we knew what the "external" and the "material" could mean here). The happening of world occurs first in the calling of language, in the gathering of the thing, in the opening up of the time-space that is also the "taking-place" of place. As it begins with something simple, so Heidegger's thinking is an attempt to address the question, and the questioning, of being in a way that remains true to being as such, but which is also true to the belonging together of being and beings, of presence and what is present, of being and human being. All of Heidegger's thought can be construed as an attempt to articulate this place of being. And in doing so, what Heidegger attempts is something that is difficult and even obscure largely because it is so fundamental, so simple, and so close: "The one thing thinking would like to attain and for the first time tries to articulate in *Being and Time* is something simple. As such, being remains mysterious, the simple nearness of an unobtrusive prevailing."[2] Elsewhere he writes:

To think Being does not require a solemn approach and the pretension of arcane erudition, nor the display of rare and exceptional states as in mystical raptures, reveries, and swoonings. All that is needed is simple wakefulness in the proximity of any random unobtrusive being, an awakening that all of a sudden sees that the being "is."[3]

One does not need to turn to great art or to the sublimity or beauty of nature to witness that which Heidegger talks about here—it can occur in the "proximity," as Heidegger says, "of any random unobtrusive being." Moreover, that occurrence "in . . . proximity" is itself an occurrence in and of place—it is an occurrence that needs no special such "place," but, is rather the happening of place as such.

In this latter respect, it seems to me that John van Buren, who has done much to draw attention to certain continuities in Heidegger's thinking, is nevertheless mistaken when he distinguishes between the very early Heidegger and the later in terms of an emphasis on the ubiquity, the "ordinariness," of the experience of being, of the Event—of what I have referred to as "place." Van Buren writes that:

In contrast to his later tendency to emphasize the mystery of *Ereignis* and the worlding of world as given in extra-ordinary meditative and poetic experiences, in 1919 Heidegger thought that not only a glorious dawn as seen from a mountain top, but rather any personal everyday situation is an *Ereignis* and a worlding-out of the world.[4]

Although it is certainly true that, in Heidegger's later thinking, the disclosing of the happening of the Event as such is not something that ordinarily happens without a certain wakefulness and attentiveness on our part—all the more so because of its constant obscuring by that particular mode of revealing that is the Framework—and so may be said to be disclosed only in certain "meditative and poetic experiences," still it is the case that the Event is there to be found in every "worlding-out" of world, every gathering of place, as that occurs in the most ordinary and everyday of situations.[5] At the same time, even in Heidegger's early thought, it is clear that the disclosedness of the happening of world, whether it occurs in the lecture hall or the mountain top, is nevertheless something that we are constantly prone to overlook, to misunderstand, and to misinterpret—indeed this is precisely why Heidegger gives so much emphasis, even in his early lectures, to "phenomenological seeing" as a way of returning to the original encounter with the thing, not as some "construction" out of the deliverances of the senses, nor as some mere posit or "value," but as the very thing that it is, in relation to which we also encounter ourselves and others, all within the overarching compass of the world.

The sort of "simple wakefulness" that is required here, the sort of wakefulness at which true "phenomenological seeing" might be thought to aim,[6] is much less easy to achieve than we might think. Not only is it threatened by our own inevitable tendency to forget even what is closest to us, but it is also constantly threatened, and often rendered completely unattainable, by the metaphysical orientation that is, in truth, a genuine response to our own being in the question of being, and yet constantly covers over that original "question"—that original emergence of meaning, of truth, of place. Whether through the idea of *ousia* as the standing fast of the being in the present, through God as the cause and reason of the world, through the realization of all things in the universality of the "idea," the "subject," or "reason" as such, or through the prioritization of the spatialized materiality of the physical universe as the only "reality," what occurs in each case is a covering over of the original and originary "giving" of being in the presencing of presence. The task of thinking, as Heidegger undertakes and articulates that task, is an attempt to recover that original "giving" of being, that original "happening" of place—as such it is also an attempt both to *dis-place* philosophy away from its inherent tendency to forgetfulness and to *re-place* thinking in relation to the place in which it always begins and to which it must also always address itself. Thinking is thus essentially a form of return home— a homecoming.

In the "Letter on 'Humanism,'" Heidegger comments on his own reading of Hölderlin, in which "home" and the "return" home are central and recurrent themes, as follows:

In the lecture on Hölderlin's elegy "Homecoming" (1943) [the] . . . nearness "of" being, which is the *Da* of Dasein . . . is called the "homeland." The word is thought here in an essential sense, not patriotically or nationalistically, but in terms of the history of being. The essence of the homeland, however, is also mentioned with the intention of thinking the homelessness of contemporary human beings from the essence of being's history. . . . Homelessness . . . consists in the abandonment of beings by being. Homelessness is the symptom of oblivion of being.[7]

Homecoming, as with homelessness, is not a theme that appears only in Heidegger's reading of poetry, but is a central element in all his thinking. Thus he writes elsewhere that:

We belong to being, and yet not. We reside in the realm of being and yet are not directly allowed in. We are, as it were, homeless in our ownmost homeland, assuming we may thus name our own essence. We reside in a realm constantly permeated by the casting toward and the casting-away of being. To be sure, we hardly ever pay attention to this characteristic of our abode, but we now ask: "where" are we "there," when we are thus placed into such an abode?[8]

Heidegger's thinking of the place of being, and his attempt to "say" that place and thereby also to recover it, is grounded in our already belonging to that place. It is this that makes the forgetting of being and the apparent obliteration of place in the face of technology an obliteration of the place, the only place, in which we can dwell and in which we already are. The need for the recovery of place, for a return home, arises, then, only because of the way in which our very being "out of place" is itself a failure to grasp our being already "in place"—a matter of our failure to grasp the very place of being, and so to grasp the place of our own being. In talking of the need to follow the "coursing" of language, Heidegger explains that:

> The way allows us to reach what concerns us, in that domain where we are already staying. Why then, one may ask, still find a way to it? Answer: because where we already are, we are in such a way that at the same time we are not there, because we ourselves have not yet properly reached what concerns our being, not even approached it.[9]

We dwell, and yet we do not dwell; we belong to being, and yet are separated from being; we are in place, and yet we find ourselves displaced; we are at home, and yet nevertheless remain homeless.

Yet what is the "home," in German the "*Heimat,*" to which we are supposed to return? Is it, to take a handful of possibilities, Heidegger's Black Forest, Wordsworth's Lake District, John Clare's native Northamptonshire, or central Australia as articulated in Pinjarra Aboriginal Dreaming? Is it to the juxtaposition of bush, hill, and sea that is so characteristic of the New Zealand North Island countryside (and of some parts of Tasmania), to the mountainous, sky-filled landscape of the Himalayas, the rocky desert country of North Africa, or the open prairie of the American West? Is it the "home" of some premodern agrarian existence, or could it possibly be found in the contemporary urban life of cities such as New York, Beijing or Sydney? In fact, the home that Heidegger is concerned with, in spite of his preference for imagery drawn from his own German life and experience, is none of these, and yet it could also be found in all or any one of them.[10] The "homecoming" of which Heidegger speaks is a return to the *nearness* of being. That nearness is not a matter of coming into the vicinity of some single, unique place, but rather of coming to recognize the placed character of being as such. Such a recognition is always articulated in and through the particular places in which we already find ourselves, and no one such place can have any priority here. Moreover, in this return to place, we are also returned to the essential questionability of being. Returning to place is a returning to nearness to things, but such nearness is a matter of allowing things to be what they are, in their closeness as well as their distance, in their unity and differentiation. Returning to place is thus not a returning to a stable and fixed spot on earth, but rather a freeing up of the essential questionability of beings and being, of thing and place, of self and other—this is the reason why returning to place, as Hölderlin makes clear,[11] stands in an essential relation to "journeying." Only insofar as we journey—and such journeying need not always be the journeying of physical distancing—do we come into nearness of the place in which we already are and which we never properly leave. Returning to place is a thus not a returning to any one place, though it may sometimes be expressed or even experienced that way, but a returning to the openness and indeterminacy of the world—a returning, also, to the experience of wonder.

At its simplest and most direct, one can say that what Heidegger hoped to accomplish in his thinking was "homecoming"—a turning back toward our own dwelling place—as such, Heidegger's thinking also expresses the hope for the convalescence, understood as a returning home, for thinking as such, a convalescence from the homelessness of technological modernity. As a homecoming, the mood of Heidegger's thinking is nostalgic—it is characterized by the desire for home or for the return to the nearness of home. Such thinking is, of course, inextricably bound to a thinking that is essentially oriented toward place and our belonging in and to place. The thinking of place, we might say, will always carry with it such "nostalgia" and will always articulate itself in terms of such a "coming home"—a coming home that will itself take the form of a "saying" of the place to which we come home in such saying. If such thinking is understood as an essential mode of philosophy, then philosophy will itself have to be understood as a form of "convalescence"—the convalescence to be found, not only in Nietzsche's Zarathustra, but also in Novalis's talk of philosophy as "homelessness" and coming to be "at home." To put matters in these terms, however, especially in terms of convalescence as "nostalgia," may seem to confirm all the suspicions that surround Heidegger's thinking in terms of its supposed character as essentially "backward-looking," as "provincialist" and rural, as conservative and "bäuerlich" (based in the thinking of the peasant and farmer)—to say nothing of its supposed mysticism and obscurity. Yet anyone who reads Heidegger closely soon learns that while Heidegger draws heavily on "ordinary" language, the way he makes use of such language is often quite "un-ordinary." When Heidegger draws on the language of "home," he does so in a way that is clearly not ignorant or forgetful of the usual connotations of the word, and yet he also appropriates that term in a way that radically reorients it. Heidegger's homecoming is thus something that is undertaken rather than completed; a return, not to what is certain and stable, but to the original question of being, and to the questionability of our own being; a turn back, not to what is familiar, in the ordinary sense, but to that which is essentially "uncanny," inexplicable, wondrous.

6.2   The Poetics of Place

The homecoming that Heidegger finds spoken of in Hölderlin is thus a homecoming that indeed consists in a remembrance of and a return to a place that properly we can never leave. Heidegger's task of thinking is to achieve, or, at the very least, to prepare the way for such a homecoming— a homecoming that must always be carried out in each and every place and time. We may choose to say that for Heidegger philosophy is such a homecoming, but we may also wonder, as Heidegger did himself, whether it is proper to speak of this still as philosophy at all. Heidegger talks of thinking, a kind of meditative thinking, that looks to preserve the place of being, to speak it, and in so doing provide us with a reminder of who and what we are, of our own being as mortal creatures, born and destined to die, and yet nevertheless given over to a world that itself shines, as Heidegger puts it, as a world—a world that shines in the truth and beauty of gathered place. Perhaps the question as to whether this remains "philosophy" is not the crucial question, and yet, inasmuch as the thinking that is at issue here seems to stand in an essential relation to philosophy and attempts to address questions that are themselves fundamental to philosophy—questions concerning our own being as well as being as such—so it seems that philosophy cannot be left out of account. In this sense, then, the turning back to place that is announced in Heidegger's thinking is also a turn back to a certain essential mode of philosophy as such—a mode of philosophy that recognizes its own relation to the poetic.

The "poetic" character of the mode of thinking that is at issue here, regardless of whether we choose to also refer to it as "philosophical," is a mode of thinking that, in turning back to place, also turns back to a certain fundamental happening of unity as differentiated and differentiating. How to understand the unity at issue here is a theme that runs throughout Heidegger's thinking. In *Being and Time*, the concern with unity is expressed through Heidegger's adoption of a transcendental mode of pro-ceeding, one largely derived from Kant, which also brings with it a focus on the phenomenon of "transcendence." The transcendental can itself be understood as already bringing a certain topological orientation with it, and yet, in spite of this, it is nevertheless predicated on a a way of understanding being that is already disjunctive—that, in its separation between condition and conditioned, between subjectivity and world, threatens the unitary character of the happening of being. The problem of such a disjunction in the understanding of being remains, however, even after Heidegger's abandonment of the framework of the transcendental, through the disjunction between being and human being and, more fundamentally, between being and beings. In Heidegger's later thinking, human being is seen as already gathered into the happening of being as such, and so as a necessary element within that happening, but as, in no way, the basis or ground of that happening.

Still, even if we think of human being as "belonging essentially" to being, the difference that remains here may seem problematic. Something of the difficulty is explored by Heidegger in "On the Question of Being." There he writes:

Presencing ("being") is, as presencing, on each and every occasion a presencing that is directed toward the human essence, insofar as presencing is a call [*Geheiß*] that on each occasion calls upon the human essence. The human essence as such is a hearing, because the essence of human beings belongs to the calling of this call, to the approach of presencing [*ins Anwesen*]. That which is the Same each time, the belonging together of call and hearing, would then be "being"? What am I saying? It is no longer "being" at all—if we attempt fully to think through "being" in its destinal prevailing, namely, as presencing, in which manner alone we respond to its destinal essence. We would then have to relinquish the isolating and separating word "being" just as decisively as the name "human being." The question concerning the relation between the two revealed itself to be inadequate, because it never attains to the realm of what it seeks to ask after. In truth we cannot then even continue to say that "being" and "the human being" "are" the Same in the sense that *they* belong together; for when we say it in *this* way, we continue to let both subsist independently.[12]

These comments bear, not only on the difference between being and human being, but on the "ontological difference" between being and beings. Julian Young argues that what is required in the thinking of this latter difference is a shift away from thinking of it as "ontological," but instead as merely "the difference."[13] Yet as Heidegger's comments in regard to the difference between being and human being suggest, the problem does not seem merely to reside in the designation of the difference as *ontological*—indeed, these comments seem to locate the source of the difficulty in the use of term "being" itself. Thus, in the Le Thor Seminar we read:

Thinking enowning with the concepts of being and the history of being will not be successful; nor will it be with the assistance of the Greeks (which is precisely something "to go beyond"). With being, the ontological difference also vanishes. Looking ahead, one would likewise have to view the continual references to the ontological difference from 1927 to 1936 as a necessary impasse [*Holzweg*].[14]

A similar point also seems to be made in the discussion *On Time and Being* in which Heidegger considers an apparent tension between the thinking of the Event and the thinking of being:

In the "Letter on 'Humanism'" . . . the term "Being itself" already names the Event. (The relations and contexts constituting the essential structure of the Event were worked out between 1936 and 1938.). . . . It is precisely a matter of seeing that Being, by coming to view as the Event, disappears as being. Thus there is no contradiction between the two statements. Both name the same matter with differing emphases.[15]

It is significant that talk of "being," as distinct from beings, does indeed take on much less prominence in the final phase of Heidegger's thinking that occurs in the period after 1945–1946. The reason for this would seem to be that Heidegger recognizes even talk of being as carrying a tendency within it that leads away from the poetic, back into metaphysics, and so back into the oblivion of being, or better, of ~~being~~ (which is one of the ways in which late Heidegger tries to deal with the difficulty in speaking that threatens here).[16]

The language of the Event, and of the simple happening of the onefold that is the fourfold, eschews the talk of being and of the ontological difference in favor of the happening of a single differentiating and differentiated unity. It is this unity that is invoked in the poetic language of Hölderlin, as well as in the increasingly explicit topological language of Heidegger's very late thinking. It is also the unity to which Heidegger seems to refer in his poem on Cézanne:

In the late work of the painter the twofoldness
Of what is present and of presence has become
one, "realized" and overcome at the same time
Transformed into a mystery-filled identity.[17]

The attempt to articulate the happening of Event is itself an attempt to articulate what also appears in poetry and art as such: the single, simple happening of world, of place, of ~~being~~.

Art and poetry always work, of course, within and through particular spaces and places—with respect to particular "works," modes, and practices. The same is true, in its own way, of the thinking of place that Heidegger attempts, and, indeed, of any such thinking. The thinking of place that is to be found in Heidegger's work is thus a thinking that, as I noted above, occurs in and through the only "place" it could for Heidegger: in the places and spaces with which he was himself familiar and in which his thinking was embedded—not only the village of Meßkirch, the city of Freiburg, and the locality of Todtnauberg in the Black Forest, but also the particular "topos" of the lecture hall, the seminar room, and of the philosophical essay. Yet here it is not merely a matter of the way in which Heidegger's thinking makes necessary reference to its own "origin," its own "place," but, more than this, the way in which the poetics of that thinking of "place" (which is, as with all places, never just a "single" place) is constituted in ways that are specific to its particular place-bound character—thus the poetics of Heidegger's thinking works through a certain philosophical tradition and vocabulary, through a particular way of doing philosophy, through a historical and topographical heritage that belongs to the South German landscape in which Heidegger was born, grew up, worked, and died, through the language and images that belong to those places and to that landscape.

That this should be so is no surprise: place only appears, and can only be spoken, in and through specific places; moreover, as Heidegger remarks in the passage I quoted in chapter 1, we can indeed only speak and think in our own language, which is to say that we can only speak the place of being through the forms in which that place is itself already articulated to us. Yet although articulated in forms that necessarily belong to particular places, the thinking of being that Heidegger attempts is nevertheless one that goes beyond any such place; while it refers itself to the forms with which it is familiar, it is not the familiarity of just those forms that is at issue. The thinking and saying of place always takes on its own local resonances, not merely in the way particular places and landscapes are glimpsed in and through our thoughtful responses to them, but also in the artistic and poetic responses to them. For myself, growing up in New Zealand rather than Heidegger's Schwabian-Allemanic countryside, the New Zealand painter Colin McCahon's work presents its own "fourfold" of New Zealand forms, a fourfold of night and day, mountain and sky, of land and sea, light and dark—a fourfold articulated in a wide range of works, including paintings such as McCahon's *Takaka: Night and Day* (1948),[18] of which McCahon himself said that "it states my interest in landscape as a symbol of place and also of the human condition."[19] In the work of McCahon's friend, the poet James K. Baxter, a similar set of elements reappears—light and dark, land and sky, death and beauty. As Baxter writes in "High Country Weather":

Alone we are born
And die alone
Yet see the red gold cirrus
Over snow mountain shine

Upon the upland road
Ride easy stranger
Surrender to the sky
Your heart of anger[20]

Here, though in a very different way from Heidegger or Hölderlin, earth and sky both appear, as do mortals, while there is also a sense of the "holiness" of the world invoked that perhaps recalls the gods—thus, in Baxter's poem, as in Heidegger's thinking, we are called to "release" ourselves to the world as that which claims us rather than being claimed by us; called to a journey that turns always homewards.

Notes

Chapter 1

1. "The Thinker as Poet," in *Poetry, Language, Thought*, trans. Albert Hofstadter (New York: Harper and Row, 1971), p. 12 (*GA* [*Gesamtausgabe*] 13:84). Although first published in 1954, Heidegger notes that the lines were composed in 1947.

2. As I indicate in the discussion below, this "middle" period includes the period of the so-called Turning (*die Kehre*) in Heidegger's thinking that is usually taken to have occurred in 1930–1936. This "middle" period can thus be construed as actually comprising two periods: what is essentially a "transitional" period from 1930–1936 and a more developed period (in which the unpublished *Contributions* volume of 1936–1938 [*GA* 65] plays a key role) from 1936–1946. See my comments below, sec. 4.1, pp. 149–155.

3. Edward S. Casey, *The Fate of Place* (Berkeley: University of California Press, 1996).

4. See Casey, *The Fate of Place*, pp. 243ff; see also my review of Casey in "Remembering Place (Edward S. Casey, *The Fate of Place*)," *International Journal of Philosophical Studies* 10 (2002), 92–100. To what extent Heidegger's pathway should indeed be viewed as "indirect" seems to me a matter open to debate.

5. Fell, "Heidegger's Mortals and Gods," *Research in Phenomenology* 15 (1985), 29.

6. See Stuart Elden, *Mapping the Present: Heidegger, Foucault, and the Project of a Spatial History* (London: Continuum, 2001), esp. pp. 1–7.

7. See Julian Young, *Heidegger's Philosophy of Art* (Cambridge: Cambridge University Press, 2000) and *Heidegger's Later Philosophy* (Cambridge: Cambridge University Press, 2002). Other recent works that are relevant include: James Phillips, *Heidegger's Volk: Between National Socialism and Poetry* (Stanford: Stanford University Press, 2005); Charles Bambach, *Heidegger's Roots: Nietzsche, National Socialism, and the Greeks* (Ithaca: Cornell University Press, 2003); and also Miguel de Beistegui, *Heidegger and the Political: Dystopias* (London: Routledge, 1998). In *Hölderlin: The Poetics of Being* (Detroit: Wayne University Press, 1991), Adrian Del Caro takes a Heideggerian

approach to Hölderlin himself (although a Heideggerian approach taken, notes
Del Caro, "with more than a grain of salt," *Hölderlin: The Poetics of Being*, p. 21).

8. Joseph Fell's *Heidegger and Sartre: An Essay on Being and Place* (New York: Columbia University Press, 1979) was one of the first works to investigate the idea of place
throughout Heidegger's work, while Heidegger's treatment of place is, as noted
above, also dealt with in Casey's *The Fate of Place*, as well as having a role, though
not taken up in any detail, in Julian Young's work referred to above—see his "Poets
and Rivers: Heidegger on Hölderlin's *Der Ister*," *Dialogue* 28 (1999), 391–416, and
"What is Dwelling? The Homelessness of Modernity and the Worlding of the
World," in Mark Wrathall and Jeff Malpas (eds.), *Heidegger, Modernity, and Authenticity—Essays in Honor of Hubert Dreyfus*, vol. 1 (Cambridge, Mass.: MIT Press, 2000),
pp. 187–204. It is notable, however, that most of the treatment of Heidegger on this
topic takes space rather than place as the main theme of investigation. To some
extent, this is true even of Stuart Elden's *Mapping the Present: Heidegger and Foucault
on the Project of a Spatial History*, even though Elden gives explicit recognition to a
distinct concept of place (*"Ort"*) in Heidegger that stands apart from space and also
from the notion of mere "location" (*Platz*)—see *Mapping the Present*, pp. 36–37.
Didier Franck's, *Heidegger et le problème de l'éspace* (Paris: Minuit, 1986) discusses the
problem of spatiality in general, although with specific reference to *Being and Time*,
while Alejandro Vallega, in *Heidegger and the Issue of Space: Thinking on Exilic Grounds*
(University Park: Pennsylvania University Press, 2003), deals with aspects of
Heidegger's treatment of space as these relate to concepts of exile and alterity. Emil
Kettering's *Nähe: Das Denken Martin Heideggers* (Pfüllingen: Neske, 1987) addresses
the idea of "nearness" as a central element in Heidegger's thinking. Specific discus-
sions of spatiality occur in: Yoko Arisaka, "Heidegger's Theory of Space: A Critique
of Dreyfus," *Inquiry* 38 (1995), 455–467 and "Spatiality, Temporality, and the
Problem of Foundation in *Being and Time*," *Philosophy Today* 40 (1996), 36–46; Robert
Frodeman, "Being and Space: A Re-Reading of Existential Spatiality in *Being and
Time*," *Journal of the British Society for Phenomenology* 23 (1992), 23–35; Friedrich-
Wilhelm von Herrmann, "Wahrheit-Zeit-Raum," in *Die Frage nach der Wahrheit*
(Frankfurt: Klostermann, 1997), pp. 243–271; Maria Villela-Petit, "Heidegger's Conception of Space," in Christopher Macann (ed.), *Critical Heidegger* (London: Routledge, 1996), pp. 134–157; and in Gjermund Wollan, "Heidegger's Philosophy of
Space and Place," *Norsk Geografisk Tidsskrift–Norwegian Journal of Geography* 57
(2003), 31–39. Heidegger's later thinking, particularly in relation to the concept of
dwelling (a concept that is clearly very closely tied to notions of space and place),
has also been an important focus for a range of discussions in architecture (see the
work of Christian Norberg-Schulz , especially his *Concept of Dwelling: On the Way to
Figurative Architecture* [New York: Rizzoli, 1985]), as well as in "humanistic" geography (see, for instance, Edward Relph, "Geographical Experiences and Being-in-the-
World: The Phenomenological Origins of Geography," in David Seamon and Robert
Mugerauer [eds.], *Dwelling, Place, and Experience: Towards a Phenomenology of Person
and World* [Dordrecht: Nijhof, 1985], pp. 15–31).

9. It is this apparent gap in the literature that *Place and Experience* was intended to fill. Earlier works that make a case for the significance of place, although they tend not to provide any detailed analysis of the concept, include: Anne Buttimer and David Seamon (eds.), *The Human Experience of Space and Place* (London: Croom Helm, 1980); J. Nicolas Entrikin, *The Betweenness of Place* (Baltimore: Johns Hopkins University Press, 1991); Tony Hiss, *The Experience of Place* (New York: Random House, 1990); Edward Relph, *Place and Placelessness* (London: Pion, 1976); E. V. Walter, *Placeways* (Chapel Hill: University of North Carolina, 1988); Yi-Fu Tuan, *Topophilia* (Englewood Cliffs, N.J.: Prentice-Hall, 1974); Edward S. Casey, *Getting Back into Place* (Bloomington: Indiana University Press, 1993). Even Casey's work has often tended more toward a descriptive phenomenological approach rather than to an investigation of the way the concepts of place and space are themselves structured—see the exchange between Casey and myself in *Philosophy and Geography* 4 (2001), 225–240.

10. As I note in *Place and Experience*, p. 30n33, to some extent this is a feature even of the pioneering work of such place-sensitive writers as Yi-Fu Tuan.

11. This is exactly the claim made by David Harvey (who also figures in the discussion below): "Places, like space and time, are social constructs and have to be read and understood as such"—*Justice, Nature, and the Geography of Difference* (Oxford: Blackwell, 1996), p. 324. Although I may be thought to be displaying a typically "philosophical" prejudice, I would suggest that the very idea of "social construct" that is invoked by Harvey here is highly problematic, all the more so when applied to notions such as place, space, and time. Are we to suppose that the "social" somehow stands outside of place, space, and time—undetermined by them, but determining of them? Indeed, the reification of the "social" that appears here, and its apparent prioritization over other concepts, threatens to turn the "social" into something fundamental and yet almost completely inexplicable.

12. In a review of *Place and Experience* in *Mind* 110 (2001), 789–792, Bruin Christensen seems to assume just such a view of place, and from it he infers the obvious falsity of the claim (advanced in *Place and Experience*) that place has any determining or constituting role in relation to self-identity. Although Christensen agrees that everything has to be "in" place, he claims that nothing significant follows from this in terms of the identity of that which is in place since places are constituted and determined by the entities located within those places, not the other way around. Yet not only does this ignore the explicitly holistic account of place and the relation between place and other elements that is advanced in *Place and Experience* (and that is also a key element in the argument that I develop in relation to Heidegger), but it also assumes a very specific understanding of place that is itself open to challenge.

13. Hence the title of the opening chapter of *Place and Experience*: "The Obscurity of Place."

14. Although it should be noted that the general account of place that I argue can be found in Heidegger and that is also a feature of my own work will be inconsistent with any account that cannot allow for what I explain in sec. 5.2 below in terms of the "iridescence" of things—the possibility for things to be disclosed in multiple ways. Consequently, reductionist approaches and approaches that insist on the unique exclusivity of certain vocabularies or of certain descriptive or analytic schemata will turn out not to be compatible with the sort of topological or topographic approach that I elaborate here and which is also to be found in *Place and Experience*.

15. John van Buren, *The Young Heidegger: Rumour of the Hidden King* (Indianapolis: Indiana University Press, 1994), p. 38. See also Thomas Sheehan, "A Paradigm Shift in Heidegger Research," *Continental Philosophy Review* 34 (2001), p. 188.

16. See especially his discussion in *The Young Heidegger*, chaps. 12–13, pp. 250ff.

17. Van Buren, *The Young Heidegger*, p. 251.

18. See John D. Caputo, *The Mystical Element in Heidegger's Thought* (Athens, Ohio: Ohio University Press, 1978).

19. The topological character of philosophical thinking is not, I would claim, peculiar only to Western thought, but basic is to any attempt at a certain "fundamental" thinking and obtains irrespective of the cultural tradition in which such thinking occurs.

20. Steven Galt Crowell, *Husserl, Heidegger, and the Space of Meaning* (Evanston, Ill.: Northwestern University Press, 2001), p. 7.

21. This is a point that seems to me to have been always implicit in my work on these topics. However, in trying to make sense of Heidegger's own use of the term "transcendental" and the special role it plays in his thinking (something explored further in chapter 4), I have sometimes used the notion of the transcendental as an idea that stands in tension with the topological—see, for instance, "From the Transcendental to the 'Topological': Heidegger on Ground, Unity, and Limit," in Jeff Malpas (ed.), *From Kant to Davidson: Philosophy and the Idea of the Transcendental* (London: Routledge, 2002), pp. 75–99.

22. See *Being and Time*, H7, H152–153.

23. *Being and Time* H1, from Plato, *Sophist* 244a.

24. See "Introduction to 'What Is Metaphysics?'" trans. Walter Kaufmann, in Martin Heidegger *Pathmarks*, ed. William McNeill (Cambridge: Cambridge University Press, 1998), p. 285 (*GA* 9:376): "By recalling the beginnings of that history in which Being unveiled itself in the thinking of the Greeks, it can be shown that the Greeks from early on experienced the Being of beings as the presence of what is present."

25. *On Time and Being*, trans. Joan Stambaugh (New York: Harper and Row, 1972), p. 7 (*Zur Sache des Denkens* [Tübingen: Max Niemeyer, 1969], pp. 6–7).

26. "On the Question of Being," trans. William McNeill, in *Pathmarks*, p. 302 (*GA* 9:400).

27. Taylor Carman, for instance, argues that, in *Being and Time* at least, being is not identical with presence at all—see Taylor Carman, "On Being Social: A Reply to Olafson," *Inquiry* 37 (1994), 203–223. Carman's piece is, as its title indicates, a response to Frederick Olafson's contrary claim in *Heidegger and the Philosophy of Mind* (New Haven: Yale, 1987), esp. pp. xvii–xviii. Olafson replies to Carman in "Individualism, Subjectivity, and Presence: A Response to Taylor Carman," *Inquiry* 37 (1994), 331–337—see esp. pp. 333–334.

28. Olafson points out that one of the complications here is that this term is also used by Heidegger to refer to the Greek *"ousia"*—see Olafson, "Individualism, Subjectivity, and Presence," 333.

29. *On Time and Being*, pp. 12–13 (*Zur Sache des Denkens*, pp. 13–14).

30. Young, *Heidegger's Later Philosophy*, p. 10.

31. Ibid., p. 12.

32. In one respect, treating "presence" as possibly referring to beings as well as to being might be taken to suggest an overlooking of the distinction between being and beings that is the "ontological difference," since if being can be construed as presence, and presence can mean beings or being, then the possibility of misconstruing being in terms of beings has already been introduced. It seems to me, however, that this actually counts in favor of using "presence" in this broad fashion—not because it condones the forgetting of the ontological difference at issue (although that difference should not be too readily assumed even in Heidegger, as will become evident in chapters 4 and 5), but because it allows us to see how that forgetting might arise.

33. See Heidegger's discussion of presence and "the present" in "Time and Being," in *On Time and Being*, pp. 11–12 (*Zur Sache des Denkens*, p. 12): "the present in the sense of presence differs so vastly from the present in the sense of the now that the present as presence can in no way be determined in terms of the present as the now. The reverse would rather seem possible (cf. *Being and Time*, sec. 81). If such were the case, the present as presence and everything which belongs to such a present would have to be called real time." Both "presence" and "the present" are being used equivocally here in a way that allows Heidegger to retain the insistence on the centrality of "presence" and "the present" in a way that seems compatible with the critique of "presence" and "the present" in *Being and Time*.

34. See, for instance, "Time and Being," pp. 9–13 (*Zur Sache des Denkens*, pp. 9–14).

35. See *Being and Time* (GA 2), H220–221. The appearance of this notion in *Being and Time* should itself indicate the way in which presence cannot be treated, even there, in the purely narrow sense of that "which is present in the present."

36. It seems to me fundamentally mistaken, although an extremely widespread tendency, to view *Being and Time* as itself the expression of a subjectivist or idealist position. The way in which Heidegger's analysis proceeds nevertheless lends itself to subjectivist or idealist interpretation, and so contains within it elements that can be seen to tend toward subjectivism and idealism. A work that already aims, from the beginning, to think "beyond" any simple distinction between subject and object, thus ends up, in a certain way, reinscribing that distinction (albeit it in a different form). For more on this issue, see the discussion in chapter 3, sec. 3.6 and also chapter 4, secs. 4.2 and 4.3.

37. A point to which van Buren gives particular emphasis in his discussion of the early Heidegger—see *The Young Heidegger*, esp. pp. 105–110, where it is discussed in relation to the use of analogy in Heidegger's habilitation dissertation.

38. "Seminar in Le Thor 1968," in *Four Seminars*, trans. Andrew Mitchell and François Raffoul (Bloomington: Indiana University Press, 2004), p. 19 (GA 15:302).

39. *Basic Concepts*, trans. Gary E. Aylesworth (Bloomington: Indiana University Press, 1993, p. 60 (GA 51:71–72).

40. In my emphasis on the centrality of unity here, I am taking issue with James Phillips's contrary emphasis in his, otherwise excellent, *Heidegger's Volk*. Indeed, on this point, Phillips seems to me to misread both Heidegger *and* Aristotle. I will return to the issue of unity in sec. 2.2.

41. Fell, *Heidegger and Sartre*, p. 209.

42. Indeed, Heidegger is a frequent commentator on his own thinking, but those commentaries, while often instructive, can sometimes also mislead if they are not integrated with a broader understanding of Heidegger's thinking as derived from the body of his writings as a whole.

43. Heidegger, "Only a God Can Save Us," trans. Maria P. Alter and John D. Caputo, in Richard Wolin (ed.), *The Heidegger Controversy: A Critical Reader* (Cambridge, Mass.: MIT Press, 1993), p. 95 (GA 16:655).

44. The list of works that deal with this issue is already considerable, and it seems that it has not yet reached an end. Much of the English-speaking controversy was sparked by Victor Farías, *Heidegger and Nazism*, trans. Paul Burrell and Gabriel R. Ricci (Philadelphia: Temple University Press, 1989). Although Farías's work had appeared in French in 1987, it drew heavily on research already undertaken by Hugo Ott, but not available in book form until 1988. Ott's *Martin Heidegger: Unterwegs zu seiner Biographie* (Frankfurt: Campus, 1988) appeared in English as *Martin Heidegger: A Political Life*, trans. Allen Blunden (London: Harper Collins, 1993). As Julian Young

points out, however, the basis for much of the case against Heidegger, namely his speeches during the 1930s, had already been compiled and published by Guido Schneeberger some years earlier as *Nachlese zu Heidegger* (Bern: Suhr, 1962), although it provoked little interest at the time—see Young, *Heidegger, Philosophy, Nazism* (Cambridge: Cambridge University Press, 1997), p. 2n4. The most comprehensive and currently definitive source is *Reden und andere Zeugnisse eines Lebensweges, Gesamtausgabe* 16 (Frankfurt: Klostermann, 2000). Much of the original documentation relevant to this issue, as well as other material, is included in English in G. Neske and E. Kettering (eds.), *Martin Heidegger and National Socialism*, trans. L. Harries (New York: Paragon House, 1990), as well as in Richard Wolin (ed.), *The Heidegger Controversy: A Critical Reader* (Cambridge, Mass.: MIT Press, 1993).

45. David Harvey, *The Condition of Post-Modernity* (Oxford: Basil Blackwell, 1989), p. 209.

46. Ibid., p. 277. Although, see also Harvey's later, and rather more nuanced discussion, in *Justice, Nature, and the Geography of Difference*, pp. 299–324.

47. Doreen Massey, "Power-Geometry and a Progressive Sense of Place," in Jon Bird, Barry Curtis, Tim Putnam, George Robertson, and Lisa Tickner (eds.), *Mapping the Futures* (London: Routledge, 1993), pp. 64, 67. Massey goes on to comment that "These arguments, then, highlight a number of ways in which a progressive concept of place might be developed. First of all, it is absolutely not static and in no way relates to the Heideggerian view of Space/Place as Being. If places can be conceptualized in terms of the social interactions which they tie together, then it is also the case that these interactions themselves are not static, they are processes. One of the great one-liners in Marxist exchanges has for long been 'ah, but capital is not a thing, it's a process.' Perhaps the same should be said also about places; that places are processes, too."

48. It is not at all clear that there is any such incompatibility, moreover Heidegger's later thinking is explicit in the way it thinks time and space together as *"Zeit-Raum"* (time-space)—see, for instance, *What Is a Thing?*, trans. W. B. Barton, Jr. and Vera Deutsch (Chicago: Henry Regnery, 1967), p. 16 (*GA* 41:16).

49. In spite of her indication of the possibility of developing a more progressive concept of place than that which she finds in Heidegger, Massey's view of place in the essay in which she discusses the Heideggerian concept seems generally rather negative. Elsewhere, however, she has advanced a much more positive conception—see for instance, her discussion in *Space, Place, and Gender* (Minneapolis: University of Minnesota Press, 1994), pp. 117–172—esp. her comments on pp. 119–123.

50. See Lyotard, "Domus and the Megalopolis," in *The Inhuman*, trans. Geoffrey Bennington and Rachel Bowlby (Cambridge: Polity Press, 1991), pp. 191–204.

51. Neil Leach, "The Dark Side of the Domus: The Redomestication of Central and Eastern Europe," in Neil Leach (ed.), *Architecture and Revolution: Contemporary Perspectives on Central and Eastern Europe* (London: Routledge, 1999), p. 151.

52. Ibid., p. 155.

53. Leach appears to assume, presumably on the basis of Heidegger's own tendency to look to rural examples, that the concept of dwelling must indeed be tied to a rural paradigm that can have no relevance to the urban. There may be a question about *how* one dwells in an urban setting, but one cannot simply assume that such a mode of dwelling is ruled out from the start.

54. Leach does quote from Heidegger at one point ("The Dark Side of the Domus," pp. 151–152), although it is significant that the quotation comes from the infamous Rectoral Address of 1933, "On the Self-Assertion of the German University," rather than from any of the later writings.

55. Young draws attention to Heidegger's complaint, in the Hölderlin lectures of 1934–1935, concerning the present "snivelling about people and blood and soil [*Volkstum und Blut und Boden*]"—*Hölderlins Hymnen "Germanien" und "Der Rhein," Gesamtausgabe* 39, p. 254; see Young, *Heidegger, Philosophy, Nazism*, p. 12n3 (it is significant that such a comment should occur in these lectures since it is here that Heidegger first begins to articulate his thinking in relation to the notion of "earth" that is so important in his later thought). Young also notes criticism of the idea of *Volk* in texts from the late 1930s. James Phillips argues, however, that "Heidegger's disillusionment with National Socialism is not a disillusionment with the notion of the "*Volk*" (*Heidegger's Volk*, p. 3), but instead arises out of a deep incompatibility between National Socialism and the concept of the "people" on which Heidegger originally saw the movement as nevertheless attempting to draw.

56. This is clear in Young's account of the "völkisch" politics that underlay Heidegger's Nazi involvement (see *Heidegger, Philosophy, Nazism*, pp. 11–51), as well as in James Phillips's detailed investigation in *Heidegger's Volk*. For an approach that takes Heidegger's thinking as nevertheless remaining compromised by a "dangerous commitment to autochthony," see Bambach, *Heidegger's Roots*, quotation from p. 217.

57. "Building Dwelling Thinking," in *Poetry, Language, Thought*, trans. Albert Hofstadter (New York: Harper and Row, 1971), pp. 143–161 (*GA* 7:145–164). This essay is itself the focus, however, for an important essay by J. Hillis Miller that does attempt to do more in the way of providing an argument for the politically dangerous character of Heidegger's place-oriented thinking—see J. Hillis Miller, "Slipping Vaulting Crossing: Heidegger," in *Topographies* (Stanford: Stanford University Press, 1995), pp. 216–254.

58. There is another element here, however, that should be acknowledged: Leach, in particular (and there is sometimes an element of this in Massey), seems to argue

that place-based thinking is out of kilter with the character of the contemporary world—in Leach's case, with the impact of technology and globalization. I would argue, and the argument is indicated at various places in the discussion over the next few chapters, that such a claim rests on a misunderstanding concerning the nature both of place and of the contemporary world.

59. For instance, Leach's claim that there have been such changes in the "ways in which we relate to the world" that "we must ask whether a concept that is so place-specific can any longer retain much authority" seems to me particularly contentious—and also surprisingly uncritical.

60. One might argue that those arguments often reduce to a form of *argumentum ad hominem* ("against the person"—an attempt to refute an idea on the basis of some fact about the person who advances that idea), or else as embodying a version of the genetic fallacy (an attempt to refute an idea based on the source or context out of which the idea comes). John van Buren, however, refers us to "the lengthy list of Heidegger's tasteless and discriminatory acts before, during and after his Rectorship (combined ambiguously with acts of kindness and generosity) that has been compiled by Farías, Ott, Sheehan and others," adding that "When conducted rightly, this historical research is not mere ad hominem argumentation, but shows within the workings of practical reason the logical consequences of the ideological tendencies in Heidegger's ontology itself and alerts us to the need to criticise his 'ideas' "—*The Young Heidegger*, p. 392. Whether there is an *ad hominem* element here does indeed depend on whether or not one can show Heidegger's actions as "logical consequences" of his "ideas." One of the ironies of this discussion is that so much emphasis seems to be placed on an implied consistency of action and idea by authors, and to some extent this is true of van Buren, who are elsewhere suspicious of the homogeneity and "unity" of thought as such. Independently of this issue, however, I think there are good reasons to suppose that the sort of "logical" demonstration that van Buren claims here is highly unlikely to be successful. Indeed, van Buren's own comments are indicative of some of the difficulties. If the "lengthy list of Heidegger's tasteless and discriminatory acts" are indeed "ambiguously combined" with "acts of kindness and generosity," then we may well take the acknowledged *inconsistency* in Heidegger's actions to cast doubt on the claim that there could be a *consistency* of the sort implied by talk of "logical consequence" between "actions" and "ideas." Moreover, between just which ideas and which actions, we may ask, is such consistency supposed to obtain? And whichever ideas and actions are the focus here, why focus on those ideas and actions in disregard of others? Why should consistency in some cases, in the face of inconsistency in others, count as adequate to support the general claim that Heidegger's discreditable actions are a logical consequence of Heidegger's "ideas"?

61. A particularly interesting example of this strategy appears in Giorgio Agamben's book, *The Open*. There Agamben discusses the work of the pioneering ethologist von Uexküll as well as Heidegger. Agamben writes of certain experimental studies by von

Uexküll that they: "follow a few years after those by Paul Vidal de la Blache on the relationship between populations and their environment (the *Tableau de la géographie de la France* is from 1903), and those of Friedrich Ratzel on the Lebensraum, the 'vital space' of peoples (the *Politische Geographie* is from 1897), which would profoundly revolutionize human geography of the twentieth century. And it is not impossible that the central thesis of *Sein und Zeit* on being-in-the-world (*In-der-Welt-sein*) as the fundamental human structure can be read in some ways as a response to this problematic field, which at the beginning of the century essentially modified the traditional relationship between the living being and its environment-world. As is well known, Ratzel's theses, according to which all peoples are intimately linked to their vital space as their essential dimension, had a notable influence on Nazi geopolitics. This proximity is marked in a curious episode in Uexküll's intellectual biography. In 1928, five years before the advent of Nazism, this very sober scientist writes a preface to Houston Chamberlain's *Die Grundlagen des neunzehnten Jahrhunderts* (*Foundations of the Nineteenth Century*), today considered one of the precursors of Nazism"—Giogio Agamben, *The Open: Man and Animal*, trans. Kevin Attell (Stanford: Stanford University Press, 2004), pp. 42–43. The way in which Agamben combines together works and thinkers who, while superficially similar in their deployment of notions of place and environment, are also representative of quite different approaches, coupled with a mode of argument that depends on little more than juxtaposition and suggestion is quite startling. And although this style of argument is not unusual in discussion of these topics, it is nonetheless a style of argument that itself seems to depend upon some highly dubious rhetorical techniques. The suggestion of a connection between Heidegger and Ratzel, and thence also between a certain form of "geographically" oriented mode of thinking and Nazi race ideology, is pursued further by Troy Paddock in "*Gedachtes Wohnen*: Heidegger and Cultural Geography," *Philosophy and Geography* 7 (2004), 237–251, and although Paddock's discussion of the historical material at issue is rather more detailed than anything in Agamben, his argument does not advance the matter much further. Paddock seems to think that the key point of commonality between Ratzel and Heidegger is a geographic rather than geometric understanding of space (*Raum*), allied with an organicist, "*völkisch*" conservatism, and that this remained even in Heidegger's late thinking, constituting a key point of affinity between Heidegger's thought and "the volkish thought" that "helped to spawn National Socialism" (p. 248). My own view is that the truth of the matter is rather more complicated in relation, not only to Heidegger (as the work of scholars such as Phillips and Young would also suggest), or indeed to Ratzel (see, for instance, Mark Bassin, "Race contra Space: The Conflict between German *Geopolitik* and National Socialism," *Political Geography Quarterly* 6 [1987], 115–134), but also to the concepts of space and place that are at issue here.

62. "Only a God Can Save Us," p. 104 (*GA* 16:668). But see my comments below, p. 385n211.

63. As in his sometime use even of anti-semitic rhetoric—see the discussion in Young, *Heidegger, Philosophy, Nazism*, pp. 39–40.

64. That all of these are to be found as elements in Heidegger's political commitments during the 1930s is explicitly acknowledged by Young—see *Heidegger, Philosophy, Nazism*, pp. 11–51. Young's account, however, is rather more moderate than that of many other critics—compare, for example, Tom Rockmore, *On Heidegger's Philosophy and Nazism* (Berkeley: University of California Press, 1992).

65. See Julian Young, *Heidegger, Philosophy, Nazism*, pp. 11–51.

66. For a detailed account of the entanglement between Heidegger's Nazi commitments and his ideas concerning university reform, see Iain Thomson, *Heidegger's Ontotheology* (Cambridge: Cambridge University Press, 2005).

67. In this respect, the tendency to look to Heidegger's account of historicality, particularly as given in sec. 74 of *Being and Time*, as the basis of his political involvement in the 1930s represents, at best, a gross oversimplification—although the tendency usually derives from Heidegger's own comment, as reported by Karl Löwith, that "historicality" (*Geschichtlichkeit*) was the basis of his, that is, Heidegger's, political involvement (see Löwith, *Mein Leben in Deutschland vor und nach 1933* [Stuttgart: Metzler, 1986], reprinted in Neske and Kettering [eds.], *Martin Heidegger and National Socialism*, pp. 157–159).

68. Julian Young points to *Being and Time*, H384, to support the identification of "people," as Heidegger uses it, with "community"—see Young, *Heidegger's Later Philosophy*, p. 33n5. Certainly, while "*Volk*" may also have other connotations in Heidegger's thinking at various times (and the use of the term during the Nazi period is, to say the least, problematic), this sense seems to capture best what is at issue in many places where the term occurs, for instance, in the Hölderlin lectures of 1934–1935.

69. See Phillips, *Heidegger's Volk*, p. 3.

70. Ludwig Ferdinand Clauss, "Racial Soul, Landscape, and World Domination," in George L. Mosse (ed.), *Nazi Culture: Intellectual, Cultural, and Social Life in the Third Reich* (New York: Schocken Books, 1966), pp. 65, 69, and 74; taken from Clauss, *Die nordische Seele: Eine Einführung in die Rassenseelenkunde*, 5th edn. (Munich: J. F. Lehmanns 1936), pp. 19ff.

71. Thus Leach comments that: "It can be seen that it is precisely in the context of an identity rooted to the soil that those groups not rooted to the soil become excluded. Traditionally, Jews and gypsies are both 'wanderers,' although each for different reasons: the gypsies largely by choice, the Jews mainly by necessity. Neither are rooted to the soil. The 'wanderer' does not fit within the concept of situatedness or rootedness to the soil and therefore does not fit within the philosophy of

the *heimat*. . . . The 'wanderer' is therefore treated as the 'other,' the excluded one, and is perceived as a threat to the nation"—Neil Leach, "The Dark Side of the Domus," pp. 152–153.

72. This marks an important point of difference between the racial psychology of such authors as Clauss, and of Nazi ideology, and the "geographical" or "environmental" determinism associated with, for instance, Friedrich Ratzel. In spite of the fact that is in Ratzel's *Politische Geographie* (Munich: Oldenbourg, 1879) that the infamous notion of "*Lebensraum*" (Living-space) is first articulated (the notion might be thought to be implicit in Clauss's claim that "every authentic racial stock is bound up with its space" since, presumably, if the racial stock is to develop and expand, so too must its space), Ratzel's thinking seems to have diverged sharply from the ideas of such thinkers as Clauss, or of Nazi thinkers more generally, precisely in its rejection of the emphasis on race—on this see Mark Bassin, "Race contra Space: The Conflict between German *Geopolitik* and National Socialism," as well as the brief discussion in David N. Livingstone, *The Geographical Tradition* (Oxford: Blackwell, 1992), pp. 196–202.

73. Although it should be noted that one recent work that focuses on the idea of Heimat, Peter Blickle's *Heimat: A Critical Theory of the German Idea of Homeland* (Rochester, N.Y.: Camden House, 2002), does indeed argue for the inherently exclusionary and reactionary character of the notion. However, in many ways, Blickle's study appears to run against the general tone of much recent scholarship in this area. Thus, in her review of the book in *Modern Language Review* 99 (2004), pp. 1121–1122, Anne Fuchs claims that Blickle's study "fails to engage with the complexity of 'Heimat' discourse which is neither intrinsically antirational and regressive nor utopian" (Fuchs, "Review of Blickle," p. 1122).

74. Celia Applegate, *A Nation of Provincials: The German Idea of Heimat* (Berkeley: University of California Press, 1990), p. 212.

75. See William Rollins, "*Heimat*, Modernity, and Nation in the Early Heimatschütz movement," in Jost Hermand and James Steakley (eds.), *Heimat, Nation, Fatherland: The German Sense of Belonging* (New York: Peter Lang, 1996), pp. 87–112; see also Rollins, *A Greener Vision of Home: Cultural Politics and Environmental Reform in the German Heimschütz Movement 1904–1918* (Ann Arbor: University of Michigan Press, 1997).

76. Applegate, *A Nation of Provincials*, p. 212.

77. See *Place and Experience*, p. 120. The primacy of place is, of course, something common to many indigenous modes of thought—see, for instance, in relation to North American Indian culture, Vine Deloria Jr., *God is Red* (Golden, Colo.: North American Press, 1994) or Keith H. Basso, *Wisdom Sits in Places: Landscape and Language Among the Western Apache* (Albuquerque: University of New Mexico Press, 1996), or, in an Australian context, Fred Myers, *Pintupi Country, Pintupi Self: Senti-*

ment, Place, and Politics Among Western Desert Aborigines (Berkeley: University of California Press, 1991) or Tony Swain, *A Place for Strangers: Towards a History of Australian Aboriginal Being* (Cambridge: Cambridge University Press, 1993).

78. "On the Essence and Concept of Φύσις," trans. Thomas Sheehan, in *Pathmarks*, p. 190 (*GA* 9:248–249). See also "Seminar in Le Thor 1969," p. 53 (*GA* 15:354).

79. In *Der große Duden, 7, Etymologie* (Mannheim: Bibliographisches Institut, 1963), "*Ort*" is given the following gloss: "Spitze (bes. einer Waffe oder eines Werkzeugs)."

80. "Language in the Poem," in *On the Way to Language*, trans. Peter D. Herz (New York: Harper and Row, 1971), p. 159 (*GA* 12:33). Translation modified.

81. This understanding of boundedness recurs at a number of places in Heidegger's thinking: see Heidegger, "Building Dwelling Thinking," in *Poetry, Language, Thought*, p. 154 (*GA* 7:156); *Parmenides*, trans. André Schuwer and Richard Rojcewicz (Bloomington: Indiana University Press, 1992), p. 82 (*GA* 54:121); "On the Essence and Concept of Φύσις," p. 206 (*GA* 9:269); "The Origin of the Work of Art—Appendix," in *Off the Beaten Track*, trans. Julian Young and Kenneth Hayes (Cambridge: Cambridge University Press, 2002), p. 53 (*GA* 5:71). It is interesting to note William Blattner drawing on just this distinction in his discussion of death as a "limit-situation" in *Heidegger's Temporal Idealism* (Cambridge: Cambridge University Press, 1999), p. 120.

82. In addition to the discussion here, especially chapter 5, see *Place and Experience*, pp. 33–34, 157–174.

83. Albert Hofstadter, in his translations of Heidegger's later essays in *Poetry, Language, Thought*, particularly "Building Dwelling Thinking," does not translate "*Ort*" as "place," but rather as "location"—one can only assume that Hofstadter, not a native English speaker himself, was not sufficiently sensitive to the difference between these terms. This might be thought to be confirmed by the fact that he uses "place" as a translation for "*Platz*," to which the English "place" is certainly etymologically related, but with respect to which there is much less semantic overlap than obtains between "place" and "*Ort*."

84. See, for instance, *Hölderlin's Hymn "The Ister*," trans. William McNeill and Julia Davis (Bloomington: Indiana University Press, 1996), p. 82 (*GA* 53:101).

85. See, for instance, Otto Pöggeler's discussion of topology in *Martin Heidegger's Path of Thinking*, trans. Daniel Magurshak and Sigmund Barber (Atlantics Highlands, N.J.: Humanities Press, 1989), pp. xv–xvi—Pöggeler notes, however, that this treatment of topology places the term "in a context which Heidegger himself did not use" (p. xvi), namely, the context of topic as it occurs in the rhetorical tradition stemming, especially, from Vico. See also Pöggeler, "Metaphysics and Topology of Being in Heidegger," in *Man and World* 8 (1975), 3–27.

86. See "On the Question of Being," p. 291 (*GA* 9:385)—the sense of "Erörterung" as "situating" or "locating" is explicitly noted by the translators, *Pathmarks*, p. 375n2.

87. *Being and Time*, H102.

88. See their note on "*Gegend*" in *Being and Time*, trans. Macquarrie and Robinson, p. 136n1.

89. "Seminar in Le Thor 1969," pp. 41, 47 (*GA* 15:335, 344): "Hence the expression *topology of be-ing* [*Topologie des Seyns*], which, for example, one finds in *Aus der Erfahrung des Denkens*; also see the text edited by Franz Larese: '*Die Kunst und der Raum*'" (p. 41). The phrase "topology of being" itself occurs only once in *Aus der Erfahrung des Denkens* (*Gesamtausgabe* 13; for the full reference, see n. 65 in chap. 4) and, although the volume also contains "Die Kunst und der Raum," that text does not itself contain the phrase at issue. Presumably the reference to the latter text is indicative of the way that text exemplifies or is a meditation upon what is at issue in such a topology.

90. "The Thinker as Poet," in *Poetry, Language, Thought*, p. 12 (*GA* 13:84).

91. "On the Question of Being," pp. 311–312 (*GA* 9:412). Here Heidegger talks of the need for a "topography of nihilism" to be preceded by a "topology: a discussion locating that locale which gathers being and nothing into their essence, determines the essence of nihilism, and thus lets us recognize those paths on which the ways towards a possible overcoming of nihilism emerge."

92. "Seminar in Le Thor 1969," p. 47 (*GA* 15:344).

93. Pöggeler, *Martin Heidegger's Path of Thinking*, pp. 232, 238 (pp. 287 and 294 in the German edition).

94. See *Place and Experience*, pp. 40–41. See also my comments in "Place and Topography: Responding to Cameron and Stefanovic," *Environmental and Architectural Phenomenology* 15 (2004), 8–10.

95. See Sheehan, "A Paradigm Shift in Heidegger Research," *Continental Philosophy Review* 34 (2001), 183–202.

96. Often the ideal of philosophical "precision" seems to depend more on a general willingness to ignore the equivocity of key terms and to operate as if the terms in question could indeed be pinned down to a limited and clear set of meanings. Yet, in fact, philosophical thinking always depends on a certain "equivocity" or "indeterminacy" of meaning even while it presents itself in terms of the "precision" and "clarity" of its terms and concepts.

97. See, for instance, J. Hillis Miller, "Slipping Vaulting Crossing," p. 229.

98. Again, see Miller, "Slipping Vaulting Crossing."

99. See Heidegger's comments in "Seminar in Le Thor 1969," p. 63 (*GA* 15:370).

100. "Anaximander's Saying," in *Off the Beaten Track*, p. 247 (*GA* 5:328).

101. "The reference in *Being and Time* (H54) to 'being-in' as 'dwelling' is no mere etymological play. The same reference in the 1936 essay on Hölderlin's word, 'Full of merit, yet poetically, man dwells upon this earth,' is not the adornment of a thinking that rescues itself from science by means of poetry. The talk about the house of being is not the transfer of the image 'house' onto being"—"Letter on 'Humanism,'" trans. Frank A. Capuzzi, in *Pathmarks*, p. 272 (*GA* 9:358).

102. A comment originally made in conversation with Marcelo Stamm. I have asked Henrich about the term myself, and while he could not recall using "*irisieren*" in this way in print, he confirmed the idea as applicable in certain respects to his own thought, as well as having, in his view, a broader philosophical significance. The image that he used to illustrate the iridescence at issue was the sheen of oil on water. Henrich also added that, in his view, Heidegger thought that the terms of Greek philosophy were especially "iridescent" in this way.

103. See Heidegger, *Being and Time*, H8—"eine merkwürdige 'Rück-oder Vorbezogenheit.'"

Chapter 2

1. From a draft appended to the elegy "Bread and Wine," in Hölderlin, *Sämtliche Werke: Historische-kritische Ausgabe*, ed. Norbert von Hellingrath, Friedrich Seebass, and Ludwig von Pigenot (Berlin: Propylaen, 1923, 2nd ed.), 4, p. 323; cited by Heidegger in "Remembrance," in *Elucidations of Hölderlin's Poetry*, trans. Keith Hoeller (New York: Humanity Books, 2000), p. 152 (*GA* 4:130).

2. See my "Beginning in Wonder," in N. Kompridis (ed.), *Philosophical Romanticism* (London: Routledge, 2005), pp. 282–298; also *Place and Experience*, pp. 196–197.

3. August 19, 1921, quoted by Kisiel in *The Genesis of Heidegger's "Being and Time"* (Berkeley: University of California Press, 1993), p. 78; original German text in Dietrich Pappenfuss and Otto Pöggeler (eds.), *Zur philosophischen Aktualität Martin Heideggers*, vol. 2, *Im Gespräch der Zeit* (Frankfurt: Klostermann, 1990), pp. 27–32.

4. Much of the discussion in chapters 2–4 of *Place and Experience* could be construed as an investigation of what concrete situatedness actually involves—the claim being that it involves spatiality *and* temporality, an objective world *and* a subjective self— that it involves, in short, a sense of place.

5. Nietzsche, *Beyond Good and Evil*, trans. R. J. Hollingdale (Harmondsworth: Penguin, 1990), p. 37.

6. *Phenomenological Interpretations of Aristotle*, trans. Richard Rojcewicz (Bloomington: Indiana University Press, 2001), p. 28 (*GA* 61:35).

7. In the *Kantbuch* of 1929, Heidegger challenges Kant's claim that this fourth question underlies the other three—see *Kant and the Problem of Metaphysics*, 5th ed., trans. Richard Taft (Bloomington: Indiana University Press, 1997), pp. 150–153 (*GA* 3:214–218). This is not because he rejects the ontological questionability that is at issue here, but because he takes issue with the specific focus on the human. The underlying question concerns something more basic than our "humanity" as usually understood—see, for instance, "Letter on 'Humanism,'" pp. 262–263 (*GA* 9:345).

8. Although it is already present quite early on, see for instance, *The Concept of Time*, trans. William McNeill (Oxford: Blackwell, 1992), p. 11E (dual English-German ed.).

9. Ibid., p. 22E.

10. *Being and Time* (*GA* 2), H7.

11. See *The Fundamental Concepts of Metaphysics*, trans. William McNeill and Nicholas Walker (Bloomington: Indiana University Press, 1995), pp. 74–167 (*GA* 29/30:111–249); "What Is Metaphysics?" trans. David Farrell Krell, in *Pathmarks*, p. 87 (*GA* 9:110); and *Introduction to Metaphysics*, trans. Gregory Fried and Richard Polt (New Haven: Yale University Press, 2000), p. 2 (*GA* 40:3).

12. See *Being and Time* (*GA* 2), H184–191, H341–346; also "What Is Metaphysics?" pp. 88–93 (*GA* 9:111–116).

13. See "What Is Metaphysics?" pp. 95–96 (*GA* 9:121); and also *Basic Questions of Philosophy*, trans. Richard Rojcewicz and André Schuwer (Bloomington: Indiana University Press, 1994), pp. 133–156 (*GA* 45:153–180).

14. "Blik der Sonne, du schönster, der / Dem siebenthorigen Thebe / Seit langem scheint," cited from Hölderlin's translation of Sophocles, *Antigone*, 5.100ff., in *Towards the Definition of Philosophy*, trans. Ted Sadler (London: The Athlone Press, 2000), p. 63 (*GA* 56/57:74). It is worth noting here the way in which wonder seems to be contrasted with the scientific attitude. In general, Heidegger seems to view wonder as always tied to an experience of the world that he takes to be ontologically more basic than that of scientific inquiry (see, for instance, the discussion of wonder in *Basic Questions of Philosophy*, pp. 133–156 [*GA* 45:153–180]).

15. From the lecture course given in the War Emergency Semester ("Kriegsnotsemester") of 1919, "Die Idee der Philosophie und das Weltanschauungsproblem," as given in the transcript from Oscar Becker and cited by Kisiel in *The Genesis of Heidegger's "Being and Time,"* p. 17; for the German text, see Kisiel, "Das Kriegsnotsemester 1919: Heideggers Durchbruch in die Hermeneutische Phänomenologie," *Philosophisches Jahrbuch* 99 (1992), 105–122, esp. pp. 106ff. An excerpt from the firsthand transcript of this lecture by Franz Josef Brecht is included in *Towards the Definition of Philosophy*, pp. 187–188.

16. *Phenomenological Interpretations of Aristotle*, p. 57 (*GA* 61:76).

17. See van Buren, *The Young Heidegger*, pp. 264ff., 291–294.

18. "The linguistic precedents for Heidegger's use of the adjective 'own' (*eigen*) for his concept of a personal *Er-eignis*, and for his notions of 'mineness' and *eigentlich* (own-ish, authentic) are to be found not in the troubled waters of subjectivism and decisionism, but rather in Scotist 'haccaeity,' Eckhartian life that lives 'out of its own,' Schleiermachean 'ownness,' and the 'ownmost own' of the 'individuity' that Natorp finds in the mystical tradition"—John van Buren, *The Young Heidegger*, p. 317.

19. Martin Heidegger and Eugen Fink, *Heraclitus Seminar*, trans. Charles H. Seibert (Evanston: Northwestern University Press, 1993), p. 126 (*GA* 15:204). See Elden, *Mapping the Present*, p. 16n28.

20. *Das Ereignis, Gesamtausgabe* 71 (in preparation) ms. 121.18, cited by Sheehan in "A Paradigm Shift in Heidegger Research," p. 193.

21. *Zollikon Seminars*, ed. Medard Boss, trans. Franz Mayr and Richard Askay (Evanston: Northwestern University Press, 2001), p. 120 (*Zollikoner Seminare*, ed. Medard Boss [Frankfurt: Klostermann, 1994], pp. 156–157).

22. Stuart Elden argues, for instance, that to interpret terms such as "Dasein" or "In-der-Welt-Sein" in terms that are taken primarily to connote notions of place or space is "too simplistic, and in certain respects inaccurate"—*Mapping the Present*, p. 16. Although it would clearly be a mistake to emphasize such connotations in ways that overlooked the existential sense that is clearly intended by Heidegger, it would also be a mistake to prioritize the existential over the "topological"—indeed part of what is at issue in Heidegger's early thinking is how to make sense of the topological origins of his thinking in the light of the existential fashion in which that thinking develops. In the end, the topological turns out to be more basic than the existential (the existential turns out, in fact, to be tied to the problematic notion of "transcendence" that is at the heart of Heidegger's rethinking of the framework of *Being and Time*—see the discussion in sec. 4.2 below).

23. See the comment in the introduction to "What Is Metaphysics?," p. 283 (*GA* 9:373), which figures at the head of chapter 4 below.

24. *Heraclitus Seminar*, p. 126 (*GA* 15:204).

25. Sheehan, "A Paradigm Shift in Heidegger Research," p. 193.

26. Inasmuch as it can be construed as emphasizing the "there" as a mode of being—"being the there." One might also suggest that there is a further set of alternatives available here that would follow from the translation of "*Da*" by "here" rather than "there." I have not given this explicit consideration above, for a number of reasons, but principally because it lacks the connotations associated with "being there" and is rather more strongly associated with a sense of immediate presence

("here, now"). In any case, neither "being-here" nor "here-being" have been much employed in the existing literature as translations for "*Dasein.*" It should also be noted that one could translate "*Dasein*" simply as "existence," as in Elden, but to do so would obscure the topological connections at issue without any obvious compensatory advantage—one of the crucial points here is that "existence" is itself topological.

27. *Being There* (1979), starring Peter Sellers, directed by Hal Ashby, screenplay (from his novel) by Jerzy Kosinski.

28. *Grundprobleme der Phänomenologie, Gesamtausgabe* 58 (Frankfurt: Klostermann, 1992), pp. 80ff.

29. See Kisiel, *The Genesis of Heidegger's "Being and Time,"* p. 27.

30. *Ontology—The Hermeneutics of Facticity,* trans. John van Buren (Bloomington: Indiana University Press, 1999), p. 24 (*GA* 63:29). The phrase "*in seinem jeweiligen 'Da'* " is difficult to render into simple and fluent English. I have chosen to use "in its own lingering 'there'" since it gives more emphasis to the "there" and yet also conveys a sense of the way in which that "there" also carries a certain "while" (it lingers) without it being the case that the "there" can somehow be separated from its "while." See also p. 5 (*GA* 63:7): " 'Facticity' is the designation we will use for the character of the being of 'our' 'own' Dasein. More precisely, this expression means: in each case 'this' Dasein in its being-there *for a while at the particular time [jeweilig]* . . . insofar as it is, in the character of its being, *'there' in the manner of be-ing.*"

31. *Ontology—The Hermeneutics of Facticity,* p. 69 (*GA* 63:90).

32. *Towards the Definition of Philosophy,* pp. 59–60 (*GA* 56/57:71).

33. *Being and Time,* H163–164.

34. Ibid., H164.

35. *Towards the Definition of Philosophy,* p. 61 (*GA* 56/57:72–73).

36. John van Buren, *The Young Heidegger,* p. 251.

37. Wittgensetein, *Tractatus Logico-Philosophicus,* trans. D. F. Pears and B. F. McGuinness (London: Routledge and Kegan Paul, 1961), proposition 1. See Heidegger's reference to (and apparent misquoting of) Wittgenstein on this point in "Seminar in Le Thor 1969," p. 35 (*GA* 15:327).

38. Maurice Merleau-Ponty, *Phenomenology of Perception,* trans. Colin Smith (London: Routledge and Kegan Paul, 1962), p. ix.

39. Thus, as Julian Young more directly puts matters: "when he [Heidegger] represents himself as 'after philosophy' he is really only representing himself as 'after bad philosophy' "—Young, *Heidegger's Later Philosophy,* p. 2.

40. See my discussion in "From the Transcendental to the 'Topological,'" esp. pp. 75–79.

41. See Derrida, "The Ends of Man," in *Margins of Philosophy*, trans. Alan Bass (Chicago: University of Chicago Press, 1982), p. 130: "Whence, in Heidegger's discourse, the dominance of an entire metaphysics of proximity, of simple and immediate presence, a metaphorics associating the proximity of Being, with the values of neighbouring, shelter, house, service, guard, voice and listening."

42. Allan Megill, *Prophets of Extremity* (Berkeley: University of California Press, 1985), p. 125.

43. *Basic Concepts*, p. 78 (*GA* 51:92–93).

44. See also Dominique Janicaud, "Presence and Appropriation," *Research in Phenomenology* 8 (1978), esp. 73.

45. *Towards the Definition of Philosophy*, p. 63 (*GA* 56/57:75).

46. "On the Nature of the University and Academic Study," in *Towards the Definition of Philosophy*, p. 174 (*GA* 56/57:206).

47. The hyphenation draws attention to the way in which "*eigen*" (own) seems itself to be a component of "ereignen."

48. In Kisiel, *The Genesis of Heidegger's "Being and Time,"* pp. 46, 329, and 458, and van Buren, *The Young Heidegger*, esp. pp. 270–294.

49. See especially *Identity and Difference*, trans. Joan Stambaugh (Chicago: University of Chicago Press, 2002, dual English/German ed.).

50. "The Doctine of Categories and Meaning in Duns Scotus," in *Frühe Schriften*, *Gesamtausgabe* 1 (Frankfurt: Klostermann, 1978); see also the discussion in van Buren, *The Young Heidegger*, pp. 108–112.

51. For a different approach to the unity at issue here, one pursued through a discussion of Proust, see *Place and Experience*, chap. 7.

52. Martin Heidegger, *Introduction to Metaphysics*, p. 26 (*GA* 40:26). See also Heidegger's comment in *The Metaphysical Foundations of Logic*, trans. Michael Heim (Bloomington: Indiana University Press, 1984), p. 221: "To philosophise means to exist from ground" (*GA* 26:285).

53. See Fell, *Heidegger and Sartre*, p. 57.

54. Ibid., p. 38.

55. Ibid., pp. 38ff.

56. Heidegger, *Zollikon Seminars*, p. 115 (*Zollikoner Seminare*, p. 150).

57. The sort of "dependence" at issue here is one according to which a priority is established between two structures such that the one structure is dependent upon the other but not the reverse. Such derivation (which I refer to below as "hierarchical dependence") is a form of grounding, but it is a very specific form. It may sometimes take the form of a reduction (indeed, it could be argued that *all* reductions are derivations of this sort in that they aim at showing a certain one-way dependence as obtaining between certain entities, processes, structures, or whatever is at issue), but not all such derivations are reductive (or at least, not all are intended to be so). In *Being and Time*, Heidegger attempts to "interpret" situatedness—the "there" of being-there—in terms of time, and so to exhibit the one-way dependence of the "there" on temporality, but this is not seen by Heidegger as a *reduction* of one to the other. For more on this, see sec. 3.5.

Chapter 3

1. "Art and Space," trans. Charles Sietert, Man and World 6 (1973), p. 4 (*GA* 13:205).

2. Heidegger does not, of course, acknowledge any connection here, but this is not unusual. Moreover, in his *System of Transcendental Idealism*, Schelling is explicit in giving priority to time over space, treating time as itself tied to the activity of the self—an idea that also has its parallels in Heidegger. See the discussion in Friedrich Kümmerl, *Über den Begriff der Zeit* (Tübingen: Niemeyer, 1962), pp. 46–47.

3. *Being and Time* (*GA* 2), H1.

4. See "Time and Being," p. 23 (*Zur Sache des Denkens*, p. 24); see also *What Is a Thing?* pp. 16–17 (*GA* 41:16–17). The attempted derivation, discussed further below, occurs in sec. 70 of *Being and Time*. Yoko Arisaka claims, however, that the arguments set out in sec. 70 do not address such a derivation at all: "The concern in this section is whether temporality founds spatiality, in the sense that temporality is the basis for having temporality"—see Yoko Arisaka, "Spatiality, Temporality, and the Problem of Foundation in *Being and Time*," *Philosophy Today* 40 (1996), 42–43n3. I can find no evidence for a clear distinction in Heidegger between "derivation" and "foundation," although, as will be evident in sec. 3.5 below, I do think Heidegger is implicitly committed to a distinction between the "derivation" associated with spatiality and ordinary temporality, and the "derivation" of care from originary temporality. Such a distinction could be put in terms of one between "derivation" on the one hand and "foundation" on the other, except that every "derivation" is surely also a mode of "foundation."

5. Heidegger, *Being and Time* (*GA* 2), H54.

6. *History of the Concept of Time: Prolegomena*, trans. Theodore Kisiel (Bloomington: Indiana University Press, 1992), pp. 157–158 (*GA* 20:211–212).

7. The connection, however, is noted by Edward Casey in his *The Fate of Place*, p. 245, as well as by Alejandro Vallega in *Heidegger and the Issue of Space*, pp. 44ff. Both Casey and Vallega provide extended discussions of the Aristotelian view— Vallega does so in connection with Plato as well as Heidegger, while, in Casey, the Aristotelian view, along with its immediate successors, is explored as part of his more general investigation of the philosophical history of place (see chapters 3 and 4 of *The Fate of Place*, pp. 50–102).

8. See my discussion in *"Kategoriai* and the Unity of Being," *Journal of Speculative Philosophy* (new series), 4 (1990), 13–36.

9. See *Physics*, 208a27–31.

10. *Physics*, 208a29–31.

11. See *Plato's "Sophist,"* trans. Richard Rojcewicz and André Schuwer (Bloomington: Indiana University Press, 1997), p. 73 (*GA* 19:105–106).

12. Aristotle, *Physics*, 212a7, quoted by Heidegger in *Plato's "Sophist,"* p. 75 (*GA* 19:108).

13. Aristotle, *Physics* IV, 5, 212a20, in *Aristotle's Physics Books III and IV*, trans. Edward Hussey (Oxford: Clarendon Press, 1983). Elsewhere Aristotle presents the same idea in slightly different form. Place is "the limit of the surrounding body, at which it is in contact with that which is surrounded" (212a36).

14. Consequently the world does not have a place since "there is nothing besides the universe [*to pan*] and the sum of things, nothing which is outside the universe; and this is why everything is in the world [*ouranos*]. (For the world is (perhaps) the universe). The place [of changeable body] is not the world but a part of the world," *Physics* IV, 212a31.

15. *Being and Time* (*GA* 2), H101.

16. Ibid.

17. Descartes, *Principles of Philosophy* 2, secs. 10, 13, in *The Philosophical Writings of Descartes*, vol. 1, trans. John Cottingham, Robert Stoothoff, and Dugald Murdoch (Cambridge: Cambridge University Press, 1985), p. 227—for the French, see *Les Principes de la Philosophie de René Descartes*, in *Œvres de Descartes*, ed. Charles Adam and Paul Tannery, vol. 9 (Paris: J. Vrin., n.d.), pp. 68–69.

18. "Into a certain box we can place a definite number of grains of rice or of cherries, etc. It is here a question of a property of the material object 'box,' which property must be considered 'real' in the same sense as the box itself. One can call this property the 'space' of the box. There may be other boxes which in this sense have an equally large 'space.' This concept 'space' thus achieves a meaning which is freed from any connection with a particular material object. In this way by a natural

extension of 'box space' one can arrive at the concept of an independent (absolute) space, unlimited in extent, in which all material objects are contained," Albert Einstein, Foreword to Max Jammer, *Concepts of Space: The History of Theories of Space in Physics*, 2nd ed. (Cambridge, Mass.: Harvard University Press, 1969), p. xiii. The modern conception of absolute space that Einstein discusses here is, of course, one that is ultimately abandoned by physics in favor of a relativistic conception. See Einstein's brief comments on this in the Foreword to Jammer, *Concepts of Space*, p. xv.

19. See Aristotle, *Physics*, IV, 2.209b6–13: "If we regard the place as the interval of the magnitude, it is the matter. For this is different from the magnitude: it is what is contained and defined by the form, as by a bounding plane. Matter or the indeterminate is of this nature; when the boundary and attributes of a sphere are abstracted, nothing but the matter is left. This is why Plato in the *Timaeus* says matter and space are the same; for the 'participant' (i.e., receptacle) and space are identical." The concept of matter that is employed here is of matter as pure mathematical extension—pure dimensionality. Such a concept of matter should not be confused with the idea of matter as that out of which something is formed, notwithstanding Plato's own use of such an analogy in the *Timaeus*—see Henry Mendell, "Topoi on Topos: The Development of Aristotle's Concept of Place," *Phronesis* 32 (1987), 213, 213–214n19.

20. See *Timaeus*, 49—see also the detailed discussion of this and the surrounding text in F. M. Cornford, *Plato's Cosmology: The Timaeus of Plato Translated with a Running Commentary* (London: Routledge and Kegan Paul, 1956), pp. 177ff.

21. Although it seems that Aristotle did once hold a more "Platonic" view of place or space. See *Categories* 6—see also Mendell, "Topoi on Topos," esp. pp. 208–210; H. R. King, "Aristotle's Theory of Topos," *Classical Quarterly* 44 (1950), 76–96, esp. 87–88; and J. L. Ackrill, *Aristotle's Categories and De Interpretatione* (Oxford: Clarendon Press, 1963), p. 93. It is notable that in the Aristotelian discussions no clear distinction emerges between *topos* and *chora*.

22. See *Physics*, 208a30.

23. See Mendel, "Topoi on Topos."

24. Heidegger, *Introduction to Metaphysics*, p. 69 (*GA* 40:70).

25. Ibid., p. 70 (*GA* 40:71).

26. *Being and Time* (*GA* 2), H54.

27. I have avoided the use of "subjective" to refer to "existential" spatiality in contrast with "objective" spatiality. There is, however, an ambiguity in Heidegger's treatment of existential spatiality that does seem to tend in this direction. See the discussion of existential spatiality in sec. 3.3, as well as the discussion of objective and "bodily" spatiality in sec. 3.6.

28. *Being and Time* (*GA* 2), H55.

29. Ibid.

30. *Towards the Definition of Philosophy*, p. 72 (*GA* 56/57:86). Heidegger adds "Analogue to the time-phenomenon."

31. *Being and Time* (*GA* 2), H54. Notice the way in which corporeality is, in this passage, deemphasized.

32. Ibid., H368. This passage goes on "In existing, it has already made room for its own leeway. It determines its own location in such a manner that it comes back from the space it has made room for to the 'place' which it has reserved" (Existierend hat es sich je schon einen Spielraum eingeräumt. Es bestimmt je seinen eigenen Ort so, daß es aus dem eingeräumten Raum auf den "Platz" zurrückkommt, den es belegt hat). Here we find "*Raum*," "*Platz*," and "*Ort*," as well as "*Spielraum*" (translated by Macquarrie and Robinson as "leeway") and "*einräumen*" closely packed together. Although the passage also seems to imply a distinction between space and place, between "*Raum*" and "*Platz/Ort*," it nevertheless appears to treat "Platz/Ort" still in terms of simple location.

33. See chapter 5, sec. 5.3 below.

34. *Being and Time* (*GA* 2), H54. The original German reads: "'in' stammt von innan-, wohnen, habitare, sich aufhalten; 'an' bedeutet: ich bin gewohnt, vertraut mit, ich pflege etwas; es hat die Bedeutung von colo im Sinne von habito und diligo. Dieses Seiende, dem das In-Sein in dieser Bedeutung zugehört, kennzeichneten wir als das Seiende, das ich je selbst bin. Der Ausdruck 'bin' hängt zusammen mit 'bei'; 'ich bin' besagt wiederum: ich wohne, halte mich auf bei . . . der Welt, als dem so und so Vertrauten. Sein als Infinitiv des 'ich bin,' d. h. als Existenzial verstanden, bedeutet wohnen bei . . . , vertraut sein mit. . . . *In-Sein ist demnach der formale existenziale Ausdruck des Seins des Daseins, das die wesenhafte Verfassung des In-der-Welt-seins hat.*" Macquarrie and Robinson note that this passage has its source in Grimm's *Kleinere Schriften* vol. 7, pp. 247ff. They also point out that it is unclear whether the reference to "*an*" in this passage is to "the preposition '*an*' (which corresponds in some of its usages to the English 'at,' and which he [Heidegger] has just used in remarking that the water and the glass are both *at* a location), or rather . . . the preterite '*an*' of *innan*," *Being and Time* (*GA* 2), p. 80n2.

35. *Being and Time* (*GA* 2), H172–173. It is worth noting the slight oddity or tension suggested by talk of a mode of being-there in which being-there "is everywhere and nowhere" (an oddity that may well be obscured in English by the retention of the German "Dasein").

36. See Kettering, *Nähe: Das Denken Martin Heideggers*, in which "nearness" is taken as a central concept through which to approach Heidegger's thinking.

37. Hubert Dreyfus, *Being-in-the-World: A Commentary on Heidegger's "Being and Time," Division 1* (Cambridge, Mass.: MIT Press, 1991), p. 43.

38. Ibid., p. 45.

39. Ibid., p. 42.

40. Ibid., p. 128.

41. Notice that this ought to be seen as leaving open the possibility that objective space may still have a role to play as part of the structure of existential spatiality—what is ruled out is the idea of objective spatiality as itself sufficient as the basis for an understanding of place or situatedness. One of the problems with Heidegger's account would seem to be a tendency, at least in his early thinking, to simply oppose objective space to the "space" of situatedness as if each stood completely outside of and apart from the other. My claim, developed in *Place and Experience*, as well as in the discussion in sec. 3.6, is that objective space turns out already to be present in the very structure of place. Place thus turns out to include within it a rich and complex spatial structure.

42. *Being and Time (GA 2)*, H66.

43. Ibid., H56.

44. Ibid., H101.

45. Dreyfus, *Being-in-the-World*, p. 129.

46. Of course, as soon as one rejects the idea that one can completely separate objective from existential spatiality, then the dilemma dissolves. That has been more or less my own strategy. Thus although I do distinguish, in *Place and Experience*, between different senses of spatiality, including what I there called "objective" and "subjective" spatiality, I also insist that these senses cannot be construed as independent of one another nor as independent of the concept of place as such. I develop much the same approach here in sec. 3.6.

47. The distinction between "spatiality" and "space" might be thought to provide an obvious way to resolve the difficulty here. Heidegger, we might say, is talking about different modes of spatiality, not different spaces—there can be only one space, but spatiality can indeed be multiple. But then the question arises as to how we are to understand the space that is at issue here?

48. *Being and Time (GA 2)*, H66.

49. Ibid., H56.

50. Ibid., H62.

51. Although the analysis of equipmentality is first set out in secs. 15ff., that this analysis is directly related to the account of existential spatiality is clearly indicated

by the fact that the discussion that is headed "Space and Dasein's Spatiality" (sec. 24—H110ff.) begins with the analysis of the spatiality associated with equipmentality.

52. *The Basic Problems of Phenomenology*, trans. Albert Hofstadter (Bloomington, Ind.: Indiana University Press, 1982), pp. 163–164 (*GA* 24:233).

53. *Being and Time* (*GA* 2), H103–104.

54. See *Being and Time* (*GA* 2), H68–70—"toward which" is "*Wozu*," in the German and "in-order-to," "*Um-zu*."

55. The fact that the same configuration of characters (for instance "gift") may figure in more than one language with possibly different meanings in those languages (in English "gift" means "something given"; in German it means "poison") does not undermine the point at issue here. The identity of a word depends, not merely on the characters of which it is composed, but the language to which it belongs (so the English "gift" is a different *word* from the German "*Gift*").

56. See *Being and Time* (*GA* 2), division 1, chapter 4, H113ff.

57. *Being and Time* (*GA* 2), H117–118.

58. *History of the Concept of Time: Prolegomena*, p. 239 (*GA* 20:329).

59. The connection between sociality and spatiality, and, more importantly, between sociality and a notion of spatiality that goes beyond the spatiality of the individual, is an important issue in exploring the role of objective spatiality; see sec. 3.6 below.

60. On this point, see also my "Space and Sociality," *International Journal of Philosophical Studies* 5 (1997), pp. 53–79.

61. See especially Henri Lefebvre, *The Production of Space*, trans. Donald Nicholson-Smith (Oxford: Blackwell, 1991).

62. What is inauthentic, of course, is only that mode of "understanding" that construes being-there purely or primarily in terms of its "public" mode of being—inasmuch as being-there has being-with-others as part of its own being, so being-there is "authentically" social.

63. *Being and Time* (*GA* 2), H126.

64. See Dreyfus, *Being-in-the-World*, pp. x–xi. Logically, it would seem that the best pairing of terms may be "dis-tance" (referring to the separation of a thing from out of an encompassing background) and directionality (referring to the grasp of the equipmental structure in which something belongs). The drawback of using "orientation" to refer to the second of these is only that "orientation" could easily be taken to cover both "dis-tance" and "directionality," whereas it seems important to

understand that Heidegger sees two complementary components at work here. I have, however, chosen to remain with Dreyfus's terminology for the sake of simplicity.

65. *Being and Time* (*GA* 2), H111.

66. Ibid.

67. Dreyfus, *Being-in-the-World*, p. 129.

68. Ibid., p. 132.

69. Ibid., pp. 131–136.

70. See Arisaka, "Heidegger's Theory of Space: A Critique of Dreyfus." Unfortunately Arisaka's account offers little in the way of an illumination of the issues at stake here. She emphasizes that "the key to understanding Heidegger's theory of space is his attempt to redescribe spatial experience without presupposing objective space" ("Heidegger's Theory of Space," p. 464), but this is really only to characterize the problem as it arises within the Heideggerian framework rather than offer an indication of its manner of resolution—it also seems not to include any recognition of the problematic character of such an attempt. In fact, Arisaka's main aim here seems less to explore the problem of spatiality as such than to make use of that problem as a means to advance Frederick Olafson's existential reading of *Being and Time* against that of Dreyfus's.

71. This seems to me an important point in general (it is a point frequently overlooked), but especially important in discussion of Heidegger since his own understanding of the question of being as one that always involves the being of questionability, and so of the one who questions, means that some notion of the "subject" (though invariably understood in terms other than those of "subjectivity" as such) is always an element in Heidegger's understanding of being. However, the fact that some notion of "subjectivity," or of human being, may be taken to be involved here does not, of itself, gives rise to any subjectivism—whether it does or not depends on just what role such "subjectivity" is seen to play here. Subjectivism implies a grounding *in the subject*, rather than in any other structure, and that means that an account that takes the grounding structure to be one that encompasses the "subject," along with other mutually determined elements, is not, as such, subjective.

72. William Blattner sees Heidegger's analysis of temporality as itself comprising a similar sequence of dependence relations: "originary time . . . *explains* ordinary time. . . . [this] explanatory dependence is in fact a chain of dependencies: ordinary time (the ticking away of purely quantitative moments) depends on world-time (the succession of qualitatively determinate Nows), whose core phenomenon is in turn the pragmatic Now (the Now that aims us into the purposive future by relying on the given past), which finally in turn depends on originary temporality"—Blattner, *Heidegger's Temporal Idealism* (Cambridge: Cambridge University Press, 1999), p. 28.

73. *Being and Time* (*GA* 2), H367.

74. Ibid., H132–133.

75. Ibid., H220. Note the use of the term "equiprimordial" (*gleichursprünglich*)—a term I discuss in more detail in sec. 3.5.

76. See *Being and Time* (*GA* 2), H219.

77. Ibid., H160—"The fundamental *existentialia* which constitute the Being-there of the 'there,' the disclosedness of Being-in-the-world, are states of mind [affectedness] and understanding."

78. See *Being and Time* (*GA* 2), H145.

79. Thus "Dasein is an entity which, in its very Being, comports itself understandingly towards that being. In saying this, we are calling attention to the formal concept of existence" (*Being and Time*, H52–53).

80. Affectedness actually comes first in Heidegger's explication of the structure at issue here. But this reflects no ontological priority and is merely a consequence of the fact that such a thing as "mood" is "*ontically* the most familiar and everyday sort of thing" (*Being and Time* [*GA* 2], H134).

81. *Being and Time* [*GA* 2], H161.

82. Ibid.: "The way in which discourse gets expressed is language." Heidegger also tells us that "the existential-ontological foundation of language is discourse" (ibid., H160–161). The exact relation between language and discourse is not at all clear—see, for instance, Charles Guignon's discussion of the place of language in *Being and Time* in Guignon, *Heidegger and the Problem of Knowledge* (Indianapolis: Hackett, 1983), sec. 9.

83. Heidegger first characterizes "falling" as one of the fundamental ontological characteristics of being-there at *Being and Time* (*GA* 2), H191—"The fundamental ontological characteristics of [being-in-the-world] are existentiality, facticity and Being-fallen [*Verfallensein*]"—but he sometimes leaves falling out of this list of fundamental characteristics altogether (as in the passage quoted above from H220), and sometimes it seems as if falling merely designates an inauthentic mode of understanding. Clearly, however, if being-there is indeed inevitably prone to falling in the way Heidegger claims (see the discussion in sec. 38), then falling must be an ontologically primitive characteristic of the being of being-there. Indeed, this seems to be the import of the discussion of falling at H179–180 in which Heidegger considers that falling might count as evidence against the existentiality of being-there, arguing that it rather constitutes evidence in favor of such existentiality and concluding that "Falling reveals an *essential* ontological structure of Dasein itself" (*Being and Time* [*GA* 2], H179).

84. See *Being and Time* (*GA* 2), H193.

85. Ibid., H12, H191.

86. Ibid., H12.

87. Ibid., H191–192.

88. Ibid., H192.

89. Ibid.

90. There is an important issue as to whether the originary temporality that is at stake here is to be identified with "authentic" temporality, but it is not something that directly affects my argument, and so I have left it to one side. In the discussion below, however, I do draw on the work of William Blattner, who argues for an understanding of originary temporality as distinct from authentic temporality—see Blattner, *Heidegger's Temporal Idealism*, pp. 98–102. In fact, I think the balance of evidence supports Blattner's reading here.

91. *Being and Time* (GA 2), H264.

92. Ibid., H299: "The Situation is the 'there' which is disclosed in resoluteness—the 'there' at which the entity is."

93. See *Being and Time* (GA 2), H325—note the translators' note in the Macquarrie and Robinson translation at p. 372n3.

94. Heidegger distinguishes "pastness," or the character of having "gone by" (*Vergangenheit*), from "having been" (*Gewesenheit*), largely, it seems, to avoid the sense of sequentiality that may be connoted by having "gone by." Heidegger thus uses "pastness" (*Vergangenheit*) to refer only to the past in this sense of "bygone" and "having been" (*Gewesenheit*) to refer to the past as it belongs to originary temporality.

95. *Being and Time* (GA 2), H326.

96. Ibid. The entire structure is summarized by Heidegger as follows: "The 'ahead-of-itself' is grounded in the future. In the 'Being-already-in . . .' the character of 'having been' is made known. 'Being-alongside . . .' becomes possible in making present"—*Being and Time* (GA 2), H327.

97. Ibid., H346: "Just as understanding is made possible by the future, and moods are made possible by having been, the third constitutive item in the structure of care—namely, *falling*—has its existential meaning in the present"; see also H328.

98. Ibid., H328.

99. Ibid., H350.

100. Ibid., H327.

101. Ibid., H329–331. This is a point that William Blattner also stresses in relation to temporality's nonsuccessive character: "Originary temporality is finite simply insofar as it is not successive"—Blattner, *Heidegger's Temporal Idealism*, p. 121; see also pp. 89ff.

102. *Being and Time* (GA 2), H379.

103. *Parmenides*, pp. 140–141 (GA 54:209–210); see also (from 1941) *Basic Concepts*, p. 103 (GA 51:120): "In Greek χρόνος means what corresponds to τόπος, to the place where each respective being belongs."

104. Heidegger distinguishes, in fact, between a number of different temporal structures: originary time (which is itself unified in the temporalizing of time in and through the temporal ecstases); "world time" (*Weltzeit*), which occupies a position analogous to that of the structure of spatiality as given in existential and equipmental space; and ordinary time, which is the leveled-out time that can be followed according to the clock—the time that is closest to objective spatiality. Indeed, just as ordinary time is a sequence of identical "nows," so one might think of objective space as a simultaneity of identical "heres."

105. The various features of ordinary temporality that Heidegger identifies as datability, spannedness, significance, and publicness (see *Being and Time* [GA 2], H406–411) are each explained on the basis of this leveled-down structure. This is, of course, a very summary presentation of a much more complex argument, but to go into the details of Heidegger's analysis would take us rather too far from the main focus of the discussion here. For a detailed analysis, see Blattner, *Heidegger's Temporal Idealism*, chapter 3, esp. pp. 164–178.

106. The entire chapter is titled "Temporality and Within-Time-Ness as the Source of the Ordinary Conception of Temporality," although the last two sections, secs. 82–83, are more general, with sec. 82 being a comparison with Hegel's account of temporality.

107. *Being and Time* (GA 2), H367.

108. Ibid.

109. See pp. 56–63 above.

110. *Being and Time* (GA 2), H367.

111. Ibid., sec. 70, H368–369. Note the appearance of "equiprimordiality" to describe the relation between "directional awaiting of a region" and "bringing-close."

112. This means that my own abilities will be relevant here just as much as the character of the tools and the workshop as such—if I lack the capacities to use some tool, then the way in which I will relate to the region in which that tool is located,

and so the associated spatiality, will differ from the way in which someone with that capacity will so relate, and from the spatiality that emerges for them.

113. Fell, *Heidegger and Sartre*, pp. 46, 48.

114. See *Place and Experience*, pp. 165–173.

115. See Blattner, *Heidegger's Temporal Idealism*, pp. 152–158.

116. As I indicated in n. 4, p. 336 above, I therefore disagree with what seems to be the implication of Yoko Arisaka's account that there is a distinction between "derivation" and "foundation" that can clearly be discerned in *Being and Time*, although there is a distinction, not obviously made by Heidegger, that can be made between those notions, but which is nonetheless somewhat different from that made by Arisaka.

117. See *Being and Time* (*GA* 2), H367–369.

118. Ibid., H329, H337, H340; see also the discussion of equiprimordiality below.

119. See *Being and Time* (*GA* 2), H331, where Heidegger describes "infinite time" as "derived" (*abgeleitete*) and *Being and Time* (*GA* 2), H329, where he talks of "derived 'time'" (*abkünftigen "Zeit"*).

120. Although this does not mean that Yoko Arisaka's claim, see n. 116 above, that the argument for the temporal character of spatiality is a matter of foundation rather than derivation is after all vindicated—see the discussion below.

121. Hegel's account of the structure of self-consciousness, particularly as exemplified in the master-slave dialectic as set out in the *Phenomenology of Mind* (sec. 178ff.), provides another instance of a form of mutual dependence (although not one that I will pursue here)—see especially Paul Redding's useful discussion of this as part of the structure of "recognition" in *Hegel's Hermeneutics* (Ithaca: Cornell University Press, 1996).

122. Yoko Arisaka contrasts the notion of equiprimordiality with that of "foundation" (using these notions in ways that more or less correspond to my distinction between mutual and hierarchical dependence), arguing that Heidegger misconstrues the relation between existential spatiality and originary temporality (as well as between originary temporality and care) as one of foundation when the two are actually equiprimordial. See Arisaka, "Spatiality, Temporality, and the Problem of Foundation in *Being and Time*," pp. 36–37.

123. Hildegard Feick, new edition by Susanne Ziegler, *Index zu Heideggers "Sein und Zeit"*, 3rd ed. (Tübingen: Max Niemeyer, 1980), p. 42.

124. *Being and Time* (*GA* 2), H131. The idea of equiprimordiality has received relatively little attention in discussions of Heidegger, although the notion is clearly a crucial one. Dieter Henrich discusses the passage from *Being and Time* cited here in

"On the Unity of Subjectivity," in Henrich, *The Unity of Reason* (Cambridge, Mass.: Harvard University Press, 1994), pp. 49ff.; originally published as "Über die Einheit der Subjektivität," *Philosophische Rundschau* 3 (1955), 28–69. I am grateful to Prof. Henrich for allowing me to discuss this issue with him in some detail during the summer of 2004, and the comments that follow derive from that conversation. Henrich emphasizes, as I have here, that what is at issue in the idea of equiprimordiality is the notion of unity in multiplicity, however, he also treats the notion as having its origins in Husserl, and as playing a key role in a critique of Husserl that can be seen to underpin much of Heidegger's account in *Being and Time*. The critique in question would run as follows: if the elements of temporality are, as Husserl seems o assume, equiprimordial, that is, "*gleichursprünglich*," then what is the nature of the "*equi-*," the "*gleich-*"—what is the basis for the unity of that equiprimordial structure? Thus Henrich sees the idea of equiprimordiality itself driving Heidegger's analysis in the direction of originary temporality, and, we might say, the ecstatic unity of temporality, in order to account for the unity of the equiprimordial elements that make up the structure of being-there. I think that Henrich's account is accurate as an account of *Being and Time*, but I also think that the difficulties Heidegger encounters in trying to work through this analysis lead him to rethink the notion of equiprimordiality so that the unity of the structure is given, not through a move back to some more primordial unity, but rather as given only through the interrelatedness of all of the elements as such—the shift from originary temporality as the ground for the unity of being-there to the way in which the unity of the "there" (the unity of the "fourfold," or of "place") is understood as occurring in and through the *Ereignis*, the "event" (for this is the shift that does indeed seem to occur in the move from early to late Heidegger), is a shift of just this sort. Unlike temporality, whose structure is explicated in terms of its own elements, the "event" of place is not explicated other than through the elements that already make it up— if we use the language of the fourfold, that means that the "event" just is the happening of belonging of earth and sky, mortals and gods. For more on this see chapter 5.

125. *Being and Time* (*GA* 2), H13.

126. Ibid., H110.

127. Ibid., H114.

128. This is a point that seems to be omitted from Yoko Arisaka's discussion of the distinction between equiprimordiality and what she refers to as "foundation," in her "Spatiality, Temporality, and the Problem of Foundation in *Being and Time*"— see esp. p. 36.

129. *Being and Time* (*GA* 2), H329, H337, H340—the first of these occurrences is quoted in the main text following.

130. Ibid., H329; see also H337, H340.

131. Notice that this means that Arisaka's contrast between "foundation" and "equiprimordiality" (mutual dependence) does not fit my use of these terms. Arisaka's distinction is closer to what I would treat as a distinction between hierarchical and mutual dependence, the former being characteristic of derivation, but the latter being consistent with a form of foundation or grounding. Arisaka characterizes foundation in terms of supervenience ("If X supervenes on Y, then X is founded on Y"), content (if the content of X is "supplied by" Y, then X is founded on Y), and conditionality ("If Y founds X, then Y is the condition for X")—see "Spatiality, Temporality, and the Problem of Foundation in Being and Time," p. 36. She presents these notions as interconnected, and so she takes dreams as "supervening" or being founded on perception inasmuch as perception supplies the content, and so is the condition, for dreams. The conditionality at issue here would seem to be a form of asymmetrical conditionality—without perception there could not be dreams, but the reverse need not hold. Arisaka's use of supervenience to describe the dependence relation is, however, a little out of keeping with the way the former notion is usually understood. Supervenience is, essentially, a form of identity relation. If X supervenes on Y, then there can be no difference in X that is not also accompanied by a difference in Y. Although supervenience itself allows of stronger and weaker versions, a minimal characterization of supervenience, expressed in terms of conditionality, would be that if X supervenes on Y, then, if there is a difference in X, it will also be necessary that there be a difference in Y (but a difference in Y need not be sufficient for a difference in X). It is not the case, however, that the supervenience relation can be described in terms of content in the way Arisaka puts it. The supervenience relation may thus hold, for instance, where the notion of content has no direct application (between states characterized, for instance, in mental and in physical terms), while the example Arisaka cites of the relation between perception and dreams is not an obvious case of supervenience at all (though one might argue that there cannot be a distinction that appears in dreams that does not also appear in perception, but this seems not to be what Arisaka has in mind).

132. Being and Time (GA 2), H323–325.

133. Ibid., H324.

134. Ibid., H151.

135. Ibid., H12.

136. See, for instance, Being and Time (GA 2), H143–144.

137. Ibid., H180.

138. See Heidegger, "My Way to Phenomenology," in On Time and Being, p. 74 (Zur Sache des Denkens, p. 81).

139. Being and Time (GA 2), H369.

140. Ibid., H334.

141. See *Metaphysics*, 1016b. Thus Aristotle's account of substance centers on living beings, taking the primary sense of substance to be that which unifies such beings in their being.

142. See "The Transcendental Circle," *Australasian Journal of Philosophy* 75 (1997), 1–20; see also "From the Transcendental to the 'Topological': Heidegger on Ground, Unity and Limit."

143. See Körner, "The Impossibility of Transcendental Deduction," *Monist* 51 (1967), 317–331. I discuss this problem, with specific reference to Körner, in "Transcendental Arguments and Conceptual Schemes: A Reconsideration of Körner's Uniqueness Argument," *Kant-Studien* 81 (1990), 232–251. Unfortunately, at the time this piece was written, I had not articulated the distinction between mutual and hierarchical dependence, nor did I bring Heidegger into the discussion. The discussion focuses instead on Körner's criticism of Kant, as well as a reply to that criticism by Eva Schaper, and a comparison of Kantian transcendental argument, as explicated by Schaper, and a form of "transcendental argument" in the work of Donald Davidson.

144. See Käufer, "Systematicity and Temporality," *Journal of the British Society for Phenomenology* 33 (2002), 167–187.

145. See "Dialogue on Language," in *On the Way to Language*, p. 51 (*GA* 12:142).

146. *Being and Time* (*GA* 2), H108.

147. *The Metaphysical Foundations of Logic*, p. 166 (*GA* 26:212). See also *Einleitung in die Philosophie* (winter semester 1928–29), *Gesamtausgabe* 27 (Frankfurt: Klostermann, 1996), p. 328.

148. *Being and Time* (*GA* 2), sec. 70, H368.

149. Ibid., sec. 70, H368. See also the discussion of *res cogitans* versus *res corporea* at sec. 19 H89–92 and the passage from sec. 12, H53 already quoted earlier.

150. See Søren Overgaard, "Heidegger on Embodiment," *Journal of the British Society for Phenomenology* 35 (2004), 116–131; see also David R. Cerbone, "Heidegger and Dasein's Bodily Nature: What Is the Hidden Problematic?" *International Journal of Philosophical Studies* 8 (2000), 209–230.

151. *Husserl, Heidegger, and the Space of Meaning*, pp. 212–213.

152. See Overgaard, "Heidegger on Embodiment," esp. p. 124.

153. Kant, "What Is Orientation in Thinking?" (1786) in *Political Writings*, ed. Hans Reiss, trans. H. B. Nisbet, 2nd ed. (Cambridge: Cambridge University Press, 1991), p. 238.

154. See his explicit discussion of Kant on orientation, *Being and Time* (*GA* 2), H109–110—the specific passage in Kant to which Heidegger refers here appears in "What Is Orientation in Thinking?" p. 239.

155. *Being and Time* (*GA* 2), H109.

156. Ibid.

157. *Being and Time* (*GA* 2), p. 137.

158. "Concerning the Ultimate Ground of the Differentiation of Directions of Space," in Kant, *Theoretical Philosophy 1755–1770*, trans. and ed. David Walford with Ralf Meerbote (Cambridge: Cambridge University Press, 1992), pp. 367–368. One could try to avoid the conclusion that space is somehow basic here by insisting that the body is itself part of the equipmental structure, but this would seem to involve a thoroughly problematic understanding of the body.

159. See, for instance, *What Is a Thing?*, p. 16 (*GA* 41:13). See also the account in *Place and Experience*, esp. chapter 7.

160. Dreyfus, *Being-in-the-World*, H368.

161. See *Place and Experience*, pp. 44ff.

162. "Seminar in Le Thor 1968," p. 32 (*GA* 15:322). See also *Zollikon Seminars* (May 11, 1965), pp. 86–87 (*Zollikoner Seminare*, pp. 113–114) in which Heidegger discusses the difference between the limits of the corporeal thing (*Körper*) and the limits of the body (*Leib*). The *Zollikon Seminars* contain an extensive discussion of what is referred to here as "bodily spatiality"—see *Zollikon Seminars*, pp. 80–89 (*Zollikoner Seminare*, pp. 105–115).

163. There is, in fact, a relation of mutual dependence here since spatiality is itself necessary, so I would claim, to the possibility of being as temporal—see *Place and Experience*, pp. 42, 105, 164. This need not prevent some sense of priority pertaining to temporality, but it will rule out any hierarchical dependence of the sort that characterizes the analysis of *Being and Time*.

164. In *Place and Experience*, I used the term "subjective" space in contrast to "objective" space, while elsewhere in the literature the term "egocentric" space is commonly employed. My own use of "subjective" space was governed by the particular manner in which the argument of *Place and Experience* proceeds since part of what is at issue in the latter work is an interrogation of the notion of subjectivity as such as it stands in relation to, and is in a certain sense, determined by, spatiality—see *Place and Experience*, esp. pp. 50–91. One way of understanding a large part of the argument of *Place and Experience*, however, is as showing that subjective space, and so also "egocentric" space, is always bodily space.

165. *Being-in-the-World*, p. 129.

166. Dreyfus, "Heidegger's History of the Being of Equipment," in Hubert L. Dreyfus and Harrison Hall (eds.), *Heidegger: A Critical Reader* (Oxford: Blackwell, 1992), p. 176.

167. Ibid., p. 182.

168. For an excellent discussion of the way in which existential or lived space is tied to bodily space, see David Morris, *The Shape of Space* (New York: SUNY Press, 2004). Morris also emphasizes the interconnection of bodily spatiality with the objective and intersubjective.

169. See the discussion of this point in *Place and Experience*, pp. 52–60. There is an interesting question as to how this point might apply in the case of fictional maps, but here I would say the same point applies, except that the way the map functions in this way must be with respect to the imagined spaces and bodies within whose context the map is itself embedded. A fictional "map" presented without any context of fictional "involvement" is no map at all.

170. An allocentric space is a space that possesses a directionality of its own, but one not based on the body; see the discussion of mappable and allocentric space in *Place and Experience*, pp. 58–59.

171. *Being and Time* (*GA* 2), H361–362; see also H112.

172. The most developed and sophisticated version of this idea is to be found, of course, in the work of Hubert Dreyfus—see especially his *Being-in-the-World*.

173. *Being and Time* (*GA* 2), H409.

174. Rouse, *Knowledge and Power* (Ithaca: Cornell University Press, 1987), p. 76.

175. Dreyfus cites examples of just this sort in support of his own more general position—see, for instance, "Heidegger's Critique of the Husserl/Searle Account of Intentionality," *Social Research* 60 (1993), 28–29. One of the difficulties here, of course, is that much depends on what we take the phenomenology to be in such cases. There is, moreover, no doubt that there is an important sense in which all skillful or "practically oriented" activity does involve an element of "unconscious" "immersion." But I think it is a mistake to take our experience of such "immersion" as given in certain forms of skillful or "practically oriented" activity as somehow giving us access to *the* fundamental mode in which we find ourselves "in" the world. A form of "immersion" is actually a feature of all activity, whether "thinking" or "unthinking," and the immersion that sometimes is experienced in practical engagement is, as I note above, never independent of the wider context of activity that includes both "theoretical" and "practical," both the "detached" and the "engaged."

176. For an account of the relation between the ready-to-hand and the present-at-hand, and so of the relation between the theoretical and practical, that, in its

general outline, is more congenial to my position here, see Joseph Rouse, *Knowledge and Power*, chapter 4, pp. 69–126.

177. Thomas Nagel, for instance, characterizes objectivity in general such that "[a] view or form of thought is more objective than another if it relies less on the specifics of the individual's makeup and position in the world, or on the character of the particular type of creature he is." Objectivity supposedly arises, on Nagel's account, through "a process of gradual detachment. . . . An objective standpoint is achieved by leaving a more subjective, individual or even just human perspective behind." See Nagel, *The View from Nowhere* (Oxford: Oxford University Press, 1986), p. 7.

178. For more on the interconnection of objective and "engaged" spatiality, see the discussion in *Place and Experience*, chap. 5.

179. See Blattner, *Heidegger's Temporal Idealism*, esp. pp. 181–184, although the argument set out here depends on the analysis that precedes it.

180. Ordinary temporality is supposed to be generated out of originary temporality through the notion of succession or sequentiality—succession thus underpins the main elements of ordinary temporality in terms of its datability, its spannedness, its significance, and its publicness. See Blattner, *Heidegger's Temporal Idealism*, pp. 164ff., esp. 173–178.

181. As should already be clear, objectivity only emerges in relation to an embodied space. This is, of course, a point that can be seen to be consistent with the account of *Being and Time*. However, I would also claim that bodily space itself emerges only in relation to objective space. It seems to me that this is true quite generally—any creature that is capable of movement must have some capacity to situate itself in relation to what is not itself, and here is the germ of the idea of the distinction between the bodily and the objective. In the case of beings such as ourselves, however, this distinction arises in a much more complex and sophisticated form.

182. See *Heidegger's Temporal Idealism*, pp. 277–310.

Chapter 4

1. *Pathmarks*, p. 283 (*GA* 9:373). There is a marginal comment included in the fifth edition, 1949 (inserted after "thought accordingly, as a place") that reads: "Inadequately said: the locality dwelt in by mortals, the mortal region of the locality." I do not see this as impugning the topological emphasis here, but rather as indicating Heidegger's concern to dispel the ambiguity in the identification of being-there with the place of the truth of being that might lead one to suppose that place was therefore something that emerges on the basis of being-there. In this respect, the marginal comment focuses on precisely the point at issue in the discussion of transcendence and subjectivity in sec. 4.2.

2. See *Introduction to Metaphysics*, p. 213 (*GA* 40:208).

3. Indeed, the thinking of the "political" is an important element in Heidegger's "re-thinking" after 1933—see James Phillips, *Heidegger's Volk*, and also Miguel de Beistegui, *Heidegger and the Political: Dystopias*. While this aspect of the turning is not one to which I can do justice here, it remains an important, if implicit, element in the development of the topological themes that are at the center of my discussion.

4. *Kant and the Problem of Metaphysics*, trans. Richard Taft, 5th ed. (Bloomington: Indiana University Press, 1997), p. 164 (*GA* 3:233).

5. Fell, *Heidegger and Sartre*, p. 169.

6. Hannah Arendt, "Martin Heidegger at Eighty," trans. Albert Hofstadter, in Michael Murray (ed.), *Heidegger and Modern Philosophy* (New Haven: Yale University Press, 1978), p. 298.

7. "Letter on 'Humanism,'" pp. 249–250 (*GA* 9:327–328).

8. Gadamer, *Philosophical Apprenticeships* (Cambridge, Mass.: MIT Press, 1985), p. 50.

9. In a marginal note appended to the "Letter" in the 1949 edition, Heidegger comments that the "Letter" itself follows a path of thinking that begins in 1936; see "Letter on 'Humanism,'" p. 239a (*GA* 9:319a). William Richardson, however, who first introduces the periodization between "early" and "late" Heidegger—see Richardson, *Heidegger: Through Phenomenology to Thought* [The Hague: Martinus Nijhof, 1963], in which Richardson talks of "Heidegger I" and "Heidegger II"—takes the turning in Heidegger's thought to begin in 1930 with "On the Essence of Truth," but to have been completed in 1935 with the lectures later published as *Introduction to Metaphysics*: "With EM [*Einführung in die Metaphysik*] Heidegger II has taken full possession"—*Heidegger: Through Phenomenology to Thought*, p. 296. *Introduction to Metaphysics* nevertheless seems still to be marked as a highly transitional work in which Heidegger is not yet in full command of the elements that characterize his later thinking.

10. See Crowell, *Husserl, Heidegger, and the Space of Meaning*, esp. pp. 215–218. Crowell suggests a periodization of Heidegger's thinking that divides it into four stages: from 1912–1917, during which time Heidegger is largely concerned with matters of logic and the question of the "meaning of meaning"; from 1917–1927 (and extending in some respects up until 1930), which sees Heidegger involved in reworking Husserlian, Diltheyan, and Aristotelian themes around the question of "the meaning of being"; 1930–1946 (although a shift is already evident in 1929), during which Heidegger attempts to disentangle himself from "metaphysics" and to reconfigure his thought around the question of the "truth of being"; from 1945 onward, which sees Heidegger's articulation of a mode of thinking that aims at the "overcoming" of metaphysics through the focus on the primordial "event" (*Ereignis*) of being (this, of course, is that in which, following Heidegger's own late

comments, I have suggested the question of the place, *topos*, of being comes to the fore). A similar four-part periodization is also suggested by Young: "Heidegger himself identifies a 'turn' in his philosophy as having begun in 1930. Since he also says, however, that it was not completed until the transition to '*Ereignis*-thinking' in 1936–1938 (see *Seminare*, GA 15, p. 344 and p. 366), he himself invites us to contemplate three (of course related) thinkers: an early (pre-1930) Heidegger, a middle or transitional thinker (1930–1938), and a late Heidegger (post-1938). . . . I shall argue for the recognition of yet another 'turn' as occurring in about 1946. So in addition to Heidegger's three, I shall identify a fourth . . . a 'post-war' Heidegger"— Young, *Heidegger's Philosophy of Art*, p. 3.

11. See Sheehan, "Kehre and Ereignis: A Prolegomenon to *Introduction to Metaphysics*," in Richard Polt and Gregory Fried (eds.), *A Companion to Heidegger's "Introduction to Metaphysics"* (New Haven: Yale University Press, 2001), pp. 3–16.

12. Ibid., p. 3.

13. Heidegger, "Vorwort" to William J. Richardson, *Heidegger: Through Phenomenology to Thought*, p. xix.

14. One might also argue, of course, for the need to be wary of Heidegger's own self-interpretations. Certainly there is a revisionist tendency in Heidegger's commentaries on his own life and work—a tendency that is perhaps most apparent in his various reconstructions of his political involvements of the 1930s, and, sometimes, in his projection of elements of his later thinking back into his earlier. Recognition of such a tendency does not imply, however, that Heidegger's self-interpretations are never to be trusted, but only that, as with all self-interpretations, they cannot provide the sole basis for the understanding of his thought and must be read in conjunction with the actual work itself. Moreover, my own reading of Heidegger's thought is one that does indeed take it to exhibit an essential consistency and unity that is itself consistent with much (though not all) of what Heidegger himself tells us about the nature of his thinking.

15. Fell, *Heidegger and Sartre*, p. 204.

16. See the discussion of the Event in chapter 5.

17. "Seminar in Le Thor 1969," pp. 40–41 (GA 15:334–335).

18. "The Origin of the Work of Art," in *Off the Beaten Track*, p. 55 (GA 5:74).

19. See "List of Sources," in *Off the Beaten Track*, p. 285.

20. In order to see exactly how it remains, see the further discussion in chapter 5.

21. *Contributions to Philosophy*, trans. Parvis Emad and Kenneth Maly (Bloomington: Indiana University Press, 1999), p. 208 (GA 65:295).

22. "European Nihilism," in *Nietzsche*, trans. David Farrell Krell, vol. 4, *Nihilism* (San Francisco: Harper and Row, 1979–1987), p. 141 (*GA* 6.2:172–173).

23. See Blattner, *Heidegger's Temporal Idealism*, p. 310.

24. Ibid., p. xv.

25. Ibid., p. 310.

26. *Being and Time* (*GA* 2), H212.

27. "Letter on 'Humanism,'" p. 256 (*GA* 9:336). I have replaced "so long" with "as long" to keep the translation consistent with that from *Being and Time*.

28. Blattner, *Heidegger's Temporal Idealism*, pp. 295–296.

29. Ibid., pp. 295–296n29.

30. Such would seem to be the implication of Blattner's argument against defining being in terms of intelligibility on the grounds that such a move would be purely stipulative, effectively assuming what *Being and Time* aims to demonstrate—see *Heidegger's Temporal Idealism*, pp. 3–6, 242.

31. "On the Essence of Truth," trans. John Sallis, in *Pathmarks*, p. 154 (*GA* 9:202). Heidegger refers to the position set out in "On the Essence of Truth," writing that "Every kind of anthropology and all subjectivity of the human being as subject is not merely left behind—as it was already in *Being and Time*. . . . rather, the movement of the lecture is such that it sets out to think from this other ground (Da-sein)." See also "Preface," in Richardson, *From Phenomenology to Thought*, p. xviii.

32. "On the Essence of Ground," trans. William McNeill, in *Pathmarks*, p. 371n66 (*GA* 9:162n59).

33. *Being and Time* (*GA* 2), H208.

34. Blattner seems to suggest that such mysticism may provide the basis for some of Heidegger's later antisubjectivism, but denies that such "mysticism" can explain Heidegger's dissatisfaction with *Being and Time* as that arose in the late 1920s; see Blattner, *Heidegger's Temporal Idealism*, pp. 309–310.

35. Since Heidegger's position stands aside from both subjectivism and objectivism (the two being tied together, as I note below), it can be misleading to characterize it as "antisubjectivist," hence my talk of "nonsubjectivist." It is a position that stands outside of the usual oppositions here. For this reason too, I would hesitate to call it a "realism," although there are strong temptations to do so. Elsewhere, however, I have been less hesitant, referring to Heidegger, along with Davidson, as a "realist," on the grounds of the way in which his thinking, as well as Davidson's, remains based in the original and prior involvement of ourselves in the world—see *Donald Davidson and the Mirror of Meaning* (Cambridge: Cambridge University Press, 1992), pp. 274–277, see also my discussion in "Holism, Realism and Truth: How to Be an

Anti-Relativist and Not Give Up on Heidegger (or Davidson)—a Debate with Christopher Norris," *International Journal of Philosophical Studies* 12 (2004), pp. 339–356. Nevertheless, it has to be acknowledged that "realism" remains, especially within the Heideggerian context—a term that brings its own problematic set of oppositions with it.

36. If subjectivism is characteristic of modernity, it is so because of the way in which modernity also seizes upon, and thematizes, the objective. This is a clear lesson to be learned from Cartesianism, in which we find the attempt at a purely "objective" understanding of the world (the prioritization of physical science) that nevertheless also gives rise to a form of subjectivism (in the prioritization of the *"cogito"*).

37. It is notable that spatiality occasionally reappears in the discussion of transcendence in ways that mirror its appearance in *Being and Time*. See, for instance, "On the Essence of Ground," p. 108 (*GA* 9:137): "Transcendence . . . means something that properly pertains to *human Dasein . . . as the fundamental constitution of this being, one that occurs prior to all comportment.* Certainly, human Dasein as existing 'spatially' has the possibility, among others, of spatially 'surpassing' a spatial boundary or gap. Transcendence, however, is that surpassing that makes possible such a thing as existence in general, thereby also making it possible to move 'oneself' in space."

38. "On the Essence of Ground," p. 371n66 (*GA* 9:162n59). Heidegger is presumably referring here to sec. 69c, "The Temporal Problem of the Transcendence of the World."

39. See *Being and Time* (*GA* 2), sec. 1, H3.

40. Ibid., H38.

41. Ibid., sec. 69c, H364–366.

42. Ibid., H366.

43. "On the Essence of Ground," p. 109 (*GA* 9:139). The comment could be seen to be partly intended as a rebuff to the charge of subjectivism, but all it actually does is to raise the problem of the unity of transcendence in a different way—as a problem about what such "co-constitution" could possibly mean. Leaving such "co-constitution" to one side, however, one of the problems that becomes increasingly evident in Heidegger's discussion of transcendence and is in fact already implicit in *Being and Time* concerns an unstable ambiguity in the notion of transcendence itself inasmuch as it seems to refer both to the essential structure of being-there and to that which encompasses both being-there *and* world. It seems inevitable that such an ambiguity will tend to resolve itself by grounding the unity of being-there and world in one or another of the two poles of the relation, and most likely in being-there.

44. "On the Essence of Ground," p. 108 (*GA* 9:137–138).

45. Ibid., pp. 121–122 (*GA* 9:156–158).

46. Ibid., pp. 108–109 (*GA* 9:137–139).

47. *The Metaphysical Foundations of Logic*, pp. 160 and 165–166 (*GA* 26:204, 211–213).

48. "On the Essence of Ground," p. 109 (*GA* 9:139).

49. Heidegger, *The Principle of Reason*, trans. Reginald Lilly (Bloomington: Indiana University Press, 1996), p. 78 (*GA* 10:115).

50. "On the Essence of Ground," p. 106 (*GA* 9:135).

51. *The Principle of Reason*, p. 78 (*GA* 10:115).

52. "On the Essence of Ground," p. 109 (*GA* 9:139–140), translation modified.

53. See *Kant and the Problem of Metaphysics*, pp. 50–53 (*GA* 3:70–75).

54. "On the Essence of Ground," p. 111 (*GA* 9:141).

55. Ibid., p. 111 (*GA* 9:142).

56. "Summary of a Seminar," in *On Time and Being*, p. 27 (*Zur Sache des Denkens*, pp. 29–30).

57. The engagement with Kant is a feature of Heidegger's work over much of the period from the late-1920s until the mid-1930s—not only does *Kant and the Problem of Metaphysics* appear in 1929, but Kant also figures prominently in a lecture course in 1926 ("History of Philosophy from Thomas of Aquinas to Kant" [*GA* 23]), two lecture courses in 1927 ("The Basic Problems of Phenomenology" [*GA* 24] and "Phenomenological Interpretation of Kant's Critique of Pure Reason" [*GA* 25]), and another lecture given in 1935 ("The Question Concerning the Thing: Kant's Teaching Concerning the Fundamental Transcendental Principle" [*GA* 41]). With the exception of the 1926 lecture, these lectures appear in English as: *The Basic Problems of Phenomenology*, trans. Albert Hofstadter (Bloomington: Indiana University Press, 1982); *Phenomenological Interpretation of Kant's "Critique of Pure Reason,"* trans. Parvis Emad and Kenneth Maly (Indiana University Press, 1997); and *What Is a Thing?* trans. W. B. Barton Jr. and Vera Deutsch (Chicago: Henry Regnery, 1967).

58. "Preface to the Fourth Edition," in *Kant and the Problem of Metaphysics*, p. xvii (*GA* 3:xiii).

59. See *Kant and the Problem of Metaphysics*, pp. 112ff. (*GA* 3:160ff.).

60. One might suppose that this is already assumed in the idea of the transcendental itself, but as I briefly indicated in chapter 3 (sec. 3.5), there is at least the possibility of understanding the transcendental, and so-called transcendental argument, in a way that need not involve such dependence, but instead takes it as

proceeding through exhibiting the integration of an otherwise differentiated unity through the mutual relatedness of the elements that make it up.

61. Joseph Fell summarizes the deficiencies in *Being and Time* in terms that also emphasize the tendency to treat the unitary structure at issue in ways that threaten the unity of that structure, while also posing a problem for the reestablishing of that unity: "First, his [Heidegger's] early thinking . . . tends to exempt itself from historical conditioning, judging Dasein's *inevitable* historicity from a transcendental-metaphysical standpoint that nevertheless attempts to isolate permanent defining characteristics (existentialia) of Dasein. . . . Second . . . a residual metaphysical permanence is assigned both to Dasein and to 'Nature,' and the two can be interpreted as irreducible relata. . . . Third . . . the construing of the ontological difference in terms of the metaphysical distinction between meaning and entity can be interpreted as in effect a split of dualism between the *source* of meaning and the *receptacle* of meaning. . . . Fourth, once these latent metaphysical distinctions have been brought to Dasein's explicit attention, Dasein must will their recombination through a "decision" that runs the risk of arbitrariness."—Fell, *Heidegger and Sartre*, pp. 166–167.

62. "On the Essence of Ground," p. 123 (*GA* 9:159).

63. *Contributions to Philosophy*, p. 226 (*GA* 65:322).

64. "On the Essence of Ground," marginal note, p. 123a (*GA* 9:159a). Note that here "beyng" (the translator's rendition of Heidegger's use of the archaic form "*Seyn*") seems to refer to this simple onefold as such, and so to be distinct from being.

65. See the reference to the "becoming one" of "the twofold of what is present and of presence" in "Cézanne," in *Aus der Erfahrung des Denkens*, ed. Hermann Heidegger, *Gesamtausgabe* 13 (Frankfurt: Klostermann, 1983), p. 223.

66. See "Seminar in Le Thor 1969," pp. 60–61 (*GA* 15:366); see also Heidegger's comments in Joan Stambaugh, "Introduction," in *The End of Philosophy*, trans. Joan Stambaugh (New York: Harper and Row, 1973), pp. xii–xiii. See also Julian Young, *Heidegger's Philosophy of Art*, p. 154.

67. *The Principle of Reason*, p. 51 (*GA* 10:76).

68. "Insofar as Being 'comes to presence' as ground, it itself has no ground. It is so, not because it grounds itself, but because any grounding—not excluding, but, indeed, rather including its own grounding—remains inadequate to being as ground. . . . Being as being remains groundless. Ground—namely as ground which grounds being—stays away from being. Being is an abyss."—*The Principle of Reason*, p. 111 (*GA* 10:166).

69. "Die Ros' ist ohne Warum; sie blühet, weil sie blühet,/Sie ach't nicht ihrer selbst, fragt nicht, ob man sie siehet," Angelus Silesius (1624–1677), *Cherubinischer Wandersmann* (Bremen: Carl Schünemann, n.d.), p. 37 (I, 289).

70. *Parmenides*, p. 28n1 (*GA* 54:42n2).

71. *Being and Time*, p. 17. See also "Letter on 'Humanism,'" p. 261 (*GA* 9:343): "It is everywhere supposed that the attempt in *Being and Time* ended in a blind alley. Let us not comment any further upon that opinion. The thinking that hazards a few steps in *Being and Time* has even today not advanced beyond that publication."

72. Although it is important to recognize that the latter is not so much a replacement for the former as an elucidation of it. Thus Heidegger says in the "Introduction to 'What is Metaphysics?'" that "'Meaning of Being' and 'truth of Being' say the same" (*Pathmarks*, p. 286 [*GA* 9:377]).

73. *The Principle of Reason*, p. 86 (*GA* 10:128).

74. Ibid.

75. Young, *Heidegger's Later Philosophy*, p. 28.

76. "The Way in the Turn," *Heidegger's Ways* (Albany: SUNY Press, 1994), pp. 129–130.

77. This is the line that appears at the head of this chapter above; it is taken from "Introduction to 'What is Metaphysics?'" p. 283 (*GA* 9:373). As I indicate in the original note above (p. 336n1), Heidegger draws attention to the need to clarify this comment so as to avoid any problematic identification of being-there with the place of the truth of being.

78. *Contributions*, p. 208 (*GA* 65:294). See also Heidegger's discussion of "the ones to come," *Contributions*, pp. 277–281 (*GA* 65:395–401).

79. See, for instance, *Contributions*, pp. 120–132 (*GA* 65:171–188) and *Basic Questions of Philosophy*, p. 131ff. (*GA* 45:151ff.). See also the discussion in Fell, *Heidegger and Sartre*, pp. 244–267. Fell notes Heidegger's emphasis on the "other" beginning as not a second beginning, but rather as identical with "the one first and only beginning that is the clearing of *aletheia*"—Fell, *Heidegger and Sartre*, p. 464n1.

80. A hyphenation that appears only occasionally in the German editions of *Sein und Zeit* (as Macquarrie and Robinson note in their translation in order "to show its etymological construction"—*Being and Time*, trans. Macquarrie and Robinson, p. 27n1), but which Joan Stambaugh, on Heidegger's own authority, employs throughout her translation of *Being and Time—Being and Time: A Translation of "Sein und Zeit"* (Albany: SUNY Press, 1996), p. xiv—something that reflects an element of the later Heidegger's reconceptualization of his own earlier thought.

81. *Contributions*, p. 219 (*GA* 65:311–312).

82. Ibid., p. 19 (*GA* 65:26)—I have used "propriative" and "propriative event" rather than Emad and Maly's "enowned" and "enowning." See sec. 5.2, for

a discussion of the difficulties presented by the translation of *"Ereignis"* and its cognates.

83. *Basic Questions of Philosophy*, p. 180 (*GA* 45:212). See also the discussion in Heidegger's very last seminar, "Seminar in Zähringen 1973," in *Four Seminars*, pp. 73–75 (*GA* 15:386–390).

84. *Basic Questions of Philosophy*, p. 181 (*GA* 45:215).

85. "Seminar in Zähringen 1973," p. 73 (*GA* 15:386–387).

86. Françoise Dastur emphasizes the way in which, from 1927 to 1935, the concept of world is "deeply transformed"—"Heidegger's Freiburg Version of the Origin of the Work of Art," in James Risser (ed.), *Heidegger Toward the Turn* (Albany: SUNY Press, 1999), pp. 128–131, esp. p. 129—in its shift away from world as the equipmental context of daily activity toward world as "holy," as the dimension of historical decision and as the setting forth of earth. Dastur also presents the concept of world as it appears in 1935–1936, in "The Origin of the Work of Art," as transitional between the world of equipmental contextuality in *Being and Time* and the world of the gathering of the fourfold in "The Thing."

87. *Being and Time*, p. 490, I.3, n.i; (H72). Kisiel points out the error in the dating here: the critical period is the War Emergency Semester of 1919—see Kisiel, *The Genesis of Heidegger's "Being and Time,"* p. 16.

88. *The Basic Problems of Phenomenology*, p. 165 (*GA* 24:234). Heidegger adds "You will think that that is a bold and presumptuous assertion. . . . How can it be that the world has not hitherto been seen in philosophy?"

89. *The Fundamental Concepts of Metaphysics*, p. 333 (*GA* 29/30:483).

90. Ibid., p. 333 (*GA* 29/30:483).

91. Ibid., p. 177 (*GA* 29/30:262–263).

92. *The Metaphysical Foundations of Logic*, p. 181 (*GA* 26:233).

93. "The Essence of Ground," p. 370n59 (*GA* 9:155n55).

94. "Seminar in Zähringen 1973," p. 64 (*GA* 15:373).

95. See *The Fundamental Concepts of Metaphysics*, esp. pp. 176–178 (*GA* 29/30:261–264).

96. *The Metaphysical Foundations of Logic*, p. 171 (*GA* 26:219–220). Heidegger adds that "this basic meaning of κόσμος—in principle first suggested by Karl Reinhardt (*Parmenides und die Geschichte der griechischen Philosophie*, 1916, p. 174f. and p. 216, note)—appears in several fragments of the pre-Socratic philosophers." Heidegger then refers to Fragment 7 from Melissos, Fragment 4 from Parmenides, Fragment 8 from Anaxagoras, and Fragment 89 from Heraklitus.

97. See *The Metaphysical Foundations of Logic*, pp. 170–181 (*GA* 26:219–233).

98. See *Being and Time* (*GA* 2), H214. The Macquarrie and Robinson translation uses "likening" for "*adequaetio*"—see *Being and Time*, trans. Macquarrie and Robinson, p. 257n2.

99. *Being and Time* (*GA* 2), H214.

100. This is an important point that is sometimes overlooked. It is particularly important in relation to Ernst Tugendhat's famous criticism of the Heideggerian account to the effect that there is no room in the understanding of truth as "uncoveredness" or "unhiddenness" ("*Entborgenheit*"—the term that Heidegger uses elsewhere to characterize the conception of truth in *Being and Time*, though not itself used in that work) to make sense of the contrast between the true and the false— there is no room for falsity as such (see "Heidegger's Idea of Truth," in Christopher Macann [ed.], *Critical Heidegger* [London: Routledge, 1996], pp. 232–233, as well as the more detailed discussion of Heidegger's account in Tugendhat, *Die Wahrheitsbegriff bei Husserl und Heidegger*, 2nd ed. [Berlin: de Gruyter, 1972]). This is, however, to miss the way in which Heidegger still maintains a sense of truth as pertaining to assertions that does indeed retain the contrast between truth and falsity, namely, the notion of truth as "correctness" (the false is that which is "incorrect"). For more on the criticism by Tugendhat, see Mark Wrathall, "Heidegger and Truth as Correspondence," *International Journal of Philosophical Studies* 7 (1999), 69–88, and also Daniel O. Dahlstrom, *Heidegger's Concept of Truth* (Cambridge: Cambridge University Press, 2001), pp. 419ff.

101. See *Being and Time* (*GA* 2), H218. This way of thinking of truth is, in fact, already an important thread throughout much of Heidegger's early thinking. For an account of the development of Heidegger's thinking of truth up to and including *Being and Time*, see Daniel O. Dahlstrom, *Heidegger's Concept of Truth*.

102. *Being and Time* (*GA* 2), H220–221.

103. Ibid., H212–213, H219–220.

104. Ibid., H225–226.

105. Ibid., H226.

106. "On the Essence of Ground," p. 106 (*GA* 9:135).

107. Ibid., p. 135 (*GA* 9:175).

108. "On the Essence of Truth," p. 147 (*GA* 9:192).

109. Ibid., marginal note in the first edition of 1943, p. 148a (*GA* 9:193a).

110. *Hölderlins Hymnen "Germanien" und "Der Rhein,"* *Gesamtausgabe* 39 (Frankfurt: Klostermann, 1980).

111. Thus, when Heidegger says that being-there is "equiprimordially" in the truth and in untruth (*Being and Time* [*GA* 2], H222), this does not mean that disclosedness is always also a concealing, but that being-there is essentially given over to falling, to fleeing, and to forgetting.

112. In "Seminar in Zähringen 1973," p. 64 (*GA* 15:372), we are told that: "The analysis of the worldhood of the world is indeed an essential step.... Yet this analysis 'remains of subordinate significance.'"

113. As Dreyfus puts it, "moods provide the background for intentionality, i.e., for the specific ways things and possibilities show up as mattering." Dreyfus, *Being-in-the-World*, p. 174.

114. *Being and Time* (*GA* 2), H343.

115. Ibid., H344: "In . . . [anxiety], Dasein is taken back to its naked uncanniness, and becomes fascinated by it. This fascination, however, not only *takes* Dasein back from its 'worldly' possibilities, but at the same time *gives* it the possibility of an *authentic* potentiality-for-Being."

116. See *The Fundamental Concepts of Metaphysics*, p. 5 (*GA* 29/30:7); the citation from Novalis is given as Novalis, *Schriften*, ed. J. Minor (Jena, 1923), II, p. 179, Fr 21.

117. The term "*Bodenständigkeit*" is often construed in ways that suggest a problematic emphasis on "rootedness" in one's native "soil" or ground (*Boden*). It is not clear that it has to be interpreted that way, however, and there seem ample indications that Heidegger does not intend it in the manner of the usual talk, which he often derides in the period after 1933–1934, of "*Blut und Boden*" (blood and soil).

118. A term Heidegger employs, as William McNeill points out, in direct relation to "solitude" in his 1933 essay "Why Do We Remain in the Province?" in *Aus der Erfahrung des Denkens, Gesamtausgabe* 13, pp. 11–12; McNeill, "*Heimat*: Heidegger on the Threshold," in James Risser (ed.), *Heidegger: Toward the Turn*, p. 329.

119. "What Is Metaphysics?," p. 96 (*GA* 9:122).

120. See *Introduction to Metaphysics*, p. 3 (*GA* 40:5).

121. "What Is Metaphysics?," pp. 95–96 (*GA* 9:121).

122. See especially the famous reference to nature as not merely "present-at-hand," at *Being and Time*, H65.

123. "On the Essence of Ground," p. 370n59 (*GA* 9:155n55).

124. See Joseph Fell, "The Familiar and the Strange: On the Limits of Praxis in the Early Heidegger," in Hubert Dreyfus and Harrison Hall (eds.), *Heidegger: A Critical Reader* (Oxford: Blackwell, 1992), p. 75.

125. *Basic Questions of Philosophy,* p. 119 (*GA* 45:137); see also *Introduction to Metaphysics,* p. 107 (*GA* 40:109).

126. "On the Essence of Truth," p. 153 (*GA* 9:201).

127. Only thus is it possible for the happening at issue here to be in any way grasped as a revealing *and* concealing, as a coming-forth *and* withdrawal, and so for concealing/withdrawal to itself be, in a certain way, evident in revealing/coming-forth. There is at least one mode of concealing-revealing, however, that does block off its character as a mode of concealing-revealing, thereby obscuring its own character in relation to ground and also obscuring the character of what is revealed in its multiplicity or "excess." This is just what occurs in the particular mode of concealing-revealing that is the essence of technology—see sec. 5.6.

128. "On the Essence of Truth," p. 148 (*GA* 9:193); see also "Seminar in Le Thor 1969," p. 38 (*GA* 15:331).

129. *Basic Questions of Philosophy,* pp. 18–19 (*GA* 45:19).

130. From the lines appended to the first page of *Off the Beaten Track,* and to *Holzwege.* In colloquial German a *Holzweg* is a path through the woods that leads nowhere, and the 1962 translation of *Holzwege* into French by Wolfgang Brockmeier is thus titled "Chemins qui ne mènent nulle part"—literally "Paths that Lead Nowhere"—a title that Heidegger himself reportedly approved. "Off the Beaten Track" captures something of what is at issue here in colloquial English.

131. See Gadamer, "Reflections on my Philosophical Journey," in Lewis Edwin Hahn (ed.), *The Philosophy of Hans-Georg Gadamer,* Library of Living Philosophers 24 (Chicago: Open Court, 1997), p. 47.

132. See Casey, *The Fate of Place,* p. 268.

133. See Gadamer, "Reflections on my Philosophical Journey," p. 47.

134. *Heidegger and Sartre,* p. 197.

135. "The Origin of the Work of Art," pp. 20–21 (*GA* 5:27–29).

136. Vincent Scully, *The Earth, the Temple, and the Gods* (New Haven: Yale, 1962), pp. 2, 3. Julian Young also cites Scully in reference to Heidegger's account—see Young, *Heidegger's Philosophy of Art,* p. 62.

137. See Alexander P.D. Mourelatos, "La Terre et les étoiles dans la cosmologie de Xénophane," in André Laks and Claire Louguet (eds.), *Qu'est-ce que la Philosophie Présocratique? Cahiers de Philologie 20* (Villeneuve d'Ascq: Presses Universitaires du Septentrion, 2002), pp. 332ff.

138. The Fourfold of earth and sky, gods and mortals, which appears to be a development out of this original "twofold" (see the discussion in sec. 5.2), is presented by Heidegger most clearly in "Hölderlin's Heaven and Earth," as mediated through

Hölderlin, but as nevertheless capturing something Greek—indeed, the poem that is the focus for Heidegger's discussion in "Hölderlin's Heaven and Earth" is Hölderlin's "Greece," and Heidegger describes Hölderlin as having knowledge "of the authentic essence of the Greeks"—see "Hölderlin's Heaven and Earth," in *Elucidations of Hölderlin's Poetry*, pp. 184–185 (*GA* 4:00). On Heidegger's use of figures from Greek thought and poetry, see also the account developed by Vincent Vycinas (an account that draws heavily on the work of Walter Otto) in *Earth and Gods: An Introduction to the Philosophy of Martin Heidegger* (The Hague: Martinus Nijhof, 1961), pp. 121ff.

139. "The Origin of the Work of Art," in *Off the Beaten Track*, pp. 55–56 (*GA* 5:73–74).

140. Jacques Taminiaux has explored the shifts that occur between the different version of the lectures with specific reference to the way in which will and decision are involved. Taminiaux sees earlier versions of the lecture as having a much more "violent" character—see *Poetics, Speculation, and Judgement: The Shadow of the Work of Art from Kant to Phenomenology* (Albany: SUNY Press, 1993), pp. 153–169. See also Clare Pearson Geiman's discussion of the more general issue of the shift in Heidegger's thinking concerning violence and force in relation to the happening of truth in "Heidegger's Antigones," in Polt and Fried, *A Companion to Heidegger's "Introduction to Metaphysics,"* pp. 161–182.

141. "Letter on 'Humanism,'" p. 256 (*GA* 9:337).

142. *Being and Time* (*GA* 2), H38.

143. "Letter on 'Humanism,'" p. 256–257 (*GA* 9:337).

144. Ibid., p. 257 (*GA* 9:337).

145. "Introduction to 'What is Metaphysics?'" p. 289 (*GA* 9:380–381).

146. See *The Metaphysical Foundations of Logic*, pp. 189–190 (*GA* 26:244).

147. "On the Essence of Truth," p. 154 (*GA* 9:201–202).

148. "Seminar in Le Thor 1969," p. 51 (*GA* 15:350–351). See also "Letter on 'Humanism,'" p. 271 (*GA* 9:357): "'Ontology' itself . . . whether transcendental or precritical, is subject to critique, not because it thinks the being of beings and in so doing reduces being to a concept, but because it does not think the truth of being and so fails to recognize that there is a thinking more rigorous than conceptual thinking. In the poverty of its first breakthrough, the thinking that tries to advance thought into the truth of being brings only a small part of that wholly other dimension to language. This language even falsifies itself, for it does not yet succeed in retaining the essential help of phenomenological seeing while dispensing with the inappropriate concern with 'science' and 'research.' But in order to make the attempt at thinking recognizable and at the same time understandable for existing philosophy,

it could at first be expressed only within the horizon of that existing philosophy and the use of its current terms. In the meantime I have learned to see that these very terms were bound to lead immediately and inevitably into error."

149. "On the Question of Being," p. 306 (*GA* 9:405).

150. As he writes in the "Letter on 'Humanism,'" p. 271 (*GA* 9:357) referring to his use of the terms and concepts of "existing philosophy": "For the terms and the conceptual language corresponding to them were not rethought by readers from the matter particularly to be thought; rather, the matter was conceived according to the established terminology in its customary meaning."

151. See "Letter on 'Humanism,'" p. 239 (*GA* 9:313).

152. "The Origin of the Work of Art," pp. 45–46 (*GA* 5:61–62).

153. "Martin Heidegger—75 Years," in *Heidegger's Ways*, p. 17.

154. Heidegger's use of etymology—his exploration of the connections between words and the "stories" that appear to belong to them—can be seen as "mythical" in a similar fashion. There too, the aim is to enable a complex structure of meaning to become evident through the evocative power of the image or the (reconceptualized) word. As Heidegger says in *Being and Time*, while we must avoid "uninhibited word-mysticism," it is nevertheless the case that "the ultimate business of philosophy is to preserve the *force of the most elemental words* in which Dasein expresses itself"—*Being and Time* (*GA* 2), H220.

155. Although not properly evident here, the way in which "*ethos*" is implicated with "*mythos*," as well as "*logos*," is important in understanding the nature of community and its relation to disclosure and concealment, particularly in terms of the gathering of the fourfold—see the discussion in sec. 5.4 below.

156. *Parmenides*, p. 70 (*GA* 54:104). Compare also Walter Otto's comment that *mythos* as it relates to *logos* "Is not merely an older expression but also stands for the older form of the essence of 'word'; it is the 'word' as the ultimate witnessing of that which was, is, and will be, as the revelation of being itself in the ancient venerable understanding which does not distinguish word and being"—Walter Otto, *Die Gestalt und das Sein* (Düsseldorf-Köln: Eugen Diederichs Verlag, 1955), p. 71.

157. *Hölderlins Hymnen "Germanien" und "Der Rhein,"* Gesamtausgabe 39, p. 88. The reference Heidegger provides at the end of this passage is to Hölderlin's *Sämtliche Werke*, 2nd ed. Norbert von Hellingrath, Friedrich Seebass, and Ludwig von Pigenot (Berlin: Propylaen, 1923)—it is the location for the notion of "poetic dwelling" which Heidegger finds originally in Hölderlin.

158. See Elden, "Hölderlin and the Importance of Place," *Journal of the British Society for Phenomenology* 30 (1999), 263; see also Elden, *Mapping the Present*, p. 36. Of course, the simple contrast between space and place that is implied here is not without its

own problems (especially given the interconnection between place and space) and can be seen, not only as a continuation of the problematic tendency to think of space primarily in Cartesian terms that was evident in *Being and Time* (and is noted by Elden), but as an ongoing difficulty in Heidegger's thinking (for more on this, see especially sec. 5.5).

159. See Young, *Heidegger's Philosophy of Art*, p. 107.

160. "Only a God Can Save Us," in Wolin (ed.), *The Heidegger Controversy*, p. 112 (*GA* 16:678).

161. See James Phillips, *Heidegger's Volk*; also de Beistegui, *Heidegger and the Political: Dystopias*, esp. pp. 87–113.

162. *Basic Questions of Philosophy*, p. 109 (*GA* 45:125).

163. Ibid., pp. 109–110 (*GA* 45:126).

164. Ibid., pp. 110–111 (*GA* 45:126–127).

165. "Postscript to 'What Is Metaphysics?'" trans. William McNeill, in *Pathmarks*, p. 237 (*GA* 9:312).

Chapter 5

1. Letter (1802), in *39 Hymns and Fragments*, trans. R. Sieburth (Princeton: Princeton University Press, 1985); the larger passage of which this is a part is discussed by Heidegger in "Hölderlin's Earth and Heaven," pp. 175–207 (*GA* 4:152–181).

2. See "Seminar in Le Thor 1969," p. 41 (*GA* 15:335) and "The End of Philosophy and the Task of Thinking," in *On Time and Being*, p. 69 (*Zur Sachen des Denkens*, pp. 77–78)—this issue is also briefly discussed below, sec. 5.2.

3. "Letter on 'Humanism,'" p. 239, n.a. (145).

4. Ibid., p. 241, n.a. (148). I have omitted the English gloss on "*Ereignis*" as "event of appropriation" that is used in the English translation of the "Letter."

5. Fell, *Heidegger and Sartre*, p. 221.

6. Henri Birault, *Heidegger et l'experience de la pensée* (Paris: Gallimard, 1978), p. 41.

7. Sheehan, "A Paradigm Shift in Heidegger Research," pp. 196–197.

8. See their comments in the "Translators' Foreword," in *Contributions*, pp. xix–xxii.

9. Emad and Maly seem to ignore this point, saying only that "We found a good approximation to *Ereignis* in the word *enowning*" (ibid., p. xx).

10. The strategy that Emad and Maly employ with respect to "*Ereignis*" is followed throughout their translation of *Contributions* (indeed, one of their reasons for

employing the translation of *"Ereignis"* as "enowning" is that it enables them to translate other terms in a similar fashion and thereby, they claim, better capture the wordplay and associations on which Heidegger draws. The result, however, not unsurprisingly, is a text that often reads as hardly "English" at all. In this respect, the English edition of *Contributions* does exactly what I aim not to do here: rather than opening Heidegger's thought up to an English-speaking audience, it serves to close it off within a isolated and rarified academic readership. From another perspective, it has also confirmed the widespread impression that Heidegger's thought, especially his late thought, is a dense thicket of obscure and impenetrable "mysticism" verging on the nonsensical—see, for instance, Simon Blackburn's review of the Emad and Maly translation of *Contributions*, "Enquivering," *New Republic*, October 30, 2000.

11. See Hofstadter, "Introduction," in *Poetry, Language, Thought*, pp. xviii–xxi.

12. Ibid., p. xxi. Various uses of *"Ereignis"* in the essays in *Pathmarks* are rendered by both "event of appropriation" and "event" (compare, for instance, the marginal note on 240[a] and that at 374[a]).

13. See *Off the Beaten Track*, for example, p. 86.

14. See *On Time and Being*, trans. Joan Stambaugh (New York: Harper and Row, 1972), pp. ix–x, 19.

15. A point noted by Hofstadter, *Poetry, Language, Thought*, p. xxii.

16. In this respect, Emad and Maly seem to me to make the crucial mistake of trying to translate *Contributions* in such a way that the translation will itself be sufficient to enable the carrying across of Heidegger's poetic speaking (that the *Contributions* is indeed an attempt to think "more poetically" seems to me to be part of what is implied by Heidegger's own characterization of *Contributions* as an attempt to speak in a "simple manner" as well as the self-evidently idiosyncratic character of the writing as such).

17. *Identity and Difference*, p. 36.

18. Indeed, "happening of belonging" seems to me a much more felicitous phrase than Emad and Maly's "enowning," while capturing much the same meaning (although, admittedly, it does not allow for the same wordplay that Emad and Maly value so highly).

19. See Young, *Heidegger's Later Philosophy*, p. 52—the embedded phrase is one Young takes from Heidegger, *Contributions*, p. 48 (*GA* 65:70). Emad and Maly render it as "removal-unto and charming-moving-unto."

20. See Young, *Heidegger's Philosophy of Art*, p. 107. Young argues that *Contributions* "is actually less fundamental than the later Hölderlin texts. Though it precedes them in the order of writing, their content . . . precedes it in the order of thinking"— Young, *Heidegger's Philosophy of Art*, p. 107n20.

21. This is not to say that the Event, which emerges dramatically in the pages of *Contributions*, is not central to this late thinking, but that the way in which Heidegger's thinking of the Event is developed and articulated, and more specifically, the topological character of that thinking, owes perhaps more (and certainly no less) to the thinking that is undertaken in the Hölderlin lectures than in *Contributions*.

22. *Towards the Definition of Philosophy*, p. 63 (*GA* 56/57:75).

23. "Seminar in Le Thor 1969," p. 41 (*GA* 15:335); see also pp. 46–48 (*GA* 15:344–345).

24. See, for instance, "Letter on 'Humanism,'" p. 243 (*GA* 9:318).

25. See "The End of Philosophy and the Task of Thinking" (first published in French in 1964) p. 69 (*Zur Sache des Denkens*, p. 76): "Insofar as truth is understood in the traditional 'natural' sense as the correspondence of knowledge with beings demonstrated in beings, but also insofar as truth is interpreted as the certainty of the knowledge of Being, *aletheia*, unconcealment in the sense of the opening may not be equated with truth. Rather, *aletheia*, unconcealment thought as opening, first grants the possibility of truth."

26. "The Origin of the Work of Art," pp. 20–21 (*GA* 5:27–29).

27. *Contributions to Philosophy*, p. 218 (*GA* 65:310).

28. The term is also used, in German, to refer to the square formed by the arrangement of walls, outbuildings, and house that makes up the characteristic farmyard.

29. "The Thing," in *Poetry, Language, Thought*, p. 173 (*GA* 7:175).

30. Ibid., p. 173 (*GA* 7:175).

31. Ibid., p. 179 (*GA* 7:180).

32. Françoise Dastur suggests that the structure that appears in "The Origin of the Work of Art" already contains all the elements present in the fourfold that appears in "The Thing." Dastur writes: "All the dimensions of the Fourfold are already present in 1935 except the sky. But we can perhaps consider that what is called in 1935 'earth' and which is understood as 'the whole' (*das Ganze*) and linked to the Greek *Physis*, i.e., to the emerging and coming into light of everything, possesses a lighted side that will later be called sky"—"Heidegger's Freiburg Version of the Origin of the Work of Art," in Risser (ed.), *Heidegger: Towards the Turning*, p. 141n21. The suggestion is not without interest, but it seems completely to neglect the way in which world seems to be understood in 1935–1936 as the lighted realm in contrast with earth (a point that also seems confirmed by the analysis of the way earth emerges as an issue in relation to world out of the considerations that preoccupy Heidegger in the late 1920s. Earth itself stands in an essential relation to the lighted realm, and is indeed to be understood in relation to nature as *physis*, but it seems mistaken to argue that earth already includes sky within it.

33. "The Thing," p. 166 (*GA* 7:167–168).

34. Ibid., p. 166 (*GA* 7:168).

35. Ibid., p. 180 (*GA* 7:181).

36. Ibid., p. 181 (*GA* 7:182).

37. Ibid., p. 180 (*GA* 7:181–182).

38. See, for instance, *Ontology—The Hermeneutics of Facticity*, p. 72 (*GA* 63:94–95).

39. John van Buren, however, sees a major contrast between Heidegger's early and later thinking precisely in terms of the way the ordinary and the everyday figures here—see John van Buren, *The Young Heidegger*, p. 314. I would suggest that it is not that the later thinking emphasizes the extraordinary experience, while the early thinking emphasizes the ordinary, but that the early directs attention to the ordinariness of the extraordinary happening of world, while the later thinking aims to bring out the extraordinariness of the happening of world even in the most ordinary. This is a point to which I shall return in chapter 6.

40. "The Thing," p. 166 (*GA* 7:168).

41. Ibid., p. 168 (*GA* 7:170).

42. It is worth noting the contrast between Heidegger's talk of containment here and that present in sec. 12 of *Being and Time*. Here the containing that is part of the essence of the jug is closely tied to the character of the jug as giving what is within to that which is without. The way in which the inner/outer distinction figures here suggests that the distinction cannot be construed simply in terms of a distinction that belongs only to "objective" spatiality.

43. "The Thing," pp. 172–173 (*GA* 7:174–175).

44. Ibid., p. 174 (*GA* 7:175). Hofstadter has "a single time-space, a single stay."

45. Ibid.

46. *Ontology—The Hermeneutics of Facticity*, p. 24 (*GA* 63:29). Translation modified.

47. "Building Dwelling Thinking," pp. 152–153 (*GA* 7:154–155).

48. Ibid., p. 152 (*GA* 7:154–155). Thus, although Heidegger may have a particular bridge in mind for some of his discussion ("If all of us now think, from where we are right here, of the old bridge in Heidelberg . . ."), his account is clearly not restricted to any instance or type of bridge.

49. "Der Feldweg," in *Aus der Erfahrung des Denkens, Gesamtausgabe* 13, p. 88.

50. Tim Ingold, "The Temporality of the Landscape," in *The Perception of the Environment: Essays on Livelihood, Dwelling, and Skill* (London: Routledge, 2000), p. 204.

51. Ingold, "The Temporality of the Landscape," p. 206.

52. In his discussion of Trakl's poem, "A Winter Evening," in the essay "Language," Heidegger also talks of the prevailing of the fourfold in the "golden-blossoming tree" that figures in Trakl's poem—see "Language," in *Poetry, Language, Thought*, p. 201 (*GA* 12:21). Although it belongs to a period in which the idea of the Fourfold has still to be properly developed, Heidegger's discussion, in his 1934–1935 lectures on Hölderlin's "Germania" and "The Rhine," of the way the river founds a dwelling place may be thought to provide a further example of the way a natural being may gather: "The river now founds in the land a characterized space and a delimited place [*Ort*] of settlement, of communication, for the people a cultivable land that guarantees their immediate being-there. The river is not a watercourse which passes by the place of men, it is its streaming, as making a land, which founds the possibility of establishing the dwelling of men"—*Hölderlin's "Germania" and "Der Rhein,"* *Gesamtausgabe* 39, p. 264.

53. Our forgetting of the dependence on the "natural" even of such a made material as plastic can be seen to be one reason for our profligate use of such a material.

54. This sense of nature as already underlying manufacture could be taken to be implied by Heidegger's account of the four causes in "The Question Concerning Technology," in which he presents the efficient cause as that which operates always in relation to the other causes. See *"The Question Concerning Technology" and Other Essays*, trans. William Lovitt (New York: Harper and Row, 1977), pp. 6–11 (*GA* 7:9–13).

55. See *Being and Time* (*GA* 2), H226–227: " 'There is' truth only insofar as Dasein is and so long as Dasein is."

56. The implication of the gods with nature should not be taken immediately to imply that natural science must somehow be connected with theology. If nature cannot be understood independently of the gods, just as it cannot be understood independently of the human, this is not because the divinities must somehow be included in scientific discourse and practice—as if we would have to make room for divine intervention, miracles, and accounts of the nature of angelic substance in our physical theory. Indeed, one of the ways in which the gods may be said to be implicated here is through the way in which scientific study of nature may actually require the setting aside of the gods, just as it will also require the setting aside of aspects of the human. Such a setting aside may be viewed as an essential part of scientific practice. At the same time, however, the gods will have a role in the structure that underpins scientific practice, as it underpins all being in the world, and in the same way that the human has such a role, that is, through being an element in the happening of world within which even the scientist is placed. This leaves open the question as to exactly how the role of the gods within the fourfold should be understood (for more on this see sec. 5.3), but it should already be quite clear that the role they play is not that of entities who enter into the natural

role to intervene or act within it. Instead, as I note above, the gods belong to the same "axis" within the fourfold as the mortals, the gods are the "immortals," and as such they embody the character of the world as it can be seen in terms of certain unified aspects, and as it has a meaningfulness that goes beyond any individual mortal life.

57. The thing can be said to have a location, but only once we step back from the way in which the thing functions in gathering a world, that is, from the way it "things," and instead see the thing simply as something located with respect to other similarly located things within a larger order of such locations. When we do this, we may well find that the analysis Heidegger gives of equipmentality in *Being and Time* will be applicable, where it is the thing as ready-to-hand tool that is at issue, as may be the analysis that would follow from the application of a purely "spatial" understanding in which the thing is construed as a present-at-hand "object." Understood in its character as a thing that "things," however, and so gathers the fourfold, the thing *is* a place—as Heidegger makes clear in "Building Dwelling Thinking" (see sec. 5.4).

58. See "The Thing," p. 180 (*GA* 7:182); also "Hölderlin's Earth and Heaven," pp. 196–199 (*GA* 4:172–174).

59. See *Truth and Method*, trans. Joel Weinsheimer and Donald G. Marshall, 2nd rev. ed. (New York: Crossroad, 1992), pp. 101–134; German edition, *Wahrheit und Methode*, 2nd ed. (Tübingen: J. C. B. Mohr, 1965), pp. 97–127.

60. "The Thing," p. 179 (*GA* 7:180–181). In *Donald Davidson and the Mirror of Meaning*, esp. p. 7, I employ a similar image to describe the holistic interrelation of attitudes, and of attitudes and behavior, as these emerge within the structure of interpretation. The image is a particularly useful one as it captures the key element in such holism, namely, the way in which a properly holistic structure is one that is purely relational—as such, the elements related cannot be construed as existing independently of the relations between them.

61. Such a shift is characteristic of what occurs when holism is taken as a feature merely of the epistemology of some domain. Understanding the structure of the domain may thus require the articulation of a set of relations between elements, but that holistic mode of proceeding finally resolves into an understanding of the elements that can then be taken in themselves.

62. "The End of Philosophy and the Task of Thinking," pp. 65–66 (*Zur Sache des Denkens*, pp. 72–73).

63. See Heidegger, *Basic Questions of Philosophy*, p. 159 (*GA* 45:184–185).

64. "Seminar in Le Thor 1969," p. 38 (*GA* 15:331).

65. See *Basic Questions of Philosophy*, pp. 147–148 (*GA* 45:170–171).

66. One may be tempted to talk of what is at issue here in terms of "transcendence." I have avoided the use of this particular term here simply because it could all too easily be confused with the sense of "transcendence" that was the focus for much of my discussion in chapter 4—the sense of "transcendence" that is tied, in Heidegger's thinking, to the idea of the transcendental and that he abandons in the early to mid-1930s.

67. "The Thing," p. 165 (*GA* 7:167).

68. *Parmenides*, p. 156 (54:232–233). In a letter from 1963, Heidegger seems to confirm the possible connection suggested here between space and the open, writing of the way in which "I regard space and spatiality as very important—because from here the phenomenon of the world can be elucidated in connection with openness [*Offenheit*]"—Letter to Medard Boss, March 20, 1963, in *Zollikon Seminars*, pp. 260–261 (*Zollikoner Seminare*, p. 326). In one of the seminars with Boss, he asks "Are space and clearing identical, or does one presuppose the other? . . . Now, that cannot be decided yet"—*Zollikon Seminars* (July 6, 1964), p. 14 (*Zollikoner Seminare*, p. 17).

69. *Parmenides*, p. 149 (*GA* 54:221).

70. Ibid. (*GA* 54:222).

71. "Building Dwelling Thinking," p. 155 (*GA* 7:157–158). Hofstadter's translation, as I indicated in an earlier note, has "*Ort*" as "location" and "*Platz*" as place. This seems to me to be exactly the reverse of what it should be ("place" being the richer and more basic term in English when compared to "location") and, consequently, I have rendered "*Ort*" as "place" and "*Platz*" as "location." I have followed this same practice in all those passages from Heidegger's work that involve these terms, and, where those passages are taken from existing translations, have adjusted the translation accordingly.

72. "Art and Space," p. 6 (*GA* 13:208).

73. "Building Dwelling Thinking," p. 154 (*GA* 7:156).

74. *Basic Concepts*, p. 41 (*GA* 51:47).

75. Ibid. (*GA* 51:48).

76. It is notable that as soon as one attempts to articulate the structure of the sort of "orientational field" that characterizes active spatiality, one immediately draws upon orientational features that are themselves tied to the differentiation of earth from sky. If any sort of concreteness is to be attached to the basic structures of up and down, left and right, front and back, periphery and center (and they are otherwise nothing but abstract constructs), one will inevitably find that that those structures are constituted in terms of earth and sky or some analogue thereof—they will also, of course, be constituted topologically.

77. "...Poetically Man Dwells...," *Poetry, Language, Thought,* p. 220 (*GA* 7:198–199). See also the comment in "Letter on 'Humanism,'" p. 254 (164): "in the determination of the humanity of the human being as ek-sistence what is essential is not the human being but being—as the dimension of the ek-stasis. However, the dimension is not something spatial in the familiar sense. Rather, everything spatial and all time-space occur essentially in the dimensionality that being itself is."

78. *Zollikon Seminars,* p. 8 (*Zollikoner Seminare,* p. 9).

79. "Art and Space," p. 5 (*GA* 13:206–207).

80. Heidegger describes the seminar in which the discussion figures as "rather a failure," *Zollikon Seminars,* p. 17 (*Zollikoner Seminare,* p. 20).

81. See *Zollikon Seminars,* "July 6, 1964," pp. 8–17 (*Zollikoner Seminare,* pp. 10–20).

82. *Zollikon Seminars,* p. 14 (*Zollikoner Seminare,* p. 16).

83. Heidegger, "Art and Space," p. 4 (*GA* 13:208).

84. See *What is a Thing?* pp. 16–17 (*GA* 41:16–17); see also "Time and Being," pp. 14ff. (*Zur Sache des Denkens,* pp. 14ff.).

85. This point has to be treated with some care, however, since there is also a sense in which exactly the opposite also holds—space gathers what time separates. To some extent, it is the latter that is the focus for the Proustian "experiment" of *A la recherche du temps perdu.* In that work, as Georges Poulet argues, it is the loss of self in time that Proust aims to overcome through the bringing of things together in space—see Poulet, *Proustian Space* (Baltimore: Johns Hopkins University Press, 1977)—although I would suggest that it is not strictly space that unifies here, but rather place. In this respect, what Proust attempts is the overcoming of the separation of time and space (itself a characteristic feature of the experience of modernity) through their "reuniting" (which is also a reuniting of Proust's narrator with himself) in place. I go some way toward setting out this reading of Proust and the reinterpretation of the relation between time and space as they relate to place in chapters 6 and 7 of *Place and Experience,* pp. 157ff.

86. The argument to this conclusion can be seen as at the core of the "Refutation of Idealism" in the B Edition of the *Critique of Pure Reason,* but the idea also appears elsewhere in Kant's writings. On the general point at issue here, see *Place and Experience,* chap. 5, and esp. pp. 114–117.

87. See *Individuals: An Essay in Descriptive Metaphysics* (London: Macmillan, 1959), esp. chap. 2.

88. See, for instance, the essays in Naomi Eilan, Rosaleen McCarthy, and Bill Brewer (eds.), *Spatial Representation* (Oxford: Blackwell, 1993).

89. *Parmenides,* p. 117 (*GA* 54:174).

90. "Letter on 'Humanism,'" p. 276 (GA 9:364).

91. Ibid., pp. 248–249 (GA 9:326); see also Heidegger's discussion in "The Nature of Language" and "On the Way to Language," in On the Way to Language (GA 12).

92. "Language," in Poetry, Language, Thought, pp. 202–203, 210 (GA 12:22–23, 30).

93. "Why Poets?" in Off the Beaten Track, p. 232–233 (GA 5:310–311).

94. In The Body in the Mind (Chicago: University of Chicago Press, 1987), Mark Johnson argues that spatial and bodily images are indeed fundamental to thought. I would prefer to say that all thinking involves what might be termed "spatialization" inasmuch as spatiality is that which enables differentiation, although such spatialization also makes essential reference to the temporal—differentiation is always a differ-ing, and is hence something worked out dynamically, while it is also a unifying.

95. "Letter on 'Humanism,'" p. 272 (GA 9:358).

96. Thus Heidegger expresses the hope that "one day we will, by thinking the essence of being in a way appropriate to its matter, more readily be able to think what 'house' and 'dwelling' are"—"Letter on 'Humanism,'" p. 272 (GA 9:358).

97. Heidegger, "Hebel—Friend of the House," trans. Bruce V. Foltz and Michael Heim, in Contemporary German Philosophy 3 (1983), 100–101 (GA 13:150).

98. Wordsworth's Lyrical Ballads contains a series of "Poems on the Naming of Places"—see Wordsworth: Poetry and Prose (London: Rupert Hart-Davis, 1955), pp. 186–208, which includes one of his most famous poems, "Michael."

99. Since Heidegger is not advancing a philosophy of language, his emphasis on the word should not be taken to imply any prioritization, in the context of semantics, of the singular term over the statement (moreover, "Wort" in German can mean "word," "phrase," or "saying"). Indeed, Heidegger does not think of the word as an isolated linguistic component but only as something that speaks—in this respect, his focus on the word as it operates in such a "gathering" might be taken to imply a focus on the word as it figures in "statements" were it not for the fact that this would put much too much of a "semantic" gloss on what is actually at issue here.

100. See Basic Concepts, p. 41 (GA 51:47), in which Heidegger talks of the way we have "our domain of residence" in the distinction between being and beings.

101. Why should the "unhomely" in the sense of the "unheimlich" be "uncanny"? From the point of view of language, the original idea of the "uncanny" is precisely that which lies outside of our "ken"—that is, outside of that which is familiar to us. One might also say that the uncanny is that which lies outside of our knowledge, especially since there is also a sense of "knowledge" as that "locality" in which we are at home—a usage that I have elsewhere noted as appearing in the work of John Clare, see Place and Experience, p. 189–190.

102. "Building Dwelling Thinking," pp. 146–147 (*GA* 7:148–149). It is worth emphasizing again, as I did in chapter 1, that the sorts of etymological considerations
Heidegger brings forth here are not to be construed as providing *arguments* for the
analyses he proposes. Rather those considerations are intended to reveal connections we might otherwise not have seen—to function as reminders of what lies
hidden in the original experience of language, of world, and of dwelling as such.

103. Ibid., pp. 148–149 (*GA* 7:150).

104. Ibid., pp. 156–157 (*GA* 7:158–160).

105. *Being and Time* (*GA* 2), H54—see the discussion in sec. 3.2 above.

106. "On the Essence of Truth," p. 144 (*GA* 9:188).

107. "Building Dwelling Thinking," p. 149 (*GA* 7:151)—Hofstadter's "sparing and
preserving" is his translation of what appears in Heidegger's German as *"schönen,"*
which carries both of these senses of sparing and preserving.

108. Ibid., p. 151 (*GA* 7:153).

109. *Being and Time*, H54—here "dwelling" as "looking after" seems to refer us to
the notion of "care" (*Sorge*) that appears later in the analysis of *Being and Time*.

110. "On the Essence of Truth," p. 144 (*GA* 9:188). That "letting be" does not mean
"disengagement from" is also an important idea in the notion of *"Gelassenheit"*
(releasement) that Heidegger proposes as the proper mode of comportment toward
technology—see sec. 5.5.

111. See, for instance, "On the Question of Being," pp. 318–319 (*GA* 9:249–250).

112. See *Basic Questions of Philosophy*, pp. 135ff. (*GA* 45:155ff.)—Heidegger refers
here, and throughout his discussion, to *"thaumazein,"* the verb form, rather than
the noun, *"thauma."*

113. See Young, *Heidegger's Later Philosophy*, pp. 63ff.

114. See "Building Dwelling Thinking," p. 159 (*GA* 7:161); see also "The Question
Concerning Technology," in *"The Question Concerning Technology"* and Other
Essays, trans. William Lovitt (NewYork: Harper and Row, 1977), pp. 12–14 (*GA*
13:13–15).

115. See "Building Dwelling Thinking," p. 159 (*GA* 7:162).

116. Ibid., p. 160 (*GA* 7:162).

117. "The Thing," pp. 178–179 (*GA* 7:180).

118. Fell, "Heidegger's Mortals and Gods," p. 32.

119. *Parmenides*, p. 111 (*GA* 54:164).

120. Otto, *The Homeric Gods*, trans. Moses Hadas (London: Thames and Hudson, 1954); originally published in German as *Die Götter Griechenlands; das Bild des Göttlichen im Spiegel des griechischen Geistes* (Bonn: F. Cohen, 1929).

121. Otto, *The Homeric Gods*, p. 161.

122. See "The Thing," p. 178 (*GA* 7:180): "The divinities are the beckoning messengers of the godhead"—see also Julian Young's discussion in *Heidegger's Later Philosophy*, pp. 94–98.

123. See "As When on a Holiday . . . ," in *Elucidations of Hölderlin's Poetry*, p. 85 (*GA* 4:63).

124. "Remembrance," pp. 126–128 (*GA* 4:103–105).

125. "The Relevance of the Beautiful," in *The Relevance of the Beautiful and Other Essays*, trans. Robert Bernasconi (Cambridge: Cambridge University Press, 1986), pp. 40–42.

126. For more on the character and role of the holiday, see Young, *Heidegger's Later Philosophy*, pp. 55–62; it also receives attention in Phillips, *Heidegger's Volk*, pp. 165–166.

127. "Letter on 'Humanism,'" p. 269 (*GA* 9:354–355).

128. See " . . . Poetically Man Dwells . . . ," pp. 222–227 (*GA* 7:201–206).

129. "Building Dwelling Thinking," pp. 158–159 (*GA* 7:161).

130. "Letter on 'Humanism,'" p. 271 (*GA* 9:356).

131. Ibid., p. 271 (*GA* 9:357).

132. See *Bremer und Freiburger Vorträge* (1949–1957), ed. Petra Jaeger, *Gesamtausgabe* 79 (Frankfurt: Klostermann, 1994).

133. The latter two are both included in *"The Question Concerning Technology" and Other Essays*. Heidegger's thinking on technology is spread across many works, but in addition to "The Thing," "The Question Concerning Technology," and "The Turning," the latter two both included in *"The Question Concerning Technology" and Other Essays*, the most important are perhaps "The Age of the World Picture" (1938), and "Why Poets?" (1946), both of which are included in *Off the Beaten Track*, and also "On the Question of Being" (1955), included in *Pathmarks*.

134. "The Thing," p. 165 (*GA* 7:167). It is useful to compare this passage with what Heidegger says about much the same phenomenon in *Being and Time* (*GA* 2), H105: "In Dasein there lies an essential tendency to closeness. All the ways in which we speed things up, as we are more or less compelled to do today, push us on towards the conquest of remoteness. With the 'radio,' for example, Dasein has so expanded its everyday environment that it has accomplished a de-severance [*Entfernung*] of

the 'world'—a de-severance [*Entfernung*] which, in its meaning for Dasein, cannot yet be visualized."

135. "The Thing," p. 166 (*GA* 7:167–168).

136. Jerzy Kosinski, *Being There* (New York: Harcourt Brace Jovanovich, 1971), p. 5. In many respects, this story, and the Peter Sellers film based on it, can be read as a fable concerning the character of modern technology.

137. "The Thing," p. 181 (*GA* 7:183).

138. The phrase "a desolate time" is used by Heidegger in "Why Poets?" in *Off the Beaten Track*, pp. 200ff. (5:269ff.), and is taken from Hölderlin's elegy "Bread and Wine," providing the guiding question for the essay as a whole: "and why poets in a desolate time?"

139. "On the Question of Being," pp. 306ff. (*GA* 9:405ff.).

140. Ibid., p. 319 (*GA* 9:422).

141. Ibid., p. 313 (*GA* 9:414).

142. In "Letter on 'Humanism,'" p. 265 (*GA* 9:349), Heidegger writes that "precisely through the characterization of something as 'a value' what is so valued is robbed of its worth." See also the discussion in *Introduction to Metaphysics*, pp. 213–214 (*GA* 40:207–208).

143. *Basic Questions of Philosophy*, p. 13 (*GA* 45:13).

144. Julian Young characterizes the destitution of the contemporary world in terms of the loss of the gods (which also means loss of community), inability to "own" death, and the "violence" of modern technology (these latter two, Young says, are both aspects of the loss of being at home in the world)—see Young, *Heidegger's Later Philosophy*, pp. 32–34. I take the loss of the gods and the inability to own death as both aspects of "homelessness" and as underlaid by the dominance of that "violent" mode of disclosedness that is evident in technology, which is itself, of course, tied to metaphysical nihilism.

145. "The Question Concerning Technology."

146. Many of these features have been seen, of course, as hallmarks of the various forms of neo-liberalism that have been so dominant within both the public and private sectors over the last two decades. Yet it is not neo-liberal thinking that is at issue here, but rather a mode of revealing that, while it may be expressed in political ideology, is no mere "ideology" as such. Indeed, many of these features are no longer seen as being associated with any particular political orientation, but have become part of the way in which the contemporary world understands itself. Indeed, why would one oppose such obvious commonsense notions as the need for greater "rationality" in decision making or improved efficiency in organizations?

Heidegger's answer is not that one should not be concerned about such things, but that one should be concerned in a way that also understands the way in which such concerns are themselves grounded, and so the limits within which those concerns are properly set. The dominance of the technological consists, in large part, in the inability for the question of such a grounding, or of the question of boundedness that comes with it, to appear *as a question*.

147. "The Question Concerning Technology," p. 17 (*GA* 7:17).

148. "Why Poets?," p. 219 (*GA* 5:292).

149. Heidegger, "The Question Concerning Technology," p. 18 (*GA* 7:18). Heidegger also emphasizes that the technological is "no merely human doing" ("The Question Concerning Technology," p. 19 [*GA* 7:20]).

150. "Seminar in Le Thor 1969," p. 61 (*GA* 15:367–368). Translation modified.

151. Clauss, "Racial Soul, Landscape, and World Domination," p. 73, taken from Clauss, *Die nordische Seele*, pp. 30–32.

152. Clauss, "Racial Soul, Landscape, and World Domination," p. 73; Clauss, *Die nordische Seele*, p. 30.

153. Clauss, "Racial Soul, Landscape, and World Domination," p. 75; Clauss, *Die nordische Seele*, p. 32.

154. For Clauss, the early Greeks seem to represent a "southern" variety of Nordic man (the Greek is thus subsidiary to the "Nordic"); for Heidegger, German culture, on the other hand, as well as European or Western culture as such, is fundamentally Greek.

155. See, for instance, Heidegger's comments in the 1946 essay "Why Poets?," p. 218 (*GA* 5:291). Heidegger's anti-Americanism is undoubtedly strongest during the 1930s and 1940s—Kisiel provides a list of anti-American references in Heidegger's work, noting that "the abuse intensifies with America's entry into the war and ebbs when Heidegger meets native Americans fluent in German and in his philosophy such as Glenn Gray" ("Heidegger's Philosophical Geopolitics in the Third Reich," in Richard Polt and Gregory Fried (eds.), *A Companion to Heidegger's "Introduction to Metaphysics"* [New Haven: Yale University Press, 2001], pp. 326–327n31). Such anti-Americanism is commonly noted as one of those objectionable elements in Heidegger's writing that reflects his provincialism, "Germano-centrism," or else "Euro-centrism." There can be no doubt of the objectionable character of much of Heidegger's anti-Americanism—it often shows quite clearly the way in which Heidegger was apparently unable to think beyond his own German loyalties. At the same time, however, the political, military, economic, and cultural dominance of the United States in the contemporary world (and it is significant that "America" does not mean the American continent as such, but rather a particular part of the political configuration of that continent), as well as the manner in which that dom-

inance seems to be accompanied by an inability on the part of many of the United States' leaders and citizens to distinguish between the interests of the United States and the interests of the rest of the world, is indicative of the problematic position of the United States in the contemporary world today—albeit, perhaps, something more evident to those outside the United States than within it. Not all forms of anti-Americanism, then, should be viewed as based in mere prejudice alone.

156. As Julian Young points out, Heidegger's critique of technology picks up on elements more broadly present as part of what has been called the "conservative revolution" in German thought and that is evident in the work of Jünger and Ludwig Klages, as well as Heidegger, prior to the 1940s. Young cites Michael Grossheim's *Ökologie oder Technokratie?* (Berlin: Duncker und Humblot, 1995) as providing an excellent account of this development, while Jeffery Herf's *Reactionary Modernism: Technology, Culture, and Politics in Weimar and the Third Reich* (Cambridge: Cambridge University Press, 1984) is also relevant. Other figures who contributed to the prewar focus on technology include Ernst Cassirer, "Form und Technik" (1930), in Ernst Cassirer, *Symbol, Technik, Sprache* (Hamburg: Meiner, 1985) and Friedrich Dessauer, *Philosophie der Technik* (Bonn: Cohen, 1927). The idea of a "philosophy of technology" appears much earlier, however, in the work of Ernst Kapp, *Grundlinien einer Philosophie der Technik* (Braunschweig: Westermann, 1877). Heidegger's critique of technology also has analogues, of course, in Weber (particularly the concept of "rationalization") and Adorno.

157. *Introduction to Metaphysics*, p. 213 (*GA* 40:208).

158. See Heidegger, "Letter to the Rector of Freiburg University, November 4, 1945," in Wolin (ed.), *The Heidegger Controversy*, p. 65 (*GA* 16:402—note that the English has Heidegger's Nietzsche lectures extending up to 1945, not 1943 as in the German).

159. Jeffrey Herf, for example, has famously argued for a view of Nazism as itself a form of modernism in *Reactionary Modernism*, while Michael Allen Thad presents an account of the melding of ideological commitment with modern organizational techniques within the SS in *The Business of Genocide: the SS, Slave Labor, and the Concentration Camps* (Chapel Hill: University of North Carolina Press, 2002). There is, of course, an influential line of argument stemming from Theodor Adorno and Max Horkheimer's *Dialectic of Enlightenment*, ed. Gunzelin Schmid Noerr, trans. Edmund Jephcott (Stanford: Stanford University Press, 2002) that sees Nazism as itself a product of the Enlightenment, and so as "modernist" in a different sense to that employed by Herf or Thad.

160. The passage (which includes the further line: "the same as the starving of nations, the same as the manufacture of hydrogen bombs") comes from the text of "The Question Concerning Technology" that was delivered as a lecture in December 1949, but which was later revised to the form that was actually published (retaining only the claim that "agriculture is now a motorized food-industry"). The passage

is cited in many places, but first appeared in Wolfgang Schirmacher, *Technik und Gelassenheit* (Freiburg: Alber, 1983), p. 25.

161. One of the lessons of the Holocaust, however, is surely that human evil persists even in the face of technological progress, and that such progress may itself amplify the capacity to do evil. Moreover, our own confidence in such progress, our own confidence in technology, may serve to obscure such persistence and may also enable the appearance of evil in ways we had not previously envisaged or encountered. In this latter respect, the way in which technology can serve to "distance" us from our engagement in the world, and so from the persons and things with whom we engage, plays a particularly important role.

162. It seems to me that there is a sense in which Heidegger's reading of Nazism in this way, particularly his reading in the postwar period, was a consequence of his own attempt to come to terms with what had happened in the 1930s and 1940s, both in terms of his personal involvement and the involvement of Germany as a whole. I am not suggesting that this was Heidegger's attempt to excuse himself or Germany from blame by demonstrating that what was at issue here was a movement of "world-history" rather than merely of German history or of personal biography, but that Heidegger may well have been incapable of making sense of what occurred in the 1930s and 1940s in any other way. Here what becomes evident, I would suggest, is the way in which even great thinkers can be hampered and blinded by the personal and historical situatedness that also enables their thought. There are, however, many commentators who take a very different view of the matter.

163. Indeed, Joseph Fell argues that the relation between Heidegger and Nietzsche can be understood in terms of the relation between the Framework (*Gestell*) and the fourfold (*Geviert*): "There is an important sense in which the Nietzsche/Heidegger relation can be read as representing the Ge-stell/Geviert relation. As the Fourfold is disclosed by a converting or re-tuning (*Um-stimmung*) of the Com-position (*Ge-stell*), so the thinking of Heidegger comes to pass from a retrieve by Heidegger of the relation of mortals to gods in the thought of Nietzsche"—Joseph Fell, "Heidegger's Mortals and Gods," p. 36. Fell thus gives a central role to Nietzsche's proclamation of the death of God as that which requires a retrieval of the holy.

164. See "Nietzsche's Word 'God Is Dead,'" in *Off the Beaten Track*, p. 178 (*GA* 5:239); also pp. 169–193.

165. Ibid., pp. 192–193 (*GA* 5:258).

166. Ibid., p. 196 (*GA* 5:263).

167. Ibid., p. 191 (*GA* 5:256).

168. "On the Question of Being," p. 321 (*GA* 9:424)—Heidegger adds "This is no war, but the Πόλεμος that first lets gods and humans, freemen and slaves, appear in their respective essence and leads to a critical encounter of Being. Compared to

this encounter, world wars remain superficial. They are less and less capable of decid-
ing anything the more technological their armaments." See also "Nietzsche's Word
'God Is Dead,'" p. 191 (*GA* 5:256).

169. See "On the Question of Being," p. 299 (*GA* 9:396). In his response to Ernst
Jünger in this essay, Heidegger quotes from a note he wrote during 1939–1940:
"Jünger's text *The Worker* is important because, in a different way from Spengler, it
achieves what all Nietzsche literature thus far has been unable to achieve, namely,
to impart an experience of beings and the way in which they are, in the light of
Nietzsche's projection of beings as will to power." And a few lines after this quotation, Heidegger says of "The Question Concerning Technology" that it "owes a
lasting debt to the descriptions in *The Worker*"—"On the Question of Being," p. 295
(*GA* 9:391).

170. Much of Heidegger's reading of Nietzsche depends on his use of this work—a
work then taken to be a legitimate part of Nietzsche's corpus, but actually a volume
constructed by Nietzsche's sister from fragments and unpublished writings in a
heavily edited form.

171. *Basic Concepts*, pp. 32–33 (*GA* 51:36–37).

172. "Letter on 'Humanism,'" p. 259 (*GA* 9:340).

173. "Building Dwelling Thinking," p. 159 (*GA* 7:161). Heidegger also emphasizes
here the character of building as always a "letting dwell."

174. See Julian Young, *Heidegger's Later Philosophy*, pp. 47–48. While it is certainly
true that work is essential to human being, it is important to recognize the possibility of different "modes" of work within which human being may be taken up.

175. Arendt, *The Human Condition* (Chicago: Chicago University Press, 1958),
pp. 126–127.

176. Albert Borgmann, *Technology and the Character of Contemporary Life* (Chicago:
University of Chicago Press, 1984), p. 125.

177. Martin Jacques, "The Death of Intimacy," *Guardian*, Saturday, September 18,
2004, p. 17. Jacques's analysis argues that the rise of "self" as the "dominant interest," "the relentless spread of the market into every part of society," and the rise of
communication technologies are eroding the "very idea of what it means to be
human." Jacques sees the erosion at issue here as evident in a wide range of phenomena from the loss of intimacy in relationships to a loss of any real encounter
with death. Jacques's analysis thus picks out many of the features to which
Heidegger's critique of technological modernity also draws attention.

178. The line of argument developed here is something explored further in my "The
Dualities of Work: Self-Creation and Self-Consumption," *Philosophy Today* 49 (2005),
256–263.

179. "The Question Concerning Technology," p. 33 (*GA* 7:34)—here, as elsewhere, I have translated *"Bestand"* as "resource" rather than Lovitt's "standing reserve."

180. "Building Dwelling Thinking," p. 152 (*GA* 7:155).

181. "Seminar in Le Thor 1969," p. 60 (*GA* 15:366).

182. "Summary of a Seminar," in *On Time and Being*, p. 53 (*Zur Sache des Denkens*, p. 57). Translation modified. See also "Seminar in Le Thor 1969," p. 60 (*GA* 15:366) and "The Way to Language," pp. 131–132 (*GA* 12:251–252).

183. In "The Question Concerning Technology," p. 22 (*GA* 7:23), Heidegger writes: "All coming to presence, not only modern technology, keeps itself everywhere concealed to the last. Nevertheless, it remains, with respect to its holding sway, that which precedes all: the earliest. The Greek thinkers already knew of this when they said: That which is earlier with regard to the arising that holds sway becomes manifest to us men only later. That which is primally early shows itself only ultimately to men." Here Heidegger is concerned to point out the way the character of any mode of revealing becomes evident only very late in its unfolding. Thus the essence of technology in ordering things as pure resource only comes to light in the extreme manifestation of technology that we see emerging in the contemporary world. This is a slightly different sense in which modes of revealing conceal themselves than the one at issue in my discussion above—my concern is with the way modes of revealing conceal themselves as modes of revealing by "blocking" access to other such modes.

184. The same point could be made using other modes of revealing, for instance, that of the Classical Greeks, of pre-European Maori or indigenous Australian culture, of medieval Islam, or of Classical China. Of course, modern technological revealing has its own origins in Greek culture, and yet, at least from Heidegger's perspective, it is distinct from it. At the time of Classical Greek culture, the essence of technology had not yet been realized, nor had the technological yet emerged as the dominant mode of revealing across the entire world.

185. This is a crucial point since if it really were the case that technology simply did away with place (as many people entranced by the power of modern telecommunications and transportation often seem to think it has), then there would be no basis on which to develop the sort of topological critique of the technological that is to be found in Heidegger. It is precisely because place (and places) remains, in spite of its obscuring by technology, that technological revealing is so problematic. This is a point for which I have argued, though from a rather different perspective, in "Acting at a Distance and Knowing from Afar: Agency and Knowledge on the World Wide Web," in Ken Goldberg (ed.), *The Robot in the Garden* (Cambridge, Mass.: MIT Press, 2000), pp. 108–125. The problematic nature of place within technological modernity is indicated by the character of locations such as the shopping mall and the airport—referred to by Marc Augé as "non-places" (see Augé, *Non-Places: Introduction to an Anthropology of Supermodernity*, trans. John Howe

[London: Verso, 1995])—both of which seem to be paradigmatic of the "placeless places" that characterize so much of the contemporary world.

186. One might argue that there are limits that have become apparent within physics, notably in respect of the very large (events on a cosmological scale) and the very small (events on the quantum scale), but the extent to which this constitutes the same sort of "unfathomability" and "mystery" that is associated with the revealing given in the world as "holy" is a matter for debate.

187. *Basic Questions of Philosophy*, p. 158 (*GA* 45:183).

188. Ibid., p. 13 (*GA* 45:13).

189. "The Turning," pp. 46–48; see also *Parmenides*, pp. 79–87 (*GA* 54:117–130).

190. See "Seminar in Le Thor 1969," p. 63 (*GA* 15:370).

191. Fell, *Heidegger and Sartre*, p. 204.

192. Alexander Koyré, *From the Closed World to the Infinite Universe* (Baltimore: Johns Hopkins, 1957).

193. See Bergson, *Time and Freewill: An Essay on the Immediate Data of Consciousness*, trans. F. L. Pogson (London: George Allen, 1910).

194. See "The Question Concerning Technology," pp. 21–22 (*GA* 7:25–26).

195. "Seminar in Le Thor 1969," p. 62 (*GA* 15:368–369).

196. The connection, via *"stellen,"* between *"vorstellen"* and *"Gestell"* should not be overlooked here. See also "The Age of the World Picture," in *Off the Beaten Track*, pp. 66–69 (*GA* 5:88–92), for more on the idea of "representation."

197. Meyrovich, "Medium Theory," in David Crowley and David Mitchell (eds.), *Communication Theory Today* (Cambridge: Polity Press, 1994), p. 67. What Meyrovich seems to miss, however, is the way in which the changes wrought by the technological do not affect the basic tie between place and human being, but only the manner in which that appears—and, of course, in the technological world, part of that appearance is such as to hide the connection with place itself.

198. In this respect, Tom Rockmore's objection to the Heideggerian analysis to the effect that Heidegger is mistaken in attributing an "essence" to technology since technology has no essence or, as Rockmore puts it, "There is no technology in general; there are only instantiations of forms of technology" (see Rockmore—*On Heidegger's Philosophy and Nazism*, pp. 236–237 [see more generally pp. 232–238]), misses a crucial element in Heidegger's analysis (which is not to say that one might not be able to argue against Heidegger on this matter, but that one would need to engage with Heidegger at a more detailed level of argument).

199. Thus the employment of concepts of "efficiency" and "effectiveness" that are so often taken as "neutral" measures of success turn out to be notions that are them-

selves completely dependent on the particular technologies with respect to which they operate. There is no "neutrality" to these notions, and what counts as efficiency within one setting may not count as efficiency in another. Indeed, increases in efficiency have often, though not always, as much to do with shifts in what counts as a *measure* of efficiency as with efficiency as such—this is all the more so when the systems whose efficiency is at issue are those that rely heavily on human interaction, for instance, in education and in most office and service-based activities.

200. For such a total ordering to be realized would also be for the image of the world as pure spatialized, measurable, extendedness to be realized—such a realization would entail, not merely the obscuring, but the obliteration, of all sense of place, and so too the complete blocking off of the Event in its self-disclosive character.

201. On the general issue of failure and the technological, see Jeff Malpas and Gary Wickham, "Governance and the World: From Joe DiMaggio to Michel Foucault," *The UTS Review* 3 (1997), 91–108.

202. Albert Camus, "Helen's Exile," in *Lyrical and Critical Essays*, ed. Philip Thody, trans. Ellen Conroy Kennedy (Vintage, n.p., n.d.), pp. 148–149 and 153.

203. In Albert Camus, *Lyrical and Critical Essays*, p. 69.

204. *Identity and Difference*, p. 33.

205. "The Turning," in *"The Question Concerning Technology" and Other Essays*, pp. 39–40 (*Die Technik und die Kehre* [Pfullingen: Günther Neske, 1962], p. 39).

206. The theme of release from the domination of technology and technological devices has, somewhat ironically, become a familiar and recurrent theme in contemporary popular culture. Thus Keanu Reeves battles against the domination of the "machines" in *The Matrix*, Arnold Schwarzenegger appears as a machine who is first an enemy and then a defender against a more sophisticated version of his kind, in the *Terminator* movies, and in *I, Robot*, Will Smith fights against a rebellion of the robotic slaves on whom human society has come to rely. Drawing on an older set of ideas and images, *The Lord of the Rings* portrays a battle against what is essentially a mode of technological domination in which the use of a certain all-encompassing technology (the "One Ring") is foresworn precisely of its dominating and transforming power. What is ironic about all of this, of course, is that the theme of the struggle against technological dominance (against "the rule of the machines") becomes a commodity produced and marketed by the very movie industry, and its increasingly diverse offshoots, that is itself a manifestation of the technological ordering of the contemporary world.

207. See "The Question Concerning Technology," pp. 25–26 (*GA* 7:26).

208. "Memorial Address," in *Discourse on Thinking*, trans. John M. Anderson and E. Hans Freund (New York: Harper and Row, 1966), p. 54 ("Gelassenheit," *GA* 16:527).

209. In this respect, Heidegger's own "turning" is a turning away from the intoxi-
cation with the power of a certain form of "technology"—that which appeared in
the form of the National Socialist "Revolution" in 1933. On the shift in Heidegger's
thinking in this respect and especially his attempt to articulate an alternative to
the violence of technological revealing, see Clare Pearson Geiman, "Heidegger's
Antigones," in Richard Polt and Gregory Fried (eds.), *Companion to Heidegger's "Introduction to Metaphysics"* (New Haven: Yale University Press, 2001), pp. 161–182.

210. Although, some caution needs to be exercised here since "democracy" is by no
means a clear or unambiguous term—see Jeff Malpas and Gary Wickham, "Democracy and Instrumentalism," *Australian Journal of Political Science* 33 (1998), pp.
345–362. Indeed, the emphasis on democratic politics as tied to power and as always
contested, limited, dispersed, inevitable, and failing itself tends toward a conception of the democratic that will not allow it to be fixed in any particular political
formation or ideological structure.

211. See Jeffrey C. Isaac, *Arendt, Camus, and Modern Rebellion* (New Haven: Yale University Press, 1992), for an account of both Camus and Arendt as converging on a
"rebellious politics"—a politics of resistance that rejects any form of violence or
ideology and instead speaks in favor of the limited and always negotiatory
character of political life.

212. It should be noted, in fairness to Heidegger (though some might think even
countenancing such a reading to be overly charitable), that one possible interpretation of the skepticism toward democracy expressed in the *Der Spiegel* interview is
to treat it in terms of a skepticism about democracy as a particular ideology—as a
determinate and already understood form of political organization and practice (this
would be to attribute to Heidegger a position that is sensitive to at least some of the
considerations alluded to in n. 209, although arriving at a different conclusion). Of
course, the argument implicit in my approach has been that democracy is itself
founded on a recognition of questionability and limit, and, understood in this way,
democracy seems in accord with a Heideggerian "topology." Yet it might be thought
that one of the important questions at issue here is precisely whether the term
"democracy" is indeed adequate to the conception of the political that emerges out
of such a "topology." My own view, which I take to be the view also, for instance,
of Camus and Arendt, is that it is adequate, but perhaps Heidegger would have
answered that it is not, or, at least, that he was not convinced of its adequacy in
this regard.

Chapter 6

1. "Who Is Nietszche's Zarathustra?" trans B. Magnus, *Review of Metaphysics* 20
(1967), 412 (*GA* 7:102).

2. "Letter on 'Humanism,'" p. 253 (*GA* 9:333).

3. *Parmenides*, p. 149 (*GA* 54:222).

4. Van Buren, *The Young Heidegger*, p. 314.

5. Van Buren seems to be misled, in part, by a failure to distinguish the everyday happening of disclosive gathering in the Event from the disclosure of that happening. The latter typically occurs only in the poetic and the meditative, whereas the former occurs irrespective of the manner of our comportment toward it. That there is indeed an issue concerning the disclosure of the disclosive gathering of the Event, while not absent from early Heidegger, is something that is much clearer and more developed in the later thinking.

6. Thus Crowell writes that "even the later Heidegger does nothing more than seek a way 'back to the things themselves' (Husserl's phenomenological slogan), and, in letting them speak, remains committed to the possibility of phenomenology"— *Husserl, Heidegger, and the Space of Meaning*, p. 221.

7. "Letter on 'Humanism,'" pp. 257–258 (*GA* 9:337–339).

8. *Basic Concepts*, p. 75 (*GA* 51:89).

9. "The Nature of Language," p. 93 (*GA* 12:188).

10. Derrida writes of Heidegger that "the solicitation of the Site and the Land is in no way, it must be emphasized, a passionate attachment to territory or locality, is in no way a provincialism or particularism. . . . The thinking of being is not a pagan cult of the *Site*, because the Site is never a given proximity but a promised one"— Derrida, *Writing and Difference* (Chicago: Chicago University Press, 1978), p. 145. What I think Derrida nevertheless misses here is the way in which what he calls the "Site" is never some abstract "locality," but always the site of our own concrete being. The task, however, is to see that the manner of our "proximity" to that "site" is not such that the site is simply given, but only appears inasmuch as it comes into question, inasmuch as it opens up into questionability, differentiation, multiplicity . . . and into unity.

11. See Heidegger's discussion of this in *Hölderlin's Hymn "The Ister,"* esp. p. 142 (*GA* 53:178): "The poetizing of the locality is the provenance of journeying from the foreign."

12. "The Question of Being," pp. 308–309 (*GA* 9:408–409).

13. See Young *Heidegger's Philosophy of Art*, p. 154.

14. "Seminar in Le Thor 1969," pp. 60–61 (*GA* 15:366).

15. "Summary of a Seminar," p. 43 (*Zur Sachen des Denkens*, p. 46). Translation modified.

16. See especially "On the Question of Being."

17. Heidegger, "Cézanne," *GA* 13, p. 223.

18. A version of which (unfortunately all too far removed from the original) appears on the dust-jacket to *Place and Experience*.

19. *Colin McCahon: A Survey Exhibition*, Auckland City Art Gallery, March–April 1972, p. 19. In many ways McCahon's work can be seen as attempting to uncover the structure of the New Zealand landscape—perhaps, one might say, to find the "fourfold" proper to it. As McCahon said: "I saw something logical, orderly and beautiful belonging to the land but not yet to its people. Not yet understood or communicated, not yet even really invented. My work has largely been to communicate this vision, and to invent the way to see it," McCahon, "Beginnings," *Landfall* 20 (1966), 360. For an introduction to the role of place and landscape in McCahon's work (as well as in that of the Australian artist Rosalie Gascoigne), see *Rosalie Gascoigne—Colin McCahon: Sense of Place* (Sydney: University of New South Wales Press, 1990).

20. James K. Baxter, *Collected Poems* (Melbourne: Oxford University Press, 1981), p. 34.

Select Bibliography

Works by Heidegger

Works in German
Gesamtausgabe (Frankfurt: Klostermann, 1976–).

Vol. 1, *Frühe Schriften* (1912–1916), ed. Friedrich-Wilhelm von Herrmann (1978).

Vol. 2, *Sein und Zeit* (1927), ed. Friedrich-Wilhelm von Herrmann (1977).

Vol. 3, *Kant und das Problem der Metaphysik* (1929—4th ed., 1973) ed. Friedrich-Wilhelm von Herrmann (1991).

Vol. 4, *Erläuterungen zu Hölderlins Dichtung* (1936–1968), ed. Friedrich-Wilhelm von Herrmann (2nd ed., 1996).

Vol. 5, *Holzwege* (1935–1946), ed. Friedrich-Wilhelm von Herrmann (1977).

Vol. 6, *Nietzsche*, 2 vols., ed. Brigitte Schillbach (1996–1997).

Vol. 7, *Vorträge und Aufsätze* (1936–1953), ed. Friedrich-Wilhelm von Herrmann (2000).

Vol. 9, *Wegmarken* (1919–1961), ed. Friedrich-Wilhelm von Herrmann (2nd ed., 1996).

Vol. 10, *Der Satz vom Grund* (1955–1956), ed. Petra Jaeger (1997).

Vol. 12, *Unterwegs zur Sprache* (1950–1959), ed. Friedrich-Wilhelm von Herrmann (1985).

Vol. 13, *Aus der Erfahrung des Denkens* (1910–1976), ed. Hermann Heidegger (1983).

Vol. 15, *Seminare* (1951–1973), ed. Curd Ochwadt (1986).

Vol. 16, *Reden und andere Zeugnisse eines Lebensweges* (1910–1976), ed. Hermann Heidegger (2000).

Vol. 19, *Platon: Sophistes* (Wintersemester 1924–1925), ed. Ingeborg Schüßler (1992).

Vol. 20, *Prolegomena zur Geschichte des Zeitbegriffs* (Sommersemester 1925), ed. Petra Jaeger (1979; 2nd ed., 1988; 3rd ed., 1994).

Vol. 24, *Die Grundprobleme der Phänomenologie* (Sommersemester 1927), ed. Friedrich-Wilhelm von Herrmann (3rd ed., 1997).

Vol. 25, *Phänomenologische Interpretation von Kants Kritik der reinen Vernunft* (Wintersemester 1927–1928), ed. Ingtraud Görland (3rd ed., 1995).

Vol. 26, *Metaphysische Anfangsgründe der Logik im Ausgang von Leibniz* (Sommersemester 1928), ed. Klaus Held (2nd ed., 1990).

Vol. 27, *Einleitung in die Philosophie* (Wintersemester 1928–1929), ed. Otto Saame und Ina Saame-Speidel (2nd ed., 2001).

Vol. 29–30, *Die Grundbegriffe der Metaphysik. Welt—Endlichkeit—Einsamkeit* (Wintersemester 1929–1930), ed. Friedrich-Wilhelm von Herrmann (2nd ed., 1992).

Vol. 39, *Hölderlins Hymnen "Germanien" und "Der Rhein"* (Wintersemester 1934–1935), ed. Suzanne Ziegler (3rd ed., 1999).

Vol. 40, *Einführung in die Metaphysik* (Sommersemester 1935), ed. Petra Jaeger (1983).

Vol. 41, *Die Frage nach dem Ding: Zu Kants Lehre von den transzendentalen Grundsätzen* (Wintersemester 1935–1936), ed. Petra Jaeger (1984).

Vol. 45, *Grundfragen der Philosophie: Ausgewählte "Probleme" der "Logik"* (Wintersemester 1937–1938), ed. Friedrich-Wilhelm von Herrmann (2nd ed., 1992).

Vol. 51, *Grundbegriffe* (Sommersemester 1941), ed. Petra Jaeger (2nd ed., 1991).

Vol. 53, *Hölderlins Hymne "Der Ister"* (Sommersemester 1942), ed. Walter Biemel (2nd ed., 1993).

Vol. 54, *Parmenides* (Wintersemester 1942–1943), ed. Manfred S. Frings (2nd ed., 1992).

Vol. 55, *Heraklit*, ed. Manfred S. Frings (3rd ed., 1994).

Vol. 56–57, *Bestimmung der Philosophie*, ed. Bernd Heimbüchel (2nd ed., 1999).

Vol. 58, *Grundprobleme der Phänomenologie* (Wintersemester 1919–1920), Hans-Helmuth Gander (1992).

Vol. 61, *Phänomenologische Interpretationen zu Aristoteles*, ed. Walter Bröcker und Käte Bröcker-Oltmanns (2nd ed., 1994).

Vol. 63, *Ontologie: Hermeneutik der Faktizität* (Sommersemester 1923), ed. Käte Bröcker-Oltmanns (2nd ed., 1995).

Vol. 64 *Der Begriff der Zeit* (1924), ed. Friedrich-Wilhelm von Herrmann (2004).

Vol. 65, *Beiträge zur Philosophie (Vom Ereignis)* (1936–1938), ed. Friedrich-Wilhelm von Herrmann (2nd ed., 1994).

Vol. 79, *Bremer und Freiburger Vorträge* (1949–1957), ed. Petra Jaeger (1994).

Die Technik und die Kehre (Pfullingen: Güther Neske, 1962).

Zollikoner Seminare, ed. Medard Boss (Frankfurt: Klostermann, 1994).

Zur Sache des Denkens (Tübingen: Max Niemeyer, 1969).

Works in English

"Art and Space," trans. Charles Siebert, *Man and World* 6 (1973), 3–8 (*GA* 13:203–210).

Basic Concepts, trans. Gary E. Aylesworth (Bloomington: Indiana University Press, 1993, *GA* 51.

The Basic Problems of Phenomenology, trans. Albert Hofstadter (Bloomington: Indiana University Press, 1982), *GA* 24.

Basic Questions of Philosophy, trans. Richard Rojcewicz and André Schuwer (Bloomington: Indiana University Press, 1994), *GA* 45.

Being and Time, trans. John Macquarrie and Edward Robinson (New York: Harper and Row, 1962).

Being and Time: A Translation of "Sein und Zeit," trans. Joan Stambaugh (Albany: SUNY Press, 1996).

The Concept of Time, trans. William McNeill (Oxford: Blackwell, 1992) (dual English-German ed.).

Contributions to Philosophy, trans. Parvis Emad and Kenneth Maly (Bloomington: Indiana University Press, 1999), *GA* 65.

Discourse on Thinking, trans. John M. Anderson and E. Hans Freund (New York: Harper and Row, 1966) (*Gelassenheit*).

Elucidations of Hölderlin's Poetry, trans. Keith Hoeller (New York: Humanity Books, 2000), *GA* 4.

The End of Philosophy, trans. Joan Stambaugh (New York: Harper and Row, 1973).

"Foreword" to William J. Richardson, *Heidegger: From Phenomenology to Thought* (The Hague: Mantinus Nijhof, 1963), pp. viii–xxiii (dual English-German text).

Four Seminars, trans. Andrew Mitchell and François Raffoul (Bloomington: Indiana University Press, 2004), *GA* 15.

The Fundamental Concepts of Metaphysics, trans. William McNeill and Nicholas Walker (Bloomington: Indiana University Press, 1995), *GA*, 29–30.

"Hebel—Friend of the House," trans. Bruce V. Foltz and Michael Heim, in *Contemporary German Philosophy* 3 (1983), 89–101 (*GA* 13:133–150).

Heraclitus Seminar (with Eugen Fink), trans. Charles H. Seibert (Evanston: Northwestern University Press, 1993), *GA* 15.

History of the Concept of Time: Prolegomena, trans. Theodore Kisiel (Bloomington: Indiana University Press, 1992), *GA* 20.

Hölderlin's Hymn "The Ister," trans. William McNeill and Julia Davis (Bloomington: Indiana University Press, 1996), *GA* 53.

Identity and Difference, trans. Joan Stambaugh (Chicago: University of Chicago Press, 2002) (dual English-German ed.).

Introduction to Metaphysics, trans. Gregory Fried and Richard Polt (New Haven: Yale University Press, 2000), *GA* 40.

Kant and the Problem of Metaphysics, trans. Richard Taft, 5th ed. (Bloomington: Indiana University Press, 1997), *GA* 3.

The Metaphysical Foundations of Logic, trans. Michael Heim (Bloomington: Indiana University Press, 1984), *GA* 26.

Nietzsche, trans. David Farrell Krell (San Francisco: Harper and Row, 1979–1987), *GA* 6.

Off the Beaten Track, trans. Julian Young and Kenneth Hayes (Cambridge: Cambridge University Press, 2002), *GA* 5.

"Only a God Can Save Us," trans. Maria P. Alter and John D. Caputo in Richard Wolin (ed.), *The Heidegger Controversy: A Critical Reader* (Cambridge, Mass.: MIT Press, 1993), pp. 91–116 (*GA* 16:652–683).

On Time and Being, trans. Joan Stambaugh (New York: Harper and Row, 1972), *Zur Sache des Denkens*.

On the Way to Language, trans. Peter D. Herz (New York: Harper and Row, 1971), *GA* 12.

Ontology—The Hermeneutics of Facticity, trans. John van Buren (Bloomington: Indiana University Press, 1999), *GA* 63.

Parmenides, trans. André Schuwer and Richard Rojcewicz (Bloomington: Indiana University Press, 1992), *GA* 54.

Pathmarks, ed. William McNeill (Cambridge: Cambridge University Press, 1998), *GA* 9.

Phenomenological Interpretations of Aristotle, trans. Richard Rojcewicz (Bloomington: Indiana University Press, 2001), *GA* 61.

Phenomenological Interpretation of Kant's "Critique of Pure Reason," trans. Parvis Emad and Kenneth Maly (Indiana University Press, 1997), *GA* 25.

Plato's "Sophist," trans. Richard Rojcewicz and André Schuwer (Bloomington: Indiana University Press, 1997), *GA* 19.

Poetry, Language, Thought, trans. Albert Hofstadter (New York: Harper and Row, 1971) (includes essays from *GA* 5 and 7).

The Principle of Reason, trans. Reginald Lilly (Bloomington: Indiana University Press, 1996), *GA* 10.

"The Question Concerning Technology" and Other Essays, trans. William Lovitt (New York: Harper and Row, 1977) (includes essays from *GA 7* and *Die Technik und die Kehre*).

Towards the Definition of Philosophy, trans. Ted Sadler (London: Athlone Press, 2000), *GA 56–57*.

What Is a Thing? trans. W. B. Barton, Jr. and Vera Deutsch (Chicago: Henry Regnery, 1967), *GA 41*.

"Who Is Nietszche's Zarathustra?," trans B. Magnus, *Review of Metaphysics* 20 (1967), 411–431 (*GA 7:99–126*).

Zollikon Seminars, ed. Medard Boss, trans. Franz Mayr and Richard Askay (Evanston: Northwestern University Press, 2001) (*Zollikoner Seminare*).

Other Works

Adorno, Theodore, and Max Horkheimer. *Dialectic of Enlightenment*. Ed. Gunzelin Schmid Noerr, trans. Edmund Jephcott (Stanford: Stanford University Press, 2002).

Agamben, Giorgio. *The Open: Man and Animal*. Trans. Kevin Attell (Stanford: Stanford University Press, 2004).

Angelus Silesius. *Cherubinischer Wandersmann* (Bremen: Carl Schünemann, n.d.).

Applegate, Celia. *A Nation of Provincials: The German Idea of Heimat* (Berkeley: University of California Press, 1990).

Arendt, Hannah. *The Human Condition* (Chicago: Chicago University Press, 1958).

Arendt, Hannah. "Martin Heidegger at Eighty." Trans. Albert Hofstadter. In Michael Murray (ed.), *Heidegger and Modern Philosophy* (New Haven: Yale University Press, 1978).

Arisaka, Yoko. "Heidegger's Theory of Space: A Critique of Dreyfus." *Inquiry* 38 (1995), 455–467.

Arisaka, Yoko. "Spatiality, Temporality, and the Problem of Foundation in *Being and Time*." *Philosophy Today* 40 (1996), 36–46.

Aristotle. *Aristotle's Categories and De Interpretatione*. Trans. J. L. Ackrill (Oxford: Clarendon Press, 1963).

Aristotle. *Aristotle's Physics Books III and IV*. Trans. Edward Hussey (Oxford: Clarendon Press, 1983).

Augé, Marc. *Non-Places: Introduction to an Anthropology of Supermodernity*. Trans. John Howe (London: Verso, 1995).

Bambach, Charles. *Heidegger's Roots: Nietzsche, National Socialism, and the Greeks* (Ithaca: Cornell University Press, 2003).

Bassin, Mark. "Race contra Space: The Conflict between German *Geopolitik* and National Socialism." *Political Geography Quarterly* 6 (1987), 115–134.

Basso, Keith H. *Wisdom Sits in Places: Landscape and Language Among the Western Apache* (Albuquerque: University of New Mexico Press, 1996).

Baxter, James K. *Collected Poems* (Melbourne: Oxford University Press, 1981).

Bergson, Henri. *Time and Freewill: An Essay on the Immediate Data of Consciousness.* Trans. F. L. Pogson (London: George Allen, 1910).

Birault, Henri. *Heidegger et l'experience de la pensée* (Paris: Gallimard, 1978).

Blattner, William. *Heidegger's Temporal Idealism* (Cambridge: Cambridge University Press, 1999).

Blickle, Peter. *Heimat: A Critical Theory of the German Idea of Homeland* (Rochester, N.Y.: Camden House, 2002).

Borgmann, Albert. *Technology and the Character of Contemporary Life* (Chicago: University of Chicago Press, 1984).

Bunkse, Edmunds V. "Saint-Exupéry's Geography Lesson: Art and Science in the Creation and Cultivation of Landscape Values." *Annals of American Geographers* 80 (1990), 96–108.

Buttimer, Anne, and David Seamon (eds.). *The Human Experience of Space and Place* (London: Croom Helm, 1980).

Camus, Albert. "Nuptials at Tipasa." In *Lyrical and Critical Essays*, ed. Philip Thody (Vintage, n.p, n.d), pp. 65–72.

Camus, Albert. "Helen's Exile." In *Lyrical and Critical Essays*, pp. 148–153.

Caputo, John D. *The Mystical Element in Heidegger's Thought* (Athens, Ohio: Ohio University Press, 1978).

Carman, Taylor. "On Being Social: A Reply to Olafson." *Inquiry* 37 (1994), 203–223.

Casey, Edward S. *The Fate of Place* (Berkeley: University of California Press, 1996).

Casey, Edward S. "Converging and Diverging In/On Place." *Philosophy and Geography* 4 (2001), 225–231.

Casey, Edward S. *Getting Back into Place* (Bloomington: Indiana University Press, 1993).

Cassirer, Ernst. "Form und Technik" (1930). In Ernst Cassirer, *Symbol, Technik, Sprache* (Hamburg: Meiner, 1985).

Cerbone, David R. "Heidegger and Dasein's Bodily Nature: What Is the Hidden Problematic?" *International Journal of Philosophical Studies* 8 (2000), 209–230.

Christensen, Bruin. "Review of J. E. Malpas, *Place and Experience.*" *Mind* 110 (2001), 789–792.

Clauss, Ludwig Ferdinand. "Racial Soul, Landscape, and World Domination." In George L. Mosse (ed.), *Nazi Culture: Intellectual, Cultural, and Social Life in the Third Reich* (New York: Schocken Books, 1966, pp. 65–75. From Clauss, *Die nordische Seele: Eine Einführung in die Rassenseelenkunde*, 5th edn. (Munich: J. F. Lehmanns Verlag, 1936), pp. 19–32.

Colin McCahon: A Survey Exhibition. Auckland City Art Gallery, March–April 1972.

Cornford, F. M. *Plato's Cosmology: The "Timaeus" of Plato Translated with a Running Commentary* (London: Routledge and Kegan Paul, 1956).

Crowell, Steven Galt. *Husserl, Heidegger, and the Space of Meaning* (Evanston: Northwestern University Press, 2001).

Dahlstrom, Daniel O. *Heidegger's Concept of Truth* (Cambridge: Cambridge University Press, 2001).

Dastur, Françoise. "Heidegger's Freiburg Version of the Origin of the Work of Art." In James Risser (ed.), *Heidegger Toward the Turn* (Albany, N.Y.: SUNY Press, 1999), pp. 119–144.

de Beistegui, Miguel. *Heidegger and the Political: Dystopias* (London: Routledge, 1998).

Del Caro, Adrian. *Hölderlin: The Poetics of Being* (Detroit: Wayne State University Press, 1991).

Deloria Jr., Vine. *God Is Red* (Golden, Colo.: North American Press, 1992).

Derrida, Jacques. "The Ends of Man." In *Margins of Philosophy*. Trans. Alan Bass (Chicago: University of Chicago Press, 1982), pp. 109–136.

Derrida, Jacques. *Writing and Difference* (Chicago: Chicago University Press, 1978).

Descartes, René. *Principles of Philosophy*. In *The Philosophical Writings of Descartes*, vol. 1, trans. John Cottingham, Robert Stoothoff, and Dugald Murdoch (Cambridge: Cambridge University Press, 1985), pp. 177–292; French edition, *Les Principes de la Philosophie de René Descartes*, in *Œvres de Descartes*, ed. Charles Adam and Paul Tannery, vol. 9 (Paris: J. Vrin., n.d.), *premiere partie*.

Dessauer, Friedrich. *Philosophie der Technik* (Bonn: Cohen, 1927).

Dreyfus, Hubert L. *Being-in-the-World: A Commentary on Heidegger's "Being and Time," Division 1* (Cambridge, Mass.: MIT Press, 1991).

Dreyfus, Hubert L. "Heidegger's Critique of the Husserl/Searle Account of Intentionality." *Social Research* 60 (1993), 17–38.

Dreyfus, Hubert L. "Heidegger's History of the Being of Equipment." In Hubert L. Dreyfus and Harrison Hall (eds.), *Heidegger: A Critical Reader* (Oxford: Blackwell, 1992), pp. 173–185.

Eilan, Naomi, Rosaleen McCarthy, and Bill Brewer (eds.). *Spatial Representation* (Oxford: Blackwell, 1993).

Elden, Stuart. "Hölderlin and the Importance of Place." *Journal of the British Society for Phenomenology* 30 (1999), 258–274.

Elden, Stuart. *Mapping the Present: Heidegger, Foucault, and the Project of a Spatial History* (London: Continuum, 2001).

Entrikin, J. Nicholas. *The Betweenness of Place* (Baltimore: Johns Hopkins University Press, 1991).

Farías, Victor. *Heidegger and Nazism.* Trans. Paul Burrell and Gabriel R. Ricci (Philadelphia: Temple University Press, 1989).

Feick, Hildegard. *Index zu Heideggers "Sein und Zeit,"* 3rd ed. New edition by Susanne Ziegler (Tübingen: Max Niemeyer, 1980).

Fell, Joseph. "The Familiar and the Strange: On the Limits of Praxis in the Early Heidegger." In Hubert Dreyfus and Harrison Hall (eds.), *Heidegger: A Critical Reader* (Oxford: Blackwell, 1992), pp. 65–80.

Fell, Joseph. *Heidegger and Sartre: An Essay on Being and Place* (New York: Columbia University Press, 1979).

Fell, Joseph. "Heidegger's Mortals and Gods." *Research in Phenomenology* 15 (1985), 29–41.

Franck, Didier. *Heidegger et le problème de l'éspace* (Paris: Minuit, 1986).

Frodeman, Robert. "Being and Space: A Re-Reading of Existential Spatiality in Being and Time." *Journal of the British Society for Phenomenology* 23 (1992), 23–35.

Fuchs, Anne. "Review of Peter Blickle, *Heimat: A Critical Theory of the German Idea of Homeland.*" *Modern Language Review* 99 (2004), 1121–1122.

Gadamer, Hans-Georg. "Martin Heidegger—75 Years." In *Heidegger's Ways* (Albany: SUNY Press, 1994), pp. 15–28.

Gadamer, Hans-Georg. *Philosophical Apprenticeships* (Cambridge, Mass.: MIT Press, 1985).

Gadamer, Hans-Georg. "Reflections on My Philosophical Journey." In Lewis Edwin Hahn (ed.), *The Philosophy of Hans-Georg Gadamer*, Library of Living Philosophers 24 (Chicago: Open Court, 1997), pp. 3–63.

Gadamer, Hans-Georg. "The Relevance of the Beautiful." In *The Relevance of the Beautiful and Other Essays*, trans. Robert Bernasconi (Cambridge: Cambridge University Press, 1986), pp. 1–53.

Gadamer, Hans-Georg. *Truth and Method*, 2nd rev. ed. Trans. Joel Weinsheimer and Donald G. Marshall (New York: Crossroad, 1992). German edition, *Wahrheit und Methode*, 2nd ed. (Tübingen: J. C. B. Mohr, 1965).

Gadamer, Hans-Georg. "The Way in the Turn." In *Heidegger's Ways* (Albany: SUNY Press, 1994), pp. 129–230.

Geiman, Clare Pearson. "Heidegger's Antigones." In Richard Polt and Gregory Fried (eds.), *A Companion to Heidegger's Introduction to Metaphysics* (New Haven: Yale University Press, 2001), pp. 161–182.

Der große Duden 7. Etymologie (Mannheim: Bibliographisches Institut, 1963).

Grossheim, Michael. *Ökologie oder Technokratie?* (Berlin: Duncker und Humblot, 1995).

Guignon, Charles. *Heidegger and the Problem of Knowledge* (Indianapolis: Hackett, 1983).

Harvey, David. *The Condition of Post-Modernity* (Oxford: Basil Blackwell, 1989).

Harvey, David. *Justice, Nature, and the Geography of Difference* (Oxford: Blackwell, 1996).

Henrich, Dieter. "On the Unity of Subjectivity." In Henrich, *The Unity of Reason* (Cambridge, Mass.: Harvard University Press, 1994), pp. 17–54. Originally published as "Über die Einheit der Subjektivität," *Philosophische Rundschau* 3 (1955), 28–69.

Herf, Jeffrey. *Reactionary Modernism: Technology, Culture, and Politics in Weimar and the Third Reich* (Cambridge: Cambridge University Press, 1984).

Hiss, Tony. *The Experience of Place* (New York: Random House, 1990).

Hölderlin, Friedrich. *Sämtliche Werke: Historisch-kritische Ausgabe*. Ed. Norbert von Hellingrath, Friedrich Seebass, and Ludwig von Pigenot, 2nd ed. (Berlin: Propylaen, 1923).

Ingold, Tim. "The Temporality of the Landscape." In *The Perception of the Environment: Essays on Livelihood, Dwelling, and Skill* (London: Routledge, 2000), pp. 189–208.

Jacques, Martin. "The Death of Intimacy." *Guardian*, Saturday, September 18, 2004, p. 17.

Jammer, Max. *Concepts of Space: The History of Theories of Space in Physics*, 2nd ed. (Cambridge, Mass.: Harvard University Press, 1969).

Janicaud, Dominique. "Presence and Appropriation." *Research in Phenomenology* 8 (1978), 67–75.

Johnson, Mark. *The Body in the Mind* (Chicago: University of Chicago Press, 1987).

Kant, Immanuel. "Concerning the Ultimate Ground of the Differentiation of Directions of Space" (1768). In *Theoretical Philosophy 1755–1770*, trans. and ed. David Walford with Ralf Meerbote (Cambridge: Cambridge University Press, 1992), pp. 361–372.

Kant, Immanuel. "What Is Orientation in Thinking?" (1786). In *Political Writings*, ed. Hans Beiss, trans. H. B. Nisbet (Cambridge: Cambridge University Press, 1991), pp. 235–249.

Kapp, Ernst. *Grundlinien einer Philosophie der Technik* (Braunschweig: Westermann, 1877).

Käufer, Stephan. "Systematicity and Temporality." *Journal of the British Society for Phenomenology* 33 (2002), 167–187.

Kettering, Emil. *Nähe: Das Denken Martin Heideggers* (Pfüllingen: Neske, 1987).

King, H. R. "Aristotle's Theory of Topos." *Classical Quarterly* 44 (1950), 76–96.

Kisiel, Theodore. *The Genesis of Heidegger's "Being and Time"* (Berkeley: University of California Press, 1993).

Kisiel, Theodore. "Das Kriegsnotsemester 1919: Heideggers Durchbruch in die Hermeneutische Phänomenologie." *Philosophisches Jahrbuch* 99 (1992), 105–122.

Kisiel, Theodore. "Heidegger's Philosophical Geopolitics in the Third Reich." In Richard Polt and Gregory Fried (eds.), *A Companion to Heidegger's "Introduction to Metaphysics"* (New Haven: Yale University Press, 2001), pp. 226–249.

Körner, Stephan. "The Impossibility of Transcendental Deduction." *Monist* 51 (1967), 317–331.

Kosinski, Jerzy. *Being There* (New York: Harcourt Brace Jovanovich, 1971). Filmed as *Being There* (1979) starring Peter Sellers, directed by Hal Ashby, screenplay (from the novel) by Jerzy Kosinski.

Kümmerl, Friedrich. *Über den Begriff der Zeit* (Tübingen: Niemeyer, 1962).

Leach, Neil. "The Dark Side of the Domus: The Redomestication of Central and Eastern Europe." In Neil Leach (ed.), *Architecture and Revolution. Contemporary perspectives on Central and Eastern Europe* (London: Routledge, 1999), pp. 150–162.

Lefebvre, Henri. *The Production of Space*. Trans. Donald Nicholson-Smith (Oxford: Blackwell, 1991).

Livingstone, David N. *The Geographical Tradition* (Oxford: Blackwell, 1992).

Löwith. *Mein Leben in Deutschland vor und nach 1933* (Stuttgart: Metzler, 1986). Reprinted in Neske and Kettering (eds.), *Martin Heidegger and National Socialism*, pp. 157–159.

Lyotard, J.-F. "Domus and the Megalopolis." In *The Inhuman*, trans. Geoffrey Bennington and Rachel Bowlby (Cambridge: Polity Press, 1991), pp. 191–204.

Malpas, Jeff. "Beginning in Wonder." In N. Kompridis (ed.), *Philosophical Romanticism* (London: Routledge, 2005), pp. 282–298.

Malpas, Jeff. *Donald Davidson and the Mirror of Meaning* (Cambridge: Cambridge University Press, 1992).

Malpas, Jeff. "The Dualities of Work: Self-Creation and Self-Consumption." *Philosophy Today* 49 (2005), 256–263.

Malpas, Jeff. "From the Transcendental to the 'Topological': Heidegger on Ground, Unity, and Limit." In Jeff Malpas (ed.), *From Kant to Davidson: Philosophy and the Idea of the Transcendental* (London: Routledge, 2002), pp. 75–99.

Malpas, Jeff. "Holism, Realism, and Truth: How to Be an Anti-relativist and Not Give Up on Heidegger (or Davidson)—A Debate with Christopher Norris." *International Journal of Philosophical Studies* 12 (2004), 339–356.

Malpas, Jeff. "*Kategoriai* and the Unity of Being." *Journal of Speculative Philosophy* (new series), 4 (1990), 13–36.

Malpas, Jeff. *Place and Experience* (Cambridge: Cambridge University Press, 1999).

Malpas, Jeff. "Place and Topography: Responding to Cameron and Stefanovic." *Environmental and Architectural Phenomenology* 15 (2004), 8–10.

Malpas, Jeff. "Remembering Place (Edward S. Casey, *The Fate of Place*)." *International Journal of Philosophical Studies* 10 (2002), 92–100.

Malpas, Jeff. "Space and Sociality." *International Journal of Philosophical Studies* (1997), 53–79.

Malpas, Jeff. "Transcendental Arguments and Conceptual Schemes: A Reconsideration of Körner's Uniqueness Argument." *Kant-Studien* 81 (1990), 232–251.

Malpas, Jeff. "The Transcendental Circle." *Australasian Journal of Philosophy* 75 (1997), 1–20.

Malpas, Jeff, and Gary Wickham. "Democracy and Instrumentalism." *Australian Journal of Political Science* 33 (1998), 345–362.

Malpas, Jeff, and Gary Wickham. "Governance and the World: From Joe DiMaggio to Michel Foucault." *UTS Review* 3 (1997), 91–108.

Massey, Doreen. "Power-Geometry and a Progressive Sense of Place." In Jon Bird, Barry Curtis, Tim Putnam, George Robertson and Lisa Tickner (eds.). *Mapping the Futures* (London: Routledge, 1993), pp. 59–69.

Massey, Doreen. *Space, Place, and Gender* (Minneapolis: University of Minnesota Press, 1994).

McCahon, Colin. "Beginnings." *Landfall* 20 (1966), 360.

McNeill, William. "*Heimat*: Heidegger on the Threshold." In James Risser (ed.), *Heidegger: Toward the Turn* (Albany: SUNY Press, 1999), pp. 319–350.

Megill, Allan. *Prophets of Extremity* (Berkeley: University of California Press, 1985).

Mendell, Henry. "Topoi on Topos: The Development of Aristotle's Concept of Place." *Phronesis* 32 (1987), 206–231.

Merleau-Ponty, Maurice. *Phenomenology of Perception*, trans. Colin Smith (London: Routledge and Kegan Paul, 1962).

Meyrovich, Joshua. "Medium Theory." In David Crowley and David Mitchell (eds.), *Communication Theory Today* (Cambridge: Polity Press, 1994), pp. 50–77.

Miller, J. Hillis. "Slipping Vaulting Crossing: Heidegger." In *Topographies* (Stanford: Stanford University Press, 1995), pp. 216–254.

Morris, David. *The Shape of Space* (New York: SUNY Press, 2004).

Mourelatos, Alexander P. D. "La Terre et les étoiles dans la cosmologie de Xénophane." In André Laks and Claire Louguet (eds.), *Qu'est-ce que la Philosophie Présocratique? Cahiers de Philologie* 20 (Villeneuve d'Ascq: Presses Universitaires du Septentrion, 2002), pp. 331–350.

Myers, Fred. *Pintupi Country, Pintupi Self: Sentiment, Place, and Politics among Western Desert Aborigines* (Berkeley: University of California Press, 1991).

Nagel, Thomas. *The View from Nowhere* (Oxford: Oxford University Press, 1986).

Neske, G., and E. Kettering (eds.). *Martin Heidegger and National Socialism*. Trans. L. Harries (New York: Paragon House, 1990).

Nietzsche, Friedrich. *Beyond Good and Evil*. Trans. R. J. Hollingdale (Harmondsworth: Penguin, 1990).

Norberg-Schulz, Christian. *The Concept of Dwelling: On the Way to Figurative Architecture* (New York: Rizzoli, 1984).

Olafson, Frederick. *Heidegger and the Philosophy of Mind* (New Haven: Yale, 1987).

Olafson, Frederick. "Individualism, Subjectivity, and Presence: A Response to Taylor Carman." *Inquiry* 37 (1994), 331–337.

Ott, Hugo. *Martin Heidegger: A Political Life*. Trans. Allen Blunden (London: Harper Collins, 1993). German edition, *Martin Heidegger: Unterwegs zu seiner Biographie* (Frankfurt: Campus, 1988).

Otto, Walter. *The Homeric Gods*. Trans. Moses Hadas (London: Thames and Hudson, 1954). German edition, *Die Götter Griechenlands; das Bild des Göttlichen im Spiegel des griechischen Geistes* (Bonn: F. Cohen, 1929).

Otto, Walter. *Die Gestalt und das Sein* (Düsseldorf-Köln: Eugen Diederichs Verlag, 1955).

Overgaard, Søren. "Heidegger on Embodiment." *Journal of the British Society for Phenomenology* 35 (2004), 116–131.

Paddock, Troy. "*Gedachtes Wohnen*: Heidegger and Cultural Geography." *Philosophy and Geography* 7 (2004), 237–251.

Pappenfuss, Dietrich, and Otto Pöggeler (eds.). *Zur philosophischen Aktualität Martin Heideggers*, vol. 2, *Im Gespräch der Zeit* (Frankfurt: Klostermann, 1990).

Phillips, James. *Heidegger's Volk: Between National Socialism and Poetry* (Stanford: Stanford University Press, 2005).

Pöggeler, Otto. *Martin Heidegger's Path of Thinking*. Trans. Daniel Magurshak and Sigmund Barber (Atlantics Highlands, N.J.: Humanities Press, 1989).

Pöggeler, Otto. "Metaphysics and Topology of Being in Heidegger." *Man and World* 8 (1975), 3–27.

Poulet, Georges. *Proustian Space* (Baltimore: Johns Hopkins University Press, 1977).

Ratzel, Friedrich. *Politische Geographie* (Munich: Oldenbourg, 1879).

Redding, Paul. *Hegel's Hermeneutics* (Ithaca: Cornell University Press, 1996).

Relph, Edward. "Geographical Experiences and Being-in-the-World: The Phenomenological Origins of Geography." In David Seamon and Robert Mugerauer (eds.), *Dwelling, Place, and Experience: Towards a Phenomenology of Person and World* (Dordrecht: Nijhof, 1985), pp. 15–31.

Relph, Edward. *Place and Placelessness* (London: Pion, 1976).

Richardson, William J. *Heidegger: Through Phenomenology to Thought* (The Hague: Martinus Nijhof, 1963).

Rockmore, Tom. *On Heidegger's Philosophy and Nazism* (Berkeley: University of California Press, 1992).

Rollins, William. *A Greener Vision of Home: Cultural Politics and Environmental Reform in the German Heimschutz Movement 1904–1918* (Ann Arbor: University of Michigan Press, 1997).

Rollins, William. "*Heimat*, Modernity, and Nation in the Early Heimatschutz Movement." In Jost Hermand and James Steakley (eds.), *Heimat, Nation, Fatherland: The German Sense of Belonging* (New York: Peter Lang, 1996), pp. 87–112.

Rosalie Gascoigne—Colin McCahon: Sense of Place (Sydney: University of New South Wales Press, 1990).

Rouse, Joseph. *Knowledge and Power* (Ithaca: Cornell University Press, 1987).

Schirmacher, Wolfgang. *Technik und Gelassenheit* (Freiburg: Alber, 1983).

Schneeberger, Guido (ed.). *Nachlese zu Heidegger* (Bern: Suhr, 1962).

Scully, Vincent. *The Earth, the Temple, and the Gods* (New Haven: Yale University Press, 1962).

Sheehan, Thomas. "A Paradigm Shift in Heidegger Research." *Continental Philosophy Review* 34 (2001), 183–202.

Sheehan, Thomas. "Kehre and Ereignis: A Prolegomenon to *Introduction to Metaphysics*." In Richard Polt and Gregory Fried (eds.), *A Companion to Heidegger's "Introduction to Metaphysics"* (New Haven: Yale University Press, 2001), pp. 3–16.

Strawson, P. F. *Individuals: An Essay in Descriptive Metaphysics* (London: Macmillan, 1959).

Swain, Tony. *A Place for Strangers: Towards a History of Australian Aboriginal Being* (Cambridge: Cambridge University Press, 1993).

Taminiaux, Jacques. *Poetics, Speculation, and Judgment: The Shadow of the Work of Art from Kant to Phenomenology* (Albany: SUNY Press, 1993).

Thad, Michael Allen. *The Business of Genocide: The SS, Slave Labor, and the Concentration Camps* (Chapel Hill: University of North Carolina Press, 2002).

Thomson, Iain. *Heidegger on Ontotheology* (Cambridge: Cambridge University Press, 2005).

Tuan, Yi-Fu. "Space and Place: Humanistic Perspectives." *Progress in Human Geography* 6 (1974), 211–252.

Tuan, Yi-Fu. *Topophilia* (Englewood Cliffs, N.J.: Prentice-Hall, 1974).

Tugendhat, Ernst. *Die Wahrheitsbegriff bei Husserl und Heidegger,* 2nd ed. (Berlin: de Gruyter, 1972).

Tugendhat, Ernst. "Heidegger's Idea of Truth." In Christopher Macann (ed.), *Critical Heidegger* (London: Routledge, 1996), pp. 227–240.

Vallega. *Heidegger and the Issue of Space: Thinking on Exilic Grounds* (University Park: Pennsylvania University Press, 2003).

Villela-Petit, Maria. "Heidegger's Conception of Space." In Christopher Macann (ed.), *Critical Heidegger* (London: Routledge, 1996), pp. 134–157.

van Buren, John. *The Young Heidegger: Rumor of the Hidden King* (Indianapolis: Indiana University Press, 1994).

von Herrmann, Friedrich-Wilhelm. "Wahrheit-Zeit-Raum." In *Die Frage nach der Wahrheit* (Frankfurt: Klostermann, 1997), pp. 243–271.

Vycinas, Vincent. *Earth and Gods: An Introduction to the Philosophy of Martin Heidegger* (The Hague: Martinus Nijhof, 1961).

Walter, E. V. *Placeways* (Chapel Hill: University of North Carolina, 1988).

Wittgenstein, Ludwig. *Tractatus Logico-Philosophicus.* Trans. D. F. Pears and B. F. McGuinness (London: Routledge and Kegan Paul, 1961).

Wolin, Richard (ed.). *The Heidegger Controversy: A Critical Reader* (Cambridge, Mass.: MIT Press, 1993).

Wollan, Gjermund. "Heidegger's Philosophy of Space and Place." *Norsk Geografisk Tidsskrift—Norwegian Journal of Geography* 57 (2003), 31–39.

Wordsworth, William. *Wordsworth: Poetry and Prose* (London: Rupert Hart-Davis, 1955).

Wrathall, Mark. "Heidegger and Truth as Correspondence." *International Journal of Philosophical Studies* 7 (1999), 69–88.

Young, Julian. *Heidegger, Philosophy, Nazism* (Cambridge: Cambridge University Press, 1997).

Young, Julian. *Heidegger's Later Philosophy* (Cambridge: Cambridge University Press, 2002).

Young, Julian. *Heidegger's Philosophy of Art* (Cambridge: Cambridge University Press, 2000).

Young, Julian. "Poets and Rivers: Heidegger on Hölderlin's *Der Ister.*" *Dialogue* 28 (1999), 391–416.

Young, Julian. "What Is Dwelling? The Homelessness of Modernity and the Worlding of the World." In Mark Wrathall and Jeff Malpas (eds.), *Heidegger, Modernity, and Authenticity—Essays in Honor of Hubert Dreyfus*, vol. 1 (Cambridge, Mass.: MIT Press, 2000), pp. 187–204.

Index

Merleau-Ponty, Maurice, 55
The Metaphysical Foundations of Logic,
    165–166, 184–185
Metaphysics, 148, 201–204, 279–280,
    313
Meyrowitz, Joshua, 296–297
Mortals, 267, 269, 273–274, 275, 311.
    See also Death; Elements (of
    fourfold); Fourfold; Human being
Mysticism, 6–8, 158, 306–307
Myth, 206–207, 365n154, 365n155

Naming, of places, 266
National Socialism, 17, 18–27, 148,
    283–285, 322–323n44, 326n61,
    379n159, 380n162
Nature, 5, 25, 192, 234–235, 237, 239,
    310, 370n54, 370n56
Nazism. *See* National Socialism
Nearness, 225–228, 248, 251, 279, 293,
    297, 310
Neo-liberalism, 377–378n146
Newton, Isaac, 294
Nietzsche, Friedrich, 161, 207–209, 283,
    285–286, 305, 310, 380n163, 381n170
Nihilism, 279–283, 285–286
Nostalgia, 56, 310
Novalis (Georg Friedrich Philipp von
    Hardenburg), 190, 310

Oak Tree (in *Der Feldweg*), 237–238
Objectivity, 141
Offenheit, 49, 50. *See also* Open
"On the Essence of Ground," 61, 148,
    162–164, 167–168, 172, 175, 182,
    184, 187–188, 192
"On the Essence of Truth," 151,
    187–188, 196, 199, 202–203, 205,
    212, 224, 269, 270
"On the Question of Being," 33, 312
"On Time and Being," 169
Ontology—The Hermeneutics of Facticity.
    See "The Hermeneutics of Facticity"

Open, 107, 126, 128, 247–248, 252.
    See also Clearing;
    Disclosedness/disclosure; *Lichtung*;
    World
Orientation, 91, 107, 126–128, 134,
    372n76. *See also* Directionality
Origin, 56, 57, 148, 150. *See also*
    Ground
"The Origin of the Work of Art," 12,
    30, 156–157, 181–182, 196–197, 204,
    207, 213, 225–229, 232, 267, 276,
    306
Ort, 29, 30, 32, 48, 69, 329n79,
    329n83, 339n32, 372n71. *See also*
    Ortschaft; Place; *Topos*
Ortschaft, 16, 30, 31, 263. *See also* *Ort*;
    Place; *Topos*
Otto, Walter, 274
Ousia, 10, 60, 308
Overgaard, Søren, 129

Paddock, Troy, 326n61
Parmenides, 103, 252, 274
Pear tree (in *The Harvesters*), 235–237
People, 8, 23, 45, 324n55, 327n68
Phenomenology, 9, 44, 45, 307
Phillips, James, 23, 324n55
Philosophy, 6, 7, 39–63, 311
Physics, 18
Physics (Aristotle), 70, 71
Place, 2–5, 7–8, 16–20, 23–37, 48–50,
    57, 65, 68–71, 78, 84, 95, 103, 173,
    177–179, 196–197, 211, 219–230,
    241, 251, 255, 262–263, 266, 302,
    305, 307–309, 314, 365–366n158.
    See also Dimensionality; *Ort*; Space;
    Time; *Topos*
    and being, 3, 8, 33
    definition of, 27–37
    and dimensionality, 27, 28
    and gathering, 28, 29, 262–263
    happening of, 219–230, 241, 251, 307,
    308